Understanding the
Castle Ruins of
England and Wales

Understanding the Castle Ruins of England and Wales

How to Interpret the History and Meaning of Masonry and Earthworks

LISE HULL

McFarland & Company, Inc., Publishers
Jefferson, North Carolina

The present work is a reprint of the illustrated case bound edition of Understanding the Castle Ruins of England and Wales: How to Interpret the History and Meaning of Masonry and Earthworks, *first published in 2009 by McFarland.*

LIBRARY OF CONGRESS CATALOGUING-IN-PUBLICATION DATA

Hull, Lise.
Understanding the castle ruins of England and Wales : how to interpret the history and meaning of masonry and earthworks / Lise Hull.
p.   cm.
Includes bibliographical references and index.
softcover : acid free paper ∞

1. Castles — England — History.
2. Castles — Wales — History.
3. Historic buildings — England.
4. Historic buildings — Wales.
5. Fortification — England — History.
6. Fortification — Wales — History.
7. England — Antiquities.
8. Wales — Antiquities.
I. Title.

DA660.H946   2016   942 — dc22   2008040568

ISBN (print) 978-1-4766-6597-9
ISBN (ebook) 978-0-7864-5276-7

BRITISH LIBRARY CATALOGUING DATA ARE AVAILABLE

© 2009 Lise Hull. All rights reserved

No part of this book may be reproduced or transmitted in any form or by any means, electronic or mechanical, including photocopying or recording, or by any information storage and retrieval system, without permission in writing from the publisher.

Cover photograph of Warkworth castle
in Northumberland, England, © 2016 Shutterstock

Printed in the United States of America

*McFarland & Company, Inc., Publishers
Box 611, Jefferson, North Carolina 28640
www.mcfarlandpub.com*

Acknowledgments

For over twenty years, I have had the good fortune and immense joy to be able to explore Britain's castles, in their myriad of shapes, sizes, and conditions. They never cease to amaze me. The work that went into excavating the earth, preparing each site, hauling the materials, and creating the finished product, particularly with the rudimentary equipment available during the Middle Ages, must have been daunting at best, back-breaking and dispiriting most of the time. I often wish I could travel back in time so that I could watch a castle being constructed, and to then see the occupied site bustling with the activities of daily life. Movies and computer-enhancements just don't quite create the effect of an actual experience. But, as time travel is presently impossible, we must make do with what has been left to us: the castle remains. Castles, particularly those in ruin, have the profound ability to affect our emotions, and we can appreciate them both for what they now are and what they once were. As my niece recently said to me, "The ruinous parts convey more of a historic feel of the land ... a soul to the place and a sense of awe, like 'wow, this place is way older than I am ... I can't even start to imagine all the things that must have gone on here.'" My hope is this book will enrich your castle experience, whether you are traveling by armchair or exploring in person, and that you too will discover that sense of awe and the true meaning of ruins.

This book would not have been possible without the contributions of many people, whose willingness to answer my questions and share their professional expertise and resources with me is appreciated more than mere words can express. First and foremost, John Kenyon has my utmost appreciation. I am honored to have made his acquaintance, even if it is only via email, and am grateful for the guidance, information, wisdom, and enthusiasm that he continues to share with me. I would also like to offer a special thank you to Neil Ludlow for his insight on various aspects of castellology, and the castles of Pembrokeshire in particular, and for generously sending me some of his artwork to illustrate this book. Neil is the author and illustrator of guidebooks for the Pembroke Castle Trust and Pembrokeshire County Council, with whom he worked closely.

My sincerest gratitude additionally goes to Jeremy Ashbee, Oliver Creighton, Christopher Dyer, Neil Guy, Skip Knox, Pamela Marshall, David Martin, and Rick Turner, who freely offered opinions and information which colored this book and enriched my personal understanding of castles, the manorial landscape, and modern attitudes towards the ruins. Howard Giles, Steve Lumb, and Penny Ward were especially helpful with my research on Bolingbroke Castle; likewise, Brian Coleman enlightened me on the efforts to restore the Manorbier fishponds. My thanks also to Councillor Robert Bevan and Dean Powell regarding the status of Llantrisant Castle, to Anita Badhan for sharing J. R. Cobb's comments and the guide to Caldicot Castle, and to Marvin Hull for being my liege man.

Finally, I want to thank Alice Ewald for being my second pair of eyes and taking time from her often unpredictable schedule to read and comment on the first draft of this book. Her help lessened my load dramatically.

Any mistakes or misinterpretations of the literature are mine alone.

Except where otherwise noted, Lise Hull owns the copyright to the images in this book.

Table of Contents

Acknowledgments v

Introduction 1

1. Castle Development 9
   Terminology in This Chapter 36
2. From the Outside 42
   Terminology in This Chapter 79
3. Exploring the Interior 88
   Terminology in This Chapter 133
4. The Manorial Estate 140
   Terminology in This Chapter 161
5. The Castle Experience 168
   Terminology in This Chapter 194

Appendix: Castles Mentioned
England 195; Wales 201; Other 204

Chapter Notes 205

Bibliography 209

Index 213

Introduction

There is something inherently alluring and mystifying about ruins. The setting where we encounter them influences our reaction to them. So does their condition, their age and their role in history (or prehistory), even if we are not aware of that role. We may feel as if we are unconsciously drawn to them, and for good reason. On a mountain-top, silhouetted against the dawning day, ruins can exude a sense of hope despite the fact of their decay. Even on a rainy, windswept day, crumbling walls, massive stone monuments and falling towers create an air of intrigue and drama. They catch our breath and our curiosity.

When we are close enough to touch them, the same ruins can seem forlorn, sad vestiges of a long gone past, lost dreams, the end of lives, the demise of civilizations. Or, they may evoke a sense of awe and inspiration as we become aware that, long ago, other humans actually stood on the same spot and handled the materials that ended in ruin. In the presence of ruins, we often gain a deeper appreciation for the past and its influence on our present.

Ruins symbolize different things to different people. Yet, they all possess one underlying trait — they physically link us to the past, regardless of the extent of their decay or whether the past was yesterday or centuries ago. No matter their age, they remain part and parcel of the original structure that once occupied the site. Their physical essence survives, and is irreversibly linked to their creators, designers, builders, owners, and the employees or residents who occupied them. They are every bit a component of the collective identity that we call humanity.

When we think of the Middle Ages, we commonly associate the era with knights, damsels, swordsmanship, sieges — and castles. Movies, television shows, novels and video games reinforce this image. Increasingly, movie and television makers are setting their stories in authentic medieval castles, as in the Harry Potter movies and the recent BBC television remake of *Robin Hood* (starring Jonas Armstrong), which gives them greater public exposure; however, the emphasis largely remains focused on the fantasy tale, which, after all, is the basis of the movie or show. Even J. R. R. Tolkein, who wrote *The Lord of the Rings* series as a fantasy about a non-existent place, albeit possibly based on real locations in Great Britain, was particularly successful at dramatizing the interplay of rival lords, their armies, their castles, and the local populace during siege time. Although the settings and the architecture in the books, and the trilogy of movies inspired by them, were fanciful and computer enhanced, much of the work gave readers and viewers a realistic appreciation for the terror and ruthlessness of medieval siege warfare.

Fantasy and drama do go hand in hand and make for great entertainment, even when it comes to dramatizing medieval history. Yet, the media can mislead as well, and it is not uncommon for visitors looking at castle ruins to complain that they are not real castles. However, the majority of Britain's castles no longer look like Alnwick Castle, which was the setting for Hogwarts, and relatively few are fit for occupation. Most lay in ruin and are scattered throughout the countryside, in towns and villages, and in open fields which they share with cattle or sheep. The irony is that, whereas the few medieval castles still used by the monarchy and British nobility, such as Windsor and Alnwick, are splendidly furnished and portions are reserved as personal living quarters, they seem cold and lifeless. Their grandeur overrides their humanity. In many ways, such castles seem associated with the immediate present more than they act as a palpable link to the past. Ruins offer a different — sensory-driven — pathway into the past. This is one of their most vital contributions. They visibly, physically, and emotionally breach the chasm between the present and the Middle Ages.

Most of Britain's greatest surviving castles have become major tourist attractions, and rightly so. Even so, many are shells of their original selves, as at Caernarfon or Conwy in Wales or Dover in England; others are ruins with enough standing masonry that they resemble their medieval counterparts, as at Kenilworth and Warkworth in England. Even the Tower of London is more empty shell than residence, most of its medieval towers no longer occupied but preserved as a tourist attraction. In many ways, the fortress physically chronicles the entire course of British history. Government money continues to be funneled to these sites not just for their ongoing preservation, but largely to entice the paying masses to them and to recoup the expenses laid out to preserve them for the future. Regardless of the numbers of visitors they attract annually, no one could deny the need for safeguarding such sites. However, the heavy, albeit essential, restoration and the concomitant throngs of visitors wearing down the medieval masonry seem to have stripped many of these castles not of building materials but of their humanity and their ties to the past, which are readily apparent at other, less heavily publicized castle sites.

The preservation and restoration of ruined castles was stimulated in the late sixteenth century with the Grand Tour and the romantic revivalism of the eighteenth and nineteenth centuries, as many citizens began to recognize the allure of ruins and also the need to prevent their further decay. The Grand Tour was essentially a fashionable rite of passage for wealthy young men heading into adulthood, who spent up to five years traveling around Europe, not only acquiring an education in the finer aspects of elite living, learning French language and manners, studying Renaissance art, and visiting ancient ruins, but also accumulating fine and unusual relics from their journeys: artwork, sculpture and books which they displayed at home. In fact, many of Britain's finest stately homes are still adorned with these treasures. By the early nineteenth century, women and men from less wealthy families also found their way into Europe to take the Grand Tour.

Exposure to Europe's great cities and newly discovered archaeological sites, such as Pompeii and Herculaneum, not only furthered the travelers' education but also sparked an interest in ancient ruins, particularly those of classical Rome which was considered the epitome of cultural achievement. Upon their return home to England, many "tourists" showed off their newfound sophistication by mimicking some of what they encountered on their travels, and, during the eighteenth century, an onslaught of new monuments based on classical designs and inspired by ruins began to appear in the grounds at stately homes and the estates of the elite. At the same time, two important cultural movements, romantic revivalism and antiquarianism, began to take hold in Britain. During the nineteenth century, people often perceived ruins as fashionable places to visit and to see and be seen by other visitors. In west Wales, for example, visitors donned their finery and headed to Tenby, a popular resort and spa town, to promenade around the castle ruins, which were encircled with a walkway for just that purpose.

While antiquarians such as William Stukeley and John Aubrey practiced their hand at archaeological excavation and the reconstruction of ancient sites, such as Stonehenge and Avebury, landscape architects, such as Lancelot "Capability" Brown, began creating wide-open parklands scattered with mock, or neo-classical, structures. More popularly known as "follies," these curious buildings resembled Roman temples and Egyptian pyramids and even prehistoric stone circles and medieval ruins, and often had embedded symbolic messages. Other architects began designing stately homes that looked like medieval castles but whose battlements were for show rather than for any defensive or military purpose.

Interestingly enough, even owners of medieval castles such as Old Wardour in England or Penrice in Wales intentionally erected sham ruins on the same property that held authentic medieval ruins. At Old Wardour, visitors will find a real prehistoric stone circle re-erected not too far from the ruined castle and an artificial stone grotto added in the eighteenth century made from pieces of the ruined castle. At the upper entrance to Penrice Castle, owners placed an eye-catching stretch of what appears to be an authentic set of ruined medieval towers connected by a curtain wall, but, in fact, they are follies. Interestingly, at Abbey Cwmhir, a sham motte dominates the grounds of the ruined abbey where the Llywelyn ap Gruffydd, the last native Welsh prince of Wales, was buried in the late thirteenth century.

One might wonder why people with plenty of money would build fake ruins if they had the financial capability to erect a much grander structure or to restore the castle they already occupied. Certainly, there is much more to a real ruin than meets the eye, and it is that essence that they were trying to reproduce by constructing sham imitations. Firstly, artificial ruins symbolically connected their owners to an ideal — or highly idealized — past, where the classical civilizations thrived culturally and controlled much of the known world. Associating oneself with the Greeks or Romans suggested virtue, achievement and power, all noble qualities a man of status should possess. Owning sham ruins or other neo-classical follies was a badge of honor in a nation where the Greeks never visited and Roman ruins were few and far between.

Sham castles shared similarities with their medieval counterparts that went beyond the superficial — owners during both eras used them to symbolically display their superior social, economic and political status. Sham ruins also suggested to visitors that the owners had a direct link to the past, perhaps even that their families had lengthy and influential pedigrees. Ownership of these curious structures signified singular status as individuals of social, cultural and/or political importance. Ironically, the same status, and the additional virtue of authenticity, makes true castles and castle ruins all the more appealing, intriguing and historic.

Public finances being what they are, scores of medieval sites have been left to endure the elements as best as possible. Many have disappeared; many more continue to erode or are overgrown with intrusive vegetation, used as junk piles, or intentionally, albeit reluctantly, ignored due to legislative restrictions that prohibit private owners from carrying out conservation. Yet, these sites still contain the past in their stone and mortar, earthworks and rubble. They are often the only surviving physical link to real people, and, regardless of the status of the medieval inhabitants, should be appreciated for the role they played in those lives. Sometimes, all it takes is a bit of basic knowledge about what you are looking at in order to recreate, at least in one's imagination if not on paper, what a ruin looked like originally, how it functioned, and what might have occurred at the site from day to day.

Sham ruins erected by Thomas Mansel Talbot in 1793 line the main gateway onto the grand estate where the ruins of medieval Penrice Castle, the Gower Peninsula's largest stone castle, occupy a ridge near Penrice House.

One can study British history, watch historical movies, read historical novels, or attend the local Renaissance faire to gain an impression of what life was like in the Middle Ages and the role castles played in medieval history. But, all the reading and movie-watching in the world can never compare to experiencing a castle in person, even when the castle is in ruins. In fact, it is essential to approach a medieval castle with as few preconceptions about the site as possible, or to at least recognize that your expectations may be based more on fantasy than on reality and then to try to explore the site without judging it based on an illusion created by the media. While castle sites have plenty in common, they are all individuals as well. Not only will the layouts differ to some degree, if not completely, from castle to castle, but their present conditions will vary as well.

Not every castle can be a Windsor Castle, nor should we expect them to be. Most castle builders were not wealthy monarchs but were men with limited resources and lesser status. However, even the rulers of medieval Britain had to keep a close eye on how much money they spent on the construction and maintenance of their castles. Though many managed to build private castles that rivaled their monarch's, most lords built smaller castles which suited their particular needs, personal preferences, and financial constraints.

That a castle is smaller or more ruined than another is really irrelevant. Each should be recognized for its individuality rather than how it stacks ups against another. To judge a site from some subjective set of standards is to miss the truly unique — and invigorating — experience of being in the presence of a centuries-old structure, walking in the footsteps of men and women who were born, lived, worked and died in the castle and on its estates, and touching the same masonry blocks and earthen mounds they also touched. To dismiss a site merely for its lack of masonry is a shame, for visitors may miss out on some of Britain's greatest fortresses, such as Fotheringhay Castle in Nottinghamshire. Now little more than two chunks of stone and a huge mound (known as a motte), this monumental castle played a critical role in history. Not only was it Richard III's birthplace, but it also imprisoned Mary, Queen of Scots, until her execution, which took place in the castle in 1587. Mary's death changed the course of British history.

The thrill of what I call "first sight," the discovery of an unexplored place (in this case, places which we personally have not explored), is like no other. Often, castles materialize ahead of you even when you are not looking for them, for example, while you are gazing from the window of a train tracing an estuary through the Welsh countryside (the author's first castle experience) or while speeding along a congested ring road around an English town. Clam-

Once a thriving castle, Fotheringhay played a key role in history. Not only was it the birthplace of the future King Richard III, it also served as the last prison and execution place of Mary, Queen of Scots. Today, the Norman motte and a few chunks of later masonry survive.

bering through dense vegetation or sidestepping anxious cows, or their patties, to then suddenly be thrust into an open area filled with ruins or grass-covered earthworks not only makes for an exhilarating challenge but startles the senses and jolts an awareness from our subconscious of the factors that shaped medieval life and, ultimately, shaped our modern world.

Wiping one's mind completely clean of preconceived notions about castles is impossible, but the goal should be to experience each castle as a unique piece of the past, by having an open mind, a sense of adventure, and appreciation for its ability to survive the centuries. If you go to a castle when a living history event is taking place, remember that the participants are using creative license to entertain and often stray from historical accuracy. Oftentimes, the activities they perform never actually took place at any castle, let alone the castle you are visiting.

Special events such as these can detract and distract from one's experience of the historical site, by diverting attention away from the structure and setting, obscuring features and blocking access to parts of the castle. On those days, it can be difficult to gain a real sense of what the castle itself was about or to come away with a clear understanding about the site. Certainly, watching the siege engines hurl missiles into the moat at Caerphilly Castle is a not-to-be-missed adventure, for similar machines played a critical role in medieval warfare. However, the ruins and their role in the history of castle building are infinitely more important and should be explored and interpreted in their own right, without the distraction of the replicas in action.

Even though most castles were built long before towns grew up around them, nowadays, they are often engulfed by urban sprawl, hidden behind village stores and residential areas. Just locating the castle can be a challenge, even when signs point you in the right direction. Generally, the best plan is to head towards a town center. If the castle is substantial, regardless of whether or not it is a ruin, the remains commonly loom like a large patch of dark gray or brown in what is otherwise a sea of green trees or an uneven jumble of lighter colored structures. Sometimes the sites rise up suddenly on a hillside; at other times, it takes some investigating or heading towards a river or stream, if there is one in the town, or some other logical place where the castle may have been situated.

Llandovery Castle in Carmarthenshire, Wales, is one example. Located alongside a parking lot behind a lengthy row of buildings in the village center, the ruins are visible briefly as you head east, but only if you have the chance to look through the openings between the densely packed structures lining the road and avoid the rush of traffic. In fact, the same buildings block your view as you drive west through the town. As at Llandovery, nearby Crickhowell Castle is similarly invisible when one drives east through the town, but the site is quite easy to spot from the opposite direction. Its riverside location helps pinpoint the location as well. Builth Castle, on the other hand, is best seen from the opposite side of the River Wye, from where it is easy to see that the castle actually towers over the congested town. Modern-day visitors might scoff at the condition of the site and claim that it is not a real castle. Once one of Edward I's great fortresses, the castle at Builth Wells is now little more than a massive earthwork mound but, in its heyday, it was much more substantial and topped with masonry and timber structures and played a key role in the king's efforts to subjugate the Welsh in 1277. Without a doubt, there is much more than meets the eye at these, and most other, ruined castles. They are well worth thorough investigation.

Historically, castles were much more than a fortified military structure. They acted as manorial and governmental centers from where their lords controlled vast estates worked by

The surprisingly extensive remains of Crickhowell Castle are partially obscured by the later buildings that line the main road through the village. Among the castle's fine features is a massive rectangular tower.

peasants and serfs. They were considerably expensive to upkeep and many owners eventually allowed them to decay, moving elsewhere to structures with modern conveniences which castles lacked. By the sixteenth century, many were derelict. A renaissance of sorts occurred in the mid-seventeenth century when many of Britain's castles were called back into action during the English Civil Wars. Many were also subjected to at least one siege, and, at the end of the conflict, many were "slighted" or rendered useless for further military action.

This book is intended to introduce readers to castle exploration, either as armchair visitors or amateur on-site investigators. Even small chunks of masonry have stories to tell, if you know how to interpret what you see. During the Middle Ages, people from all levels of society, from the owners to the peasants, knew (often unconsciously) how to interpret castles; the symbolism might be blatant or subtle, but nevertheless was there for all to notice. In fact, castle builders went to great lengths to ensure visitors as well as occupants recognized the meaning behind decorative features, the structural differences between various parts of the castle, how they were used, who used them, and how to distinguish between different chambers. The key parts of a castle were identifiable from the outside, and passersby were often enticed along special pathways designed to go by certain parts of the castle, so that they could "read" the visual clues, interpret them, and know what might await them inside.

Today, even humps and bumps underneath the ground can be interpreted, for despite their differences, castles had many features in common, features that are identifiable even in ruin. You don't have to take the Grand Tour to enjoy and learn to value medieval ruins. At times, you will find them without even trying when driving through villages or in the countryside. Some actually hide in plain sight on grassy verges that overlook motorways!

Ruins are tangible relics of a past that has shaped modern lives. They have endured what is generally considered uncontrollable: the passage of time, the disruption of weather, and the destructive practices of later cultures, such as intentional abandonment, plowing, bulldozing, and bombardment. Ruins are often the only physical evidence of lives that history might have otherwise failed to record. They represent human persistence, permanence, impermanence, and perseverance. As such, they are every bit as vital to the story of the past as the more complete castles. As we shall see in this book, even though many — indeed, the majority — of Britain's castles are fragmentary, they are no less castles in the fullest sense of the term.

1

Castle Development

Castle studies is currently in a state of flux. Whether the present trend towards drastically revising ("deconstructing") long held theories about the purpose of castles is the natural outcome of scholarly curiosity or a way for some researchers to make a creative mark in academia is unclear. However, what is clear is that castellologists (castle scholars) have very disparate opinions about castles, which they vigorously defend.

The traditional view is that castles in Britain were fortified "military" residences which were owned and built for private individuals, the monarch or a lord, during the Middle Ages. They were an essential part of feudal society and, even though they were erected for a variety of crucial reasons, above all, every castle performed the same two primary functions at the same time: they were private homes *and* they were fortifications. The degree to which they were fortified depended upon the builder's personal preferences, and other circumstances, and so did the extent to which they accommodated full-time residents. Some castles were more military than home; others were more home than fortress. But, without possessing both elements, none of these structures should be classified as a "castle." It is more appropriate to call them "houses" or "stately homes"—or in some cases, "palaces"—or to call them "fortresses" or "forts."

The long held notion that all castles served a "military" purpose is probably the one issue that has caused the most consternation among the newer members of the castle studies field. Traditionally, castles have been defined by their military nature, their heavy defenses and the roles they played in siege warfare and conquest. Indeed, history supports the contention that conquering kings erected castles to keep their new subjects in line and that, while castles were the targets of sieges, sieges were also staged from castles. Lords needed sturdy defenses to prevent an enemy from taking their castles, and castles helped a lord maintain control of his lordship. However, during peacetime, the emphasis shifted away from warfare and militarization. The same lords then used their castles as residences and as places from which they administered their lordships. In fact, most castles were never heavily garrisoned, particularly during peacetime; oftentimes, a skeleton staff manned the site, particularly when the lord and his entourage were away at his other manorial estates or at the royal court.

Such contradictions between the role of the castle during war and during peace have recently led some castellologists to the curious conclusion that castles actually had no military role at all. Yet, this thinking is completely at odds with the historical documents that have passed down the ages. That castles were residences made them no less "military" in nature. Perhaps, the use of the word "military" is the real problem for modern castellologists, who have been christened as "revisionists" for their new theories and twists on traditional approaches to castles. Rather than being characterized as military structures, perhaps castle studies would be better served by identifying castles by their offensive (as opposed to defensive) role.

Another concern for revisionists is the question of what makes a castle "fortified." As is still evident today, some castles, like the Tower of London or Dover Castle, were heavily guarded with numerous towers, gateways, thick walls, moats or ditches, and features such as portcullises, murder holes, and arrowslits. They also functioned as royal residences, treasuries, mints, prisons, and armories, and had chapels and substantial garrisons. Clearly, these sites were fortified, and served a military purpose. They rightfully deserve to be classified as castles.

However, other structures, such as Weobley Castle in Wales and Bodiam and Kirby Muxloe Castles in England, straddle the fence with their less substantial defenses, and many castellologists classify them as "fortified manor houses" rather than true castles. Yet, these simpler buildings did possess many, if not all, of the same basic features that justify labeling other structures as castles. Weobley, Bodiam and Kirby Muxloe were fortified. No one questions that. And, they were homes of lords. No one debates that either. It's the matter of the extent of fortification that is used to differentiate between fortified and non-fortified buildings. Generally, residences with walls over five to six feet thick and other castellated features have been classed as castles; yet, some sites with exterior walls measuring three feet in thickness have also been accepted as castles. Unfortunately, short of traveling back to the Middle Ages and taking a survey of lords and their masons, no one today can state with certainty when a wall-

Begun by William, Lord Hastings, in about 1480, Kirby Muxloe had the main features of the typical stone castle, including a gatehouse, corner towers, and a drawbridge, which spanned the enclosing moat. Even so, many researchers consider it to have been a fortified manor house.

was too thin to be considered fortified or when a moat was too shallow to be a barrier to an attack or when a tower was too weakly battlemented. Medieval documents do not clarify this issue. Consequently, any determination would be arbitrary at best and still open to debate.

For the purposes of this book, then, the definition of a "castle" is a "fortified military residence," and they simultaneously performed as a private house and a fortification. Archaeological excavations support this definition, and so does the recorded history of medieval siege warfare. That castles also functioned as manorial and administrative centers and were used by their builders for symbolic purposes, particularly to display their wealth and superiority over other people, in no way lessens the singular importance of these two primary functions. Unless a castle no longer survives to any degree or only the scantiest of ruins remain, pieces of structures that helped fulfill the defensive and the residential requirements of a lord are often easy to spot. Fireplaces or chunks of carvings, for example, reveal the location of kitchens or the great hall. Earthen embankments may indicate the location of the outer defenses or the remains of a support structure, such as a fishpond. Even slight rises in the ground can suggest the survival of foundations of buildings that once served the basic needs of castle residents.

Retracing the Norman Invasion

The Norman invasion of England was the culmination of a series of events that began many years before Duke William of Normandy sailed his fleet across the English Channel in September 1066 to claim what he believed to be his rightful place as ruler of the Anglo-Saxon kingdom. The path to the throne was barred by Harold Godwinson, the newly crowned Saxon king, whom the ailing King Edward the Confessor had chosen as his successor shortly before his death in January 1066. Nothing short of controversial, Edward's choice was the spark that led to the Saxon downfall later that year and the ascendancy of the Normans in Britain.

Among other responsibilities, the Anglo-Saxon council of noblemen known as the witan or witenagemot[1] was tasked with selecting a new monarch. Generally, they followed the law of primogeniture, whereby the eldest son or closest male blood relative inherited the throne upon the king's death; however, they were free to choose whichever man they felt was right for the position. Edward the Confessor's marriage to Edith, a daughter of Godwin, Earl of Wessex, who some historians identify as the power behind the Saxon throne and certainly the most powerful land owner in England, had produced no children to which to pass the title. However, several men, including Harold, who was Godwin's son and Edith's brother, felt they had strong enough ties to the monarchy to be considered the rightful heir, ties worth fighting for.

The year 1066 was not the first dispute over the Saxon throne. Some fifty years earlier, a similar situation occurred when Knut of Denmark invaded England and was chosen by the witan as the replacement for the Anglo-Saxon king, Aethelred, who died in 1015. Aethelred actually had several sons, including Edmund Ironside, his eldest by his first wife, Aelfgifu, and Edward, by his second wife, Emma. For a brief time, Edmund ruled the southern part of England while Knut had the north. However, Edmund died within six months, and Knut became the sole ruler of the Anglo-Saxons. Taking Emma as his second wife, Knut promptly sent Emma's children by Aethelred to Europe. Her son, Edward, headed to Normandy. There, he was schooled in the cultural and social mores of the Normans and made many solid friendships. This experience eventually shaped Edward's reign in England and, ultimately, changed the course of British history.

By 1042, Knut's bloodline had run out of direct heirs to the Saxon throne. Edward had returned from exile several years earlier and, when Harthaknut, Knut's son with Emma, died suddenly, Earl Godwin proposed that Edward, the last surviving male child from the lines of either Knut or Aethelred, be made king of Saxon England. Even though Edward, later known as "the Confessor," was an Anglo-Saxon, much of his reign was couched in what he had learned while living in Normandy, including the French language, which he apparently spoke more frequently than he did English. He also brought with him several Norman friends, who were probably responsible for constructing the few pre–Conquest castles that have been identified in England.

After Earl Godwin's death in 1053, his son, Harold, became the Earl of Wessex and took over his father's role as the king's primary advisor. Harold's brother, Tostig, became Earl of Northumbria. Not surprisingly, Harold had expected to be appointed as heir apparent, partly because it was quite evident that the king would never sire a son of his own and also because Harold was already ruling the kingdom on Edward the Confessor's behalf. His expectations seemed justified, especially after the title, *Dux Anglorum* (meaning Earl or Duke of the English), was created just for Harold. A widespread search for blood relatives of the king revealed that another Edward, the son of Edmund Ironside, had fathered children while in exile in Hungary. He was brought back to England in 1057, but he promptly died and his children passed into the care of the king. As the only son, Edgar (the Aetheling), was a viable candidate to become the next king of England. As a result, the Godwins faced something of a familial crisis, for they had planned to place their own heir on the throne.

When Edward the Confessor finally died on January 5, 1066, the Godwins got their wish. Harold Godwinson became King Harold II the next day. The Confessor had made it clear on his deathbed that the earl was the man he preferred to "protect" his wife and his kingdom. Yet, another individual—William, Duke of Normandy—believed Edward had made it clear enough to him in private conversations held in late 1051 that he would become the next king of England. Not only that, but in 1064, Harold himself had reputedly sworn an oath of loyalty and fidelity to William, so it came as something of a shock when, four days later, the duke learned that Harold had stepped onto the throne that should have been his. Enraged by the news, Duke William began plotting his response to Godwinson's effrontery.

In the meantime, Harold's brother, Tostig, began searching for an army to support an assault on the monarchy. Having been in exile since the previous year, Tostig first attempted to curry favor with several royal courts in Europe, hoping to regain the earldom of Northumbria—if not the kingdom itself. When he failed, Tostig made one final appeal, this time to the King of Norway, Harald Hardrada ("Hard in Council" or "Hard Bargainer"), to come to his aid. Hardrada agreed, and began assembling a fleet of Norsemen to cross the North Sea and invade England, not so that Tostig could seize the throne, but so that the brutal Norse king could instead.

The Norman victory over the Saxons was largely the result of a series of happenstances and not, as many people might think, due to the complete superiority of the Norman army over that of the Saxons. Had weather conditions been different; had Harold's men been prepared to march back and forth across England over the course of just a couple of weeks, first fighting the Norse and then battling the Normans; and had William not received the backing of the pope to his claim to the English throne, perhaps there never would have been a Norman Conquest. That said, all the circumstances and miscalculations inevitably led to the Norman victory and the death of the Saxon king near Hastings on October 14, 1066.

Within two weeks of each other, enemy armies attacked the Saxons on two fronts. Both fleets had to wait until the weather produced just the right winds to push their ships across the sea to the English shores. The Norse fleet, led by King Harald Hardrada, landed on the eastern coast of Yorkshire on September 18 and the Normans (who were descended from the Norse) landed at Pevensey on the southern Sussex coast on the 28th. Initially, Harold II had stationed an army and his fleet at the Isle of Wight to wait for the Normans. However, the contrary winds had forced Duke William to delay embarking for England for four months, during which time the Saxons depleted their supplies and came to the erroneous conclusion that the Normans were not going to invade after all.

Disbanding his troops on September 8 and returning to London, Harold discovered to his dismay that several days later all was not well in Yorkshire. The Norwegians had landed several days later in Yorkshire. Shortly thereafter, they scored a victory over the Saxons at Fulford Gate and seized York on the 20th. The Saxon king then made the brash decision to march on York, a 190-mile trek from London, and immediately called together an army. Five days later the Saxons surprised the Norwegian forces, which had stationed themselves seven miles southeast of York, at Stamford Bridge. The rout of the Norwegians was complete, the victory sweetened by the deaths of Hardrada and Tostig, the traitor.

Even so, Harold could not rest on his laurels, for the long-anticipated Norman fleet had finally crossed the English Channel, reaching the shores of the Saxon kingdom on September 28. The king probably reached London on October 5 or 6, and immediately replenished his tired army with more men and supplies before beginning his march to Hastings, a distance of almost 60 miles, five days later. The Saxon army arrived at Hastings late on Friday, October 13. However, they were exhausted by their rapid journey and in need of recuperation before their encounter with the Normans.

Having to wait four months to embark on his invasion of England gave Duke William plenty of time to contemplate how to best stage his assault. Even though only a few documents have been passed down to us which reveal what the Norman leader thought and how he planned to defeat the Saxons, we know a great deal about the effort thanks to the preservation of a remarkable, hand-sewn length of cloth known as the Bayeux Tapestry. The 230-foot long series of embroidered panels is the closest thing historians have to a photographic record of the event, and covers all sorts of activities, from the preparations in Normandy to the gathering of the fleet to castle-building to the defeat of the Saxons and the coronation of Duke William as king of England. The colorful tapestry brilliantly recreates the scenes and gives us a real sense of what was involved in organizing the campaign, how the men were dressed, what supplies they took, and how they fought the Battle of Hastings.

Today, the tapestry is on display at the Centre Guillaume le Conquérant in Bayeux, France. Possibly commissioned by Odo, the Bishop of Bayeux and William's half-brother, and embroidered by several women, including Matilda, William's wife, the stylized but highly detailed wool and linen tapestry is biased in favor of the Normans. Even so, it is without a doubt our best glimpse into the events that preceded that fateful day in mid–October, 1066, which ended with the defeat of the Saxons and the arrival not only of a new aristocracy into England but also the construction of scores of castles.

Though historians still debate the exact reasons why the Norman fleet landed at Pevensey and whether the winds played a role in the choice when William went ashore on September 28, his journey to meet the Saxons had only just begun. His original destination was probably Hastings, which was on the edge of estates held by the Norman monks from the Abbey

Many of William the Conqueror's castles were constructed on the remains of Roman-era sites, as at Pevensey, where the Norman invaders first landed on English soil. The ruins of the Roman fort were incorporated into the later stone castle erected by William's cousin, Robert de Montain, shown here.

of Fecamp as a grant from King Knut.[2] The invaders took about three days to reach Hastings, after first building an earthwork castle at Pevensey inside the remains of Anderida, a third-century Roman fort. Today, the castle site is dominated by the Roman walls and the remains of a later Norman castle, built by Robert de Mortain, another half-brother of William of Normandy, well inside the fort. The only surviving traces of William's castle probably include a ditch located just outside the Roman west gate,[3] which would have provided additional protection for the interior of the site. The Normans may have briefly occupied the fort before splitting into two groups and ravaging several villages as they made their way east to Hastings. At Hastings, Duke William erected his second castle by first cutting a deep ditch across the narrowest part of a steep-sided hillock and then digging other ditches and piling the spoils into a mound; at the same time, his army prepared to battle the Saxons.

For William, building a castle implied much more than merely needing defensive cover. It was no coincidence that he decided to erect his first castle, albeit a very simple crescent-shaped earthwork and ditch that would probably be best classified as a "siege castle," on British soil using the remains of a Roman fort as its backdrop. Not only did the site offer ready-made defenses, its association with Rome was of particular significance for the man who would be king of England. Planting a castle inside a Roman ruin implied that the Normans were at least on a par with—if not superior to—that great classical civilization. William repeated this practice when he constructed castles elsewhere in England, choosing former Roman sites as the settings for his castles, as at Londinium and the Roman temple of Claudius, where he built the Tower of London and Colchester Castle. He also erected castles on top of Saxon settlements, tearing down scores of houses and other buildings, as at Dover and York, and even building castles on Saxon cemeteries, as at Cambridge. William intended these actions to symbolically and quite physically demonstrate his supremacy over his new subjects.

Today, the battlefield site where the Saxons clashed with the Normans is largely obscured by later construction, but the positions where the two armies established themselves are quite easy to identify from the hilltop alongside Battle Abbey. (Despite the traditional name of the battle, it actually took place a few miles north of Hastings; the village nearest the battlefield is known as Battle, for obvious reasons.) For several years, re-enactments of the historic event have been staged at the battlefield site.

During the early hours of October 14, 1066, the Normans learned that Harold II had stationed his army on a ridge on the northern side of a marshy valley. Marching from Hastings to meet the Saxons, Duke William established his troops on the opposite side of the valley and prepared to launch his assault on the Saxons. Even though both armies probably numbered about 7,000 to 8,000 men, they differed greatly in composition, quality and strategy. Leading the Saxon army were some 4,000 "house-carls," professional fighters who were housed and fed by the king and carried shields and wielded battle-axes with incomparable skill. Behind the house-carls stood the rest of the army, the "fyrd," who provided their own arms and supplies and had little to no fighting skills. Their strategy was simple: the front ranks of house-carls would form a shield wall to prevent penetration from Norman arrows, javelins or missiles, and thereby retain control of the ridge as they cut down the attackers with their axes. As their men died, the Saxon ranks would close up and continue to fight.

With 5,000 foot soldiers, including archers, and 2,000 mounted horsemen — the knights — separated into three divisions, the Norman army was much better prepared for battle. In the center were the Normans themselves, led by Duke William and his half-brother, Odo. To their left stood a contingent of Bretons, soldiers from Brittany commanded by Count Alan Fergant, and to their right were the French and Flemish (men from Flanders), led by Count Eustace of Boulogne. Each of the three main divisions was also divided into three sections. The archers led the way with short bows and, possibly, with crossbows. They were followed by the foot soldiers, who wore chain mail and carried swords and pikes, and then the armored horsemen with their swords, shields, lances, and iron maces. Ironically, their horses turned out to be the knights' weak points. Unarmored, the vulnerable animals were easy targets for the battle-axes.

Despite the seeming superiority of the foreign army, the Saxons, with their impenetrable shield wall and butchering battle-axes, resisted the Normans. After several hours of bloodshed, the Breton flank of the invading army began to flee the scene, but abruptly found themselves stuck in a mud-filled ditch. Seeing this as an advantage, a portion of the Saxon army charged down the hill towards to squirming soldiers. Ironically, at the same time, a rumor that Duke William had been killed ran rampantly through the Norman contingent, who likewise started to retreat. Only when William tore off his helmet to prove that he was still alive did his men stop, regroup, and turn around to kill the Saxons chasing them. After a lull in the action, the French and Flemish division launched the next assault, but the section of the Saxon line closest to the action charged after them and forced them to retreat. This time, however, the Norman army anticipated such a response from the Saxons and turned around to challenge them. Their retreat, in fact, was a tactical sham, intended to make the Saxons think they had won the day.

One of England's first Norman castles, the motte at Ewyas Harold dates to about 1052, when the Saxon king, Edward the Confessor, still ruled Britain. The site has never been excavated.

The battle raged throughout the day, the shield wall still intact but barely so, as the Normans pounded the Saxon fighters head on and also fired arrows strategically aimed on an arced path to impale the crowd of Saxons amassed behind the wall. One of the arrows struck a Saxon in the eye. Tradition reinforced by the Bayeux Tapestry claims that the victim was King Harold II himself. Blinded, the man was completely vulnerable to what next beset him. According to tradition, Duke William, Count Eustace, and two other knights rode their horses up the hilltop, where they stabbed, disemboweled, and hacked the king into pieces and effectively defeated the Saxons. Two and a half months later, Duke William of Normandy was crowned the first Norman king of England. Allegedly penitent for his brutality, William I then ordered the construction of the great Benedictine abbey where the battle occurred. The high altar at Battle Abbey reputedly stood on the site where King Harold died. Today, a stone slab marks the historic spot.

Most historians mark the Norman invasion as the moment in history when castles appeared in Britain. As mentioned earlier, however, Edward the Confessor's Norman associates erected a few castles in the decade prior to the Conquest, but they appear not to have had an impact on the Saxons, who made a few notations about them in the *Anglo-Saxon Chronicle*. Started between 850 and 890 A.D. on the orders of King Alfred (the Great) of Wessex and added to until the mid-twelfth century, when King Stephen ruled Britain, the *Chronicle* indicates that three or four castles — probably those at Ewyas Harold, Richard's Castle, and Hereford in Herefordshire and possibly Clavering in Essex — were built by "the French" in about 1052. The timber structures have long since vanished, but the earthen mounds that formed the focal point of the castles can still be explored — except for the motte at Hereford, which has been leveled. The bailey, however, does survive as a bowling green.

An artist's rendition of the first castle at Pembroke, which was erected by Arnulf de Montgomery, son of one of the Conqueror's most important supporters, the Earl of Shrewsbury, during the Norman "invasion" of west Wales. The earth and timber castle may have been built in about 1092 on the site of an Iron Age fort (courtesy Neil Ludlow).

Why these few castles were built remains something of a mystery, but at least one castle historian speculates that these Normans were preparing to combat a rebellion by supporters of Earl Godwin. Even so, the Saxons felt no need to emulate the Normans and build their own castles. They had their own system of defended settlements, known as "burhs," which had adequately served them long before the Battle of Hastings.

Rather than enclosing a private residence with thick walls and massive structures designed to provide defensive might, the Saxons chose to enclose entire settlements with fortifications. Inside, both subject and Saxon chief lived in fairly close proximity. Even though the chief's house would have been the most impressive, and possibly would have had some extra protection, the overall function of the burh was quite different from that of the castle, which was in its entirety a lord's private residence. True, as shall be shown later in this book, castles bustled with activity on a regular basis and, similar to a settled community, provided accommodation for all sorts of residents besides the lord's family and also received a variety of guests, from other lords and their households to local subjects attending the lord's court. Nevertheless, at the end of the day, a castle was primarily a private (fortified) residence whereas the burh was a (fortified) settlement, inside of which the leader of the group and his subjects resided.

Even though William had defeated Harold II to finally take the English throne, the Saxons were not completely ready to accept a new king. It took several decades for the Normans to finally subdue their new subjects, not just in England but in Wales as well. One of their most important weapons was the castle. The Normans introduced two types of earth and timber castles to Britain: the ringwork and the motte and bailey castle. Of these two types, William's castle at Pevensey can be classified as a partial ringwork and his second stronghold, Hastings, was dominated by its motte. Of the pre–Conquest castles mentioned above, Ewyas Harold, Hereford, and Richard's Castle were definitely motte castles; however, there is some question whether the fourth castle, Clavering, was a motte or not. Generally more visible in the landscape than ringworks, motte castles have long been considered *the* Norman castle; yet, many of Britain's major stone castles began as ringworks. Both mottes and ringworks can be found off the beaten track in open fields and behind village shops throughout the British Isles.

Ringwork Castles

In addition to Pevensey, William the Conqueror erected a series of castles soon after his victory at Hastings, largely in an effort to secure his new capitol city, London, as the power base for his kingdom. Pevensey was not the only site where William's army reused earlier fortifications to bolster their defenses. Two of his most important ringwork castles were established on Roman sites at Dover and London; they eventually became England's mightiest stone castles. Both are open to the public throughout the year. Traces of the original earthwork castles at these monumentally important sites are now difficult to identify, but they probably occupied the sites on which the two great keeps now stand. William probably also ordered the construction of two other castles, mottes, which may have reused Saxon fortifications, at Canterbury and Berkhamsted, as he made his way around southeastern England before heading into London for his coronation on Christmas Day 1066.

The tactic was not only symbolic but it was practical as well, for the remains of Roman, Saxon and Iron Age forts often contained substantial earthen embankments and masonry walls originally erected for the same purpose that the Normans were employing them. The structures not only enhanced a ringwork's defensive capacity, but they also helped the Normans establish their power bases as they marched across southern England to take formal control of London.

During 1067, King William I returned to Normandy for almost ten months. During his absence, his men built another castle, a ringwork, at Winchester, which had been both a Roman town and the Saxon capital. Here again, the construction symbolically reiterated the new Norman king's position, replacing both the Romans and Saxons as the most powerful force in the realm. Upon William's return later that year, he personally selected Exeter, also a former Roman and Saxon site, for his next castle, yet another ringwork. By now, the Norman king had made it clear to his new subjects that he was in command and in England to stay.

Interestingly, even though they are most often acclaimed for the introduction and prolific construction of motte castles, in the years immediately after the Conquest, the Normans predominantly built ringwork castles to consolidate their control of England and Wales.[4] William the Conqueror found ringworks of particular value in securing and controlling an area. They were easy and economical to build, constructed with locally available natural resources, needed only unskilled laborers, and, at least in theory, could be raised in a matter of days. A partial ringwork such as at Pevensey was erected so that the arc faced outward towards the likely

The powerful earthen embankments and deep ditch forming the ringwork castle completely dominate the great twelfth-century keep at Castle Rising.

direction from which an enemy would stage an assault. Behind the curved banks and timber defenses, encamped soldiers could shield themselves, at least for a time, from advancing forces and use the embankments as cover while firing upon the attackers.

Also known as an earthen enclosure castle, a ringwork castle was a low-lying oval or round-shaped mound encircled by an earthen bank and at least one ditch. The main ditch was located on the outer side of the embankment. Builders often also dug a ditch on the inner side. The summit of the mound was scooped out so that the center of each ringwork's was lower than the enclosing embankment. This feature gave the structure its name. A timber palisade, positioned around the perimeter of the mound, defended the interior of the site, which held timber structures. Whereas several ringworks later acquired masonry structures, many others did not. They were eventually abandoned or neglected in favor of more substantial sites. Some ringworks were actually converted into baileys and used to support adjacent mottes.

Arguably Britain's finest surviving ringwork can be explored at Castle Rising in Norfolk, where visitors will also discover one of Norman England's most impressive castle keeps. Almost entirely swallowed up by massive earthen banks, the great Norman keep, which stands 50 feet high, barely peeks above their summit. Begun in 1138 by William d'Albini, Earl of Sussex, shortly after his marriage to Henry I's widow, Adeliza de Louvain, Castle Rising was built to engulf the existing Saxon settlement at the site, which the Romans had occupied even earlier. The Norman castle covers an area of over 12 acres. Rising some 60 feet from the base of the ditch, the earthen banks which form the inner bailey stand about 30 feet above the level of the interior ward. A mammoth structure that would easily have dwarfed its inhabitants, the ringwork contained all of the castle's main domestic buildings. It also enclosed the late-eleventh-century church, probably held by Stigand, Archbishop of Canterbury from 1052 until his replacement in 1070 by Odo, the Norman Bishop of Bayeux, William the Conqueror's half-brother. Standing inside the well-preserved embankments of one of the three enormous baileys at Castle Rising, visitors will gain a real appreciation for the defensive might that ringworks could offer their residents.

The primary purpose of these castles was military; their use as residences was a secondary consideration at best, at least in the earliest months of the Norman campaign to consolidate England against the Saxons. For the time being, at least, the Normans had subjugation on their minds, not making themselves at home. Shortly thereafter, however, these earth and timber strongholds acquired new buildings, including residences and other domestic chambers, and were used as castles, as defined above. For example, almost immediately after conquering the Saxons, William granted Pevensey to his half-brother, Robert, Count of Mortain, who transformed the site into a masonry castle. And, soon after his return from Normandy in 1067, William began erecting of one of his most famous buildings, the White Tower, which still dominates the Tower of London, one of the world's greatest castles.

The Normans built ringworks well into the twelfth century and continued to occupy

In 1139, King Stephen unsuccessfully besieged Corfe during his civil war with the Empress Matilda. Just a mile away from the castle, Stephen's forces built an intriguing set of earthworks, known as the Rings, seen here from the battlements inside the castle. From the Rings, Stephen carried out what proved to be a futile siege.

them much later. Why some lords erected ringworks and others built motte castles is unclear. Some researchers speculate that the reasoning was as simple as the personal preference of the builder, but there is also some evidence that topographic features also played a role in the decision-making process. In southern Wales, for example, there appears to be a distinct difference in which type of earth and timber castle was built. All of the ringworks were constructed either in the Vale of Glamorgan or near the southern coast of the Gower peninsula, in fertile lowland areas underlain by limestone. Geological conditions evidently precluded the construction of mottes in these areas. On the other hand, the more rugged upland areas were characterized by the presence of glacial deposits, ridges of rock that could be more easily reshaped into mottes. At least twenty-eight ringworks were constructed in lowland Glamorgan, where the Normans primarily established themselves in the late eleventh century; only a handful of mottes were built in upland Glamorgan, where the native Welsh were forced to live after the Normans arrived in Wales.

Sadly, knowledge about how ringworks were constructed is limited because relatively few of the sites have been excavated and there is little information on them in the historical record. Despite that, excavations at Chateau des Marais undertaken in the late 1970s identified the series of steps taken to build a thirteenth-century ringwork on the Isle of Guernsey.[5] After burning the land clear of vegetation, builders marked out the plan of the castle with large stones, which they placed to indicate the midway point for the earthen ramparts to be built over them. Then, they piled up heaps of turf to form the embankment, over which they laid a mass of clay mixed with granite chunks to form the outermost coating of the rampart.

The relative speed with which ringwork castles could be constructed, or at least partly

Best recognized from the eastern side of the site, the low ditch and ring-bank at Llantrithyd Castle enclose almost the entire ringwork, which had a diameter of about 184 feet.

completed, made them quite useful as siege castles. Oftentimes, a besieging army had to dig in and wait for the defenders inside a castle to either surrender or gain enough support from their lord's allies (assuming he had some) to go ahead with the siege. In the meantime, the earthen embankments provided temporary protection until the situation came to a head or was resolved. One of the finest examples of a ringwork designed for use during a siege is located within view of Corfe Castle in Dorset. Known as "the Rings," the ringwork and bailey castle was built in 1139 during the Anarchy to shelter King Stephen's men, who besieged the formidable masonry castle on the nearby hilltop, which was held by supporters of the Empress Matilda during her fight for the English throne. Even though their efforts proved unsuccessful, their ringwork castle has survived the ages.

Besides their role in warfare and the establishment of the Norman kingdom in the decades just after 1066, many ringworks were the defended homes of lesser lords whose income prevented them from constructing masonry castles but who, nonetheless, wanted to showcase their status in a socially acceptable and visual way. Ringworks fulfilled that role for them. The elevated structures stood above ground level and were capable of supporting a wide range of buildings inside their circular embankments. Today, virtually all traces of these interior structures, primarily constructed with timber, have vanished but archaeological excavations have offered insight into living in a ringwork castle.

Even though the tiny hamlet of Llantrithyd presently contains only a few residences, the spot is a treasure trove of medieval sites, including a modest ringwork castle. Probably built in the early twelfth century by the de Cardiff family, who were followers of the Norman Robert Fitzhamon, Earl of Gloucester and Lord of Glamorgan, the grass-covered ringwork can be reached via a public footpath behind a house on the eastern side of the settlement. The site measures about 184 feet across and consists of a low bank and ditch. Even though the western side has been quarried and portions of the northern side slope directly downhill to Llantrithyd Brook, the rest of the castle survives in good condition.

Not surprisingly, the ringwork lacks its original timber structures, but humps and bumps on the surface indicate where they once stood: archaeological excavations during the 1960s revealed that an array of buildings originally peppered the site. A six-post timber structure on the southern side of the enclosure may have been the original gatehouse or a granary or a storage building. On the opposite side of the ringwork, evidence was uncovered for at least three other structures, including a large ten-post, six-bay aisled hall partly embedded in the earthen bank on the northwestern edge. Measuring about 52.5 feet by 33 feet, this hall was surrounded by a drystone wall and probably had a thatched roof. Archaeologists also discovered a circular structure on the northern side of the site, which was embedded in the earthen ramparts. The unusual building measured 16 feet across; it may have been an observation tower, a kitchen, or a dovecote. It stood alongside yet another building, the purpose of which remains unclear.

Many earth and timber sites such as Llantrithyd are deceptively small. However, excavations have proven that they were often crowded with buildings and activity, and were occupied for centuries prior to their destruction or abandonment in favor of larger, more comfortable residences. At Llantrithyd, for example, the remains of Llantrithyd Place, a grand Tudor manor house fitted with formal gardens, orchards, and an extensive set of ornamental fishponds, exist midway between the ringwork site and a fine medieval church dedicated the St. Illtyd, which contains the tombs of former castle owners among its treasures. Individually, each of the historical sites at Llantrithyd offers a doorway into the past. When experienced together, like pieces of a puzzle, they help visitors recreate a picture of what life may have been in the lordship of minor lords such as the de Cardiffs or their heirs, the Bassets and Mansels.

Motte Castles

As depicted on the Bayeux Tapestry, Duke William of Normandy's first motte castle in England was erected on a hillock overlooking Hastings, where his army settled to wait for the arrival of the Saxon army. While there is no proof that the traces of what was a fairly small motte and a set of earthen embankments date to the Norman invasion, they more than likely are the remains of William's castle. By 1069, William had granted custody of the site to Robert, the second Count of Eu, who was also lord of the County of Eu on the Norman side of the English Channel opposite Hastings. Prior to construction of the castle mound, a Saxon burh, known as Haestingaceaster, may have occupied the site. However, there is better evidence for pre–Conquest occupation of the hilltop well before the Saxons, for the castle actually occupied the site of earthworks that at least partly date from the Iron Age.[6]

Hastings Castle was the first of scores of motte castles that still dot the British Isles. The classic motte and bailey castle was essentially circular in plan, surrounded by a ditch (either wet — the moat — or dry), and had at least one oval or kidney-shaped bailey, an area enclosed by earthen embankments crowned with timber palisades and an outer ditch, inside of which the main activities of daily life took place. All mottes were artificial mounds constructed, as mentioned, either with the spoils from the surrounding ditch, or by reshaping an existing natural structure, a hillock or glacial deposit, so that the flat-topped summit could support one or more timber structures or a stone ring-wall known as a shell keep. Around the summit, a timber palisade provided protection for the residents who lived on the motte, normally the lord and his family. Mottes were not only used to house the lord, but were also excellent observation points from which a guard could watch over the surrounding countryside and sound an alarm when necessary.

As William began to parcel out his new kingdom to the loyal lords who fought by his side against the Saxons, motte castles began to appear throughout England and in Wales. In fact, in order to gather enough men for his army, Duke William had probably promised his most important supporters that they would receive large parcels of land if they accompanied him to England and helped defeat Harold II. In exchange, William expected nothing less than complete fealty from the men. The bargain was the basis of the feudal system that William enforced in his new kingdom.

Initiated in Europe by Charlemagne, the Holy Roman Emperor, in the ninth century, feudalism was a political and economic system under which land was granted by the monarch or another high-ranking nobleman to a person in exchange for military service, avowed loyalty, and other, sometimes financial, obligations. A monarch such as William the Conqueror divided his kingdom into parcels known as "fiefs," and granted tenancy or the right to use the land to favored subjects, known as "vassals," whose power in an area was based on having land, which he held "in feud" and administered from his castle. The vassals were obligated to their ruler, but, in turn, governed a class of "serfs," who tilled the lands and labored for their lord. Serfs were actually bound to the land. Vassals could parcel out their estates to lesser vassals, in a process called "subinfeudation," whereby the feudal obligations were comparable to those owed by the greater vassals to their king. The men were required to pay homage — to swear complete loyalty — and to fight for their king on a moment's notice. They were also obligated to provide a specific number of knights, drawn from their own landholdings, to fight in the king's army. Although these noblemen acquired their power from the king, many acted as "kings" of their own estates and doled out punishment, levied taxes, minted coins, and waged wars from their castles. The most powerful of William I's feudal lords were Roger de Montgomery, Earl of Shrewsbury, Hugh d'Avranches, Earl of Chester, and William FitzOsbern, Earl of Hereford.

Whereas ringworks had superficial similarities to defended fortifications that the Anglo-Saxons were accustomed to seeing (the burhs), motte castles were something of a novelty. However, they were even more an unwanted intrusion in the landscape which the Normans used to solidify their feudal kingdom and as the centers of their new lordships. The Saxons must have interpreted these unfamiliar structures as symbols of Norman oppression and a constant reminder that they were no longer free in their own homeland. Certainly, the Normans appreciated both of these factors and had few qualms about building castles wherever they pleased. Varying in height from a low of five to six feet to well over 50 feet high, mottes physically dominated an area, just as the Normans politically — and physically — controlled their new subjects. Scores of motte castles were erected in borderlands and political and cultural frontier regions,[7] such as the Welsh Marches, where place names such as Bishop's Castle and Castell Caereinion reveal the presence of a medieval castle. These were areas of frequent conflict between the Norman overlords and the local populace,[8] and castles were used to maintain control over the lands held in feud on behalf of their king. The new lords had found new prosperity, and had little desire to relinquish their power to the native inhabitants.

When William I returned from his ten-month visit to Normandy late in 1067, he found a kingdom still in the throes of dealing with having been conquered. In fact, the conquest was not settled overnight. Even though King Harold II had died at Hastings, Saxons all around England had no intention of being ruled by a foreigner, no matter how strong his claim to the throne had been, and discontent continued to foment. Consequently, in an effort to quell the tension, William decided to construct more castles. Now, motte castles began to dominate the countryside from southern England all the way north to York, where the Normans erected mottes on either side of the River Ouse.

Not only did the king build substantial motte castles at Warwick, York, Lincoln, Huntingdon, Cambridge, and Nottingham, his co-regent, William FitzOsbern, built his own motte castles at Berkeley, Monmouth, Clifford, and Wigmore, rebuilt the pre–Conquest castle at Ewyas Harold, and began building the great hall-keep at Chepstow, one of Britain's earliest stone castles. Other motte castles were constructed at Chester, Stafford, Oxford, Gloucester, Norwich, Worcester, and Shrewsbury, as the Normans progressively consolidated the kingdom under the rule of King William I.[9] William also began building the motte that is still the focal point of England's largest continuously occupied royal castle, Windsor. Located some 20 miles west of London, Windsor was strategically positioned to defend the capital city. William's castle took its name from the Saxon village of Windlesora (also known as Old Windsor), which overlooked the River Thames at the edge of the Saxon royal hunting ground and forest that had attracted the king to the spot to build his castle.

Like ringworks, motte castles were easy and inexpensive to build, needing only unskilled laborers to excavate a large, round ditch and heap the materials dug from the ditch into the center of the circular area it enclosed. The pile of earth and other materials formed a mound, the motte, which might vary from five or six feet in height to well over 50 feet. Summits measured from 20 feet in diameter to 380 feet across, as at Norwich Castle in Norfolk. At many mottes the basal diameter was twice that of its height.[10]

Like ringwork castles, building a motte was a fairly simple, inexpensive project that required no special materials and few, if any, skilled laborers. In fact, the labor pool was largely drawn from the local area: the recently-defeated Saxons were pressed into service as the brawn for the building projects, which undoubtedly fueled their resentment of the Normans. However, the effort involved in erecting a motte castle was much more labor- and time-intensive than building a ringwork. At one time, it was thought that a motte could be built in as little as eight days, but, unless the king or lord could muster 500 men to work on the project at the same time,[11] it would have actually taken several weeks to several months to build the average motte castle. One study estimated that it would have taken 42 days for 50 men working a ten-hour day to complete the motte at Lodsbridge in Sussex, which now stands about 16 to 17 feet high and had a base measuring about 129.5 feet across.[12] The enormous investment in time is one reason why it made more sense for William I to begin taking control of England with ringwork castles, which could be raised more quickly.

Though heavily stylized, the depictions of motte castles in the Bayeux Tapestry offer insight into their construction. In one panel, the construction of the motte at Hastings is shown in considerable detail: laborers busily pick the ground and scoop materials upwards to pile onto the partly completed mound, which is already crowned with either to be a tower or a timber palisade. The rounded mound features a series of horizontal bands of different colored soil laid on top of each other; an outer layer of material, which appears to encase the entire structure, perhaps even including the tower/palisade. The image makes sense, when we consider that, in order to prevent a pile of earth from collapsing, particularly when it must support several buildings and the people who live in them, something more substantial than merely tossing the loose dirt into a mound was necessary to keep them upright.

Archaeological excavations have revealed that, as the Tapestry suggests, a variety of substances were in fact used to erect a motte. At some castles, builders covered the initial level of material, which came from the ditch, with a thick layer of turf, to keep the unconsolidated pile in place. Then, they covered the entire structure with a top layer of clay, which held the mound together. Some castle builders alternated layers of gravel, clay, and chalk in order to consolidate the soil and turf mounds. It is not surprising that many mottes were created by reshaping craggy hills, which contained bedrock or naturally occurring layers of stone. The mounds would have been less prone to collapse from the weight of the timber buildings they supported and from the erosive effects of wet weather. The image of Hastings Castle on the Tapestry lacks an encircling ditch, which is an indispensable feature of most motte castles; however, close examination of the other castles in the tapestry, at Dol, Dinan, Rennes, and Bayeux in France, reveals the presence of the ditch and the outer bank that defended them.

The fact that so many motte castles survive in the countryside, albeit without their original timber structures, attests to their strength and that the building technique described above was viable. Portions of the outside of some mottes were revetted, or faced with timber or stone, which also helped prevent them from slumping. Excavations at the motte castle at South Mimms, which Geoffrey de Mandeville, Earl of Essex, probably erected in about 1141 during the Anarchy, revealed that the 10- to 12-foot high mound was actually enclosed with timber shuttering, which prevented anyone outside from seeing most of the motte. The shuttering enclosed only the top of the motte, which was comprised of chalk, flint, and clay,[13] and also surrounded a tall timber tower, part of which was actually embedded in the mound. The

motte had a basal diameter of about 110 feet across, and the castle could only be entered through a 26-foot-long tunnel cut into the mound which opened into the base of the tower.[14] Whether this design was common to other motte castles remains uncertain. Walls of stone still completely disguise the mottes at Berkeley Castle and Farnham Castle, but visitors can identify their locations by their roundish shape and prominent positions in the centers of the sites.

Each of the castles on the Bayeux Tapestry is crowned by a timber structure. The structure under construction on top of Hastings Castle probably depicts a tower similar to those shown on the French mottes rather than a palisade. Even so, mottes were known to have supported both types of structures at the same time. The inner tower would have served as the lord's residence, the strong point of the castle, and as an observation post, while the surrounding timber palisade would have provided a barrier to an attack, and also a screen, which hid activities on the summit from general view. The building of some towers actually began before the motte was solidified; the timber footings were set into the ground and then the earth for the motte heaped up around them. At other castles, the towers were embedded into the summit after completion of the motte.

Even though they ranged from 20 feet in diameter to an immense 380 feet across (Norwich Castle), the summits of most mottes were relatively small and could hold only a limited number of buildings. To compensate for the limited space, most motte castles had at least one bailey, which was joined to the motte with a timber bridge that also spanned the ditch. The baileys were the true hubs of activity at most castles and contained a number of timber buildings, including a hall, the kitchen, stables, workshops, the smithy, and accommodation for servants and members of the garrison. They also served as obstacles to successful assaults on the motte. Many motte castles only had one bailey, but others had two, as at Windsor, and some, such as Clun, had even more. Only three British castles are known to have had two mottes: Lewes and Lincoln in England and Nevern in Wales.

Even though many more motte castles have been excavated than ringworks, few have been as extensively examined as Hen Domen, which is located on the Welsh side of the border with England in Montgomeryshire. One of Roger de Montgomery's earliest castles, Hen Domen was built in about 1070 to overlook the important fording spot of Rhydwhiman close to the former Roman site of Forden Gaer.[15] The substantial motte and bailey castle stood about 26 feet high, had a basal diameter of 131 feet, and had a summit which stretched 21 feet across. It was occupied almost continuously until well into the thirteenth century, when it was superseded by the impressive stone castle situated on a hilltop just a mile to the south. When the stone structure received the name Montgomery Castle, the earth and timber motte castle became known as Hen Domen, which means "the old mound."

Archaeological teams led by Robert Higham and Philip Barker conducted excavations at Hen Domen for almost thirty years, beginning in 1960. Their findings startled scholars, who had come to believe that the standard motte and bailey castle was a fairly simple structure with few ancillary buildings. During the excavations, archaeologists uncovered a wealth of evidence to prove that the grassy open areas we see today actually teemed with activity and were often crammed full of the buildings that supported daily life at the castle and also helped occupants prepare for war when necessary.

Opposite: The development of Lewes Castle dates to about 1068 during the tenure of the Warennes at the site. Consisting primarily of two motte castles and an associated bailey, Lewes is a masterpiece of early Norman construction and one of England's earliest motte castles.

Today, visitors to the site will find Hen Domen obscured by roadside hedges and vegetation. Like most other motte and bailey sites, it is grass-covered and lacks any traces of medieval structures, which were built with timber and have long since rotted or burned away. However, the buildings left evidence of their existence, in form of post holes, inside the bailey. Located on the eastern side of the motte, the bailey was enclosed by two turf-covered clay embankments and a ditch and defended with timber palisades.[16]

The number and types of structures erected in the bailey at Hen Domen varied with the needs of the times. Just after the Conquest, the castle consisted of the motte, which was enclosed by a ditch, and also featured a forebuilding, which stood more or less perpendicular to the bridge connecting the bailey to the motte and spanning the ditch. The forebuilding may have held the main hall or functioned as a barbican.[17] Other buildings, including what was possibly a house, lined the northern side of the bailey (the southern side was not excavated) during the first building phase. Then, in 1095, the Welsh attacked and devastated the castle so that the timber defenses had to be rebuilt. At that time, the owners apparently added a timber wall-walk or fighting platform and a timber tower at the northwestern corner of the bailey near the motte.[18]

During the mid-twelfth century, the northern half of the bailey at Hen Domen acquired over fifty new buildings (the southern half probably received its fair share as well). As a result, the site was almost overflowing with timber structures, probably roofed with thatch, containing a large hall with a portico; a second hall away from the motte, which was probably one of several structures built specifically to accommodate servants and/or a garrison; numerous houses; a water cistern; a guardroom; and possibly a granary.[19] In the later 12th or early 13th century, more buildings were added or replaced earlier structures, including what may have been the chapel and another house.

Interestingly, during the final building phase at Hen Domen, the bailey contained fewer structures than it had in the previous century, quite possibly because its role as a major castle declined when Henry III's stone castle at nearby Montgomery became the center of the lordship. At least for a time, though, Hen Domen may have continued to act as an observation post for the larger castle and was only manned by a small garrison. Excavations near the motte ditch uncovered traces of two buildings, which may have housed the soldiers, and another building on the opposite side of the bailey.[20]

Today, visitors to Hen Domen, Llantrithyd, or any one of dozens of earth and timber castles in Britain will encounter only the earthwork remains. The timber structures no longer survive, at least above ground, to prove to modern skeptics that many of these sites were once formidable barriers to an assault and once buzzed with daily life. And age and the weather have taken their toll on the mottes, ringworks, and the earthen banks of their baileys. All have been eroded and stand somewhat lower than they did in their medieval heyday, and, in many cases, slumping earth and the natural accumulation of vegetation has filled in their ditches. Yet, it should always be remembered that, just like their mightier stone counterparts, these sites housed real people. They governed an area and a local population, who supported the castle dwellers with their labor and their products. They endured sieges, oftentimes burning to the ground only to be rebuilt with stronger or more complex defenses; or, they were replaced by stone castles built from scratch a short distance away, as happened at Montgomery.

Some earth and timber castles have survived due to later incorporation into stone castles, such as occurred at Windsor, Warwick, or Arundel. Many motte castles, such as Wiston, Berkhamsted, and Pickering, have been cleared of their vegetation and made accessible

Enclosed by an extensive earthen embankment and associated ditch, the elliptical bailey at Wiston Castle covers an area of approximately two and a half acres. The motte and shell keep stand on the northern side of the bailey.

to the public. When we wander their remains and contemplate how they were used, we can gain a real appreciation for the hardiness of the people who lived in them and were governed from them and for how well these structures served them. In many ways, it is a wonder that ringworks and mottes continue to survive some 900 years after their construction. Despite their primitive appearance and lack of above-ground structures, they are repositories of history and humanity and have much to teach us about our collective past.

Exploring the Remains

Castle hunting is a pastime anyone can enjoy. For castles off the beaten track, an Ordnance Survey map — especially one of the Landranger or Pathfinder series — can be a visitor's best friend. Yet, seeking out and finding the castle is just the beginning of the adventure. Many castles, particularly earth and timber sites, can be found by examining the place names in a region. For example, in Pembrokeshire, the place names New Moat, Henry's Moat, Castlemartin, and Walwyn's Castle hint at their origins as medieval castles. Oftentimes, it takes just driving into the village to spot the castle, many of which are accessible to the public via public footpaths or a simple knock on the door of the property owner (many ringworks and motte castles are now on private property but most owners are happy to allow access to the sites — indeed many are veritable treasure troves of knowledge about their castles). Sometimes, the site is obscured by trees or off the roadway so that it takes detective work to locate it. Besides a village name, another indicator of the presence of a castle is the name of a farm or house, such as Talyfan Farm, where Castell Talyfan can be explored.

Wiston Castle is a typical motte and bailey castle. Managed by Cadw, the governmental agency in charge of historic monuments in Wales, the motte has been cleared of bracken and a set of wooden steps allows access to the summit, as it may have been reached in the Middle Ages. The site itself is nestled in a quiet spot not too far north of the A40 roadway that runs between Haverfordwest and Carmarthen. The castle is located immediately across the lane from the medieval church, which has a small parking lot and makes an excellent landmark when hunting for the site. Once through the stile and onto the site, visitors come face to face with a large earthen embankment and a gap — possibly the medieval entrance — which opens into the bailey. Nowadays, the elliptical bailey, which encloses an area of approximately two and a half acres, is cluttered with grazing cattle and mucky patties. During the early twelfth century, when Wizo the Fleming occupied the site, the enclosed area would have held the castle's main support buildings, possibly including a hall, the kitchen area, a stables, workshops, and living quarters. The ramparts surrounding the bailey probably date to the early thirteenth century, when they would have been topped with a timber palisade.

Across the bailey, the massive motte still dominates its surroundings. Its steep sides and the 10-foot-deep encircling ditch would have made it challenging at best to reach the top, especially for armored attackers. The ditch created a gap between the bailey's embankments and the motte. Quite possibly, a timber bridge linked the two structures at this point; from there anyone could access the motte via a set of timber stairs. Even with the aid of modern steps, it is an exhilarating experience to climb to the flat-topped summit of the motte, which has a diameter of over 59 feet and stands almost 30 feet high. Originally, the motte would have been surrounded with a timber palisade, inside of which a timber tower would have stood; however, it was refortified with a round stone ring-wall, known as a shell keep. When the castle was occupied, the stone wall would have enclosed a variety of structures designed to make the lord's life easier. A gaping hole in the now ruinous structure offers views of the bailey below and to the countryside well beyond the castle. Standing on top of the motte, one can easily understand why this type of castle was built. A lord certainly felt as if he were on top of the world — or at least on top of his piece of turf. A motte castle visibly reinforced his domination of an area and of the people who lived there.

Yet, throughout Britain, including at Wiston, it quickly became evident that timber defenses were insufficient to prevent rebellion and the torching of castles. Timber was flammable and subject to decay. As seen above at Hen Domen and Llantrithyd, some owners frequently replaced or added new timber structures to their castles. However, many more chose to rebuild the timber defenses and interior structures with a more durable building material — stone. Others started from scratch and built massive stone castles, as at Caerphilly and Goodrich. Even then, timber remained an essential part of the castle-building process, for it was required for flooring, ceilings, and roofs, and for defense features such as hoarding.

One should not get the impression that William the Conqueror was the only Norman king to build earth and timber castles. Rather, he was the instigator. His sons, William I and Henry I, were also prolific castle-builders, as were dozens of Norman lords and later monarchs, from the Angevin to the Plantagenet dynasties. However, as times changed, so did castle-building, and stone increasingly became the preferred building material for new castles. Motte and ringwork castles continued to be occupied, but many were greatly altered by new owners and new building styles. Along with these changes came the expectation that lords would apply to the king for a "license to crenellate," or formal permission to erect a new castle or strengthen one already standing. Although never mandated by the monarchy nor a common practice until after 1200, applying for a license to erect a castle or to fortify an already extant residence indicated not only that the applicant had the self-confidence to approach the king, but also demonstrated that he possessed the financial and personal status that came with the ability to build a castle.

Stone Castles

During the twelfth century, an important shift occurred as builders increasingly began to choose stone over timber for their new castles and to replace or rebuild timber defenses and other timber structures in castles already standing. Even though earth and timber castles continued to be built and used into the thirteenth century — and later at some sites, stone castles increasingly began to dominate the English and Welsh landscape. Not only was timber prone to rot and fire, which could come from a castle's own hearths as well as from an enemy attack, but stone was better able to withstand the pounding of siege engines and could also be shaped into features for both defensive and decorative purposes. Not surprisingly, many motte and ringwork castles were refortified with stone defenses, including the stone shell keeps mentioned earlier, and also stone walls, stone towers, and, most notably, stone keeps or great towers, one of the most recognizable features of a Norman stone castle, then and today.

Though it seems logical that a lord would choose a sturdier building material such as stone when making repairs to damaged timber structures, in many cases, as at Hen Domen, some rebuilding efforts were done with timber. In fact, some lords were reluctant to use stone at all, as at Clifford's Tower in York, where the Saxons destroyed a timber tower on the massive motte on five different occasions before it was refortified with stone defenses. As the Normans began to feel more settled in their new kingdom, they no longer felt the same urgency to throw up new earth and timber strongholds and instead began strengthening their castles with stone. In fact, almost all of the approximately 100 Norman earth and timber castles built in the eleventh century were substantially rebuilt in stone.[21] Many developed into the realm's greatest fortresses.

For example, even though the extensive masonry fortifications give the impression that Windsor Castle is a stone fortress, it is in fact a motte and bailey castle: topped by the Round Tower, the great motte still dominates the center of the formidable fortress. On either side of the motte, the two baileys contain the major buildings, including the State apartments. A towered curtain wall forms the outer defenses where the timber palisades once stood. Similarly, Arundel and Warwick Castles originated as motte and bailey castles. Today, both retain their original mottes and shell keeps; their baileys were later enclosed with extensive and expensive residential buildings and towered walls. When exploring these castles, imagine them without the stone structures or as if they are heavily ruined — though they seem considerably larger than the average motte castle, they would appear exactly the same and much like the scores of motte sites scattered throughout Britain. Though grandiose by comparison, particularly with their stone buildings intact, these better known masonry castles contain the same features that we easily identify with the smaller motte and bailey castles. Even though the timber structures no longer survive or the sites are no longer occupied, they are all castles.

Unlike earth and timber castles, which can be divided into two basic categories based on stylistic differences, it is difficult to distinguish stone castles by type, and in many ways, they are best all categorized as "enclosure castles" or "stone enclosure castles," regardless of their specific plan. Fortunately, at least when dealing with basic terminology, "ringwork" is an adequate alternative to "earthen enclosure castle," and thus eliminates the confusion that could arise if stone castles were known as "stone enclosure castles." However, just labeling them as "stone castles" seems inadequate, for the plans of these castles vary greatly. Some stone castles are also known as quadrangular castles, because their basic design features four, more or less, square sides, with corner towers and a main gatehouse. This design appeared late in British castle-building and is best exemplified by Bodiam Castle, which was built in the late fourteenth century. Ironically, most castellologists now consider the towered, moated, gated, battlemented structure at Bodiam to be a fortified manor house rather than a true castle. Another variety of stone castle is the concentric castle, which appeared in Britain in the late thirteenth century, and is exemplified by Caerphilly and Beaumaris Castles in Wales. Other castles, such as the Tower of London and Dover Castle, acquired the concentric design over the course of their complex building histories, but Caerphilly was the first of its kind in Britain to be built from scratch. Today, it is a grand ruin.

Both of the above stone castle designs can be classified as "enclosure castles," as can all other stone castles, which were neither concentric nor quadrangular but which characteristically had a stone curtain wall enveloping the entire site, as well as other stone structures. Unfortunately, there is no one all-encompassing word comparable to "ringwork" to adequately cover enclosure castles predominantly built with stone. Moreover, the issue becomes even hazier when one considers the great stone castles that originated as earth and timber sites, such as Arundel, Warwick, or Windsor. Should they be considered as motte and bailey castles or as stone enclosure castles? The short answer is "yes," these sites are both types of castle. Over time, they developed from motte and bailey sites into substantial enclosure castles, with baileys surrounded by stone curtain walls and at least one ditch or moat, entered through a primary gateway cut into the enclosing wall, and containing all the main castle structures. The mix of structures inside the walls has nothing to do with the site's identification as an enclosure castle. In fact, as some researchers point out, the main factor that distinguishes earth and timber castles from stone castles is the choice of dominant building material,[22] not the particular plan. In reality, timber was widely used in the construction of stone castles. So, for the purposes of this book, the term "enclosure castle" will apply to all stone castles; individual variants will be mentioned when applicable.

A lord's choice to use stone was based on several factors, none of which could he afford to take lightly: his income; his immediate and long term goals; the availability of building materials; the threat of attack from his subjects or from a rival; his relationship with the monarchy; and his ego and social status. During the twelfth century, when the price of building stone began to rise significantly, many lords chose to continue living in their castles, making necessary repairs rather than beginning major rebuilding projects or building afresh in stone. If a castle had just withstood an assault, he would initiate repairs as quickly as possible to make the place defensible and livable and, perhaps most importantly, to retain his grip on the lordship. But, depending on his financial status, he might opt to rebuild in timber rather than make the switch to stone. Be that as it may, many lords, whose incomes (which averaged less than £1000 a year) were far less than their king's, felt that it was much more important to spend the money to build stone castles than it was to worry about a financial shortfall; so, in the late twelfth and early thirteenth centuries, Britain experienced a surge of stone castle-building.

Building with stone was much more complicated than constructing a motte or ringwork, especially when building from scratch, and created a series of concerns for the castle owner. Extensive planning was required before the lord actually embarked on such a project. Whereas the construction of earth and timber castles depended on locally obtained natural resources and the unskilled labor of workers largely forced into service (at least during the years immediately after the Conquest), stone castles were much more resource- and labor-intensive, and, hence, much more costly. Unlike earth and timber, stone was not always locally available, and the costs of transporting stone could be exorbitant. Even if there were local quarries, the type of stone might not suit castle construction — it could weather or shatter easily or be difficult to shape — and, even when obtained from the local area, it could be pricey. Unless the king or lord owned the local quarry, he would have to make substantial purchases or lease the site from its actual owners, oftentimes a monastic community. If the site had previously been used as a fort or burh by the Romans or Saxons, some building materials might have been available for reuse in the new Norman castle, which would have helped reduce the expenses of obtaining stone from a distance while also fulfilling a symbolic role for the lord. Today, Roman brickwork and red tiles can often be identified in the walls of Norman castles.

In addition to finding a reliable source of building stone, a castle-building lord had to locate, hire and bring in skilled laborers, such as quarrymen (also known as quarries), rough masons, freemasons, carters, barrowmen, hodmen, layers, setters, and slaters, to quarry the stone, haul it to the castle site, shape it, and lay it in place. A master mason not only supervised the building activities but often designed the castle as well. In addition, woodmen and hewers had to be hired to fell trees, which meant that the lord had to own plenty of forest land or had to purchase woodland for his own use, and then pay for the wood to be brought to the site. Timber was used for a variety of purposes, including as scaffolding, braces for archways, for bridges, the main doors, shuttering, and interior doors. Other materials, such as lead, iron, lime, and charcoal, also had to be purchased and transported to the building site, and other specialists, such as carpenters, miners, smiths, limeworkers, plumbers, tillers, and thatchers, had to be hired.[23] Interestingly, Henry II, a prolific castle-building king, continuously employed a select group of skilled workers who traveled from site to site to build castles,[24] which must have been a considerable expense, but one which the king undoubtedly thought well worth the price.

Not only did the castle owner have to pay the costs of purchasing and transporting the materials to the building site, they also paid the workers' wages, purchased livestock, other supplies, tools, and equipment, and covered any other relevant expenses. Depending on the laborer's specialization, wages varied greatly. For example, master masons and master carpenters could expect to receive six pence a day, a retainer fee of three pence a day, and a gown allowance.[25] Some masters also received extra monetary payments, grants of land, and, in a few cases, as with James of St. George, Edward I's famed master mason, key positions as castle constables. Carpenters and masons were paid four pence a day, and quarrymen and miners received three pence a day (during the thirteenth century).[26]

Besides paying workers' wages, the lord had to ensure they had plenty of tools and equipment, the amount of which would vary according to the enormity of the project. Each specialist required a set of tools, such as wedges and mallets (or malls), stone cutters' pickaxes, saws and chisels, shovels, hammers, hoes, trowels, levels, carpenters' axes, and even measur-

The great round towers at Rhuddlan Castle splendidly demonstrate the differences between ashlar and rubble building stone.

ing sticks.[27] Carts and wagons were essential for transporting raw and shaped materials to the building site, where wicker baskets, handcarts, wagons, and wheelbarrows moved lighter loads and cranes and winches hoisted the materials upwards. The expense of providing all of these items, which were not necessarily costly in themselves, would mount up and greatly add to the financial burden already placed on the lord or king.

In all, about 25 percent of the total expense of erecting a stone castle went to purchasing building materials; another 25 percent was spent on transporting the materials to the building site; and the remaining 50 percent was used for the actual construction effort.[28] During his reign (1154–1189), Henry II spent almost £21,500 on new construction and maintenance. Of the 90 castles mentioned in the Pipe Rolls, 30 received £100, while Dover, Newcastle-upon-Tyne, Nottingham, Oxford, Winchester, and Windsor each received over £1000. Of these six castles, Henry spent some £6400 on Dover, which covered, among other projects, the construction of his mammoth great keep,[29] which still dominates the castle. For the times, when the king's annual income was £20,000, such expenses drastically strained the royal coffers and often meant levying taxes and collecting rents from tenants, or dedicating the entire income from more than one manorial estate to a castle project. Many stone castles could take at least a decade to complete, so the enormity of the expense could be astronomical.[30]

The actual process of building a castle was straightforward. After the site was chosen, the master mason, who was in some ways comparable to a modern-day architect, would design the castle, making sure it suited the requirements and expectations of the new owner. He then used field stones or other materials to mark out the plan on the actual property. At the same time, workers would be summoned; quarries, woodland, materials and supplies purchased; and stone and trees prepared for use and transported to the site. The first structures to be built included accommodations for the workers and essential defenses, including earthworks and the ditch, which would help forestall a sudden assault. (This strategy did not always work: in 1267, Welsh rebels destroyed Earl Gilbert de Clare's first castle at Caerphilly, which was in the early stages of construction; the destruction prompted the Lord of Glamorgan to rebuild. The final product was — in the author's opinion — Britain's greatest concentric castle.) Then, workers would lay the foundations for the main structures, dig the well (if the castle were to have one; surprisingly, not all did), and level the surface of the site.[31] Finally, work on the walls would begin in earnest.

Two basic forms of stone were used to construct castle walls: ashlar and rubble. A form of dressed stone, ashlar covered the outermost sides of walls, whereas the random rubble consisting of stones of different sizes and shapes and formed the core of the walls. Cut from bedrock and chipped to smooth out their faces, ashlar was laid in horizontal rows which gave the castle a more appealing appearance. Sometimes, the leftover chips were added to the rubble, which was framed with timber shutters and bound together with mortar, a combination of lime, sand, and water. The lime for mortar was produced by burning limestone in kilns fueled by charcoal or sea-coal. The circular remains of the kilns can be identified at many castles.

Walls took shape gradually. When they became too high to manage easily, workers would erect scaffolding, or timber frameworks, the ends of which were placed into squares, known as putlog holes, cut into the walls. The diagonal lines of these holes are easy to spot at castles such as Conwy, Edward I's great castle in North Wales. The scaffolding was strong enough to support workers, tools, and building materials. Once they had finished the walls, workers "washed" or painted them with a solution of lime, which left the towers and curtain walls a bright white — hence, the term "whitewash" and the names White Castle and the White Tower in London. Today, most of the plasterwork, whitewash, and paint have long since disappeared from the medieval walls, but alert visitors can recognize remnants of plaster and faded paintings, particularly in the chambers that served as chapels and private apartments,[32] but also on exterior walls.

The presence of herringbone masonry is an identifying feature of Norman castles and, therefore, it can reliably date the wall or a particular building to the late eleventh century. A characteristic feature of Norman-era architecture, herringbone masonry consisted of flat stone or brick diagonally laid in the mortar and alternating with horizontal layers of thin stone. It was often arranged in a zigzag pattern resembling the skeleton of a fish. Examples survive at Arundel, Corfe, and Richmond Castles and other sites, including Norman churches in Britain.

In addition to ashlar, other dressed stone enhanced a castle's overall sense of elegance and unique character. Used for intricate carvings and corbels, window frames (tracery), moldings, and other special elements, dressed stone created charm in an otherwise harsh environment and also displayed the owner's stylistic sophistication. Many lords imported the very costly Caen stone, a light-colored, creamy yellow limestone from across the English Channel in France, for these features. In many cases, the dressing or sculpting of the stone was completed prior to shipping the pieces to Britain. Though now often heavily eroded, Caen stonework adorns many castles, most notably at the Tower of London, and was especially treasured for the windows in great halls and chapels, and, at times, in a lord's private apartments.

Now largely stripped of their finer building materials, many castles no longer display their original ashlar stone and their decorative carvings have disappeared. As a result, the coarse rubble core now appears on the outside, giving visitors the impression that it also served as the original, medieval exterior. However, looking closer, visitors often discover remnants of the ashlar still secured to the wall face higher up on the side of a keep, as at Peveril Castle, or along the upper courses of gate towers, as at Rhuddlan Castle, where the lowest levels were quarried for their ashlar. Raglan Castle, on the other hand, retains vast quantities of ashlar, even on the great hexagonal keep, which was partly destroyed in 1648 after the English Civil War. Other castles retain traces of carvings, such as the stylized heads of King Edward II, Queen Isabella and Hugh le Despenser, which adorn the walls in the great hall at Caerphilly Castle or the elaborately carved springers in the great hall-keep at Chepstow Castle.

Most castles are products of several building phases, which were undertaken by successive lords who sought to leave their own, permanent mark on history. In some cases, changes in basic building stone reflect changing priorities and changes in ownership, as at Goodrich Castle, where the great keep, a hulking, light gray tower, visibly contrasts with the dark reds of the massive corner towers and curtain wall. At many other castles, different structures represent the influence of different owners and the introduction of different building periods. The Tower of London, for example, expanded as monarch after monarch added new buildings, which both extended the defensive might and added to the complexity of the castle and also reiterated the power and status of the monarchy within the kingdom and in the wider world as well. Lordship castles likewise developed as a series of owners added their own personalities to the site. From its beginnings as a simple hall-keep, William FitzOsbern's great castle at Chepstow acquired an imposing main gatehouse, a substantial barbican, round towers, a state-of-the art apartment complex, and one of the most impressive corner towers ever built at a castle, as subsequent owners, the Marshals and Bigods, sought to leave their own marks at the site during the late twelfth and thirteenth centuries.

In all, it is important to recognize that, even though earth and timber castles did dominate the decades immediately after the Conquest, the construction of stone castles had in fact begun as well. The concept of building stone castles did not evolve from earth and timber castles, but, rather, the two building styles co-existed. Earth and timber castles served a vital purpose in implementing and solidifying the Norman conquest of the Saxons and restricting Welsh independence by allowing the new rulers to establish themselves quickly and with relative ease. That stone castles generally appeared later than timber castles had more to do with their builders' perceptions of the political situations they found themselves in, their personal ambitions, and, ultimately, their need to draw attention to their newly assumed superior status over their subjects.

TERMINOLOGY IN THIS CHAPTER

Anglo-Saxon Chronicle: One of Britain's oldest surviving and most important records, the document is actually a series of manuscripts reputedly first ordered by Alfred the Great, King of Wessex, in the late ninth century and added to by various monastic communities until 1154. The Norman invasion is among the many events it chronicles.

The Anarchy: From 1135 to 1154, England was embroiled in a civil war that pitted supporters of King Stephen, the nephew of the recently deceased Norman king Henry I against the Empress Matilda, Henry's daughter, who was married to Geoffrey, fifth Count of Anjou.

Ashlar: Neatly trimmed, rectangular building stone having a flat cut surface and square edges.

Bailey: Whether made of earth or stone, the typical medieval castle featured at least one defended courtyard or ward, the bailey. Some castles featured an outer bailey and an inner bailey, the functions of which varied depending on their position relative to the heart of the castle and the structural complexity of the site itself. The bailey was often an enclosed area adjoining a motte or an open area enclosed by masonry walls or earthen embankments in which the main activities of daily life in the castle took place.

The inner bailey commonly contained the hall and kitchen block, residential chambers, and the chapel, whereas the outer bailey typically held workshops, stables, and other ancillary facilities. In castles with only one bailey, the enclosed area would normally hold all of these facilities; residential chambers might also fill towers along the curtain wall enclosing the bailey. Some castles, such as Chepstow Castle, featured lower, middle and upper baileys, which were added and expanded by succeeding owners during the entire history of the castle. The earliest portion of the castle, now the upper bailey, contained the great tower. As times changed, and more space was needed for defensive strength and comfortable accommodation, Chepstow Castle expanded to include a middle bailey, which was actually created by the construction of an inner wall and gate, and then the lower bailey, where the great gatehouse still welcomes visitors. Windsor Castle in England also contains three baileys. The upper and lower wards enclosed the main residential structures and gateways, whereas the middle ward held the original motte and shell keep, which filled almost the entire bailey.

Barbican: Generally located just outside the main gate, the barbican was a defensive outwork which in some cases extended a gateway already in place, as at Exeter Castle. In other cases, the structures stood as separate buildings apart from but fronting the main gate, as at Arundel, Goodrich and Warwick Castles. Barbicans prevented or stalled enemy access by confining the attackers to an area outside the castle. They were also places where the garrison could gather to stage a sortie. Numerous examples exist throughout Britain.

Bayeux Tapestry: A 230-foot-long series of well-preserved embroidered panels which intricately details the Norman takeover of England, from the preparations in Normandy to the gathering of the fleet to castle-building to the defeat of the Saxons and the coronation of Duke William as King William I of England.

Burh: A defended settlement erected and occupied by the Anglo-Saxons; many were destroyed or reoccupied by the Normans and centered with castles.

Caen stone: A light-colored, creamy yellow, fine-grained limestone quarried in and transported from Caen, France, favored by William the Conqueror and used by the Normans in Britain and in France as building material both on castles and churches.

Campaign castle: A temporary earthwork fortification erected by a besieging army to protect them during the siege.

Carboniferous limestone: A common building stone extensively used to construct castles. Formed during the Carboniferous period by the accumulation of shell and coral deposits, the limestone was deposited in much of England and Wales, and parts of Scotland, Ireland, and Europe.

Carpentarius: A carpenter; skilled worker who built flooring, roofing, siege engines, furniture, panelling for rooms, and scaffolding.

Carters: Workmen who used a cart or wagon to bring wood and stone to the site of a castle under construction.

Castle: A properly fortified medieval military residence built for an individual rather than a settlement of people. As a privately defended fortress, a castle served a variety of purposes as administrative, manorial, governmental, and residential centers, in addition to being a fortress. As such, they contained the buildings the lord considered as essential to the operation of his lordship. How the buildings were laid out and the image the castle presented to others were as important to their owners as their military and domestic capabilities.

Cementarius: Stonemason.

Cistern: Generally located in the inner bailey or within the kitchen block, cisterns were stone-lined containers that collected and stored rainwater.

Concentric plan: Devised as the perfect barrier to a successful assault on a castle, the concentric plan consisted of a walls-within-walls design whereby a lower line of defense (for example, a curtain wall with towers and a gatehouse) enclosed a higher inner defensive wall (also comprised of towers and at least one gatehouse). Some sites, such as Caerphilly and Kenilworth Castles, shrewdly interspersed water defenses with the stone defenses to create a series of daunting barriers which at the very least kept the enemy at bay and had the potential to confound the most experienced warrior.

Soldiers defending the stronghold had an obvious advantage with this type of castle and could concentrate firepower onto a specific spot from several vantage points, without firing upon their comrades. The attacking enemy had the task of breaching the barriers while also avoiding the firepower of the defenders.

Constable: As the castle governor, the constable was responsible for all aspects of castle administration, its contents and facilities in the lord's absence. Also known as the captain, castellan, or warden.

Domesday Book: One of the great records of William the Conqueror's reign, documenting the results of the extensive survey undertaken in 1086 to identify who owned what in explicit terms, purportedly so that each person could be taxed properly but, just as importantly for William, to document the extent of what he controlled in his kingdom.

Dovecote: Often associated with castles or monasteries, the dovecote was a medieval pigeon house created from bricks or cut stone. Inside, the building was lined with pigeon holes used to breed doves and squab (as young pigeons, the most prized for their meat) for castle food supply.

Dressed stone: Stone worked into a smooth or molded face; used to outline angles, windows, and doors.

Earth and timber: Phrase used to describe motte or ringwork castles, which were primarily built with earth and timber resources normally found in the local area, as opposed to stone castles, which had substantial masonry structures as well as earth and timber elements and contained materials often brought to the site from a long distance.

Earthen enclosure castle: An alternate term for ringwork castle.

Earthworks: Ramparts or fortifications largely made from earth and underlain with other materials, such as chalk, wood or stone; includes mottes and ringworks, prehistoric hillforts, and Anglo-Saxon era dykes.

Edwardian: Castles built during the reign of Edward I which share certain characteristics, such as twin-towered gatehouses.

Embankment: An earthen wall or slope which enclosed an area or formed the walls of a ditch or enclosing ramparts; often revetted with timber or clay and topped with timber palisades. Also known as a bank.

Enclosure: (1) An area associated with a castle which is surrounded by a stone wall or an earthen embankment; (2) a ringwork castle; (3) a general term for a stone castle, having a stone curtain wall enclosing or embracing the castle's other structures, such as the gatehouse, keep, and residential suites.

English Civil Wars: A series of battles and sieges between supporters of King Charles I (known as Royalists or Cavaliers) and those who backed Parliament (Parliamentarians or Roundheads) which occurred between 1642 and 1651. Numerous castles were brought back into active service during the conflict, and used in aid of both causes. In the end, the Parliamentarians were victorious and the king was executed. Scores of castles were slighted so that they could never be reused in military action against the new heads of the government.

Fealty: An oath pledging the complete fidelity, or loyalty, given by a vassal to his lord or monarch.

In Feud: Land held in exchange for the military service of a single (one) knight.

Feudalism: A political, social and economic system under which land was granted by a landowner to a person in exchange for military service or other duties (the feudal obligation). See Chapter 4.

Fief: Land held by a knight or other landowner, in exchange for the military service of one knight; a fee.

Fighting platform: See *hoarding*, Chapter 2.

Forebuilding: A projecting defensive work that screened the entrance to the keep or other structures and blocked a direct attack at that point.

Fortified manor house: Comparable in many ways to a castle, in that the structure was both a residence of a person of status and had defensive features; however, the defenses were weak at best and often purely for show.

Fossatore: Ditcher or miner; person who dug the castle ditches and building foundations.

Foundations: The masonry substructure of a building; often the only surviving remains of a castle or its inner structures.

Freemason: A skilled laborer subordinate to the master mason who cut freestone into specified shapes to conform with construction requirements.

Freestone: Soft stone, such as fine grained limestone or sandstone, which was easily cut and molded into building blocks.

Gabion: A large wicker basket used to haul building materials, such as earth and stone, from the ground to upper levels.

Granary: A building used to store grain.

Guardroom: Chamber used by guards when on duty; normally located in the castle gatehouse, often on either side of gate passage or in a gate tower.

Hall: Dining, entertainment and occasional sleeping center of the castle, where guests were feasted; also used as an administrative chamber.

Hall-keep: An early version of the rectangular keep, where the keep was shorter than it was wide and was dominated by a large hall on the first story above ground level. Fine examples exist at Chepstow and Manorbier Castles.

Harald Hardrada: The King of Norway in 1066, who sought the English throne when Harold II succeeded as King of England after the death of Edward the Confessor. Led a fleet of Norsemen on an invasion of England, landing on the coast of Yorkshire and moving inland. Fought and killed by the Saxon army at Stamford Bridge, near York.

Harold II (Harold Godwinson): The Anglo-Saxon lord who gained the English throne after the death of Edward the Confessor in 1066. His rise to the kingship led to the Norman invasion later that year, the defeat of the Saxons, and Harold's death at the Battle of Hastings, which resulted in the coronation of Duke William of Normandy as King William I of England.

Herringbone masonry: An idenfitying characteristic of Norman-era architecture, featuring flat stone or brick laid diagonally in mortar rather than horizontally. It was often arranged in a zigzag pattern resembling the skeleton of a fish.

Hewer: The laborer responsible for splitting timber beams and shaping them into usable pieces.

Hillfort: A prehistoric fortification normally crowning a hilltop which defended a settlement with earthen ramparts and ditches. Often reused by later peoples, including the Normans, as ready-made defenses.

Hoarding: A timber fighting platform fitted to the parapet of a curtain wall or tower which provided defenders with a covered area from which to fire down upon an enemy without fear of being vulnerable to return fire. See Chapter 2.

Hodman: The laborer who hauled supplies to masons or brick workers using a hod, or strong box with a long handle supported on his shoulders.

Homage: A public show of respect and declaration of loyalty or indebtedness to another.

Ingeniator: An engineer; the master mason.

James of St. George, Master: As far as Edward I's crucial late-thirteenth-century castle-building program in Wales was concerned, the architectural power behind the throne was James of St. George. James, a little-known but nonetheless important historical figure, was a master mason summoned from the Continent to implement the king's plans. Born around 1230, he worked on a number of great European castles including the fortress of St. George d'Esperanche (in Savoy on the French-Swiss-Italian border) from which he took his full name.

Master James was directly responsible for at least twelve of the seventeen castles in Wales which Edward either built, rebuilt, or strengthened. Rhuddlan was James' first venture, Beaumaris his last, by which time he had perfected the symmetrical, concentric "walls within walls" design which characterized the castles of the period. The king evidently appreciated his work, for he paid James the handsome daily wage of two shillings, an amount which an ordinary craftsman would receive for a whole week's work. In 1284, his payment rose to three shillings a day for life. Master James of St. George died in 1308.

Keep: As the main citadel or great tower of a castle, the keep was a fortified, self-sufficient tower containing living quarters, which could be used as the last line of refuge in a siege. Mostly square or rectangular in shape, some keeps stood over 80 feet high and had walls over 17 feet thick. Designed in a variety of sizes and shapes, including the shell keep, the rectangular keep, the round or cylindrical keep, and the polygonal keep. Also known as the donjon.

Throughout the medieval period, living in the keep or the dominant mural tower at a castle was a mark of status normally reserved for the lord and his family. From the earliest motte castles, with their timber towers or shell keeps, to the finest stone castles of the Middle Ages, the great tower quite visibly distinguished its occupants from other castle dwellers. See Chapter 3.

Kiln: An oven-like structure used to burn lime for use as a component of mortar or to process corn and other grain for brewing.

License to crenellate: Formal permission to erect a castle or to fortify (crenellate) a residence. The first license to crenellate was possibly issued for Bishopton Castle in 1143, though earlier licenses gave permission to strengthen an existing castle. The last license was granted to Sir William Fitzwilliam for Cowdray Castle (House) in 1533.

Mason: Laborer who prepared rough stone for shaping by a freemason; he often etched the stones with identifying symbols or marks, which are still identifiable today. Also known as a rough mason.

Masonry: Castle stonework bonded together with mortar.

Minator: A miner; the person who dug the ditch, building foundations, mines or tunnels.

Master craftsman: Expert in his field in charge of workers tasked with jobs under his area of expertise and responsibility; in addition to the master mason, master craftsmen who worked on the construction of castles included master carpenters and master plumbers. These men had the authority and skill to designate a work as a "masterpiece" of craftsmanship.

Master mason: The individual responsible for designing and overseeing the building of a structure, including the castle itself. Much like an architect, the master mason was probably the most important figure in the castle-building process, second only perhaps to the owner himself, who often had direct input into the final layout of his fortified military residence.

Moated site: A manor house or farm surrounded by a water-filled moat, sometimes used for defense but often decorative.

Molding: A continuous ornamental contour decorating a surface or the beveled edge of a wall; often adorned the great hall, private chambers, and the chapel.

Mortar: The substance formed from the combination of lime, sand, and water used to seal building stone together. Some castles featured drystone masonry, which did not use mortar as a sealant.

Motte: Typically an artificially sculpted, flat-topped mound, packed with earth and often revetted with timber and stone or a reshaped natural hillock or pile of field stones created from the upcast of the enclosing ditch. The Normans introduced the widespread building of motte castles to Britain in the decades immediately after the Conquest in 1066.

Palisade: Timber fencing or defenses normally erected on top of earthen ramparts or a motte; a continuous length of pointed wooden poles joined together with leather or other material to prevent them from collapsing. Their pointed or crenellated tops increased the defensive capability of the structure.

Partial ringwork: The inland-facing embankment(s) of some ringworks, particularly those at the edge of a steep cliff or waterway, which were crescent-shaped; rather than needing to construct a complete ringwork, builders relied upon the cliff or riverside to act as natural defenses.

Pipe Rolls: Financial records created by the English government in the twelfth century and used until 1833. They were so named for their shape as rolled up parchment documents.

Plaster: A mixture of lime and water and other substances such as sand, which was commonly used to smooth over and seal walls or ceilings in castles and medieval houses to give the structures a white color from which some took their names (for example, the White Tower at the Tower of London, and White Castle in Wales). Plastered interior walls were often painted with bright colors, heraldic emblems, human figures or scenes to brighten up the otherwise drab atmosphere and also chronicle historic events and people associated with the castle.

Putlog holes: Square holes or notches carved into the masonry which supported timber scaffolding (the putlogs); now identifiable by their diagonal arrangement along a curtain wall (and occasionally on towers). Their placement gives modern onlookers a sense of how a castle may have been constructed, even though the scaffolding has long since been removed.

Portico: A covered porchway situated in front of an entrance into a building.

Post holes: Holes dug into the ground into which timber beams were fitted; post holes normally survive as circular patches in the earth, where wood from the buildings the beams once supported has long since disappeared but left its mark behind.

Quadrangular castle: A late medieval castle consisting of a roughly square plan, which normally had towers at the corners and a main gatehouse.

Quareator: Quarrier; quarryman.

Ramparts: (1) Battlements or protected fighting platforms for castle defenders; (2) a defensive bank of earth or rubble, topped with timber fence.

Ringwork: An earth and timber fortification introduced to Britain by the Normans; similar to a motte but having a dished out summit encircled by earthen banks topped with timber palisades.

Rough mason: Laborers who fashioned rough, uncut stone into workable shapes. They also were responsible for mortaring finished blocks to solidify walls and other structures.

Rubble: Stone of various shapes and sizes used to form the core of the walls of a castle, bound together with mortar to stabilize them.

Scaffolding: A temporary timber framework erected along a wall, which supported laborers and supplies during construction.

Siege castle: An earthwork structure erected for the protection of a force besieging a castle; popularly used during the Anarchy in the twelfth century and the English Civil War in the 1640s. Also known as a siegework or campaign castle.

Siege engine: One of a variety of timber-framed machines operated by a combination of human strength, torsion or tension, ropes, chains or pulleys to propel a projectile at a target, such as a curtain wall or tower; includes ballistas, mangonels, springalds, trebuchets, perriers, petraries, onagers, and scorpions.

Slaters: Laborers responsible for laying slate on roofs and as otherwise needed.

Subinfeudation: Similar to subletting, whereby a tenant, often a lord, grants parcels of his own land (held in feud) to lesser lords or men of lower status, who then owe feudal obligation, such as military service or rent, to the greater lord. See Chapter Four.

Thatcher: The worker responsible for securely covering roofs with thatch, such as straw or reeds.

Tostig (Godwinson): Harold Godwinson's upstart brother who rebelled against Harold's accession as king of England and joined forces with Norwegian King Harald Hardrada to invade England in September 1066. Harold marched his army to Stamford Bridge, just southeast of York, where he defeated the invaders but paved the way for the Norman victory a few weeks later. Tostig was among those killed during the battle.

Tower house: A significantly fortified residence built to thwart brief assaults rather than prolonged sieges; architecturally similar to a rectangular keep. Commonly constructed in the border region between England and Scotland, but also found in Wales (rarely) and Ireland.

Tracery: Decorative or curving stonework commonly associated with the windows of a great hall or castle chapel.

Vassal: A feudal tenant who acquired the use of land in exchange for military service and avowed loyalty to the lord or monarchy. A lord was a vassal of the king whereas tenants were vassals of the lord.

Wall-walk: See Chapter 2.

William I (Duke William of Normandy): Led the Norman invasion of England in October 1066, and defeated the Anglo-Saxon army led by Harold II at the Battle of Hastings. William was a prolific castle-builder and consolidated control of his new kingdom by constructing ringwork and motte castles and parceling out the countryside to his loyal supporters while imposing feudalism upon them.

2

From the Outside

Despite being only about twenty miles west of London, Windsor Castle is clearly visible just south of the M4 motorway, where it still dominates the now-urbanized, low-lying landscape alongside the River Thames. As today, medieval travelers would have been able to spot the royal fortress from quite some distance and make assumptions about its occupants based on their understanding of the role of castles — and themselves — in society. Closer to the castle, the same visitors would begin to identify specific parts of the castle, not only those built for defense and military might but also those built for luxury and status. Throughout medieval Britain, visitors and passersby would have been sure to notice a castle's position in the landscape, for its builder would have taken special care to choose a site that clearly emphasized his presence.

The Castle and Its Setting

Castle builders deliberately positioned their castles to fulfill particular needs, which included both practical requirements, such as defensive support and the availability of raw materials and a labor force, and personal ambitions, such as their need to maintain control of their lordship and dominate their subordinates, while at the same time impressing friends and rivals. A castle's location was often its first line of defense, in terms of preventing an enemy from approaching the site, for staging counterattacks and foraging in the local countryside, and for obtaining reinforcements and additional supplies (and a reliable source of drinking water) when under siege.[1] As was discussed in Chapter 1, many lords located their castle in or near Roman or prehistoric fortifications, which the original builders had chosen for their naturally defensive positions. The settings also provided medieval builders with a ready source of construction materials and symbolically linked them to the ancient cultures, a factor which reinforced the lord's power over the locals.

Many people today have the impression that most castles were built on hilltops — and movies, magazines and books reinforce this perception. In fact, this was not so. Most castles were actually built on valley sides and at the ends of promontories[2]; they stood in the midst of towns, alongside waterways, and, surprisingly enough, on flat ground. Certainly, hilltop locations had both strategic and symbolic potential. The abrupt slopes made it difficult for an enemy to assault a castle, while the presence of a castle towering over the heads of the local populace visibly emphasized the lord's supremacy over them — daring them to rebel. The high-rise position also afforded distant views: guards inside the castle could keep an eye on the activity in the area and raise the alarm if needed, and people traveling in the vicinity of the castle would become aware of its presence well before they passed by the site or arrived at the main gate.

Many other castles were intentionally placed to overlook rivers or the shoreline, from where they could receive provisions and other necessary items and have access to a constant water supply and a natural moat. They could also regulate human movement through the immediate area, and to and from the castle as well—water gates and sally ports not only accommodated the distribution of supplies from ships docking alongside the castle, they also could be used as escape hatches or openings through which the garrison could launch a surprise attack on an unsuspecting enemy.[3]

Several castles were erected alongside ancient fording points[4] or on commonly traveled roads constructed by the Romans or by prehistoric peoples whose feet wore down trackways that later groups continued to follow. During the Middle Ages, such routes remained essential because they not only enhanced military readiness but they also facilitated the movement of people (lords could travel from estate to estate, for example, with little trouble) and allowed vital information to pass from place to place with relative ease. Today, many of these routes have been transformed into motorways or designated as hiking trails.

Controlling these routes with a well placed castle vastly increased a lord's command of a region. Some noblemen, like William de Braose, the lord of Bramber Castle, built timber bridges over waterways flowing near their castles to block passage and collect tolls from ships sailing by.[5] Others, such as King Edward I, deliberately rerouted rivers to pass closer to their castles. At Rhuddlan, a three-mile stretch of the River Clwyd was diverted so that the castle could be accessed and provisioned by sailing ships. This monumental effort required the tal-

The construction of Rhuddlan Castle took about five years and £10,000 to complete. Not only was it a huge task to erect the structure, but in order for ships to reach the castle, Edward I also ordered the excavation of a navigable channel which redirected the course of the River Clwyd.

ents of a master *fossatore* (ditcher or digger) named William who supervised the labors of 968 diggers for the three years that the project took place. An average of 66 diggers working continuously six days a week were required to complete this masterful undertaking.[6] Then, the king easily commanded all movement along the river at this point.

Nowadays, regardless of whether a castle is ruined or still occupied, the first thing a visitor still notices (albeit often accidentally) is its place in the surrounding landscape. Cliffside and hilltop settings are easy to recognize, not just visually but by the strenuous trek to the site. Riverside settings create an air of romance, yet they were much more than attractive, as discussed above. Modern urban settings can obscure the medieval look of a site, but in many cases, just entering onto the property has the ability to shift one's perception away from the encroachment of buildings and traffic. When approaching any castle from a distance, visitors should try to imagine how the setting would have affected medieval observers. Then, when walking onto the castle site, consider why the original builder chose the particular spot, and try to identify any natural defenses (steep slopes, waterways, etc.), possible quarries, many of which were on the castle site, and the position of the castle relative to other geological and topographical features.

Every castle contained a main entry point, living chambers, and fortifications, elements of which could be identified from the outside. Other members of the aristocracy would have been more than familiar with castles, at least in generic terms if not the specific design and furnishings of the site they were preparing to visit. The peasantry who had the opportunity to work inside the castle might share their knowledge of the site with their families and friends, and point out locations as they passed the castle on one side or the other. When working neighboring fields, they might pause to glance at the hulking structure, think about life inside, and envision where different chambers were located. Moreover, members of besieging armies often lived in their own castle or worked near one. As a result, they would have been familiar with the kinds of defenses they might encounter during a siege and also what other structures commonly comprised a castle and would have used this knowledge to their advantage when preparing for and conducting a siege. Even so, in order to be most effective and efficient when staging a siege, commanders and their soldiers had to have at least a cursory knowledge of a castle's particular design and what defenses they might face, so they could plan how best to stage the assault.

Identifying the Outer Defenses

Even today, when the structure is a ruin, a castle's manmade defenses are its most recognizable features. Depending on its actual design, in order to reach the inner core of the castle, where the most important business was conducted and the lord's private apartments were normally located, people had to navigate their way past and through a variety of structures, often beginning with the outer bailey, which functioned as a defensive outwork, before progressing inward to the main gate and the inner bailey beyond. In between, not only did guests, attackers, servants, and residents have to deal with the moat or ditch and the drawbridge, but also with any outer defenses that stood in the way. The point of the exercise, simply enough, was to prevent unwanted access.

Most modern visitors can easily spot the moat (known as the ditch, if it is dry), unless it has been filled in and covered over by later construction or the natural accumulation of bracken and rotting vegetation over the centuries. Even though historians cannot firmly state

Designed by master mason John Cowper, the plan of the quadrangular castle at Kirby Muxloe included towers built at each of the four corners, a curtain wall linking the towers to the gatehouse, and other towers placed midway along each length of wall. Around the entire complex, the moat provided defense against intrusion.

that most castles were defended by ditches, many were, and even when filled in, the original positions of a moat or ditch can often be identified. Castle ditches varied greatly, and many were water-filled, as at Bodiam, Rhuddlan and White Castles, which were flooded by springs or re-routed rivers.

Some ditches transformed into moats at high tide. Flint Castle, for example, was built immediately alongside the Dee Estuary so that the waters would fill the moat and also allow ships carrying supplies to sail up to the castle. The ditch enclosing the inner bailey at Ogmore Castle was strategically placed to fill at high tide, when the waters of the neighboring River Ewenny would rush inland. To regulate the flow so that the interior of the castle would not flood, dams or movable barriers known as sluice gates were fitted into place and manually operated from inside some castles. Some sluice gates are still visible, as at Caerphilly Castle, where they have been restored; at Ogmore, where a stone wall embedded in the ditch apparently blocked rising waters; and at the small motte castle at New Moat, where remnants of a stone-built dam and sluice survive on the eastern side of the site.

The construction of the moat at Kirby Muxloe Castle, which is still filled by water diverted from two brooks at the site, is particularly interesting. To ensure the moat filled and emptied properly, builders installed two masonry dams, sluices, and an intriguing set of hollow oak logs, which could be blocked with leather-ringed wooden plugs. They also placed a screen across the mouth of the little brook to prevent blockage from leaves and other items.

In the early twentieth century, when work was done to consolidate the site, one of the plugs, a tapering block of wood covered with leather, was discovered in place, still doing its original job.

At some castles, the waters that once flowed right up to the foundations have long since subsided, leaving the castle high and dry at a distance that seems way too far from the nearest water source. For example, even though Edward I intentionally erected his great castles in North Wales at sites that were accessible by sea, two of his most impressive fortresses, Beaumaris (which means "fair marsh") and Harlech, now stand at a distance away from the water. Today, the marshy land that separated the estuary and Beaumaris Castle (which retains its water-filled moat) is occupied by a series of parking lots, a road, and some buildings. Even so, when visiting the site, it is easy to imagine that the waters of the Menai Strait, which split the Isle of Anglesey from mainland Wales, flowed up to the castle and filled the moat.

The same cannot be said for Harlech Castle. A considerable chunk of dry land, now occupied by buildings, stands between the castle's current position, high atop an isolated crag known as Harlech Dome, and the waters of Tremadog Bay, which is visible from the battlements. During the thirteenth century, however, the waters flowed much closer to the base of the castle rock. Today, visitors can still climb up the "way from the sea," a laborious set of 108 steps that lead from the water gate, where medieval ships delivered their supplies, to the upper gate, which opened into the outer grounds of the castle.

At Pembroke Castle, the River Pembroke still runs close to the site; however, it too has receded. Today, visitors can walk a path around the outside of the castle where the river once flowed. At a point along the northwestern side, a large cavern known as the wogan opens from underneath the bedrock supporting the castle. Researchers believe the dank hole acted as a water port of sorts and that large ships laden with supplies sailed directly into the wogan. From inside the cavern, the materials—and soldiers—could be hauled up the narrow spiral staircase into the castle itself. Interestingly, Pembroke Castle did not have a well. Rather, inhabitants used a system of lead pipes that allowed water to pass from the river into the castle to obtain their drinking water.

At some castles, the ditch survives as little more than a slight depression in the ground that may stretch around the castle or in front of the main gate. At other castles, marshy but walkable land or an area that frequently floods or stays very moist may mark the location of the ditch (as at Skenfrith and Tretower castles).

On the other hand, deep rock-cut ditches still enclose many castles. In many ways, they are more impressive than their water-filled counterparts, for they reveal the bedrock and foundations that supported the massive stone structures above them and also emphasize the enormity of the task that confronted the ditchers who were responsible for their excavation. They also demonstrate just how daunting a foe they could be to an enemy attempting to storm the castle. The stunning ditch at Goodrich Castle, which may date to the 1150s, measures about 60 to 70 feet wide and is 20 to 25 feet deep. Just digging a ditch of this size would have been a monumental task for workers equipped only with the simplest of tools. The sheer, cliff-like walls of the rock-cut ditch rose almost vertically to meet the base of the powerful curtain wall and massive corner towers that were added to the stronghold in the early thirteenth century. Since they would have been virtually impossible to scale, there was no need to fill the ditch with water. Stone cut out of the ditch was used to construct portions of the castle that the ditch enclosed. Today, visitors can walk in the ditch and visualize for themselves just how daunting the prospect of besieging such a strongpoint would have been, especially for men heavily laden with armor and weapons.

Its outer defenses rising from rocky outcrops, Harlech Castle seems more like one of Snowdonia's peaks than a manmade fortress. The proximity of the sea, which once washed the base of Harlech Dome but has long since retreated, provided Edward I with an ideal site for a castle.

Cilgerran Castle commands a promontory site underlain with slate and overlooks a steep-sided gorge cut by the River Teifi on the north and the rushing waters of the River Plysgog, which shaped the sloping hills on the western side of the site. Even though nothing remains to verify that a ringwork originally occupied on the northern side of the site, it seems reasonable to conclude that the inner ward, which is separated from the outer ward by a natural fracture in the bedrock, may have contained the earliest Norman stronghold, which was in existence by 1108. The fracture was modified into an imposing ditch and later revetted (or faced) with stone. Today, the ditch is crossed by a wooden bridge, which leads visitors from the outer bailey into the residential inner ward, which is scattered with medieval foundations and dominated by two enormous thirteenth-century round towers.

Quite unlike the moats and ditches described above, the huge water defenses at Caer-

Cut into sandstone bedrock, the great ditch at Goodrich Castle encloses almost the entire site. Pyramidal buttresses support the formidable round southeast tower, alongside of which the ruinous latrine block once dumped its waste into the ditch.

The lake-like moats at Caerphilly Castle were inspired by the great mere, which defended Kenilworth Castle during the barons' rebellion against King Henry III. The Ministry of Works reflooded the lakes in the 1950s.

philly Castle were the size of lakes, so that, during a siege, when the drawbridges were raised, attackers would have had to swim (carrying their weapons and wearing armor) or sail across. Gilbert de Clare II, who began Caerphilly Castle in 1268, took his inspiration from the complex defenses he saw at Kenilworth Castle two years earlier. Now completely ruined but still in fine enough condition that visitors can visualize how it looked in its heyday, mighty Kenilworth Castle was once entirely surrounded by a manmade body of water, known as "the great mere." The enormous lakes, which measured over 100 acres in area, were so impressive that they formed an effective barrier to an assault, as was demonstrated during the Siege of Kenilworth in 1266, which de Clare witnessed. Three centuries later, the great mere acted as the backdrop for a fantastic water spectacle which Robert Dudley, Earl of Leicester, arranged as the main event of a nineteen-day stay by Queen Elizabeth I (and her entourage of several hundred people) in 1575.

Clearly, one of a castle's most important defenses was the drawbridge, which could be moved away from the moat or ditch in order to create a large enough gap. Without it, anyone wishing access would have tremendous difficulty — and probably get quite wet — trying to reach the main gate. Used to connect outer and inner baileys as well as to access the gatehouse, drawbridges were made from timber and drawn up with chains or ropes and either human power or the aid of a pulley system and a windlass (a winch or hoisting mechanism). Most medieval drawbridges no longer survive but archaeological excavations have uncovered remnants of the timbers at several sites. The timbers not only provide evidence of the placement of the bridge but can help date the structure through tree-ring analysis.

At many castles, including both Goodrich and Cilgerran, immovable footbridges now

To gain access to the inner ward at Cilgerran Castle, visitors crossed a drawbridge which spanned the rock-cut ditch. Today, the modern bridge is stationary, but the medieval abutments survive.

cross the same spot as the original bridge. At others, only the drawbridge pits or footings of the original structure mark the original location. The facades of some gatehouses also retain the tall grooves that once held the drawbridge fittings when the bridge was raised into place or small pivot holes through which the chains passed when moving the bridge. Excellent examples are visible at Caerlaverock Castle and at Raglan, where the great keep was accessed via two separate drawbridges. Earth and timber castles also used drawbridges; the motte and bailey site at Hen Domen actually featured a series of rebuilt bridges, dating from as early as the 1070s and continuing until the thirteenth century.[7]

Several types of drawbridges defended castles in Britain. The earliest and easiest to manipulate were removable lifting bridges. When necessary, defenders could simply lift and pull back the timber platform into the castle, leaving a gap between the gate and the outer ward, which would have made it difficult at best for besiegers to cross. Pivot bridges used pulleys to haul them into place. Used increasingly from the late thirteenth century, this complex system used counterweights, a pivot, and chains or ropes to maneuver the bridge in and out of position. Oftentimes, extra space was needed to move the weighted end into place, so builders excavated deep pits into the bedrock or earth underneath the bridge site. Turning bridges had hinges on their inner sides and used ropes or chains and pulleys to hoist the timber platforms towards the gatehouse until they rested flat against the wall, completely closing off the entranceway. Guards operated windlasses positioned in a chamber over the gate passage to power the pulley system.

Once across the bridge, access to the interior of the castle was achieved by walking through a narrow channel, the gate passage, which led visitors, friend or foe, through the gateway or gatehouse and was equipped with a variety of defensive devices. Positioning the main gateway took careful planning. If the site had natural defenses, such as steep sides or a riverside location, builders situated the main gate on the opposite, inland-facing side of the property, which was most vulnerable to attack and required the most substantial defenses to keep out an enemy.

The earliest castle gateways were simply defended, mere arches cut into the stone curtain wall; heavy timber doors or small rectangular or square towers barricaded the simple, ground-level passageway leading into the castle. However, as time progressed and the needs of the owners changed, so did the complexity of the castle gate. By the early thirteenth century, twin-towered gatehouses equipped with numerous defensive mechanisms and living quarters on their upper levels became fashionable.

An examination of the walls lining a gate passage — and even fallen chunks of masonry — frequently provides clues to which mechanisms were used to thwart access to a particular gatehouse. Even at castles where the entry point was little more than a simple archway, as at Newcastle Bridgend, evidence often survives to identify the methods guards used to keep out unwelcome visitors. For example, square holes cut into the stone door jambs reveal that timber doors were used to bar access. To prevent the doors from opening (they normally opened outwards), guards pushed iron bars into the holes, which held the ends securely. These features are known as drawbar holes and are often the only physical evidence left which indicates that there were doors at a particular spot.

Another popular defensive device, frequently used in tandem with pairs of timber doors, was the portcullis, a framework of thick spikes made from oak, iron, or a combination of the two materials, which was raised or lowered by winches (the windlass or winding mechanism) usually located in a chamber immediately above the gate passage. Like the doors positioned behind them, most portcullises no longer survive. Yet, the grooves or slots that held the chains or ropes that hauled the heavy grates into place often still frame both sides of the gate passage, close to the drawbar holes. At some castles, two or more sets of grooves are visible, sometimes positioned at opposite ends

Few castles retain their original portcullises, which were built with timber and subject to rot or burning. Backed by heavy double doors normally made from oak, the combination of portcullis and barred doors posed a significant obstacle to a battering ram.

Cut into walls and battlements, arrowslits were designed so that defenders could fire upon an enemy without being seen. During the thirteenth century, the ends of the slits were often carved into round shapes and were known as cross-oillets (or eyelets).

of the passageway. If men on duty in guardrooms on either side of the passage could coordinate their timing, they could trap attackers between the two sets of portcullises. Then, they could use carefully positioned murder holes and arrowslits to bombard the men into submission.

Murder holes were large openings in the ceilings of gate passages through which defenders dropped hot liquids or stone missiles onto the heads of unsuspecting or trapped attackers. They were probably also used to quench fires started by the enemy. Nowadays, visitors should always be on the lookout for these devices, and scan not only the walls but also the ceilings above them. Also called meurtrières, murder holes are easy to identify when standing in the gate passage — one can just imagine the impact a stone missile would have on a helmetless head. And, when in the chamber overhead, visitors can peer down through the same openings to the passageway below and imagine pouring liquids on fires or dropping stones onto unwary victims.

Arrowslits, on the other hand, can be found not only on gatehouse walls but also on towers and at positions all along the curtain wall, inside of which passageways allowed both residents and defenders to move around the castle without being seen from the outside. The slender openings were constructed in a variety of shapes, ranging from simple slots with squared ends to cruciform designs known as cross-oillets, which may have better accommodated crossbows while also giving defenders a larger opening to see through.

From the outside, the narrow slits seem as if they would have interfered with a soldier's view, let alone offer enough space for him to accurately fire upon an attacker. However, many castle walls measured from six feet to over twenty feet wide, so they could easily incorporate splayed openings known as embrasures. Forming the inner side of many arrowslits, embrasures were often deep enough for an entire person to stand inside of them. Others could accommodate at least the upper half of a person, who could then support himself on the stone recesses, observe the enemy below, and fire upon them with relative comfort.

Interestingly, when hand guns and muskets were finally introduced to medieval Britain in the fourteenth century, castle owners often modified the lower ends or centers of existing arrowslits to fit the new weapons; these features are generally described as gunloops. Later, castles were frequently fitted with gunports, circular openings backed by embrasures through which guns and small cannons could be fired.

At many castles, builders placed wall towers close to an especially vulnerable main entrance so that defenders on the battlements and behind the arrowslits could aim their firepower directly onto attackers. In addition to intensifying the defensive capabilities of the main gate, towers of all sizes and shapes became essential features of medieval castles. Mural towers were erected at strategic points along the curtain walls, and freestanding towers, known as keeps, donjons, or great towers, dominated many inner baileys. They often stood taller than the enclosing curtain walls. Besides the gatehouse, the towered curtain wall is a castle's most obvious—and most critical—feature. Curtain walls fitted with mural towers had a clear advantage over those that did not. Plain walls had numerous blind spots which enabled an attacker to approach the wall without being detected. Towers, particularly those that projected outward from the line of the wall, broadened the defender's field of vision by allowing them to see points on the ground normally obscured both below them and at a distance, effectively eliminating most blind spots. Mural towers became increasingly common during the thirteenth century.

Early stone towers were generally either square or rectangular in plan. Even though they were easy to construct, their angular corners made them vulnerable not only to battering but also to undermining, a siege technique whereby enemy sappers, soldiers trained to dig tunnels, would burrow under the walls, prop the tunnels up with timber, load them with flammable materials, ignite the materials, and cause the walls above to collapse with the crumbling timbers. Undermining was an effective way to create a breach in the walls, through which attackers could then storm the castle. Rounded walls, on the other hand, not only deflected missiles and withstood battering more easily; they were also difficult to pull down by undermining.

Common during the twelfth century, square and rectangular towers were often positioned alongside simple gateways to bolster their ability to withstand an assault, and others actually served as gate towers. At Dover Castle, Henry II enclosed his masterful great keep, the enormous rectangular tower that stood at the center of his royal fortress, with a curtain wall fitted with fourteen square mural towers. Four of the towers flanked the two gateways guarding the inner bailey, now named the Palace Gate and the King's Gate. Built in the 1180s and 1190s, they are said to be the earliest twin-towered gatehouses in England.[8] After Henry's brother, John, assumed the throne, Hubert de Burgh, his chief justiciar and the castle's constable, furthered the work at Dover and enclosed the entire site with another towered wall. John's wall featured both square and round towers, the new fashion of the times, massive gatehouses with round towers, and an innovative triangular structure known as a redan.

One of the highlights of castle development during the thirteenth century was the use of round mural towers (and keeps) and the widespread construction of gatehouses. At Pem-

Round towers improved a castle's ability to withstand bombardment by catapulted missiles and undermining by enemy sappers. William de Valence added the round dungeon at Pembroke Castle in the late thirteenth century.

broke, in about 1208 William Marshal the Elder built his enormous, 80-foot-high round keep in the inner bailey. Then, he left construction of the outer bailey defenses, including the main gatehouse and the towered curtain wall, to his sons and their successor, William de Valence, who became Earl of Pembroke in 1246. Probably erected by de Valence, the curtain wall around the outer bailey featured five round towers, placed at corners where the stone wall bent around the promontory site, a bastion with two small round towers, and, inside the castle, a round dungeon tower. Interestingly, the sophisticated gatehouse, which was constructed sometime in the mid- to late thirteenth century, was defended by a simple barbican and fitted with a variety of defensive devices (including portcullises, arrowslits, murder holes and doors), but only had one gate tower facing outside the castle. Fittingly known as the Bygate Tower, the round-fronted structure projected outwards from the western side of the gatehouse and stood partly inside the barbican. Another round mural tower, named the Barbican or Town Tower, does overlook the eastern side of the gatehouse and the plain outer gate which led into the barbican. Perhaps added as an afterthought, the Barbican Tower actually connected to the upper floors of the gatehouse; like the Bygate Tower, it would have provided positions from which defenders could fire at an approaching enemy. Two round turrets on the inner side of the great gatehouse face towards the bailey. They create the impression that this is indeed a twin-towered structure; however, they only contain spiral stairways.

By the end of the thirteenth century, round flanking towers were considered integral features of a castle gatehouse. The seven gatehouses at Caerphilly Castle were all fitted with twin round towers. Four massive circular towers also guarded the inner bailey. The innovative round design provided defenders with a wider field of fire and was quickly adopted for use as a key part of the great twin-towered gatehouses that dominated castles such as Harlech, Beeston, and Dover — and so many others — and wall towers also built during the century. While many survive in solid condition, other twin-towered gatehouses are heavily ruined. In many cases, the crumbling remains and ground level foundations reveal the might that made these castles so difficult to overpower.

Like Beeston, Bolingbroke Castle was built in the 1220s by Ranulf de Blundeville, Earl of Chester. It was equipped with an impressive twin-towered gatehouse and five D-shaped mural towers positioned at each corner of the hexagonal enclosure, the walls of which were about thirteen feet wide.[9] During the early fourteenth century, the castle became the property of the earls of Lancaster. Having been the birthplace of Henry Bolingbroke, the future King Henry IV, it was destined to play a key role in the Wars of the Roses. Today, the gatehouse and rounded mural towers survive but are heavily ruined, having been slighted by Cromwell's troops after the English Civil War. Even so, Bolingbroke Castle remains a remarkable site, not just because the lowest levels of the castle and other earthworks at the site (which, according to latest theories, were probably erected during the English Civil War) can still be identified but also because it is a direct, physical link to one of Britain's most historic families and events that changed history.

By the end of the thirteenth century, polygonal towers had become common, especially octagonal and semi-octagonal designs.[10] Even the shell keep at Lewes Castle acquired polygonal corner towers, which may have provided defenders with a wider choice of positions from which to fire upon an enemy. However, the design may also have been used by the Warennes, Earls of Surrey, to create a more pleasing visual effect for this relatively simple, double-motted castle. Edward I also used polygonal towers for his imperial headquarters at Caernarfon. The imposing royal castle was carefully and meticulously planned to become the king's finest

A fine example of a D-shaped, or apsidal, tower can be explored at Bolingbroke Castle. Despite the ruinous condition, the low-lying foundations allow visitors to imagine the original appearance of the tower, which would have stood at least three stories high.

fortress in Wales, so that each feature reminded passersby of the stature of the warrior king, whose armies had finally subdued the Welsh.

Begun in 1283, the elongated figure-eight-shaped castle had thirteen polygonal towers, four of which fronted the two great gatehouses, the King's Gate and the Queen's Gate. Added in 1316, nine years after Edward's death, turrets rising from the tower rooftops were also designed with multiple sides. The overall effect was one of grandeur, innovation and power. Nothing less would have suited this king. Yet, none of his other Welsh castles feature polygonal towers. Even masterful Conwy Castle, which rivals Caernarfon for its visual and engineering excellence, was defended with circular towers. However, the main gatehouse at the lordship castle in Denbigh, built by Henry de Lacy, Earl of Lincoln and one of the king's right-hand men, in some ways resembles Caernarfon Castle, for it also has polygonal towers and an unusual checkerboard pattern to its masonry (Edward's is said to emulate the walls of Constantinople, the king visually bonding himself with the Holy Roman Emperor, Constantine). Perhaps de Lacy's intention was to show off his supposedly close, personal relationship with Edward I.

Polygonal towers appeared with increasing frequency late in the history of British castle

Opposite: Polygonal towers became popular late in the history of castles as builders sought to create more impressive facades. Thomas Beauchamp, the Earl of Warwick, ensured his stone fortress featured the trendy but impractical design, which he used on his twin-towered gatehouse, the barbican, and corner towers, including Caesar's Tower, which held the dungeon.

building. During the fourteenth and fifteenth centuries, castles such as Warwick and Alnwick, the fortified residences of two of the most important noble families in Britain, the earls of Warwick and the dukes of Northumberland, acquired their signature features. On either side of the barbican and gatehouse at Warwick Castle stand its two most impressive towers: Caesar's Tower, a 147-foot-high irregular quatrefoil (or clover-shaped) tower rising three stories (and having a basement-level dungeon), and Guy's Tower, a twelve-sided, five-story, 128-foot-tall tower. Constructed by Thomas de Beauchamp, Earl of Warwick, in the fourteenth century, both towers also had hexagonal guardrooms.[11] The façade of the so-called Ghost Tower, the Watergate tower which overlooks the River Avon on the opposite side of the castle, also features polygonal turrets, as does the barbican discussed previously.

Alnwick Castle began its existence, like Warwick Castle, as an eleventh-century motte and bailey castle but over the centuries acquired a masonry curtain wall and other stone structures. During the early fourteenth century, Henry Percy bought the castle from the bishop of Durham and began a huge rebuilding program, which included the construction of the multi-sided keep that still dominates the core of the site. Crowned with battlements and stone soldiers who, even today, present the image that the castle is heavily defended, the structure features a twin-towered entry point, similar to a gatehouse and fronted with octagonal towers. Constructed in about 1350 by Henry Percy, second Lord Percy, the towers are decorated with armorial shields of families associated by marriage with the second lord of Alnwick. The passage between the two towers retains its medieval portcullis grooves and a seventeenth century pair of timber doors. Interestingly, the curtain wall is a mixture of tower shapes from different eras but predominantly dating to the fourteenth century and to reconstruction efforts undertaken during the nineteenth century. It features square, rectangular, and polygonal designs.

The construction of polygonal towers reached its zenith at Raglan Castle, during the fifteenth century, when Sir William ap Thomas, the "Blue Knight of Gwent," and his son, William Herbert, transformed the site into a palatial fortress. Even in ruin, Raglan remains one of Britain's grandest castles and one that Edward I would certainly have envied. Hexagonal and semi-hexagonal towers dominate the entire castle, from the eye-catching twin-towered gatehouse and enormous closet tower to the east, which held the prison, residential chambers, and possibly the treasury, to the kitchen tower beyond the gatehouse, and finally to the monumental great tower, which is surrounded by its own moat and turreted apron wall, immediately to the south of these other structures. Even in ruin, one cannot help but admire the elegance of the site, particularly its machicolations, fine carvings, and the enormity of the great keep, known as the Yellow Tower of Gwent (or the Twr Melyn Gwent), which in many ways was a castle in its own right. Raglan Castle remains a lasting testament to the success of ap Thomas and his son, who later became the earl of Pembroke, and their successors, the Somersets, dukes of Beaufort. The prolific use of polygonal towers both physically and symbolically displayed the achievements of its owners, in terms of political stature, financial status and cultural sophistication. Today, even in ruin, the castle is one of Britain's grandest ruins, and clearly reflects its medieval splendor.

During the Middle Ages, a castle's battlements (or crenellations) were among its most defining features. Even today, when people spot the tooth-like features that crown the tops of towers and curtain walls, they automatically associate them with castles. Indeed, during the eighteenth and nineteenth centuries, several wealthy entrepreneurs modeled their mansions on castles, symbolically and physically attempting to tie themselves to the Middle Ages

Hexagonal and semi-hexagonal towers abound at Raglan Castle. The machicolated Closet Tower, built next to the great twin-towered gatehouse, overlooks the pitched stone court. It may have housed an entire suite of rooms for the castle steward.

and feudal authority with features sometimes known as sham or mock battlements. Flimsy in comparison with their medieval counterparts, these modern variants were erected to emulate a style that associated the owners with the medieval aristocracy, and not for any defensive purpose.

Medieval castle battlements were functional, and not merely for show. The upright crenels created a stone barrier behind which defenders could safely prepare their weapons and plan their next moves. When ready, they moved quickly into the openings, the merlons, to fire upon an attacker, or, perhaps, to push an advancing enemy's scaling ladder away from the wall before they could reach the wall-top and leap into the castle. Some crenels had openings that functioned like arrowslits, which gave them additional protection behind the upright block of stone. From outside the castle, the crenellations disguised the wall-walks; they were always one of a castle's most important features, useful for both defensive and domestic purposes. A stone walkway, known as the wall-walk, ran the length of the curtain wall behind the battlements and was used by defenders and residents to move between different areas of the castle. At many sites, wall-walks still trace much of their original circuit around the castle; at others, they are fragmentary or too dangerous to walk upon. Some retain unusual features, such as carefully positioned latrine chutes or access to spiral stairways

Two other devices enhanced the defensive capabilities of the battlements: covered fighting platforms, known as hoarding, and stone projections at rooftop level, known as machicolations. Whereas machicolations survive on the rooflines of many castles, the hoarding, which

Timber fighting platforms known as hoards or hoarding enabled defenders to drop missiles and fire arrows upon besiegers through openings in the wooden flooring. This replica at Caerphilly Castle lines both the interior and exterior battlements.

were made of timber and served a temporary purpose, have long since disappeared. At some castles, the line of the holes that held the timber support beams for the fighting platforms can be identified on the exterior curtain wall beneath the battlements. A portion of the northern curtain wall enclosing the inner ward at Caerphilly Castle now supports a modern reconstruction. Visitors can gain a real sense of how these platforms would have hidden the defenders and enabled them to drop missiles or fire upon attackers on the ground beneath them. Much like murder holes but projecting from tower rooftops rather than being positioned inside the gate passage, machicolations seem more like ornamentation than defensive features. Yet, during a raid, defenders could pour hot liquids or drop missiles onto the heads of attackers and thwart their assault.

Having a single entry point allowed defenders to focus their firepower on that spot, which was the main target of attackers during a siege. Therefore, in addition to erecting defended gateways and towered walls, builders often constructed structures known as barbicans, on the outer side of the moat or in front of the main gatehouse to keep besiegers at bay. Some barbicans functioned much like a gatehouse, as at Lewes, whereas others were little more than curved curtain walls enclosing the open area just outside the gatehouse, as at Pembroke. Some were simple enclosed areas fronting a gateway, as at Chepstow Castle, where William

Opposite: Outworks known as barbicans were strategically situated to cover the main gateway and also to confuse attackers as they tried to breach the defenses. At Pembroke, a simple oval-shaped barbican projected outwards from the great gatehouse. It was designed to entrap the enemy and prevent them from gaining access to the gate passage.

Marshal added a substantial barbican and massive round tower to the western end of the site, and at Conwy Castle, where Edward I ensured both gateways were fronted by barbicans, the easternmost of which faced the sea and also contained an herb garden. Others barbicans had simple D-plans or enclosed rampways. Barbicans were intended to confuse and trap attackers in a confined space outside the castle, while the defenders decided their fate. Many barbicans incorporated a series of sudden turns, as at Denbigh, Beaumaris, and Carreg Cennen, which pushed the enemy along a pathway that ended in their entrapment. Defenders also used barbicans as staging points, where they gathered to form up and rush the enemy.

Much like their medieval precursors, visitors to concentric Beaumaris Castle now encounter a blank wall after they pass through what appears to be the main gate, known as the "gate next to the seas." However, to locate the true entry point, they must then turn to the right, where yet another wall, this time with a doorway, faces them. Yet, the challenge continues inside this simple barbican, for once again, they must turn, this time to the left, where, finally, the entrance into the impressive southern gatehouse opens before them.

At Denbigh Castle, an unusual barbican defended the upper gate, a secondary gateway into the great thirteenth-century site. Anyone attempting to gain access at this point first had turn abruptly to the left to enter the now ruined postern gate, the lowest entrance into the castle, and then trudge up a severely sloped bridge which spanned a rock-cut ditch and led to the upper gate. Nowadays, a modern footbridge covers the spot, but the remains of the drawbridge pits and footings are visible below. Only after crossing the bridge could visitors reach the upper gate, a narrow gateway defended by yet another tower. The unusual plan was intended to disorient attackers and expose them to the garrison's firepower.

Barbicans were often well equipped with their own defenses. Warwick Castle's twin-towered, late-fourteenth-century barbican resembles the great gatehouse to the rear, but is smaller and more elongated. The four-story-high barbican is battlemented, secured by a drawbridge and ditch, and contained a portcullis, a pair of thick timber doors, several murder holes, and arrowslits. It is one of the finest examples of its kind still standing in Britain.

One of England's most easy to recognize barbicans can be explored at Goodrich Castle. Now standing to about half its original height, the helmet-shaped structure was probably built by William de Valence in the late thirteenth or early fourteenth century and based on his earlier barbican at Pembroke Castle. Projecting outwards on the eastern side of the imposing rock-cut ditch, the simple structure had its own entrance gate, portcullis, and drawbridge designed to ensnare advancing besiegers when slammed shut. Today, the rear of the barbican links to a bridge, which spans the intimidating ditch and leads to the main gatehouse. At one time, this side of the barbican was further defended with two portcullises, murder holes, and a guard chamber.[12] If an enemy had made its way through the first gateway, he would still have to contend with these additional defenses. In the meantime, he would have been effectively contained inside the barbican.

A similarly designed barbican once protected the western corner of the Tower of London. Known as the Lion Tower because it housed the monarch's menagerie of wild animals until 1834, only the layout of the D-shaped structure, set out in cobblestones, survives in the adjoining roadway. The main entrance and visitor center presently occupy the site. A causeway built by Edward I in 1278 led from the Lion Tower across the then water-filled moat to the Middle Tower, which had its own drawbridge and regulated the flow of water into the inner moat, and then progressed onward to the main gateway, the Byward Tower, the entry point into the outer bailey. This creative combination of outer structures, causeway, and drawbridges posed a substantial challenge to an enemy attempting to storm the castle. Closing off any of those points along the causeway would have prevented besiegers from moving farther ahead into the great fortress.

Of course, no castle gateway stood in isolation; rather, each was an integral part of the curtain wall, the most important and most vulnerable part but nonetheless just one part of the larger whole, which consisted of a walled enclosure and its interior structures. Once an enemy breached the main gate, the most significant and difficult phase of the siege was complete. Many garrisons would surrender at this stage, recognizing the futility of further resistance. Yet, prior to their surrender, valiant defenders would have done their level best to withstand the assault, manning the battlements, racing along the wall-walks, and raining their firepower upon the besiegers. An ordinary wall posed little threat to an attacker, and could be battered with relative ease. However, adding battlements, fighting platforms, and barbicans, and strategically placing towers and strengthening the walls gave the defenders at least a fighting chance against an enemy army. In many cases, besiegers found it more advantageous to blockade a castle, prevent provisions from reaching the garrison, and starve them into submission. Much depended on who was heading the siege and what they hoped to gain from defeating the people inside the castle.

When approaching even the most heavily ruined stone castles, most visitors can identify the location of the original main entrance. Of course, at many castles, the agency that manages the site has made it obvious by channeling visitors along footpaths that lead to the medieval gateway or locating the ticket booth inside the gate. However, to reach that point, visitors often first pass through an outer bailey, which may or may not now be enclosed with a curtain wall, in order to proceed onward to the main gate. If the wall no longer survives or is little more than earthworks or foundations, visitors may not realize they have entered the outer bailey.

Exploring the Outer Bailey

The overall layout of a castle depended on the needs, preferences, wealth, and grandiosity of the lord who built it. Nonetheless, most medieval castles in Britain had at least one outer bailey that visitors had to pass through in order to reach the main part of the castle, where the lord and his family lived and where he performed any official or ceremonial duties. Today, thanks to urban sprawl and the construction of roadways, many outer baileys have been covered over with asphalt or buildings. Consequently, they are often difficult to recognize. Many times, we can identify the probable position of the outer bailey by signs in the landscape, for example, the route a road takes around a site, the presence of earthworks, hedges or fencing which delineate the medieval perimeter of a site, or the layout of houses near the remains of a castle. As we become familiar with the general design of castles, whether they were primarily built with earth and timber or stone, it becomes increasingly easy to imagine where a bailey might have been situated.

Most outer baileys were positioned to provide defensive support for the interior of the castle; similar in some ways to a barbican, they acted as defensive outworks which left an advancing enemy vulnerable to attack from defenders. The inner bailey was generally positioned against the most dangerous side of a site for an enemy to attack, where there were cliffs or other factors that made it less likely for an assault to come from that direction. Outer baileys normally occupied the inland side of a castle, from where it was easier for an army to approach the site in order to stage a siege.[13]

Of even greater importance was the outer bailey's role in the day-to-day activities carried out inside the castle, for they usually contained essential ancillary structures such as stables, workshops, secondary halls, and accommodation for servants and members of the garrison. Initially, these structures were timber-framed, set on stone foundation, and backed against the curtain wall or earthen embankment that enclosed the bailey; in time, many acquired stone walls or were built largely with stone to begin with. Not surprisingly, if they survive at all, most of these fairly fragile buildings are now identifiable only by their foundations or certain structural features, particularly from the side that abutted the curtain wall. Indeed, many outer baileys — and also many inner baileys — seem so wide open that visitors today may justifiably come away with the notion that they were nothing more than large empty areas that simply added to the overall size of the lord's residence.

However, such interpretations are flawed, as a visit to Windsor Castle would show. During the Middle Ages, outer baileys bustled with activity and noise, as servants and laborers went about their daily routine, made repairs to the castle, forged iron for swords and horseshoes, and completed other jobs. The craftsmen, including masons, carpenters, plumbers, and other laborers, who focused on maintaining the castle itself, had their workplaces in the outer bailey. Blacksmiths forged and sharpened tools and weapons, beat out dents in armor, made hinges for the doors and window grilles, and tipped the portcullises with iron points. Close by, attiliators made crossbows, coopers and hoopers made barrels, billers made axes, cobblers made shoes, and glaziers cut and shaped glass.

One of the most important members of the castle's outer household was the marshal, the officer in charge of the lord's horses, stables, carts, wagons, and other containers. He oversaw the activities of the "outside servants," the farriers (or blacksmiths), armorers, grooms, boy attendants, carters, and messengers, who largely worked in the outer bailey.[14] The marshal also managed the transport of goods and sometimes supervised the work of clerks. Eventually, the marshal became a high-ranking member of the royal court: William le Marischal (and better known as William Marshal, Earl of Pembroke, and, among other things, regent to Henry III) derived his name not only from his father, John, who was King Stephen's marshal, but also from his own position in the courts of the kings of England. Nowadays in Britain, the Earl Marshal is responsible for ceremonial procedures and state functions. The Howard dukes of Norfolk, who reside at Arundel Castle, have been the hereditary Earls Marshal of England since the late seventeenth century.

The constable, often a lord in his own right or a man of notable status, was in charge of all aspects of the castle's administration, as well as its contents and facilities, in the lord's absence. Normally residing in a chamber over the gate passage, he monitored the activity in the outer bailey, at the main gate, and also inside the castle, and responded to a crisis if needed. Also known as the castellan, warden, or custodian, he wielded considerable power, not only with castle residents but in the surrounding area as well. At many castles, the position became hereditary. Among the constable's subordinates was the porter (door-ward or "durward"), who was responsible for taking care of the doors and the guardrooms, and also opened and closed the main doors and ensured that no one entered or left the castle without proper permission.

Many castles contained only one outer bailey, particularly those that originated as motte or ringwork and bailey strongholds and were refortified with masonry defenses. Today, we can identify these castles not only by the presence of the motte or ringwork embankments, shrewdly incorporated into a later stone castle, but also by the design of the castle. For exam-

Once through the great gatehouse, visitors to Pembroke Castle find themselves thrust into the wide-open outer bailey. At one time, a number of structures would have occupied this space, but recent archaeological investigations have been unable to verify building locations or what uses they would have served.

ple, the motte at Warwick Castle, which was built shortly after the Conquest, stands at the southwestern end of the later stone fortress on the opposite side of the castle from the gatehouse. When the timber defenses were replaced with the towered curtain wall that still encloses the outer bailey, builders made sure to incorporate the northeastern side of the motte into the stone fortress by constructing the wall so that it crossed over the top of the mound. From inside the castle, modern visitors might not recognize that the tree-covered hill is the original motte built by William the Conqueror, but a path on the exterior of the castle weaves its way to the summit. From there, it is easy to identify the physical relationship between the massive mount, now called Ethelfleda's Mound, and the rest of the castle, which originally formed the outer bailey but later served as the main seat of the earls of Warwick and became the inner bailey of their castle. The post-medieval state and private apartments line the eastern side; the rest of the bailey has long since been cleared of any other structures.

Unlike Warwick Castle, which was occupied until the twentieth century, modern visitors to Pembroke Castle, now largely a shell and occupied by ruined structures, might find the experience of passing through its seemingly complete gatehouse into the wide-open, empty outer bailey rather disconcerting. Now enclosed by the towered curtain wall built by the de Valence earls of Pembroke in the late thirteenth century, the sprawling grassy area was originally enclosed with earthworks and timber defenses. It is unclear what buildings once occupied the outer bailey; however, recent archaeological excavations have provided evidence that

Framed by the battlements that defended the mighty castle, William Marshal's innovative round keep identified the Earl of Pembroke as a man of power, stature, and influence not just in West Wales but within the greater kingdom over which he served as Regent during the minority of King Henry III.

the area once was crowded with a variety of structures, such as barns, stables, storerooms, workshops, and animal pens. And, according to historical records, a dovecote and a garden also were located in the outer bailey.

Once inside Pembroke Castle, visitors today have the option of exploring the curtain wall and its towers, or making their way across the outer bailey — after first attempting to imagine what structures stood here and what types of activity would have taken place on a daily basis — to reach the inner bailey, which is dominated by William Marshal's great round keep and the main domestic buildings. In fact, the inner bailey probably marks the site of the original earth and timber castle at Pembroke, built by Arnulf de Montgomery, the son of the Earl of Shrewsbury, in about 1093. Medieval visitors would have originally accessed this part of the castle by walking the roadway up the steep hillside to the postern gate, which William de Valence later incorporated into his masonry curtain wall where his new watergate and Monkton Tower still stand. A pathway from the opening still leads to the Horseshoe Gate, which is now represented only by its D-shaped foundations cut into limestone bedrock. Access into the inner ward was through this unusual gate tower.

Like Pembroke Castle, Edward I's Welsh headquarters at Caernarfon Castle was erected on the site of a motte and bailey castle, which Hugh d'Avranches, Earl of Chester, built in about 1090. In fact, Edward's new castle so totally engulfed the earth and timber stronghold that it is surprising to realize that the motte, which was lowered to make way for the stone castle, actually survives underneath the Cistern Tower. It is best viewed from outside the castle.

The plan of Caernarfon Castle resembles an elongated figure eight. Positioned at the midpoint between two oval baileys, the King's Gate still acts as the main gatehouse into the stronghold. The jagged masonry on either side of the inner end of the gate passage shows that the gatehouse was never complete. The builders had intended for the twin-towered gatehouse not only to contain a highly complex set of defensive devices, but they also planned to erect a cross-wall to separate the two baileys, known at Caernarfon as upper and lower wards.

The King's Gate actually leads modern visitors into the upper ward, away from the king's private residence. Had the cross-wall been built, more than likely the area would have functioned as an outer bailey, as did the same feature at Conwy, and prevented all but the most welcome guests into the lower ward, which was the king's domain. Indeed, except for the location of the gateways and the reversed positions of the inner and outer wards, the two great castles essentially duplicate each other. Interestingly, whereas the great hall and kitchen block at Conwy were placed in the outer bailey, they were situated inside the lower ward at Caernarfon, closer to the towers designated for the king and queen. And, rather than using a kitchen tower to supplement work in the kitchen block located in the bailey, as at Conwy, the comparable tower at Caernarfon contained the well, which was intentionally positioned so that ships could sail alongside the castle and unload their supplies into the waterside basement. The well at Conwy was centrally located in the outer bailey alongside the cross-wall.

Some castles had a bailey on either side of the innermost ward. Windsor Castle is an excellent example. Visitors actually pass through the twin-towered King Henry VIII Gate into the triangular lower ward, which is dominated by St. George's Chapel and five round mural towers erected during the reign of Henry III. To move further around the castle, they must then make their way around the middle (or innermost) ward containing the original motte castle and its twelfth century round keep to reach the royal and state apartments that surround the upper ward, where several medieval towers were largely reconstructed during the 1820s.[15]

As at Windsor, the stately residence of the dukes of Norfolk at Arundel Castle features two large baileys positioned on either side of the enormous motte, which is crowned with a well-preserved Norman shell keep. Interestingly, each bailey has its own gateway, the most elaborate of which opens into the "Quadrangle." Dating originally to the twelfth century, this lower bailey consists of a courtyard completely enclosed by the duke's private residence, the reconstruction of which began in the late eighteenth century and continued for well over a hundred years.[16] The twin-towered barbican built by Richard FitzAlan, first Earl of Arundel, in 1295, still defends its entry point. The "Tilting Yard" on the opposite side of the motte forms the upper bailey. Enclosed by a less substantial battlemented wall with fragments dating to the twelfth century, it is normally not open to the public.

When visiting a castle, never expect a standard layout or that the placement of the baileys, where more than one exists, leads in a straight line from the outermost to the innermost area of the castle, as is the case at Chepstow. Castles were built creatively and their design was based on the lay of the land, the structures already present on the site, and the needs of the owner at a given time. Corfe Castle, with its outer bailey, west bailey, and inner ward, is a case in point. The now boot-shaped castle completely engulfs the lofty hilltop on which it stands, extending all the way to the village at its base, which is separated from the castle by a ditch dug in 1214. To reach the inner ward from the main entrance, the outer gatehouse, visitors still must cross the severely sloped outer bailey, a broad open area heavily defended with a towered wall on its less severely sloped western side. At the upper end of the outer bailey, the great ditch marks the location of southern side of the southwestern bailey, which was destroyed in the thirteenth century to make way for the ditch and once extended around to the west bailey.

Top: Even though the modern appearance can distract visitors from the medieval remains, Arundel Castle is an outstanding example of a motte castle with two baileys. The Duke of Norfolk's state and private apartments now line the Quadrangle, one of the original medieval baileys at the great castle. *Bottom:* Now heavily ruined in large part due to slighting after the English Civil War, Corfe Castle was once one of the realm's most spectacular castles. Though only rising to half its original height, the outer gatehouse was defended with arrowslits, machicolations, a portcullis, and massive double doors, and also had a timber hoard around its first story.

Then, visitors must make their way to the ruined southwestern gatehouse, which leads to the west bailey, and from there trudge still further uphill to finally turn to the right, only to continue climbing up the slope to reach level footing inside the inner ward. The jumble of ruins ahead once formed Henry I's great keep and King John's gloriette, both of which were so completely destroyed by Parliamentarian troops in 1646 that even present-day archaeologists and architectural historians have had a difficult time making sense of the puzzle. Modern visitors should investigate as much as possible of the remains to gain an overall impression of the majesty and military might of this important structure. (Having a castle guidebook will help sort out the confusion.)

At some castle sites, the entrance into the outer bailey is marked by the remains of a small outer gatehouse. At White Castle, the outer gatehouse partly stood in the ditch that surrounded the outer bailey. The fairly short twin-towered structure, which was probably built by Prince Edward, the future King Edward I, in about 1257, was fronted by a drawbridge, the pit for which is still visible, and contained a portcullis (as evidenced by the presence of a groove), two pairs of timber doors, positioned to barricade each end of the gate passage, a guardroom, and stairs, which led to a latrine that dumped into the ditch. When he acquired the castle, Edward remodeled the entire site, so that the main entrance, which had been on the southern side of the castle, now stood on the northern side. It was at this time that Edward added the small outer gatehouse. Such a dramatic alteration can play havoc with the minds of modern visitors, who would be none the wiser about this change, except if they read the guidebook or start to question just why there is a gaping hole in the rear wall of the castle. Once functioning as the main entrance into the twelfth-century castle that predated Edward's alteration of the site, the opening was converted into a postern gate when the prince rearranged the layout of the site and constructed the imposing twin-towered great gatehouse on the opposite side.

At Kenilworth, visitors who choose to go directly into the castle rather than first exploring the surroundings, where the great mere and other features were located, are directed along the medieval causeway, which was occasionally used as a tiltyard (also known as the lists) for men wanting to practice—or show off—their jousting skills, and through the remains of Mortimer's Tower, a small outer gatehouse which controlled access to the outer bailey. Like the outer gate at White Castle, Mortimer's Tower featured two outward-facing gate towers and a portcullis, the grooves for which survive. At the outer end of the causeway, nearest the new ticket point at the main parking lot, visitors can also identify the Brays, an area enclosed by earthwork embankment and ditch inside of which melees and other tournament events took place.

Pembroke Castle stands at the western fringes of the adjoining medieval walled town, which grew up alongside the castle and connected to it at two points on the curtain wall. A modern visitor's initial impression of the castle depends upon the direction from which he or she arrives in the town and also which parking lot is used. When arriving from the north, views of the magnificent castle are blocked by the natural layout of the land, trees and houses, until visitors reach the Mill Bridge, where the north gate once stood. The tidal Mill Pond once flowed past the northern side of the castle. It acted as a natural moat and also powered a corn mill. As one crosses the bridge, almost without warning, the hulking castle pops into view on the right (western) side of the bridge. The massive great keep and towered wall dominate the scene, but only for an instant, for the traffic swiftly charges uphill to circuit around the town, where portions of the town walls are quite visible.

William Marshal's imposing domed round keep towers well above the outer curtain wall at Pembroke Castle. The rise and fall of the River Pembroke created a natural moat around the formidable fortress.

After parking, visitors can opt to head directly to the main entrance into the site; investigate the exterior from a distance by walking a footpath on the opposite side of the River Pembroke, which formed the southern and western moats; or examine the structure up close by taking the pathway at the base of the castle. They may also choose to explore the extensive remains of the medieval walls, which once enclosed the entire town and connected directly to the castle. Today, they are in fine condition and allow visitors to gain an appreciation for the relationship between the medieval town (and borough) and its castle. Each approach to the castle offers a different perspective, and gives an indication of what thirteenth-century visitors or besiegers might have contended with when arriving at the earl of Pembroke's main fortress. Clearly the castle stood head and shoulders above any other structure and prospects for storming its walls would have been daunting at the very least. Indeed, the final trek up the steep slopes of Westgate Hill to the main gate required an extra burst of energy, as it does to this day.

Whether standing alongside the curtain wall or viewing it from a distance, it is immediately apparent that Pembroke Castle was a powerful structure. As in the Middle Ages, the great castle towers well overhead and exudes an air of intimidation as well as lordly domination. The castle of the earls of Pembroke would have seemed quite impregnable, particularly when the waters of two tidal streams flowed at the base of the castle. They have receded enough to allow construction of the walkway around the perimeter of the site.

In reality, no castle was ever completely impervious to an assault, and even the best defended sites could fall if the attack was well-planned and intensely focused. So, Pembroke Castle's builders armed the main gateway with a variety of defensive mechanisms as well as a barbican, to thwart the best efforts of a besieging army or a rebellion by the Welsh. Beyond the ticket office, visitors approach a simple archway, which serves as the outer gate and leads into the remains of the barbican probably built by William de Valence in the latter part of the thirteenth century. Curiously, the flat, battlemented entry point, which was reconstructed in the late nineteenth century, is so innocuous that it is easy not to notice it at all, especially if one is in a hurry to explore the rest of the castle or is distracted by the presence of the larger, and far grander, towers to the right and further ahead. Even so, the archway leads into one of the most important structures at the castle, the D-shaped barbican, an open area enclosed by the curtain wall which was positioned in front of the gatehouse in order to corral attackers trying to make their way through the outer entrance. Today, the barbican seems unremarkable, for it is little more than a cramped shell; however, it is well worth examining before turning right to face the gate passage as it provides a good impression of how such structures could have kept an enemy at bay.

Even without its portcullises, heavy timber doors, and soldiers manning the parapet, Pembroke Castle's formidable great gatehouse remains an imposing structure. Though not a true twin-towered gateway, its does feature two flanking towers, one of which (the Bygate Tower) projects into the barbican, while the other (the Barbican Tower) stands just a brief distance away on the eastern side of the gatehouse. Having been destroyed in about 1648 by Parliamentarian troops at the end of the English Civil War, the exterior of the D-shaped Bygate Tower was restored during the early twentieth century, as were the exteriors of the Westgate Tower, the Henry VII Tower, and the Northgate Tower, all of which had round plans. Interestingly, the exterior of the round Barbican Tower remained unscathed. Instead, Parliamentary troops damaged a portion of the interior and rendered it useless for further military action.

Inside the gate passage, visitors can easily identify the two sets of portcullis grooves and the drawbar holes that once secured the gatehouse and prevented unwelcome guests from entering the rest of the castle. Arrowslits on either side of the passage and murder holes positioned overhead allowed defenders to fire upon or drop missiles and hot liquids onto anyone trapped between the two portcullises. Prisoners might temporarily find themselves confined in one of the guardrooms located on either side of the passage. When the portcullises were raised using the winding mechanism located in the chamber above the passageway, residents and invited guests could make their way into the outer bailey or choose to climb spiral staircases located inside the turrets at the inner end of the gate passage to reach the upper levels. Today, visitors have the same two options.

During the 1880s and again in the 1920s and 1930s, extensive restoration work was carried out at Pembroke Castle (see Chapter 5 for more information). Without the efforts of antiquary J. R. Cobb and Major-General Sir Ivor Philipps, the seat of the earls of Pembroke (and the birthplace of the future King Henry VII) might now be a complete ruin, perhaps comparable to the sites that, because of their ruinous condition, many people now criticize for not being true castles, such as Bolingbroke, Fotheringhay or Pontefract, to mention only three of the dozens of heavily ruined but historically significant medieval fortresses. At one time, all of these structures were the pride of their owners, featured defenses and residential units, and commanded the surrounding landscape and the populace who lived on it. The same can be said about earth and timber castles. Warfare, abandonment in favor of a new home, the pilfering of stone, or the expense of the castle's upkeep all played a role in creating the ruins that can be explored throughout Britain. Each was and is a castle in its own right.

The Visual Effect

Some castle researchers now believe that medieval castle-builders constructed their castles in accordance with the social expectations of the times: a lordly residence was supposed to exude power and status, which military features such as crenellations, towers, and a moat fulfilled. Therefore, so the theory goes, just as medieval warfare was the purview of the aristocratic class, so was their architecture — the mere presence of military structures, regardless of their defensive capabilities, distinguished a nobleman's home from those of other classes.[17] Lords of substance were pressured by society to build castles in order to confirm their social and political stature. Presumably, the bigger and more imposing the defenses, the more impressive the lord who had built them would seem to his rivals. Lesser lords with fewer financial resources to turn to would still make an effort to construct a castle with the showiest defenses he could afford.

If it is true that medieval castles were built according to an unwritten set of aristocratic expectations, then when visitors approached a castle, the owner would have anticipated some sort of emotional response from them which they hoped to provoke with the construction of certain architectural features. Awe, intimidation, respect, jealousy — a myriad of feelings could have been prompted by the vision of a castle as a visitor approached the main gate. Even though we cannot know with complete certainty what was experienced by those guests, we can imagine their responses by noticing our own reactions as we explore castles today.

One of the clearest impressions I have of a castle is my first view of Haverfordwest Castle, as I rode downhill from the train station towards the center of town. As the car I was riding in rounded a curve in the road, I was immediately confronted with the remains of the castle, which still commands a hilltop above the bustling town and traffic chaos. Saying I became enamored with the sight does little to describe my feeling; yet, over the decades that have passed since I first arrived in Haverfordwest, the vision has not dimmed.

Even though the remains of Haverfordwest Castle may not rival a more complete site, such as Windsor Castle, or even a site like Pembroke Castle, which is located only about 15 miles away, who really cares? Even Pembroke Castle deceives its visitors, for it is heavily restored, a ruin that has been rejuvenated thanks to the far-sighted efforts of the men who restored the site in the nineteenth and early twentieth centuries. Approaching a site such as Haverfordwest Castle with an attitude of wonderment and curiosity does it more justice than carelessly dismissing the site because its impressive northern front somehow fools us into thinking it is more substantial than it really is. We can more meaningfully imagine that, as they approached from the north, medieval visitors would have seen something akin to (and certainly even more impressive than) what we see today and probably experienced the same awe still exuded by the sight.

When it came to royal visitors, owners normally went all out to impress their guests; some spent so much money to repair, rebuild, and decorate their castles that they bankrupted themselves. However, depending on the political situation of the times and the personality of the reigning monarch, the construction of a lordship castle, particularly one with substantial defenses, could be interpreted by the king as a personal threat or, at the very least, that the lord was implying that the two men were of equal status. One can presume that Gilbert de Clare II had this notion in mind when he set about erecting Caerphilly Castle, which predates Edward I's great fortresses in North Wales by several years. While the enormity of the castle, which is Britain's second largest castle after Windsor, may imply that de Clare considered the unruly Welsh to be a potent threat to his lordship in Glamorgan, it seems even more likely that de Clare wanted to call attention to his political stature as one of the realm's most powerful lords and, perhaps, to provoke the king, with whom he had long had a contentious relationship.

At Orford in Suffolk, Henry II erected arguably one of England's most pretentious great towers, which he began in 1165 in order to re-establish a physical presence in the region and to send a clear message to two upstarts in East Anglia: William de Blois, fourth Earl of Warenne and King Stephen's youngest son, whose properties in East Anglia had been seized by the king, and Hugh Bigod, first Earl of Norfolk and lord of Framlingham Castle. Henry's main goal was to prove to the men that he was superior to them as a ruler, and as a castle-builder as well.

Prior to his invasion of England, Duke William was well aware of the threat castles posed to his rule in Normandy, where tensions in the aristocracy had been a significant problem for decades. In Normandy, the law of the land was largely on the duke's side, and William had the legal authority to regulate who administered his castles. Whereas earlier dukes had chosen men they believed had the highest noble status, counts and viscounts, and other trusted supporters[18] to manage Normandy's castles, William appointed family members, who should have been trustworthy. Yet, even with this cautious approach, the castle-holders did rebel, and many brazenly constructed their own castles. William's response was not only to demolish the castles of these untrustworthy barons but also to garrison some of the castles with his own men.[19]

In the years immediately after William's death, his sons, Robert of Normandy and William (Rufus) II, King of England, vied for control of Normandy's castles. In 1091, they drew up a document identifying ducal rights and customs for Normandy, known as the *Consuetudines et Iusticie,* which reputedly were in effect during their father's rule. It placed specific restrictions on castle building: no one could dig a ditch (*fosse*) greater than "one shovel's throw in depth," nor raise "more than one line of palisading," nor build battlements,[20] nor, for that matter, erect a *"fortitudinem,"* a strong place, on bedrock or on an island.[21] In fact, the duke of Normandy had the right to take over any lord's castle, in essence, when the mood struck, in a process known as rendability. Enforced elsewhere in France and also in Britain, rendability had a symbolic function as well as a practical use, for it allowed the duke — and in Britain, the monarch — to restate his power over a lesser lord.

Clearly, William the Conqueror and his son, Rufus, were aware of the threat that unregulated castles could pose. In Normandy, where there was an overabundance of castles, these restrictions were essential to the duke's continued control. However, in England and Wales, where the Normans wanted to impose themselves over the newly conquered populace, similar rules were not needed. Rather, William's followers were encouraged to build castles in the new lordships they acquired from their king. They were well aware, however, that the monarchy always retained the right to take back any castle or lordship that had been granted to them.

Nonetheless, political circumstances changed and later Norman kings and their successors inevitably perceived certain castles and their owners as threats to their authority. During the Anarchy (1135–1154), when the Empress Matilda battled Stephen, the last Norman king, for control of England, many castles were strengthened and new strongholds, largely of earth and timber, were raised in the countryside. Estimates of the number of these new sites, traditionally known as "adulterine castles," vary wildly from less than a hundred to over a thousand.[22] In 1154, the Anarchy concluded with the coronation of Matilda's son, the first Angevin king of England, who was crowned Henry II.

In the aftermath of the Anarchy, Henry II set about imposing order in the realm. He not only demanded the destruction of scores of adulterine castles, which had no place in his kingdom (but still linger in the countryside), but he also began investing — to the tune of over £20,000 — to repair and construct his own castles and great towers, including those at Scarborough, Newcastle-upon-Tyne, Dover, and Peveril,[23] in his effort to reaffirm his role as England's supreme leader.

Despite his best efforts to the contrary, Henry felt threatened by the existence of certain castles throughout his entire reign, not surprisingly, because he continued to have to deal with discontented barons. After putting down another barons' rebellion in 1174, the king reputedly asserted the royal right of rendability and seized all of the castles in England, manning them with his own custodians.[24] Two years later, he ordered the demolition of at least twenty baronial castles. Henry's actions dramatically heightened the power of the monarchy and seemed to lessen the threat he felt from his barons, at least as symbolized by their castles.

Yet, Henry's concerns proved valid, and civil war continued to plague his successors, most notably during the reigns of his son, John, and grandson, Henry. The Magna Carta wars began a few months after the pope agreed to void the Great Charter, which King John had signed in June 1215. By 1216, opponents of the king had proclaimed the French prince, Louis, as king of England. Hoping to add Britain to his holdings, the future King Louis VIII of France and the rebel barons besieged several castles, including Rochester and the Tower of London, and managed to capture much of England, if not the castles. When John died later that year, his nine-year-old son, Henry, was crowned king; it was up to his regent, William Marshal, Earl of Pembroke, to settle the score with the barons and their French leader.

One of Henry III's first acts (as maneuvered by William Marshal) was to reconfirm the provisions of the Magna Carta. The move only temporarily satisfied the barons. Marshal also began to re-establish the monarchy's authority over the barons by adding a clause to the end of the Magna Carta, which ordered the immediate destruction of all adulterine castles, specifically those built or rebuilt since the beginning of the wars between King John and the barons.[25] He also forced Louis to retreat back to France. Though some castles were destroyed, the fortifications of others were restored to their pre-war (and, hence, pre-adulterine) condition. During the 1220s, Henry III and his chief advisor, Hubert de Burgh, set out to recover the royal castles that had been lost during the barons' rebellion and to thereby reassert royal authority on a wider scale.[26] For almost thirty years, Henry and his barons co-existed in a state of relative peace. When civil war between the monarchy and the barons again erupted, this time led by Simon de Montfort and Gilbert de Clare, castles had a crucial impact on the final outcome.

Some four centuries later, castles again played a crucial role in the struggle between Britain's ruler, this time King Charles I, and the barons, whose key leaders served in Parliament. In 1642, the conflict erupted into full-scale warfare, known as the English Civil Wars. Many castles were repaired and prepared for battle, garrisoned with soldiers supporting one or the other side of the fray. After finally defeating the royalist army in 1648, parliamentary leaders, most notably the new Lord Protector, Oliver Cromwell, instituted a widespread policy of

Once enclosed by substantial towered stone walls, a barbican, and a gatehouse, the royal castle at Pontefract is now little more than a series of masonry foundations and a motte, which was once topped with a multi-lobed shell keep. Richard II (the Lionhearted) died under mysterious circumstances while imprisoned at the castle.

destroying castles in order to prevent them from being reoccupied and used against them in future battles.

Whereas some castles were "slighted," so that defensive structures, such as the outer curtain wall or towers, were rendered useless while the rest of the castle remained intact, as at Pembroke, other castles were completely pulled down. Obliging the request of the town's residents, who had endured three sieges in four years and wanted to avoid further turmoil, parliamentary troops in 1649 so extensively devastated the imposing royal fortress at Pontefract that modern visitors will find it almost impossible to believe that a substantial fortress equipped with a twin-towered gatehouse, a barbican, and mural towers ever occupied the site. The castle site is now dominated by a large motte and ruined great tower. The four-lobed shell keep once stood three stories tall but is now little more than a few feet high. The expansive bailey still contains foundations from several stone structures, including the great hall, chapel, kitchen and bakehouse, and one of the towers. Careful examination of the masonry, however, does reveal features such as a portcullis groove, a latrine (garderobe), ovens, and a mason's mark.

At first glance, it may be difficult to imagine that the remains of an earth and timber castle or a jumble of stone ruins may once have posed a serious threat to a monarch. Yet, historical documents and archaeological evidence have proven that many of these now forlorn sites changed British history. Whether symbolically or physically, scores of castles and the lords who owned them continued to endanger the stability of the kingdom as long as they could be repaired easily and re-garrisoned. Clearly, the destruction of these castles, which included the earth and timber strongholds erected during the Anarchy, allowed the monarch (or the Lord Protector) to exhale with relief, for the castles no longer could be used against them and their attention could be focused elsewhere.

The Peasant's View

Besiegers were not the only people who interacted with a castle's outer defenses. Besides the occupants, a lord's superiors and subordinates had reason to visit or investigate a castle, as invited guests, rent payers, to take part in legal matters, to perform castle work or guard duty, and for a variety of other purposes that had nothing to do with a siege. In fact, sieges were relatively rare during the Middle Ages; daily life in a castle generally occurred in a peacetime environment and oftentimes while the lord was away taking care of business or in residence at one of his other castles. Nonetheless, the administration of the encompassing lordship and manorial estates continued to be carried out, and people from all sorts of backgrounds continued to approach the castle during the lord's absence. Their attitudes towards the owner would have been influenced by the design and dimensions of the defensive structures that stood in their way as they headed to the gateway for permission to enter the castle or pay their fees.

Nowadays, we would reasonably imagine that members of the peasantry would have had a hostile response to the presence of a castle. However, we must be careful not to base our opinions on our own projections of what peasant life would have been like during the Middle Ages. In fact, what we know comes from interpreting documents written by literate members of the upper class, whose biases largely color their writing. A few medieval chroniclers, such as Ordericus Vitalis and the writers of the *Anglo-Saxon Chronicle*, condemned the oppression of the peasantry that accompanied castle-building. The 1137 entry in the *Anglo-Saxon Chronicle* reveals the despair caused by castle-building at the start of King Stephen's reign:

> and they filled the land full of castles. They cruelly oppressed the wretched men of the land with castle-works; and when the castles were made, they filled them with devils and evil men. Then took they those whom they supposed to have any goods, both by night and by day, laboring men and women, and threw them into prison for their gold and silver, and inflicted on them unutterable tortures; for never were any martyrs so tortured as they were. Some they hanged up by the feet, and smoked them with foul smoke; and some by the thumbs, or by the head, and hung coats of mail on their feet. They tied knotted strings about their heads, and twisted them till the pain went to the brains. They put them into dungeons, wherein were adders, and snakes, and toads; and so destroyed them. Some they placed in a crucet-house; that is, in a chest that was short and narrow, and not deep; wherein they put sharp stones, and so thrust the man therein, that they broke all the limbs. In many of the castles were things loathsome and grim, called "Sachenteges," of which two or three men had enough to bear one. It was thus made: that is, fastened to a beam; and they placed a sharp iron [collar] about the man's throat and neck, so that he could in no direction either sit, or lie, or sleep, but bear all that iron. Many thousands they wore out with hunger. I neither can, nor may I tell all the wounds and all the pains which they inflicted on wretched men in this land. This lasted the nineteen winters while Stephen was king; and it grew continually worse and worse.[27]

Certainly, even if only a few — or none — of the above indignities occurred, the peasant class in medieval Britain had reason to be angry. The Normans had seized the kingdom and become their overlords. Norman castles were built with the sweat of Anglo-Saxon laborers, oftentimes on top of Anglo-Saxon settlements. No matter their size, castles were perpetual symbols of the defeat the Saxons had suffered at the hands of the Normans. They had not only lost their leader, Harold II, but also experienced the demise of their own aristocracy, many of whom died at Hastings or at Stamford Bridge. Still others lost their lives during the short-lived rebellions that plagued William's reign until his death in 1087 or fled into exile. With some exceptions, the Anglo-Saxon elite who remained in England lost their fortunes and landholdings, which were taken over by the Normans, and found themselves among the peasant class. A rare few, some of whom were involved in the major building projects initiated by the Normans (not only castles, but churches and cathedrals as well),[28] or were granted positions as subtenants on estate lands[29] actually prospered.

Even though historians have long argued that feudalism arrived with the Normans, it is now widely accepted that the Anglo-Saxons had a similar system in place prior to the Conquest and that the peasants were accustomed to government by a king, now in the guise of William of Normandy, and strong lords. In Anglo-Saxon England, the king, earls, and thegns comprised the upper class, whereas the peasantry, known as the ceorls, occupied the lowest level of society. Before the Conquest, the Anglo-Saxon aristocracy owned the land and performed military service, whereas the peasantry worked the land and provided the elite with food and other resources; after the Conquest, the aristocracy — now Normans — performed those same roles. In many cases, the Normans simply opted to maintain the status quo and administered their new lordships as they had been managed prior to 1066. Dispersed as they were in the countryside, many peasants would not have felt much of an effect from what actually amounted to a superficial change of ownership.[30] Indeed, the placement of many Norman castles was directly related to the patterns of settlement and land tenure already in place prior to the Conquest. For the most part, the Anglo-Saxons probably accepted the power of the new lords and carried on with their lives; the presence of the castle in their midst probably seemed an extension of the lord himself. Though the Anglo-Saxons did not have castles, the upper crust did live in fine houses, which they defended with ditches and palisaded embankments.[31] Over time, however, the Norman lords began demanding greater productivity and exorbitant (and extortionate) rents from the peasantry; not surprisingly, the rumblings of discontent eventually turned into open revolt.

On a day-to-day basis, the ordinary folk generally had little contact with castles, and even less with their lords, many of whom were not in residence on a regular basis. Instead, much of the peasantry would have spent their days working in the villages and fields for their own sustenance or were assigned to work for the lordship and manorial estates. That work would have kept them fully occupied; however, during certain times of the year, they were also obligated to provide specific services to the lord, close to or inside the castle walls. "Weekwork" and "boon-work" required them to work the lord's lands (known as demesne lands) for a specified number of days each week or during harvest season. Some peasants were required to maintain the herrison, a dangerous area in the outer bailey filled with stakes.[32] Others would have been assigned to make repairs to the castle. And, when it came time to pay rent or fines or attend the manorial court, some members of the peasantry might have had to approach the castle. Even then, their inferior status might prohibit them from entering the castle — on those rare occasions when they did go to the castle, they had to hand their fees to the reeve (also a member of the peasantry) or another official representative, or, even more rarely, the lord himself, standing at the main gate. Normally, however, reeves or bailiffs collected rents in the villages and turned them over to the Receiver, an official on the lord's central staff who would in turn pass it on to the lord, who was often absent from a castle for over a year.[33]

So, how did the Anglo-Saxon peasantry perceive castles? No one knows for certain. Yet, one can reasonably presume from the above discussion that their attitudes towards their lord's castle would have influenced their attitudes about how their lord treated them and how they felt about their subordinate social position. Furthermore, the architectural grandiosity of the castle would not have escaped their attention. Those who worked directly for the lord as his representative, such as the reeve, might view a castle as a place of opportunity, where power and money could be acquired. On the other hand, those who had lost their aristocratic status, paid exorbitant rents, or tilled the lord's fields would have undoubtedly viewed their Norman lord's castle with considerable hostility and resentment, but perhaps also with at least a smidgen of awe and intimidation, not that they would ever have admitted to doing so.

As their leaders recognized the futility of further revolt, went into exile, or lost their property, the Anglo-Saxon populace that occupied England prior to the Conquest became part and parcel of the new Norman kingdom, albeit as members of the peasantry. The native Welsh, however, faced a different set of circumstances, as the Normans gradually made their way across the borderlands into the farther reaches of the British countryside. And, they reacted to castles in a much different way from the Anglo-Saxon peasantry, for whom everyday life continued largely unchanged by the presence of their new lords.

In Wales, however, the Normans generally chose the most fertile lowland regions for their new lordships, and pushed the Welsh into more rugged terrain, where life was harsher. They also established planned towns centered on castles, which they then colonized with outsiders from England and the Continent. For example, Henry I encouraged the Flemings, from what is now Belgium, to migrate to Pembrokeshire and establish their own communities, such as Haverfordwest and Wiston, both of which were built by Flemings. The native Welsh were pushed into the hinterland. It is not surprising, therefore, that the history of medieval Wales is marked by repeated rebellions, which targeted the castles of their unwelcome overlords, as they struggled to regain control over their homeland and to remain independent. For them, castles symbolized subjugation, defeat, denial, and dispossession. Unlike the Anglo-Saxons, who seem to have adapted to feudalism and the intrusion of castles in their landscape, the Welsh never accepted the loss of independence.

As in England, castles arrived in Wales with the Normans. However, unlike in England, the Welsh were still ruled by native princes, who refused to turn over their homeland without a fight. Even though they erected several earth and timber castles during the late twelfth and early thirteenth centuries, their leaders largely continued to live in lightly defended halls known as *neuaddau*. However, by the early thirteenth century, the native princes had begun erecting their own stone fortresses, which tended to be much simpler than their English counterparts, and included sites such as Carreg Cennen, Castell-y-Bere, Dolwyddelan, Ewloe, Dolforwyn, and Powis. In the end, the English, led by Edward I, subdued the Welsh, and — to their minds — effectively ended the Welsh quest for independence with the construction of several enormous fortresses and the large-scale takeover of several Welsh-built castles, including Caergwrle, Criccieth, and Carreg Cennen, which Edward's men refortified and converted into English strongholds. The construction of Conwy, Caernarfon, Harlech, and Beaumaris Castles, four of the realm's most powerful fortresses, was meant to symbolize Edward I's supremacy over the Welsh. The massive nature of these mighty monuments likely also reflected the king's respect for the resiliency of the Welsh and his fear of future uprisings.

Indeed, revolts continued to pepper the Welsh countryside, the last attempt to oust the English coming in the early fifteenth century with the Welsh rising led by Owain Glyndwr, whose fortified residence at Sycharth was actually a motte and bailey castle. Like his predecessors, including Llywelyn ap Iorwerth and Llywelyn ap Gruffydd, Glyndwr targeted castles during his twelve-year-long campaign against the English. Besides taking Aberystwyth and Criccieth Castles, Glyndwr's finest moment took place in 1404, when he seized Edward I's great castle at Harlech after a lengthy siege. Glyndwr and his family occupied the castle, which served as the Welshman's headquarters for almost five years, when it was retaken by English forces led by Henry of Monmouth, the future King Henry V. Even though Glyndwr disappeared from history shortly after this event, his fame never waned. Neither have Welsh hopes for independence.

Perceptions

Approaching a castle during the Middle Ages must have stirred a variety of emotional and intellectual responses, based on the individual's purpose, status, and expectations. Even today, though we cannot com-

The D-shaped Welsh Tower at Ewloe Castle, possibly built by Llywelyn ab Iorwerth in the early thirteenth century, dominates the upper bailey. At the opposite end of the castle, the round West Tower built by his grandson, Llywelyn ap Gruffydd, retains traces of its original white plaster.

pletely erase our preconceptions of what a REAL castle should look like, we can do our best to understand that all castles, regardless of their present condition and their original design, have value as relics of a historic past that involved real human beings, most of whom left nothing of themselves to posterity. Many castles, such as Raglan and Kenilworth, impress despite their ruination, and we can imagine besiegers or visitors making their way to the site, assessing the power of the battlements and the potential for danger or for welcome. We can appreciate the obstacles they faced, both in daily life and, quite literally, in confronting the castle before them. We can have a similar experience at motte and bailey and ringwork castles, and also at stone castles where only fragments survive; though no longer as imposing as they were centuries ago, they all performed the same basic functions.

TERMINOLOGY IN THIS CHAPTER

Adulterine castles: Castles erected without royal permission, thereby lacking a license to crenellate; commonly associated with the Anarchy and the reign of King Stephen (1135–1154). Stephen's successor, Henry II, ordered their widespread destruction after he became king.

The Anarchy: The civil war lasting from 1135 to 1154 which pitted supporters of King Stephen, the nephew of the Norman king, Henry I, against the Empress Matilda, Henry's daughter and the wife of Geoffrey, the fifth Count of Anjou.

Apsidal tower: A D-shaped tower. Often associated with Welsh-built castles, the name derives from the shape of a church's apse.

Arms: (1) Weapons which were generally portable and handheld, such as handguns, pickaxes, swords, or crossbows.

During the twelfth century, the three most common weapons were swords, battle-axes, and spears (or lances); but, the crossbow was rapidly gaining popularity at the same time. Combined with the increased prevalence of horse warfare (which eased movement and gave an advantage to its warring riders who carried spears) and the introduction of massive siege engines, handheld weapons allowed an enemy to overawe less technologically-advanced peoples. Peasants, on the other hand, generally fought with the only weapons they had—the tools that they used to till their fields and tend their homes: hayforks, flails, sickles, axes, clubs with spikes, and boar-spears.

With the thirteenth century, the technology of sword-making improved and swords became sturdy enough to slice through a knight's protective armor. Short stabbing daggers were also used, as were a variety of axes (some equipped with spikes), clubs, maces, spears, crossbows, and the sling. The most significant development during this century was the longbow, which was used to great success at Agincourt.

During the early fourteenth century, the introduction of gunpowder forever changed weapons, by making possible the development of artillery weapons, including cannons, and guns. Initially, cannons were designed as long metal cylinders and fired "gun-arrows," but they quickly evolved into versatile killing machines which could launch balls weighing 200 pounds. Over the next 100 years, these metal monsters became more mobile and more accurate. And, resembling miniature cannons, small handguns also made their appearance at this time.

Even though the cannon and handguns had greater firepower, timber siege engines remained part of the monarch's arsenal through the late Middle Ages. Blunt and sharp-headed lances were used in "jousts of peace" (tournaments) and "jousts of war." And swords, axes, maces, and hammers with spikes never disappeared from the medieval weapons inventory.

(2) A heraldic emblem used to distinguish status and familial or political affiliations, which was sewn onto or otherwise attached to a uniform or armor; evolved into the phrase "coat of arms."

Arrow: A projectile consisting of a straight wooden shaft ending in a pointed head made of stone or iron, which was fired from a bow; the opposite end was often adorned with goose feathers, known as "fletchings." Varying the size and composition of the arrowhead allowed arrows to penetrate chain mail, some armor, and horse flesh.

Arrowslit: A narrow, vertical or cross-shaped groove which penetrated castle walls at strategic locations and allowed crossbowmen to watch and shoot at an attacker while shielded behind the curtain or tower walls; also known as "arrowloops" or "crossloops." Rare before 1190, arrowslits were often less than two inches wide and between three and twelve feet long. Over time, the design was modified but the purpose remained unchanged: arrowslits were used to defend the castle. Many featured a short horizontal slit or circular opening known, as an oillet, about midway along their length or at the base.

During the fourteenth century, some arrowslits were widened to accommodate handguns and larger artillery. The slots then became known as "gunloops" or "gunports."

Bailey: Whether made of earth or stone, the typical medieval castle featured at least one defended courtyard or ward, the bailey. Some castles featured an outer bailey and an inner bailey, the functions of which varied depending on their position relative to the heart of the castle and the structural complexity of the site. A bailey was often an enclosed area adjoining a motte or an open area enclosed by masonry walls or earthen embankments in which the main activities of daily life in the castle took place.

The inner bailey commonly contained the hall and kitchen block, residential chambers and the chapel, whereas the outer bailey typically held workshops, stables, and other ancillary facilities. In castles with only one bailey, the enclosed area would normally hold all of these facilities; residential chambers might also fill towers along the curtain wall enclosing the bailey.

Some castles, such as Chepstow Castle, featured lower, middle and upper baileys, which were added and expanded by succeeding owners during the entire history of the castle. The earliest portion of the castle, the upper bailey, contained the great tower. As times changed, and more space was needed for defensive strength and comfortable accommodation, Chepstow Castle expanded to include a middle bailey, which was actually created by the construction of an inner wall and gate, and then the lower bailey, where the great gatehouse still welcomes visitors. Windsor Castle in England also contains three baileys. The upper and lower wards enclosed the main residential structures and gateways, whereas the middle ward held the original motte and shell keep, which filled almost the entire bailey.

Ballista: A siege engine powered by twisted skeins of rope, hair, or sinew, which hurtled heavy stones, bolts, and spears along a flat trajectory. Easy to fire accurately, smaller ballistas were effective anti-personnel weapons that could skewer warriors to trees. Large ballistas could send a sixty-pound stone at least four hundred yards to pummel castle walls. Invented by the classical Greeks, who called it the scorpion, and adapted by the Romans, who passed their knowledge to the Middle Ages.

Barbican: Generally located just outside the main gate, the barbican was a defensive outwork which in some cases extended a gateway already in place, as at Exeter Castle. In other cases, the structures stood as separate buildings apart from but fronting the main gate, as at Arundel, Goodrich and Warwick Castles. Barbicans performed a dual defensive-offensive role, for they were intended not only to prevent or stall enemy access by confining them inside the area but outside the castle itself, but were also places where the garrison could gather to stage a sortie. Numerous examples exist throughout Britain.

Belfry: A wooden tower or framework standing several stories tall mounted on wheels or rollers and covered with iron plates or animal hides soaked in mud and vinegar. Used to protect the soldiers stationed inside the structure as they approached an assault from a castle's walls. Also known as a siege tower.

Battering ram: See ram.

Battlements: The toothlike stonework protecting the wall-walk and the tops of towers, consisting of crenels and merlons. Also known as crenellation.

Blockade: To block or prevent the defenders from receiving supplies, such as food and arms, or reinforcements to support their fight in order to starve them out and force them to surrender.

Boon-work: Work done by the peasantry on the lord's demesne lands on special days, such as at harvest time, when the lord's fields had priority. See also Chapter Four.

Bore: An iron-tipped pole similar to a battering ram but generally lighter in weight. Also known as a pick. See ram.

Carpenters: Laborers who built flooring, roofing, siege engines, furniture, paneling for rooms, and scaffolding.

Carters: Workmen who brought wood and stone to the site of a castle under construction.

Cat: A squat, hide-covered framework used to approach a castle and to protect miners or soldiers wielding a battering ram during a siege. Also known as rat, mouse, sow, tortoise, or weasel.

Catapult: A large crossbow-like weapon that fired (or catapulted) darts or missiles towards a human target defending a castle. Often used as a generic term for siege engine.

Concentric plan: Devised as the perfect barrier to a successful siege, the walls-within-walls design whereby a shorter, outer line of defenses (for example, a curtain wall with towers and a gatehouse) enclosed a taller, inner defensive wall (also comprised of towers and at least one gatehouse). Some castles, such as the Tower of London and Dover Castle, acquired concentric plans over time as builders, such as Edward I and King John, bolstered the defenses. Caerphilly Castle was the first concentric castle built from scratch in Britain.

Soldiers defending the stronghold had an obvious advantage with this type of castle, for they could concentrate firepower onto a specific spot from several vantage points, without firing upon their comrades. The attacking enemy had the task of progressively breaching each barrier that they confronted as they moved into the interior of the castle while also avoiding the firepower of the defenders on the successively higher battlements. Had Edward I completed Beaumaris Castle, it would have been the most perfect example of its kind in Britain. Today, it is largely a shell, but even in ruin, it remains one of Edward's finest creations.

Constable: The lord's representative and commander of the castle in his absence.

Conventions: The generally accepted set of standards followed when waging a siege.

Counterweight: A loaded basket or other weight affixed to the opposite end of the timber beam holding missiles ready to be catapulted towards a stone wall or into the castle from a trebuchet or mangonel.

Crenel: The opening between a pair of merlons (the upright or toothlike sections of crenellation) through which defenders could observe activity on the ground below or fire down upon an attacker.

Crenellations: The battlements, a series of crenels and merlons that formed a toothlike pattern which provided protection for guards on the wall-walk and tower tops.

Crossbow: Also known as an arbalest.

Crossbowmen: Soldiers skilled in firing a crossbow.

Cross-oillet: A cross-shaped arrowslit featuring a rounded or eye-hole shape at its base which broadened the field of vision for a defender standing inside the castle and, when large enough, could accommodate a cannon or other firearm.

Curtain wall: A stone wall erected which enclosed a bailey which consisted of sections of masonry linked together or hung between two towers (like a curtain), the main gateway, and other structures; one of the castle's most valuable defenses. Also known as a "courtine."

D-shaped: Apsidal; see apsidal tower.

Defenders (stone): Life-sized carved stone figures resembling the garrison which occasionally adorned the battlements of castles, as at Alnwick and Chepstow. Historians believe these sham defenders presented the impression of a formidable force prepared to defend the castle from advancing attackers.

Demesne: The portion of a manorial estate reserved for the lord's personal use.

Ditch: A dry moat surrounding the outer perimeter or fronting the main gatehouse of a castle; many were cut out of bedrock.

Ditcher: Laborer or soldier who dug out the castle ditch or moat, mines, and building foundations. Also known as a "fossatore" or digger.

Donjon: The French word from which "dungeon" derives; the great tower or keep of a castle; the main citadel of a castle.

Doors: Normally composed of heavy oak beams, most castles' gate passages had pairs of doors which were reinforced with iron straps and could be barricaded shut with drawbars. Castle doors frequently featured iron studs, which were embedded in the timber and thwarted the hacking of axes. At least one pair of double doors was situated in the gate passage immediately behind a portcullis. The combination created a stronger barrier to an enemy's progress through the gatehouse and into the castle itself.

Drawbar: A sliding wooden or iron bar, which guards moved into place to secure doors in a closed position. While the drawbars often have not survived, the holes into which they were inserted are often visible in door jambs located in the gate passage.

Drawbridge: A movable timber bridge which spanned the moat or ditch and could be raised or drawn upwards with the aid of a pulley system and a windlass to prevent unwelcome entry through the gatehouse. Types include the removable bridge, pivot bridges, and turning bridges.

Dungeon tower: Oftentimes, the castle dungeon or prison was situated in a specific tower. The word itself derives from the French, "donjon," which in fact is one of the names for the castle's great tower or keep, the ground levels of which sometimes contained guardrooms and the prison. More often, builders designed a castle so that the prison was as far away from the inner core as possible to prevent unwanted access from a prisoner. Consequently, prisons were often placed in a chamber in the main gatehouse. Basement levels often contained the pit prison or "oubliette," a cramped, dimly lit chamber from which escape was virtually impossible. The ceiling had a trapdoor which opened into the chamber above, from which prisoners were lowered by a rope into the pit and received their food and water. Some oubliettes sat below the water table and frequently flooded.

Edward I (ruled 1272–1307): Arguably Britain's greatest castle-building king. Employing the most advanced castle-building technology of the times and the engineering talents of some of the medieval world's most creative architects, including Master James of St. George, who had made his name in Savoy, France, Edward left a lasting mark on the history of British castle building. Edward is perhaps best known for constructing a series of imposing fortresses, several of which were associated with walled towns, in Wales, believing he had conquered the Welsh and that his castles would keep them under his thumb. During two separate building periods, which occurred shortly after Edward put down major rebellions for Welsh independence, the king erected Flint, Rhuddlan, Aberystwyth, Builth, Conwy, Caernarfon, Harlech, and Beaumaris Castles. In 1986, UNESCO designated the castles and town walls at Conwy, Caernarfon, Harlech, and Beaumaris as World Heritage Sites. In fact, Edward made significant modifications to many castles in Wales, England, and Scotland, including the Tower of London, to which he added several towers, which extended the area of the castle and transformed it into a concentric fortress. The Tower of London is also a World Heritage Site.

Embrasure: A defensive feature consisting either of a splayed opening in a wall or parapet or a slit cut into a merlon. Through the embrasure, defenders could observe action in the area or fire upon an enemy from a position of relative safety.

Enclosure: See Chapter 1.

Engineer: Comparable to an architect. An individual skilled in designing castles and constructing siege engines. Also known as an ingeniatore. See also master mason.

English Civil Wars: A series of battles and sieges between supporters of King Charles I (known as Royalists or Cavaliers) and those who backed Parliament (Parliamentarians or Roundheads) which occurred between 1642 and 1651. Numerous castles were brought back into active service during the conflict and used in aid of both causes. In the end, the Parliamentarians were victorious and the king was executed. Scores of castles were slighted so that they could never be reused in military action against the new heads of the government.

English Civil War fortifications: Even though new castle building had ceased well before the 1640s, when the Parliamentarians fought the Royalist supporters of King Charles I, medieval castles experienced a rebirth of sorts when they were called into action to serve both sides of the post-medieval conflict. Besides making essential repairs to the castles, garrisons during this time also constructed additional defensive structures, including "redans" and "ravelins," V-shaped earthworks which pointed outwards from the fronted of the castle. While shielded behind the embankments, defenders could get closer to the attacking army than they would have been inside the castle and fire upon them with a sense of safety. Sometimes, traces of these earthworks (also known as siegeworks) are still visible at castle sites, as at Carew, Manorbier, and Raglan.

The besiegers also erected fortifications to protect themselves while assaulting a castle. Remnants of these structures, which varied in design from relatively simple square shapes to more elaborate star designs, can often be identified in locations not too far from castle sites and also at several towns, such as Newark-on-Trent and Newcastle-upon-Tyne.

These earthen structures, known as "redoubts" and "sconces," were similar in concept to earlier siege castles. In fact, King Stephen's siege castle, The Rings, was modified by Parliamentarian troops besieging Corfe Castle. Usually square or polygonal earthworks, redoubts temporarily fortified a spot so that attackers could approach close enough to a castle to lay siege to it. For example, Parliamentary forces probably erected the rectangular redoubt on the point of land just northwest of Caerphilly Castle, on the opposite side of the moat from the hornwork. Their redoubt featured two corner bastions, each of which would have supported cannons. After they captured the castle, the Parliamentarians apparently continued to occupy the redoubt in order to keep abreast of the activity inside the castle and to prevent the occupants from rebuilding the stronghold.

When a castle centered a substantial town, it was not uncommon for residents to erect siegeworks to withstand the impact of cannon fire and interfere with the progress of an advancing army. Still in outstanding condition, the Queen's Sconce occupies a hill at the southern end of Newark-on-Trent. Composed of banks and ditches, a sconce was similar to but more complex than a redoubt and was only built during the English Civil War. While basically square in plan, the Queen's Sconce had large diamond-shaped bastions at each corner which produced an overall star-shaped design. Fronted by a thirty-foot-wide ditch that measured between twelve and fifteen feet deep, the sconce may also have featured "storm poles," sharpened timber stakes embedded in and projecting outwards horizontally or at an angle from the earthen embankments, which would have made a close approach rather unpleasant.[34] Though demolished at the end of the Civil War, the King's Sconce was comparable to the Queen's Sconce and once defended Newark's northern side. Only partly excavated, modern construction covers much of the site.

An even more complex series of siegeworks once enclosed Colchester. In 1648, Parliamentary soldiers built a series of some twenty siege forts (or redoubts) connected by a lengthy trench to conduct an eleven-week siege. From the forts, they blockaded and bombarded the town during what turned out to be a vicious assault. Thus far, only two or three have been located; at least one of the sites was star-shaped.[35]

Escalade: An assault on a curtain wall or palisade using scaling ladders normally made of timber or rope. Normally employed during the initial stages of a siege, the onrush would take place at several spots along the curtain wall in hopes of splitting up the garrison, diverting attention, and gaining access at a weak point.

Feudal summons: An official decree requiring fulfillment of a lord's military obligation.

Feudalism: A political and social system under which land was granted by the monarch or a high ranking landowner to a person in exchange for military service and avowed loyalty. See Chapter 4.

Fighting platform: See Hoarding.

Foraging: Scouring the countryside for food and other supplies and freely taking or seizing whatever is available, regardless of the loss to the local population.

Fortifications: The castle's main defenses.

Fossatore: See ditcher.

Gabion: A large wicker basket used to haul building materials, such as earth and stone, from the ground to upper levels during castle construction.

Garderobe: An alternative term for the latrine chute, privy, or castle toilet; originally a room to store personal items. Derives from "wardrobe."

Gateway: The main entry point, protected with at least modest defensive structures, such as timber doors.

Gate passage: A narrow channel which led visitors, friend or foe, through the gateway or gatehouse. Complex gate passages contained a mix of defensive devices, such as arrowslits, murder holes, a portcullis, and timber doors, which allowed the garrison to bar unwanted visitors and create a killing field in case of an enemy attack.

Gatehouse: A strong, multi-story structure containing a fortified gate, the portcullis chamber, and accommodation for the castle constable; often contained other residential units as well as defensive mechanisms, guardrooms, and, at times, a prison.

Guardrooms: Chambers specifically used by guards when on duty, commonly located in the castle gatehouse, often on either side of the gate passage. Some guardrooms were equipped with arrowslits and other defensive devices, but they often lacked fireplaces and latrines to give the soldiers some degree of comfort.

Gunloop: Often little more than a modified arrowslit, a rounded opening in a wall through which a gun or cannon could be fired at an enemy. Also known as gunports, gunloops appeared in England in the fourteenth century in anticipation of assaults from France.

Gynour: A soldier who operated the siege engines. Also known as a gunner.

Hoarding: A timber fighting platform fitted to the parapet of a curtain wall or tower which provided a covered area from which to fire down upon an enemy from a position of safety. Gaps in the flooring of the platforms allowed defenders to observe the activities underway beneath them and to shoot crossbows or drop stone missiles onto enemy heads. The wooden walls protected the men from enemy fire and functioned much like battlements, having openings similar to crenels through which they defended the castle. A fine example of a reconstructed hoard lines the battlements on the northern side of the inner bailey at Caerphilly Castle.

Hornwork: An earthwork barrier or platform situated outside a castle entry point to impede advancing attackers; two fine examples survive at White Castle and Caerphilly Castle in Wales.

Ingeniatore: See engineer.

Justiciar: An officer of the king's court who had the power to run his own law court and act as a judge. The Chief Justiciar was comparable to today's Prime Minister.

Keep: The main citadel or great tower of a castle; a fortified, self-sufficient tower containing living chambers. Most keeps were square or rectangular in shape, although there were round and polygonal keeps. Some keeps were over eighty feet high and had walls over seventeen feet thick. Throughout the medieval period, living in the keep or the dominant mural tower at a castle was a mark of status normally reserved for the lord and his family. Also known as the donjon. See Chapter 3.

Knight: A vassal, soldier, or man-at-arms who fought while mounted on horseback.

Latrine: Also known as the garderobe or privy chamber, the medieval version of the modern toilet. Human waste dropped down a chute to the moat or land at the base of a tower containing the latrine, where a cesspit might contain the material until cleaned out. See Chapter 3.

Lists: Open space alongside curtain wall where soldiers practice their swordsmanship and other fighting skills. When enclosed, the lists became an arena of sorts for jousting and tournaments. Also known as the tiltyard. The present approach to Kenilworth Castle passes through the original tiltyard.

Lord: The male owner or holder of a feudal estate; the landlord.

Machicolations: Projections lining the tops of gate towers or other structures, which consisted of a series of openings and functioned much like murder holes, allegedly allowing defenders to safely toss missiles or water down onto enemies or fires below. They were also decorative in nature.

Magna Carta: "The Great Charter" signed by King John in 1215 in order to appease the barons and Pope Innocent III regarding the rights the king could assert over his subjects.

Mangonel: A siege engine employing a long timber arm or beam, held in place by skeins of tightly twisted rope stretched between two sides of the frame, to hurl projectiles at a target, such as a castle. The medieval counterpart of the Roman siege engine known as an onager.

Mason's marks: Specific marks or symbols carved into dressed stone or masonry blocks which identified a particular mason. Mason's marks survive at many castles and can be used to track the work of individual men around a site and their movement from castle to castle.

Menagerie: Comparable to a private zoo but inside a castle, where wild and exotic animals presented as gifts from other monarchs were kept.

Mercenary: Someone who makes their living as a paid soldier.

Merlon: The toothlike, upright projections located between the crenels or embrasures, which safeguard defenders from missiles and arrows fired by an attacker.

Meurtrières: See murder holes.

Miner: See sapper.

Missiles: Large stone projectiles or other heavy objects thrown at an enemy through murder holes or with a siege engine.

Moat: A water-filled ditch enclosing or partly surrounding the castle, which was kept full by a nearby water source, such as a spring, lake, stream, or river, the purpose of which was to inhibit a siege. A corruption of the French term "motte."

Mural passage: Passageways constructed within the thickness of a wall so that residents could move easily from place to place while also providing cover for defenders as they observed and fired upon a besieging army.

Murder holes: Gaping openings in the ceilings of gate passages, through which soldiers stationed in the chamber overhead could drop missiles and pour liquids onto attackers or fires below.

Onager: Roman-era siege engine consisting of a heavy timber trestle mounted midway on a horizontal timber frame. It hurled a missile in an overhead arc, similar to the effect produced flinging peas with a spoon. When fired, the engine's rear kicked upward—hence the name, which means "wild ass." See also mangonel.

Oubliette: The pit prison in a castle, most commonly associated with the dungeon. See dungeon tower.

Outwork: Any defensive structures, such as a barbican, made of earth or stone and erected beyond the castle walls and ditch that provided an added obstacle to an enemy assault on a castle.

Palisade: See Chapter 1.

Parapet: The battlemented shielding wall attached to the outer edge of the wall-walk.

Portcullis: A movable grille made out of spikes of oak, iron, or a combination of the two, and covered and linked together with iron, which could be lowered into place with the aid of a windlass stored in an overhead chamber and grooves cut into the sides of the gate passage to direct and secure their placement. Situated to protect an entrance to a gatehouse or, at times, a private chamber within the castle, a pair of heavy timber doors normally stood close to each portcullis.

Postern gate: A secondary gateway or back doorway used for quick escape or to receive supplies and reinforcements, often strategically located so that ships could easily and surreptitiously move to and from the castle.

Quarrel: An iron-tipped dart or bolt fired from a crossbow.

Ram: A heavy timber beam tipped with an iron head that often resembled the horns and head of a ram, a male goat. Suspended on chains from a timber framework or carried by besiegers protected inside a cat or penthouse, the ram was swung back and forth to slam into a gateway or the most vulnerable angles along a curtain wall. Also known as a battering ram.

Reeve: Supervised the work on the lord's property, checking that the peasants began and stopped work on time, and ensuring nothing was stolen. Senior officer of a borough. See Chapter 4.

Rendability: The monarch's right to take back a castle from a lord.

Revetment: An outwork, ditch, embankment or wall faced with a layer of timber or masonry.

Revetting: Stone or timber facing applied to a wall or bank.

Sapper: A skilled laborer who dug tunnels or mines underneath a curtain wall or tower in order to bring down the walls or open a breach through which besiegers could storm the castle. Also known as a miner or underminer.

Sally port: A secondary gateway or small door, usually some distance from the main entrance of a castle or bailey; often hidden along the curtain wall to allow defenders to enter and exit (or "sally forth") without detection to surprise attackers. An interesting example survives at Denbigh Castle.

Scaling ladder: Made from rope and wood, these flexible ladders were used by besiegers — laden with armor and weapons — to scramble up curtain walls as quickly as possible and leap onto the battlements (during an escalade) while trying to avoid arrows or burning straw thrust at them by the defenders, who were also frantically trying to push the ladders off the wall.

Scutage: A fee or tax paid by an individual in lieu of military service. Also known as a shield-tax.

Siege: The process of investing or assaulting a castle in order to force its surrender.

Siege castle: See siegework.

Siege engine: One of a variety of timber-framed machines operated by a combination of human strength, torsion or tension, ropes, chains or pulleys to propel a projectile at a target, such as a curtain wall or tower; includes ballistas, mangonels, springalds, trebuchets, perriers, petraries, onagers, and scorpions.

Siege tower: See belfry.

Siege train: An assemblage of military personnel, livestock, and the wagons carrying the weaponry and supplies needed by a besieging army, traveling by sea and on land to the site of the siege. Also known as a baggage train.

Siegework: An earthwork structure raised for the protection of a force besieging a castle; popularly used during the Anarchy in the twelfth century and the English Civil War in the 1640s. See English Civil War fortifications.

Slighting: The process of deliberately rendering a castle useless, which involved dismantling a fortification by undermining, breeching, battering, or using gunpowder to pull down the walls. The policy ruthlessly enforced by Oliver Cromwell and Parliamentarian forces after the English Civil Wars to ensure the realm's castles would be impotent in the event of further warfare. Many modern castle ruins resulted from this demolition.

Sluice gate: Gates designed to regulate the level and flow of water passing through a channel or into a moat which opened or closed by sliding into place.

Splay: A sloping face or slant of stone; an aperture that widens as it progresses inwards; normally associated with windows.

Springald: A variant of the ballista; a tension-driven device closely resembling a crossbow in function and used to fire javelins or large bolts. A vertical springboard was fixed at its lower end to a timber framework. Soldiers manually retracted the board, which moved like a lever; when released, the springboard smacked the end of the projectile, propelling it toward its target.

Spur: A pointed masonry projection positioned to strengthen or buttress the base or low end of a tower and deflect missiles.

Stables: Buildings housing the lord's horses, which were kept ready for the next part of the journey on the annual itinerary, for the hunt, or to do battle. Some castles had more than one stable block. Today, little more than foundations survive from most medieval castle stables.

Tiltyard: See lists. The tilt was another name for a joust.

Tower: A multi-level structure built from timber or stone with squared or rounded sides situated at points along the curtain wall (and known as mural towers) in order to extend a defender's view of the area immediately outside the castle both at the base of the curtain wall below them and to either side of the tower. Their positions prevented blind spots or dead ground where the enemy could sneak up to the castle without being detected. Mural towers also allowed the defenders greater flexibility in firing at an attack, particularly at some distance from the castle. Over the course of castle-building history, they became an essential component of the main gatehouse. Towers also contained domestic units, prisons, and other facilities. Freestanding towers, known as keeps or great towers, dominated many Norman castles, and timber towers occupied positions of importance atop mottes and were used as observation posts as well as the lord's residence. See Chapter 3.

Trebuchet: A highly effective stone-hurling siege engine powered by a counterweight mechanism invented during the Middle Ages. Able to accurately hit targets at a range of five hundred yards with missiles exceeding three hundred pounds in weight, the trebuchet could relentlessly pound a curtain wall until it broke open.

Truce: Cessation of hostilities for a specified period of time, as agreed upon by both sides of a siege.

Turret: A small tower often added onto a larger tower to provide additional chambers or extending above a tower for use as an observation post, when it is also known as a "crow's nest."

Twin-towered: Describing a gatehouse with matching round, or drum, towers flanking either side of the gate passage.

Undermining: The process of digging a tunnel or mine underneath a curtain wall or tower and then burning its timber supports to force the wall to collapse, after which besiegers could rush in and seize the castle.

Unlicensed: A castle erected without royal permission (the license), which was subject to seizure or fines.

Wall-walk: The stone walk lining the inner side of the battlements at the top of the curtain wall, which enabled defenders and residents to move easily from place to place into other parts of the castle and to allow the garrison to keep track of an advancing enemy and approaching visitors.

Ward: A courtyard or bailey enclosed within castle walls.

Wars of the Roses, the: From 1455 to 1487, the Houses of Lancaster and York fought each other for control of the English throne, both claiming lineage back to Edward III and thereby asserting the legal right to the rule the kingdom. Known as the Wars of the Roses, many of history's most significant battles occurred during these years, including the Battles of Mortimer's Cross, Towton, Tewkesbury, and Bosworth Field, where Harri Tudor defeated King Richard III, became King Henry VII, and initiated the Tudor Dynasty.

Water gate: A secondary gateway or opening in the curtain wall or castle foundation allowing access to and from a neighboring waterway through which people and supplies were moved.

Week-work: Regular work performed on the lord's demesne lands in addition to that done on the peasant's own parcel of land. See Chapter 4.

Wicket: A small gate or doorway positioned in the framework of a portcullis, which allowed only individual access to the castle without forcing the raising of the portcullis.

Windlass: A mechanical device used to raise or lower a drawbridge or portcullis. Operated by a series of ropes, chains, pulleys, and a winding drum, the powerful machine made use of grooved slots carved into the walls of the gate passage to ensure the sides of the portcullis or the arms of the drawbridge were correctly secured into place.

3

Exploring the Interior

Even when the exterior of a medieval castle appears to be solid and intact, the interior is often an altogether different matter. Passing through the main gate can confuse modern-day visitors, who may expect the interior to be just as complete. Bodiam Castle is an excellent example. One of Britain's most photographed castles, the exterior of Edward Dalyngrigge's fortified residence seems to represent the ideal castle, its fine condition a testament to its builder's pride and status. The well-preserved walls, battlemented towers, and impressive gateways, all enclosed by an expansive moat, present a vision of castellated splendor. Yet, appearances in this case are deceiving: Just beyond the impressive gatehouse, visitors are greeted with a cramped, empty shell littered with foundations and the ruined remains of buildings that once provided all the domestic needs of the residents. Today, one's initial impression of the site may combine surprise and disappointment. Even so, closer examination and some well-informed imagination can reveal the complexities of life at this fifteenth-century quadrangular castle.

Likewise, Edward I's powerful castle at Conwy seems to be in perfect condition, the massive towers and lengthy curtain walls standing to their original height. However, most of the towers are now empty cylinders connected by roof-level walkways; the great hall (in the author's opinion, the most impressive structure inside the castle) is little more than an open area without a roof; the kitchen block survives only as foundations; and the chambers in the inner ward, the king's residence, consist mostly of unroofed chambers and fragmentary walls with window openings. Yet, despite these factors, the castle is a masterpiece of engineering genius; the ruined interior cannot alter that fact.

In many ways, these unenclosed, unrestored chambers allow us to envision how different structures were interrelated and how builders attempted to position them both to make the most of the physical limitations of the site and to accommodate the residents according to social status and the jobs they performed. At Conwy, the outer ward, which faced the adjoining town and comprised almost two-thirds of the castle, was intended for the permanent garrison. The inner ward, situated alongside the Conwy estuary for ease of movement to and from the opposite side of the site, housed the king and his retinue when in residence. In fact, Edward I always made sure his castles had direct access to the sea. At Bodiam Castle, on the other hand, residential suites, which contained halls, living chambers, bed chambers and also an adjoining tower, framed the inner courtyard. The lord's chambers and the chapel filled the eastern side, while his retainers and members of the garrison and other servants occupied the opposite western side; other important dignitaries and their retainers may have occupied the northeast tower and north range of domestic suites and halls. The great hall lined the southern end of the courtyard in front of the postern gateway. The kitchen,

Bodiam Castle's well-preserved exterior belies the ruinous condition of its interior. Each side of the quadrangular castle was lined with residential units, assigned according to the occupant's status level.

pantry and buttery stood to the west of the hall and the southwest tower beyond contained the well and a dovecote; to the east of the great hall, guests or members of the lord's family probably stayed in the southeast tower. These arrangements were intentional, and symbolically reminded everyone in the castle of their position relative to the lord.

Fortunately, despite the differences in their specific layouts and their builders' individual preferences, medieval castles in Britain did have certain stylistic consistencies which have helped archaeologists and architectural historians interpret the purposes of chambers even when only foundations survive, basing their decisions partly on their relationships to neighboring structures and partly on physical clues — and partly on evidence in historical accounts. Regardless of whether a castle was built with stone or earth and timber, at the minimum, they contained several standard chambers, elements of which can be identified by modern visitors, as they were identified by medieval visitors who might also need a "road map" to find their way around an unfamiliar castle. Interestingly, as castles became increasingly common visions in the landscape, most people could also pick out the main residential chambers from the outside of the castle. The nature of these chambers was signaled by features such as large, ornate windows, or their placement relative to other structures, such as the main gate. Visitors today can enjoy a similar experience, distinguishing different castle buildings based on their placement, their ornamentation, and other details.

Trundling through the Towers

Before heading into the inner ward when visiting a castle, first explore the outer bailey (see Chapter 2) and, wherever possible, climb into the towers. Tower plans varied from castle to castle, and even within individual castles. However, most towers generally had several basic features: Two or more stories; a single chamber filling a single level; staircases (spiral and straight) located in the thickness of the outer wall or at a corner connecting the levels; doorways opening to the wall-walk; latrines discretely positioned in a wall-passage or the corner of a room; and windows, which became progressively larger on higher levels. At some castles, such as Bolingbroke, where only tower foundations survive, the shape of the remains can help visitors form an impression of the structure that once stood on the spot.

Today, many castle towers have reconstructed floors that allow visitors to wander through the upper stories and imagine how each room may have looked, without its furnishings, during the Middle Ages. Fireplaces, windows, and even medieval painting or plasterwork often survive, especially in upper chambers that were reserved for the most important residents and their guests. Many times, the relative position of the fireplaces, seemingly planted one on top of another, indicate the divisions between two stories. However, some rooms lacked fireplaces, and we can speculate that they were occupied by guards or lower-class servants, who may have carried braziers, portable heaters filled with charcoal or kindling, into the communal bedchambers. Many towers, even at the best-preserved sites, such as Conwy and Pembroke Castles, still lack flooring. This is not necessarily a bad thing, for visitors can gain a real sense of the enormity of the structures and visualize for themselves the original location of the different levels within the tower. The great round keep at Pembroke, for example, is now an empty cylinder which, at over 80 feet in height, dominates the entire castle. When standing at ground level, one can identify the corbels and determine the positions of the medieval floors. When on top of the domed roof, which is accessible by a lengthy spiral staircase constructed in the walling of the keep, panoramic visions of the medieval town and the surrounding countryside are possible.

Castle residents, soldiers, servants, and guests had a variety of options when it came to moving from one level in a structure to another level — or to an altogether separate

Even though a building may be an empty shell, the different stories can be distinguished by the placement of certain features, such as these fireplaces.

building. Spiral and straight staircases built into the thickness of the walls, some used the cover of a forebuilding to reach upper stories, and some rose in their own towers or turrets specifically designed to contain the stairways, with entry/exit points positioned at each story of the main structure. They provided access from room to room, level to level, or to the wall-walk without having to retreat outside. On the other hand, doorways into staircases also allowed movement at ground level from the inner bailey into towers, mural passages, and other structures. Wooden ladders or stairs were used in early castles, often to reach the wall-walk. As defensive devices, they could be easily removed if an enemy attempted to breach security. Non-movable wooden ladders were often used inside the castle, where they were less prone to rot or burning.

Though more expensive to construct and maintain, stone staircases were durable and practical. Even today, where other structures have fallen or disappeared, stair towers and fragments of spiral staircases often endure. Better known as a spiral staircase (or a "turnpike staircase" in Scottish castles), the newel stair consisted of rectangular, triangular, or keyhole-shaped steps barely wide enough for a booted shoe, which were positioned on top but offset from each other and wound around a slender but solid central post, the newel. They were often designed to ascend clockwise, which in theory forced attackers to expose their bodies as they fought while holding their swords in their right hands. Elaborate stairways and enclosed porches were often constructed more for display than merely to accommodate movement within the castle. They created an air of drama and anticipation, particularly as guests made their way into the great hall or great chamber.

Modern visitors may find it difficult at first to distinguish one story from the next in ruined structures where the floors do not survive. So, it is important to look for clues which indicate where floors and ceilings would have separated the levels from each other. Variations in the texture of the masonry—for example, where two different types or sizes of stone were used to form the walls at different levels within a tower—often indicate the location of a floor. Related structures, such as fireplaces or windows, which appear to be positioned one on top of the next, also differentiate adjacent levels.

The best indicators of the exact positions of upper floors are joist holes. These rectangular slots were placed at the same level in the outer wall of a room and held the ends of timber joists, horizontal beams laid side-by-side across the chamber, which supported the room's flooring. A room's floor also functioned as the ceiling for the room below. Flooring for upper stories normally consisted of wooden planks covered with rushes, or possibly rugs; ground floors were generally made of beaten earth or flagstones.

Castle builders also used stone corbels, small brackets or platforms that projected outward from a wall, to support timber joists and roof-beams. They were positioned directly across a chamber from each other and in straight lines along a wall. Many corbels were plain, whereas others featured carved designs, including gargoyle figures and human faces, sometimes of real people, such as King Edward II, Queen Isabella, and Hugh le Despenser, whose faces overlook the activity in the great hall at Caerphilly Castle. Corbels also supported other features, such as machicolations, on exterior walls.

The ceilings of "undercrofts," basement or ground level chambers, and some special rooms such as the chapel, were often vaulted, meaning they were arched rather than flat spans. Gate passages were often vaulted as well. The simplest type of vault is the barrel vault, which, as its name suggests, is shaped like a barrel or a cylinder cut in half lengthwise and supported by straight walls. The design also resembles a tunnel. Developed by the Romans, barrel vault-

Positioned underneath the base of a fireplace, a row of corbels — small platforms projecting from the wall face — reveal where a ceiling once separated two stories. The ends of timber beams rested on the corbels and created a sturdy framework to support the ceiling.

ing is typically associated with Romanesque, or Norman, architecture. Other types of vaulting actually developed from this basic design. Groined vaults consist of two interlocking barrel vaults, placed at right angles to each other. Ribbed vaulting features a vaulted ceiling subdivided by ribs, or independent arches, to form individual bays. The type of vaulting, particularly when it survives only as fragments, can help visitors identify the function of the chamber they are exploring. Many times, only the springers, the masonry blocks or points from which a vault (or an arch) started, survive from a vaulted ceiling.

Many castle towers now also have reconstructed rooftops, which allow visitors to experience what it was like to climb to the summit, take in the views, and imagine the approach of an enemy army or the routine passage of people through the area. At some castles, the layout of the medieval town associated with it can be identified from the top of a tower. Some tower roofs were domed, some flat. Other buildings in the castle would have had pitched or gabled roofs. (The triangular area beneath the pitched roof is the gable.) At many castles, fragments of masonry still outline the point where a pitched roof from one structure connected to the wall of an adjoining building; they are often the only evidence that such a building stood on that spot. Conical roofs were rare in Britain.

Tower roofs were timber-framed: A series of timber beams, known as joists, were set into squarish holes or grooves in the stone walls to form a framework which spanned the open area at the top of the tower. The framework was then covered with materials such as oak shingles, slate, thatch, flagstone, or clay tiles to complete the roofing.[1] The earliest known examples of earthenware roof tiles, dating to the early twelfth century, were found during excavations of the hall at Goltho Castle in the 1980s.² The vulnerability of such roofs to fire, and also to rain and wind, motivated many builders to opt for lead roofs, even though they were considerably more expensive than timber. Today, the timbers no longer survive, except perhaps for a few splinters, but rooflines can be identified by the presence of joist holes, openings in the wall which held the beams in place. Many castles also had rooftop gutters and downspouts, some of which were shaped like gargoyles. Both functional and decorative, they are easy to spot at many castles.

Even though it is reasonable for us to expect that castle towers would have been enclosed on all sides with masonry, this was not always the case. Many towers were "open-gorged," meaning the side facing the inner bailey was closed only from the ground to wall-walk level and then open for the rest of their height.³ For example, of the thirteen mural towers at Framlingham Castle, erected by Roger Bigod II, Second Earl of Norfolk, in about 1190, ten were open-gorged towers, meaning the upper part would have been covered with timber-framed walls, which could be removed to prevent unwanted access to adjacent parts of the castle.

Builders fit timber beams into this line of joist holes in order to support the ceiling of the lower chamber. The platform also acted as the flooring for the upper chamber, which is decorated with Norman arches.

The impressive towered town wall at Conwy reveals just how useful this type of tower could be during an assault. The three-fourths-mile circuit had three twin-towered gateways and twenty-one round towers deliberately placed at fifty-yard intervals. A continuous wall-walk fitted with removable timber bridges linked the towers together. In the event of an attack, defenders could remove boards, which were temporarily affixed to the rear of each open-backed tower, and effectively isolate that tower and the adjoining length of wall. The inventive design impeded enemy progress and also created a self-contained unit from which the defenders could safely continue to resist the attack.⁴

In contrast to the above, some castles had completely solid mural towers. At Conisbrough Castle, built by Hamelin Plantagenet, Henry II's half-brother, in the late twelfth century, at least five solid round towers projected outwards from the curtain wall. From the front of the stone keep at Pevensey Castle, believed to have been built by Richard I in about 1190, two bastions projected into the inner ward. Probably added to the keep shortly after its comple-

Top: Carvings of historic figures and mythological creatures adorned corbels and also the openings of roof gutters, as at Raglan Castle, where machicolations on the roof of the great gatehouse are decorated with gaping gargoyles. *Bottom:* Little remains of the rectangular Norman keep at Pevensey Castle, with the exception of the solid bases of the unusual late twelfth-century bastions, which face into the inner bailey.

tion, the D-shaped bastions are similar in appearance to a twin-towered façade; however, the structures were solid at ground level. Their design is said to have been inspired by bastions in the outer wall of the Roman fort inside of which the Normans built their castle.[5]

Oftentimes, as at Pembroke, the names given to a castle's towers reflect their position rather than the function they actually performed during the Middle Ages. Monkton Tower faced Monkton Priory, the ruins of which survive across the river west of Pembroke Castle. Westgate and Northgate Towers overlooked two of the gates into the medieval town, the walls for which actually connected to the castle at the towers. The Barbican Tower, as mentioned earlier, overlooked the barbican and provided defensive support for the eastern flank of the main gate. On the western side of the gatehouse, the Henry VII Tower is so named because of its reputation as the birthplace of Harri Tudur, who defeated Richard III at Bosworth Field to become king of England in 1485. More recently, historians have come to believe that the king was probably born in a chamber inside the great gatehouse. In any case, the interior of the tower, with its impressive fireplace and heraldic emblems, displays the castle's historic association with the Tudor Dynasty, which also spawned the likes of Henry VIII and his daughter, Queen Elizabeth I.

Indeed, the names of many castle towers commemorate notable people. The Plukenet Tower at Corfe Castle derives its name from the presence of the carved heraldic emblem of Alan de Plukenet, who served as constable from 1265 to 1270.[6] The Amble or Montagu Tower at Warkworth Castle was named after John Neville, Lord Montagu, Earl of Northumberland, who acquired the castle in 1464. Felton's Tower at Caerphilly Castle honors Sir John de Felton, the constable who held the castle on behalf of Edward II when it was besieged by Queen Isabella's forces in 1327. Ironically, Ethelfleda's Mound at Warwick Castle was named for the daughter of Alfred the Great, the Anglo-Saxon king. Historians believe that the Norman motte was erected on top of fortifications, probably a defended settlement (a burh), built by Ethelfleda in about 914 to protect residents from Danish invaders. The notion is credible; as was discussed in Chapter 1, William I had a habit of replacing Anglo-Saxon sites with his own castles.

Towers also acquired their names from their roles in daily life, including use as latrines. For example, many of the mural towers at Caernarfon Castle were named for the personnel they served, the roles they performed, or their position relative to the adjoining town. The wall enclosing the upper ward (the outer bailey) features granary tower, northeastern tower, watch tower, cistern tower, and black tower. The chamberlain tower (also known as the treasury tower and the record tower) stands midway between the two baileys. The lower ward (or inner bailey) features the well tower, eagle tower (the king's residence), and queen's tower. Whether the granary tower actually held a granary is unclear as is the derivation of the name of the black tower; however, it is quite clear that the eagle tower acquired its name from the presence of carved stone eagles on the battlements. The birds symbolized Edward I's affinities with the Roman Empire.

At Conwy Castle, in addition to the northwest and southwest towers which protected the main gate, visitors will find the kitchen tower and prison tower (also known as the debtor's tower) on either side of the outer ward, the bakehouse tower and stockhouse tower midway between the baileys, and the chapel tower and king's tower in the inner ward. Unlike the towers at Caernarfon, the ones at Conwy contain structural elements that explain how they received their names: The stockhouse tower acquired its current name during the sixteenth century, when two pairs of stocks were installed in the tower to restrain prisoners. It is impor-

Top: The original Norman motte at Warwick Castle is largely overawed by the grander masonry castle, much of which was erected during the fourteenth century. Known as Ethelfleda's mound, the motte survives in fine condition despite being covered with trees. *Bottom:* The inner bailey at Caernarfon Castle provided separate accommodations for the king in the eagle tower, at the far end of the site, and for his queen, in the queen's tower, to its left. The adjoining watergate afforded rapid escape by sea in the event of a landward attack.

tant to remember that, even though a tower might have contained a kitchen or the stocks or the well and received its name on that basis, other chambers in the same tower (normally located on the uppermost levels) performed other functions; most often they were living quarters. Some towers also stored the lord's treasury or contained a small mint (a privilege bestowed upon only a few of the greater lords).

As mentioned earlier, the Tower of London contained a zoo, which housed a menagerie of wild animals, many of which were gifts presented to Henry III by foreign monarchs. Founded by King John in the early thirteenth century, the royal zoo existed for over 600 years. In 1235, the Holy Roman Emperor, Frederick II, reputedly presented the king with the castle's first lions to honor his marriage to Henry's sister, Isabella, and, quite possibly, to symbolically acknowledge the power of the king himself. In 1277, Edward I built the so-called Lion Tower, a semi-circular structure which housed the great cats. Interestingly, in 2005, archaeologists discovered the skulls of three medieval cats, two lions and a leopard, in the moat; the oldest skull has been dated to between 1280 and 1385. In early 2008, scientists from the Natural History Museum in London used DNA analysis to determine that two of the skulls were male Barbary lions, which came from North Africa.[7] Edward's Lion Tower probably stood alongside the moat at this point.[8] The Duke of Wellington closed the zoo in 1835,[9] and the surviving animals were transported to Zoological Society's Gardens in Regent's Park, now known as London Zoo.

Distinguishing the Great Tower

In many ways, the castle keep was the ultimate tower. In fact, for much of their history, these imposing towers were known as "great towers," the "turris magnus." It is easy to see why, for keeps were always the largest and most impressive towers in any castle. Even though "keep" is now commonly used to describe the great tower, it was only late in the Middle Ages that the word was adopted. In fact, in addition to "great tower," the French word, "donjon," was most widely used. It derives from the Latin, "dominarium," which means "lordship"— its application to the great tower implied a direct link between the building and the authority of the lord who owned it.[10] While some castles, such as Flint, still apply the French word to the great tower, "donjon" was corrupted over time into the better known, "dungeon." The fact that many early keeps contained the castle prison may have had a lot to do with why the French term became associated with the dank pit prison that most of us think about when considering the word today.

Most great towers served as the lord's private residence. However, many were built for ceremonial purposes or to dramatize the lord's power and had both public and private functions.[11] While no two keeps were exactly alike nor used for identical purposes, the majority seem to have been built according to the same generic plan: The basement level (ground floor) contained store rooms; the first floor above the basement contained a hall (often the great hall), and sometimes a solar or private chamber and/or a chapel; and the upper stories held private rooms which were heated by fireplaces (and, if not, residents used portable braziers) and nicely decorated. The rooftop was by and large reserved for military purposes. The main entrance was normally situated on the first story and reached by a detachable ladder or a protected forebuilding, which aided in the defense of the keep. Movement between levels was accomplished via a spiral staircase built into the thickness of the walls. Latrines were discreetly positioned down short mural passageways. Windows were generally small but increased in

When exploring the inner bailey at White Castle, try to imagine how the rectangular keep would have looked when it had walls. Now, only foundations survive. The original main gate opened immediately to its right.

size to some degree the higher their positions within the keep. Wooden shutters kept out the cold, wind and rain. Glass was rare and expensive, its use usually relegated to the chapel or great hall; it was removed and carted from castle to castle as the lord moved from one residence to another during the year.[12]

Generally positioned to dominate the inner bailey, the great tower stood well above the other towers and much higher than the battlemented curtain wall. It was normally quite visible from outside the castle. The reason for this visibility was twofold: As the most important person living in the castle, it was only proper that the lord occupy the largest and most evident tower and, as the most important person in the lordship, it was only proper that his status and wealth be displayed so that anyone passing by or approaching the castle had to see it, and thereby be forced to consider — and acknowledge — the lord's powerful position not just in the region but in the wider feudal kingdom as well. Even today, most great towers — regardless of their overall condition — are easy to separate from the other buildings in the inner bailey. However, some are only shells, parts of walling left standing; others, such as the rectangular keep at White Castle, are nothing more than the barest of foundations. Even so, we must always keep in mind that, at one time, they were the pride and joy of their builders, who spent their fortunes to ensure their castles were fitted with the best buildings money could buy.

In addition to shell keeps, which were discussed in Chapter 1, some early Norman castles contained "hall-keeps," rectangular buildings that were longer than they were high. One of the finest examples is the late eleventh-century great tower at Chepstow Castle, which still dominates the site. Regardless of whether one is standing inside or outside the site, the keep at Chepstow is clearly the focal point of the castle. Undoubtedly that was its builder's intention: No matter where anyone stood, even if it was on the opposite banks of the River Wye, the great keep would have grasped their attention—as it does today. Once inside the castle, medieval visitors were intentionally drawn to the structure along the pathway that led from the great gatehouse into the lower bailey, through the middle gateway and bailey, onwards to the hall-keep. Walking up the steeply sloping pathway to the keep forced visitors to look upwards towards their goal. The great tower—and its lord—stood head and shoulders above them. Indeed, everything about the site draws one's attention up the slope to the keep.

The hall-keep at Manorbier Castle performed the same function as its counterpart at Chepstow, but on a more modest scale. Erected by William de Barri early in the twelfth century, the three-story hall-keep was the castle's most impressive building. As soon as visitors made their way through the gate passage, the first sight they would have seen was the hall-keep, which stood immediately across the inner ward from where they stood. Bordered by the kitchen range on one side and private chambers on the other, the hall-keep was essentially a residence unto itself. The basement level contained a group of what may have been storerooms. The level above held the great hall, with the lord's chamber and access to the watergate (and latrine turret) on one side and the buttery and pantry on the other. Inside those rooms, servants would prepare the food and drink for their final presentation to the lord and his guests. The great hall itself actually took up two stories; the solar (the lord's withdrawing chamber) actually occupied the outer end of the second story of the hall.

Some castle builders incorporated their keeps into the curtain wall. At Ludlow Castle, the original gateway, probably erected by Roger de Lacy in the late eleventh century, was blocked sometime during the twelfth century and converted into the four-story rectangular keep that still dominates the entrance into the inner bailey. Immediately to the right (east), the de Lacys cut an opening into the curtain wall enclosing the inner bailey to create a new entrance. The simple archway was altered again during the fourteenth century.

As at Ludlow, during the twelfth century, the rectangular keep at Richmond Castle replaced the original eleventh-century gatehouse and a new gateway was cut into the curtain wall just east of the two-story keep. Interestingly, Richmond Castle was one of the few early Norman castles built entirely of stone. Probably begun by Conan the Little, the impressive keep was completed by Henry II in the 1170s. It stood over 100 feet tall and had walls some eleven feet thick.

Probably the most common type of great tower, the freestanding, rectangular design was similar to the hall-keep but was taller than it was wide. Rectangular keeps varied in height from three to five stories, their walls ranged from six to over twenty feet thick, and, at least initially, access was at first floor level (the story above basement or ground level). Today, rectangular keeps are fairly easy to identify, for they tower well above the other structures in and around the inner bailey. Sadly, some are only shells or fragmentary walling; others, such as the rectangular keep at Llanblethian Castle (also called St. Quintin's or St. Quentin's Castle) consist of little more than a jumble of rubble, but visitors can presently identify the fine quality of building stone that once formed the keep, including pieces of a straight staircase. The following discusses a few of the realm's finest, more intact examples.

Constructed during the reign of Henry I, the three-story keep at Canterbury superseded the motte castle erected by William I shortly after the Conquest. Even though there is some

Erected by Henry II in the mid-twelfth century, the tall rectangular keep at Richmond Castle is a classic example of its type. Built over the original gateway, the keep is deceptive, for it only contains two full stories. During the World Wars, it served as a prison.

speculation to the contrary, it is more than likely that the mound known as Dane John, which dominates a nearby park and has been landscaped and reshaped to some degree, was the original castle erected by the Normans. The great stone keep was added to the outer bailey of the original castle during the early twelfth century. Standing on a platform of flinty rubble and Roman brick, the imposing building originally rose well over 80 feet high. Decorated with pilaster buttresses, the walls ranged from nine to fourteen feet in thickness. The keep contained two levels above the ground floor, and, like most early keeps, was only accessible at the first floor level, via a masonry forebuilding. The first story held the great hall and associated kitchen range and a residential chamber. It also featured two large fireplaces and had its own chapel. The ground floor level was probably used for storage. The uppermost story no longer survives. Discovered during excavations in the 1970s, the ditch was once spanned by a drawbridge.

In 1170, Henry II began using Dover as the primary royal castle, so Canterbury's keep was converted into the jail for the sheriffs of Kent. In 1227, Henry III granted the castle to Hubert de Burgh for his entire lifetime. Successfully assaulted on two occasions, Canterbury Castle fell to the French Dauphin, Louis, in 1216 but reverted to the Crown when the prince was defeated in his efforts to remove King John from the English throne. In 1381, local peasants rebelled, freeing the prisoners and imprisoning the constable instead. During Bloody Mary Tudor's reign in the mid-sixteenth century, when scores of people were imprisoned for their religious beliefs, they often starved to death inside Canterbury Castle or were burned at the stake after a lengthy incarceration. The rectangular keep remained the county jail until

3. Exploring the Interior 101

Often overlooked because of the presence of the historic cathedral, Canterbury Castle still preserves its three-story great keep, built by Henry I. Not too far away, the original Norman motte, known as Dane John, stands alongside the medieval city walls.

the eighteenth century, when the prison was moved to another site and the castle fell into ruin. The curtain walls were demolished, the ditch filled in, and houses built on the site late in the same century. Further demolition efforts in 1817 destroyed the upper story and the stone forebuilding. Today, visitors to Canterbury are likely to bypass the castle, which is on the opposite side of the city from the cathedral and its precincts. Well within walking distance, the great keep is certainly worth a visit, for it played a critical role in shaping British history and remains in solid condition. Dane John can be explored a brief distance away from the stone castle.

Also in Kent but much closer to London, Rochester Castle contains England's tallest keep. In many ways, the great twelfth-century keep is a classic example of its type. However, as at Canterbury, Rochester's castle is largely overshadowed by the marvelous cathedral that stands alongside the ruins. Even so, its place in history was considerable and the ruins are quite substantial. Like Canterbury, Rochester Castle was built on the site of Roman remains, in this case a Roman town once known as Durobrivae, "the stronghold by the bridge," which provided ready-made defensive walls for the Normans who settled there a thousand years later.

Shortly after the Conquest, William I bestowed upon his half-brother, Odo, then the Bishop of Bayeux, the title of first Earl of Kent. Odo quickly began building a motte castle at Rochester, overlooking the River Medway and the road to London, which crossed the river at this point. In 1088, Odo led a rebellion against his half-nephew, William II, and was forced into exile; his successor, Bishop Gundulf, then took on the enormous task of enclosing Rochester Castle with a stone wall. Another motte, known as Boley Hill, stands just outside the castle walls. At one time, it was believed to have been the original motte at Rochester, but reassessment of the site has led to the conclusion that it was part of the defenses constructed by William II to besiege Odo's castle.

It took another forty years for construction to begin on the great tower. Encouraged by Henry I, a prolific castle-builder in his own right, William de Corbeil, Archbishop of Canterbury, began the massive project after the king granted him custody of the castle in 1127. When it was completed, the four-story keep stood 113 feet and measured 70 feet square. Riddled with stairways, windows, mural chambers and garderobes, the great keep resembles a maze-like shell. Its massive walls, which vary from 11 to 13 feet in thickness, once enclosed four levels of chambers, the most important of which, the second story, held the great hall and great chamber, and quite possibly the archbishop's state apartments. The castle remained under the control of the Archbishops of Canterbury until 1215, when it became the focus of the barons' rebellion late that year.

Seizing Rochester Castle in order to prevent the king from returning to London, William d'Albini, Earl of Sussex, garrisoned the site with rebel supporters. In response, King John swiftly marched to the castle and personally commanded Royalist troops in one of England's most noteworthy medieval sieges. Effectively employing great stone-throwing machines, John's men breached the curtain wall, but when the garrison refused to surrender, the king then ordered sappers to undermine the southeastern angle of the great tower. Propping the mine with timber beams, the men packed the tunnel with 40 fatty pigs and set them alight. The raging fire burned the timber props, causing the earth to collapse beneath the angular corner, which also crumbled. The rebels retreated to the opposite side of the keep and continued to resist. On the verge of starvation and forced to eat horseflesh, the defenders finally capitulated after almost two months of resistance. To prevent future attempts at undermining and enhance the castle's ability to withstand an assault, John ensured the southern tower was rebuilt to a round plan.

In the early twelfth century, Henry I granted Norman-built Kenilworth Castle (probably a motte and bailey) and the surrounding estates to his chamberlain and treasurer, Geoffrey de Clinton. De Clinton added a defensive ditch to the castle and also erected a priory nearby. By mid-century, his son, another Geoffrey, replaced the timber defenses with a rectangular stone keep and a simple masonry curtain wall. The two-story, battlemented keep was a formidable structure: Its red walls measured seventeen feet thick and had powerful, 100 foot tall towers at the four corners. Buttressing not only provided extra support, but also interfered with an enemy's undermining. An internal spiral staircase allowed movement between the main story and adjoining levels; each of the upper stories held a single, plain chamber. The northwest tower contained three levels of latrines, which serviced the entire keep. In 1173, Henry II took back control of the castle and set up a garrison. Meanwhile, the de Clintons moved to Buckinghamshire. In time, the addition of the great mere and other defensive structures transformed the castle into one of the kingdom's mightiest strongholds, as Henry III discovered in 1266 during yet another barons' rebellion against the monarchy. For six long months, the rebel garrison managed to thwart the king's army, only surrendering after sickness, starvation, and thirst had taken their toll.

Today, the great keep at Kenilworth survives but is an empty ruin, thanks to slighting by Parliamentary troops led by Colonel Hawkesworth, who also drained the great mere, in the aftermath of the English Civil War. The castle had supported King Charles I, who actually stayed there in 1644. Even though it pales when compared to the much more ornate, yet

Though lacking its western wall, which Parliamentarian forces slighted in the seventeenth century, the sheer power of Kenilworth Castle's great keep remains self-evident.

equally ruinous, structures added by John of Gaunt and Robert Dudley in the fifteenth and sixteenth centuries, the hulking keep still exudes physical strength and demonstrates the ability of its builder to dominate a locality.

Seeking new ways to understand castles, some present-day researchers are trying to prove that the great rectangular towers, particularly those erected during the twelfth century, such as Canterbury, Rochester, Kenilworth, and mighty Dover, were built solely as showcases of power and status rather than for defensive purposes or for use as private accommodation. Some castellologists[13] claim that the austere facades, still crowned with battlements and lined with thick walls but now stripped of their decorative elements, have created the false impression that keeps were used as refuges, places of last resort from which defenders could continue to battle besiegers who breached the main gate.

Surprisingly, a few castle historians have even gone so far as to claim that Henry II's expensive tour de force at Dover Castle was not intended for siege warfare nor as a regal residence but instead was built primarily as a symbol of the king's supremacy over his own subjects and over anyone daring to cross the English Channel to challenge his absolute authority. An examination of the structure itself reveals its true nature.

A masterpiece of medieval ingenuity conceived by Maurice the Engineer, Henry II's keep is the finest example of a medieval great tower still standing in England. Rising some 95 feet and measuring about 98 by 96 feet near the base, the heavily defended rectangle served capably both as the castle's central strongpoint and also as the grandiose residence of the reigning monarch. The powerful stone walls measured between 17 and 21 feet in thickness, necessitating the construction of a battered plinth splayed at the base of the tower to support the heavy walls, which were crowned at the four corners by battlemented turrets.

To gain access to the interior, visitors must climb three straight flights of stairs inside the huge forebuilding, which scales the entire eastern side of the keep; the first set of stairs stop at a vestibule at the first floor level, which leads into the smaller of two highly ornate chapels in the keep, and then proceeds across a drawbridge upwards to the main entrance in the vestibule on the second story. Both the first and second stories were residential in nature, with the king's main apartments, including garderobes, the great hall, the upper chapel, and, interestingly, the well chamber occupying the uppermost level. The plan of the first floor essentially mirrored the arrangement of the chambers above. The fairly plain ground level basement was probably used for storage. Today, portions of the keep have been transformed into interactive history presentations, which partially obscure the medieval structure, but some of the chambers have been refurbished to present an impression as to how they may have looked during the Middle Ages.

Certainly everything about Dover's great tower shouted "huge" and "indestructible" and reflected not only how Henry felt about himself but how he would have wanted his rivals, his subjects, and anyone thinking about seizing the throne to perceive him. Henry had no qualms about further fortifying the site with a powerful curtain wall, evenly pierced with ten rectangular towers and two twin-towered gateways, including the King's Gate, which opened into a substantial D-shaped barbican on the northeastern side of the keep and provided access into the outer bailey. Henry's son, King John, later enclosed the outer bailey with another heavily defended circuit of wall towers and gateways. Like his father, John demonstrated his power to the lords in his own kingdom and to his rivals in France by adding to the fortifications at the castle.

It is a mistake to reject the notion that keeps (such as at Rochester, Kenilworth and Dover) had no defensive role. Certainly, defense and personal comfort were not the only purposes served by the great towers, but they were fundamental to their existence. It is reasonable to state that these imposing buildings, which were basically castles in their own right, showcased the power and wealth of their lords, whether they were the kings of England, whose great keeps at Dover and London are arguably the most impressive examples of their type, or the realm's lords, who sought to demonstrate their personal achievements by building their own rectangular keeps, as at Hedingham, Castle Rising, and elsewhere in the kingdom.

As with Dover Castle, castellologists have recently taken a new look at the function of the fine rectangular keep at Hedingham Castle and, out of this research, have come up with some new conclusions about castle keeps in general. Just as any new aristocrat was expected to do, Aubrey de Vere III erected the great tower at Hedingham to mark his new status as the first Earl of Oxford, which the Empress Matilda had bestowed upon him in 1141. On the surface, the formidable structure looks much like any other rectangular keep (it even had 12-foot-thick walls), but several decorative elements and the interesting interior chambers give lie to that fact, for the tower actually lacked living quarters.[14]

Originally four stories tall, with a fifth story added in the fifteenth or sixteenth century,[15] the impressive structure was apparently all about power and prestige — the new earl of Oxford wanted to ensure that everyone who entered the great keep was more than aware of his new status. The building is now believed to have been intended as a giant ceremonial structure.[16] It originally contained a simple basement level (probably for storage); a heated, first floor lower hall; and an upper hall and gallery which essentially occupied the two uppermost levels and was open to roof level. An elaborate forebuilding led visitors to the main entry point at the first floor level, which opened into the unremarkable lower hall. To reach the upper hall (probably a public reception room) and the lord himself, they evidently then had to climb a set of wooden stairs, which de Vere could order blocked to keep out unwanted guests. The gallery was similarly accessible: from there, visitors could gaze on the activity below them in the hall. The great hall was a spectacle unto itself, with numerous archways penetrating the walls on both levels; an enormous arch spanning some 28 feet dominated the center of the chamber.

Closer examination of the decorative features has led researchers to speculate that the builders intended to force visitors in an anti-clockwise direction around the gallery. Interestingly, the gallery also features the most elaborate windows in the keep. Having no room behind them, it is likely that they were deliberately situated so that arriving guests would see them, admire the new earl's taste, and, hopefully, reflect on his sophistication, wealth, status, and political clout.[17] After all, only men of position and substantial financial means were able to erect a keep, even one of modest proportions. De Vere's great tower demonstrated he had achieved much more than the average citizen. Hedingham Castle's keep seems to have been a one-of-a-kind structure: a rectangular great tower that lacked accommodation for the lord and his family and performed a purely ceremonial role for its owner.

Undoubtedly, many keeps ostentatiously — and quite intentionally — displayed a lord's "coming of age," signaling his arrival into the upper reaches of society. The construction of a structure worthy of his achievement — a great keep — placed him literally and figuratively head and shoulders above his associates, at least until they were standing next to him! We see this situation again and again, not just at Hedingham Castle but also at Castle Rising, where William d'Albini (d'Aubigny) began constructing one of England's finest Norman keeps shortly after his marriage to Henry I's widow, Adeliza de Louvain, in about 1138. William's massive 50-foot-high keep still dominates the enclosure created by the well-preserved ringwork. Among its most intriguing features is the stylish forebuilding which was designed to guide guests to stopping points between the two staircases it contained, from where they could be turned back or allowed to progress into an entrance vestibule into the exquisitely decorated great hall on the first story. Beyond a cross-wall at the opposite end of the hall hid the lord's private chamber and a magnificent chapel, which today features skillfully carved Norman arches, ornate diamond and chevron patterns (typical of Norman architecture), decorative columns, and traces of red paint. D'Albini's impressive keep was certainly a symbol of his personal achievements, not just for having served as Henry I's chief butler, but for his marriage to the king's widow and his political stature as the first Earl of Arundel, where another of d'Albini's castles survives.

Freestanding keeps dominated castle construction from the late eleventh century and throughout the twelfth century. They continued to be built, albeit to a lesser degree, until the fifteenth century. Even though the design of the great tower seems to have developed over time from rectangular to round to polygonal shapes, castle researchers now believe that the changes had more to do with the personal ambitions and inclinations of their builders than that they were evolutionary modifications prompted by improvements in siege techniques. This author believes both factors had equally important roles in the decision-making process: Rounded towers could certainly better deflect missiles and thwart the efforts of miners and attackers battering their walls with picks or other handheld tools, and they could also dazzle the eyes and impress visitors, much like rectangular keeps. One only has to look at William Marshal's great round keep at Pembroke Castle to recognize the power of the design.

On the other hand, polygonal keeps often contained many straight sides and 90 degree

One of England's most unique great towers, the polygonal keep at Warkworth Castle dominates its surroundings. During the nineteenth century, owner Algernon Percy, fourth Duke of Northumberland, converted part of the keep into a private residence.

angles, so even though some castellologists have claimed that their development was an improvement necessitated by changes in warfare technology, that explanation makes little sense, because they offered even more flat and angled walls to attack than did the rectangular keep. A key role for the polygonal keep, which for the most part appeared late in the history of British castle-building, must have been to symbolically demonstrate a lord's political achievements, personal wealth, and cultural refinement in a very public way. Two impressive examples can be explored at Warkworth and Raglan Castles, both of which, even as grandiose ruins, still reflect the good taste and political clout of the men who ordered their construction.

Warkworth Castle originated as a motte and bailey fortress, but was converted to stone beginning in the twelfth century. In the late fourteenth or early fifteenth century, Henry, fourth Lord Percy and first Earl of Northumberland, began his magnificent polygonal great tower, which was erected on top of the motte, possibly on the site of an earlier keep. From above, the complex keep takes the form of a cross superimposed on top of a square (which measures 69 feet square and has beveled corners), the four semi-octagonal ends of the cross projecting outwards about midway along the walls of the square. The building stands three stories tall, has eight-foot-thick walls, and a maze of passageways led to the great hall, kitchen block, lord's solar, bedchambers, a chapel, and other rooms. Clearly, Percy intended this tower, which completely dominates the site, to fulfill a dual role as his private residence and also as the center of pomp and circumstance at the castle. Visitors now, as during the Middle Ages, cannot help but marvel at the unique structure, which is still adorned with the Percy lion, the heraldic symbol that defined the family. Percy's other great castle, at Alnwick, remains occupied by the dukes of Northumberland. It also features a polygonal keep and octagonal towers, and visitors will find the heraldic lion there as well.

Like the elaborate great tower at Warkworth, Raglan's keep was erected in the early fifteenth century, partly as a response to the increasing hostilities of the Wars of the Roses. Oddly enough, the heavily defended, self-sufficient structure stood on its own outside the curtain wall, and possibly occupies the site of an earlier motte. Known as the Twr Melyn y Gwent, or the Yellow Tower of Gwent, for its yellow-colored sandstone, the great keep at Raglan Castle once stood five stories tall but today only rises four stories, due to undermining by Parliamentarian troops after the end of the English Civil War. Surrounded by an apron wall with six turrets (similar to a low curtain wall), one of which contained a postern gate and gave access to the encompassing moat, the hexagonal keep was accessible only via drawbridges, which once crossed the moat from inside the castle and led into a forebuilding.

Even though the interior of the Yellow Tower of Gwent is largely a shell, visitors can pinpoint a variety of features which will help them determine the functions of each level: The basement, with its huge fireplace (and a fine latrine), contained the kitchen and a small chamber, added later, which may have contained the treasury; upper levels, with fireplaces, latrines, and increasingly wide windows, held accommodation — the great chamber on the first floor and the lord's private bedchambers on story above. The sheer magnificence of this polygonal keep cannot be disputed; however, neither can its defensive power, which defied the pounding of cannons and mortars fired by Parliamentarian troops, during the siege of 1646.

Both of the polygonal keeps discussed above grandly displayed the fact that their builders had "made it," politically, socially and financially. For Henry Percy, the fabulous design of his keep may have in some way symbolized his parity with the monarch; after all, he was the most powerful man in northern England and had the enormous responsibility to keep the kingdom free from Scottish rule. It would have seemed only fitting for him to build one of the most fantastic keeps of his era. For William ap Thomas, a Welshman from a minor gentry family who had made his name (the Blue Knight of Gwent) fighting alongside Henry V at Agincourt and made his fortune by marrying Elizabeth Bloet, the widow of Sir James Berkeley and heiress to the Bloet estates of "Raggeland," erecting the mammoth keep marked the acquisition of a knighthood and also his advancement into noble society. The Yellow Tower of Gwent was his badge of honor, one that combined all the features expected of a keep into a remarkably strong, physically appealing, residential structure.

When examining even the smallest keeps, such as Peveril Castle (the "Castle of the Peak"), or more complicated structures such as Tretower Castle, keep in mind that they were once undamaged, occupied buildings that contained separate stories with floors and individual, furnished chambers complete with carved architectural features and decorations designed not just to create a pleasant living atmosphere but also to express certain symbolic meanings. Their size is just one aspect of the overall picture. Look closely at the features that survive even where the floors do not. They often provide clues to the function of a room that no longer exists.

Peveril Castle is small in comparison to many of the better known fortresses in Britain, which is surprising, considering it was the stronghold of several kings. Nevertheless, the fortress was prized for its location as a buffer between the Penines and Cumbria in an area which was a rich source of lead (from which silver was extracted). Consequently, the stronghold had an eventful history. Just after the Normans conquered Britain, William I granted

The compact keep at Peveril Castle was an anomaly for the prodigious castle-building king, Henry II, who also built the mammoth keep at Dover. Even so, Henry used the keep to impress guests, such as Scotland's king, and to administer the rich mining region commanded by the castle.

the site to William de Peverel, said to have been an illegitimate son of the Conqueror, as a reward for services during the Conquest.

Completed by 1086, Peverel's castle originally consisted of a stone curtain wall enclosing a triangular site; it was well placed to make full use of its natural and manmade defenses. The castle remained a Peverel possession until 1155, when William Peverel the Younger lost favor with the Crown and also lost claim to the estates at Peveril and nearby Bolsover Castle. William was charged with complicity in the poisoning of Ranulf, the Earl of Chester (there is speculation that Peverel was framed), and was banished to life in the monastery. King Henry II then took control of the castle, made significant modifications, and created much of what survives today.

Although not one of his primary strongholds, Henry II took a personal interest in the refortification of Peveril Castle. He visited the castle in 1157, 1158, and 1164 and added the "old" hall, chapel, east gatehouse (today's entrance), and, most notably, the fine keep. Not surprisingly, the small, rectangular keep is the castle's most imposing structure. Begun in 1176, a few years after Henry's wife, Queen Eleanor of Aquitaine, and their sons led a rebellion against her husband, the keep took about two years to build at a cost of under £200.[18]

Surely the highlight of the castle, the great tower stands just west of the original entrance onto the site. Though small for a royal castle, measuring 40 feet square by 60 feet tall with only a single upper story above the basement level, it is a typical rectangular keep. Sadly, much of the exterior masonry has been pilfered or fallen due to neglect; however, at the top and on the southeastern facades, well-preserved fragments of the fine-cut ashlar blocks that adorned the entire keep adorn the walls. Remains of decorative sculpture and the projecting stone box that held the latrine chute are also visible. Visitors may climb a modern staircase to explore the interior of the keep, which was never equipped with a forebuilding but probably had a moveable ladder for access during medieval times. A slot in the masonry jamb reveals that the keep had drawbars to latch the heavy wooden door. Overhead, a double arch added style to the otherwise plain façade—a heavily eroded face is all that remains of the two carved heads adorning the doorway. Inside, sharp-eyed visitors will notice two small rooms at the north and south corners. The southern chamber held the latrine. On the eastern side, a spiral staircase once gave access to the basement and also to the wall-walk.

It is curious that Henry, the builder of several of the realm's most powerful keeps, chose to erect such a simple tower at Peveril Castle. Even though the keep dominates the rest of the property, it was devoid of all the comforts and facilities normally found in the typical great tower. Instead, the king erected a range of structures to the south of the great tower to provide these services. Today, the group of structures seems more a jumble of ruins than the remains of several distinct buildings; but at one time, the area held the twelfth-century "old hall" and the castle's chapel; two round watch towers added in the thirteenth century. Of these structures, only foundations remain, along with eleventh-century masonry, identifiable by the herringbone pattern of stones along the base of the curtain. (The northern portion of the curtain wall also features herringbone masonry. Dating to the late eleventh century, these stones are excellent examples of Norman stonework and would have been constructed by William Peverel.)

Other buildings constructed during the thirteenth century include the "new" hall, the kitchen and service block, and domestic chambers, now little more than foundations along the northern and western curtain walls. Among the unusual remnants are pillar bases and "slops," chutes for draining waste away from the area, and a large central open hearth in the hall. The dais occupies the opposite or "high" end of the hall, where the lord, his family, and special guests dined. These remains offer intriguing insight into the lifestyle of the rich and famous during the Middle Ages. However, they do not explain why Henry II built such a small keep.

Certainly, Henry could not have been trying to impress his family, friends, subjects, or rivals such as Scotland's sixteen-year-old king, Malcolm IV, who paid homage to the English king at the castle in 1157 after being forced to relinquish his control of Cumberland and Westmorland.[19] Whereas Henry's other great towers were obviously much more impressive, here at Peveril Castle, the diminutive size of the keep actually could have implied the opposite, that the king was a small, weak ruler. But Henry never would have allowed his reputation to be represented that way. The position of the castle, which existed prior to the construction of the keep, was not particularly conducive to building a large keep, for the rocky point of land would never have been able to support it.[20] The king would have wanted to add his mark to the site, which was in the heart of an area rich in mineral ore. Recognizing the limitations of the site, the great castle-building king opted not to build a completely new castle and instead chose to add a compact keep, one with fine-cut stone and a towering position in the uppermost corner of the site, factors which would exhibit his—and the monarchy's—ongoing control of the region.

Interestingly, the Castle of the Peak was owned and frequented by the likes of Henry III, who made extensive repairs during the thirteenth century and added several key buildings, such as a horse mill; his wife, Queen Eleanor of Provence, who granted the castle to Simon de Montfort, the leader of a notorious rebellion against the king; Queen Eleanor of Castile, who was required to pay an annual rent of £100 for the estate and the castle; and Piers Gaveston, Edward II's controversial courtier. In time, it passed to John of Gaunt and became part of the Duchy of Lancaster, which it remains to this day.

Unlike at Peveril Castle, where the great tower is structurally similar to larger rectangular keeps in the kingdom, including Henry II's greatest at Dover Castle, visitors to Tretower Castle may find the site rather perplexing, partly because much of the medieval castle has eroded away due to later construction on the property but even more so because of the unusual design of the medieval great tower(s) which still dominates the surroundings. During the thirteenth century, the Picards erected a tall cylindrical keep inside the twelfth-century shell keep at the site, which had replaced the original timber tower that stood atop a low-rising mound of earth and contained a kitchen, the hall, and a range of apartments, evidence of which survives. It is possible that the Picards erected the new building as a way to keep up with the times, when round towers were becoming fashionable and more common. Lesser lords like the Picards, owners of the castle from the late eleventh century, probably hoped to demonstrate their accomplishments, such as they were, and to impress other lords. With the construction of the innovative round tower, the design of which was becoming increasingly popular, especially in the Welsh Marches, the Picards probably intended to enhance their status within the region. It must be noted that, when the male line of Picards died out, the castle passed to Ralph Bloet. His daughter, Elizabeth, married Sir William ap Thomas, as mentioned above, and not only brought Raglan Castle but also Tretower Castle to the marriage.

Today, the ruins of Tretower's polygonal shell encircle the taller, cylindrical keep. Why the thirteenth-century owners kept the shell keep is unclear, for at best it must have created an uncomfortable home and the disturbing awareness of the physical limitations of the structure; stifling, claustrophobic living conditions. Perhaps, the shell keep was thought to provide an extra barrier to an assault. (Apparently, later residents could not tolerate the cramped conditions and built spacious Tretower Court as a substitute.) Though portions of the original Norman shell keep were demolished to make room for the inner tower, the remains of some of its domestic buildings have survived on the inner wall, including the outlines of windows and the fireplace. When exploring the site and others where only walling survives, visitors should always remember to examine the interior wall. At Tretower, one can identify features from the kitchen, such as a semi-circular fireplace and a drain, the hall and solar block (which originally projected into the area framed by the shell keep), and traces of the wall-walk. The taller round tower, which once stood three stories high and contained fine apartments, also retains evidence of occupation, including fireplaces and windows with seats on its inner wall. The exterior walling should also be examined for remnants of the gabled rooftop, which apparently covered a wooden bridge that led to the wall-walk on the adjacent shell keep.

In the fifteenth century, Sir Roger Vaughan was granted ownership of Tretower Court, the castle, and surrounding estates. One of his first actions was to initiate an extensive building program to upgrade the fading and very simple Tretower Court, which had been built in the early 1300s. Extending the house, he created a marvelous residence fit for a man of status. As far as his castle went, Vaughan neglected its upkeep and it finally fell into ruin. Interestingly, his status eventually plummeted and, in 1471, Sir Roger lost his head after the Battle of Tewkesbury. His son, Thomas, fortified Tretower Court and the Vaughan family continued to live there until the eighteenth century.

The cylindrical keep at Tretower Castle clearly dominates the older shell keep. Once rising three stories, the taller keep contained fine apartments furnished with fireplaces and windows with seats. The top level provided support for a timber hoard.

The Tower House: Keep and Castle

Always remember that looks can be deceiving at castle ruins, and even at still-occupied castles. Despite your best efforts, you might identify a structure as one type of site only to discover that it is something else entirely. For example, some people classify tower houses as "keep castles"; however, tower houses are actually a separate architectural development which resembled rectangular keeps but had several distinctive features. As such, it is important for visitors to be aware of the differences and to assess each site they explore with those distinctions in mind. In some ways, the tower house was a peculiarly Scottish structure, which developed as a response to an increased need for protection from sudden, brief assaults or raids by local reivers and clan rivals rather than for thwarting prolonged sieges. As early as the late thirteenth century, tower houses began appearing throughout the countryside, particularly in the border regions of Dumfries and Galloway. It has been estimated that some 700 tower houses once existed in Scotland, some 80 of which were in Dumfries and Galloway.[21] Two of the finest examples are Threave and Hermitage Castles.

Whereas the poorer population generally lived in unfortified, single-level dwellings, tower houses were marks of the authority and higher status of the landed gentry. Like rectangular keeps, they contained at least three levels and stood an average of 40 to 80 feet high. Some were built to a round plan. Unlike rectangular keeps, tower houses were modestly defended independent structures and not part of a larger castle. If additional defenses were needed, owners built a walled courtyard known as a barmkin, which was similar to but normally much smaller than the typical bailey and primarily used for holding livestock. Early tower houses were very plain, with few windows, battlements, walls averaging six to seven feet thick; the main entrance opened on the first story above ground level. Each level served a single function: The ground floor held the basement or was used for storage, and had no access to the upper stories, except through a trapdoor in the ceiling; the hall or kitchen occupied the next story; and the laird's private apartments filled the uppermost levels.

During the late fourteenth and fifteenth centuries, a variety of modifications were introduced which made tower houses more spacious while remaining secure, and attention was also given to the ornamentation on the exterior walls. The two most significant developments were the L-plan and the Z-plan, whereby extensions of the basic tower house design were added to provide more living space. Once the extra wings became routine additions, rooms like the kitchen — with its well, sink and fireplace — the hall, and the chapel could be relocated to the annexes. Structural variations became increasingly popular, as did flamboyant features such as conical roofs and elaborate machicolations, which lost their defensive function and became purely decorative elements, as at Crathes or Inveraray Castles.

During the early 1400s, the Irish also started constructing tower houses, which dominated the landscape for the next two centuries and eventually numbered as many as 3,000 structures. Irish tower houses share certain similarities with those in Scotland, but they also have distinct differences. Like those in Scotland, they developed in response to the political and social conditions of the times. As in Scotland, clan warfare was a considerable problem, and local raids were commonplace. Ireland's tower houses were simple, solidly fortified residences, primarily rectangular in plan, which rose several stories. A few round tower houses have survived in Ireland as well. Irish tower houses contained from three to six levels; the distinctive top story featured stepped battlements and a double-gabled roof at the center. Walls ranged from six to eight feet in thickness, but, unlike in Scotland, the main entrance was at ground level. Upper levels contained the great hall, fireplaces, mullioned windows with seats, and latrines. Some had corner turrets which held staircases or offered additional space. Bunratty and Blarney Castles are two of Ireland's finest examples.

From the late sixteenth to the mid-seventeenth centuries, a horizontal version of the tower house, called a "stronghouse," appeared in the Irish countryside. Much wider than the standard tower house, many of these fortified structures stood five stories high. They are identified by their numerous gables and a focus on comfort rather than defenses. However, many had gunports installed at strategic locations around the walls to combat an assault.

Welsh tower houses were rare. Located just north of the parish church, Angle Castle is the tower house left in Wales. Probably erected in the late fourteenth century, the machicolated structure stood over 34 feet high and had three-foot-thick walls. A single living chamber, measuring almost ten feet square, filled each of the upper three stories. Each contained a fireplace, small, unglazed windows, and arrowslits, but only the first story had a garderobe (latrine). A movable drawbridge apparently allowed access at the first floor level, and then a spiral staircase in the rounded turret at the northeastern corner allowed passage from one level to the next. Visitors to Angle should also look for the remains of the barmkin, a dovecote, and an unusual ruin on the southern side of the main street, which may have been a medieval hall-house.

Standing about 35 high and constructed with three-foot thick walls, Angle's machicolated tower house provided single living chambers on each of the upper three floors. Note the putlog holes on the exterior wall. A domed dovecote peeks through the undergrowth behind the tower.

Entering the Inner Sanctum

The goal for anyone entering a castle, whether friend or foe, medieval or modern, has always been to make it into the inner bailey, the vital core of the site where the lord and his family made their home and from where the lord meted out justice, administered the lordship, and entertained important visitors. At many royal castles, for example, the inner bailey often contained the monarch's private and state apartments, the queen's private and state apartments, and any essential support structures, such as the main chapel. Lordship castles featured the same basic configuration of structures, the most important and most impressive — the lord's personal and public chambers — dominating the center of the castle.

One would assume that, because the most important buildings generally lined the walls of the inner bailey and also filled adjoining mural towers, the castle owner would make sure his most heavily defended gatehouse stood at the entrance into the core of the site. However, that was not always the case. Much depended on the needs and preferences of the builder himself. At some castles, such as Pembroke and Rochester, the outer gateway was the more substantial, whereas at others, such as Laugharne and White Castle, the inner gatehouse was by far the more formidable of the two. Sometimes, the disparity reflected the age differences between the structures, where one or the other of the gateways was erected before the other or by different builders; sometimes it reflected the relative importance of the two parts of the castle. And, at other times, it was a key part of the overall plan of the castle, particularly if construction involved a concentric design, as at Caerphilly, where all of the gatehouses were

Overlooking the bending river immediately behind the great gatehouse, Roger Bigod III's complex hall-block at Chepstow Castle was really two buildings in one. The complex structure embodied medieval affluence. The ornate hall still contains traces of paint and elaborately sculpted windows.

heavily defended, but the largest and most complex of the lot guarded the main, eastern entrance into the inner ward.

Furthermore, where one lord might have erected a keep and also placed other vital buildings in the inner bailey, others added similar structures to other parts of the castle later in its history, as at Chepstow, where Roger Bigod III built an elaborate apartment complex and powerful corner tower in the lower bailey, well away from the great hall-keep. Still other owners, such as Henry de Lacy, opted for keepless castles, in which, as at Denbigh Castle, the lord's residential chambers were situated inside wall towers and in ranges lining the perimeter of the inner bailey. Some of these castles had substantial gatehouses and comparatively meager residential ranges; others, particularly quadrangular castles built later in the history of British castle-building, such as Bodiam and Bolton, had meager gatehouses and comparatively substantial residential ranges.

Even though each castle was distinct, planned for individual owners to their specifications, medieval castle builders made sure to include certain key buildings somewhere in the inner ward: a hall or great hall, the lord's private apartments, a solar, the kitchen block, a well, and a chapel. Not only were these structures essential to daily life and useful for more than one purpose (for example, halls also functioned as sleeping chambers), they were also used to present a certain image to visitors, particularly if the guests were royal. Walking into the inner bailey of a castle today, visitors may discover that many of these buildings survive only as foundations or are considerably ruined. Yet, during the Middle Ages, history was often made inside these seemingly vacant inner enclosures: Treaties were signed, monarchs abdicated or were held under house arrest, and fantastic celebrations were staged. Perhaps most important of all, routine activities—from cooking and cleaning to eating and sleeping—occurred in and around the inner ward. For that reason, the surviving stones have stories to tell; one just needs to know what clues to look for and how to interpret what he or she sees. Then, the stories become accessible.

Even in castles with well-preserved exteriors, as at Conwy and Bodiam, the interior structures are often little more than foundations or ruined shells; the decrepit conditions make it difficult at best to place the remains in their proper context. Even so, many have left behind distinguishing features which allow us to make assumptions about their medieval functions and place within castle life. When exploring the baileys, also be sure to take a close look at the walls and associated foundations and not just at the larger, more obvious features such as towers, for you will miss clues to other types of structures that played a role in the castle's history. Staircases and doorways that seem to go nowhere once had destinations: Sometimes, they even headed into discreetly located latrines. The remains of an especially large fireplace or ovens reveal the position of the kitchen or, perhaps, the bakehouse. Remnants of a large central hearth point to the location of the great hall, as can extra large, ornamented windows. Sometimes, only the mantle pieces survive to pinpoint bed chambers. Masonry that forms an inverted "V" indicates where a roof once connected to a wall.

At Pembroke Castle, the outline of a high-pitched roof is still quite visible on a wall in

Originally leading into the first floor of the great hall from an antechamber, this spiral staircase at Raglan Castle now seems to lead to the heavens. Ashlar blocks and the rubble core are visible on the exterior.

the rectangular courthouse (also known as the chancery building) that stands alongside the great keep in the inner bailey. A horizontal line of small square holes reveals where the ends of timber beams would have been placed to support a ceiling or upper story; so do small stone projections, known as corbels, which were often carved with floral designs or facial features. At Denbigh Castle, carvings in the shape of a lion's face and an imp's head adorn corbels in the southern room and a maiden's head forms a corbel in the northern room of the so-called Green Chambers, which now exist only as foundations and fragments along the curtain wall. Keen-eyed visitors can visualize the placement of upper stories by spotting these architectural features in the remains of domestic chambers and towers lining the bailey.

Arguably the most important building in the inner bailey besides the keep was the hall, inside of which residents and guests ate and drank — and sometimes slept, particularly in the early days of castle-building in Britain. Halls not only served as the castle's main dining center; they functioned most importantly as its business and administrative centers. Some castles contained a great hall and a lesser hall; at others, separate blocks of residential chambers had their own halls. Some castles had freestanding halls, the most impressive of which is the only physical evidence of Winchester Castle's existence. Many if not most, masonry halls were built against the curtain wall, which formed the fourth side of the building, which was normally rectangular in plan.

If builders erected the hall against an outer wall which angled or turned slightly, they adjusted the plan, as at Conwy, where the walls of the majestic great hall form a broad V-shape which mirrored the site's perimeter. Even though the elongated structure lacks a roof and floors, the walls stand to their full height. Today, visitors enter at ground level, which not only accentuates the enormity of the building but also creates a feeling of disorientation. The sensation is probably not surprising, since the interior is largely gutted. Overhead, a single stone arch stretches across the hall, the last of eight arches added in the 1340s to support the roof. Remnants of the others, known as springers, project from their rooftop locations; with some imagination, visitors can recreate a mental picture of the medieval ceiling built for the Black Prince (Edward of Woodstock, Edward III's eldest son) by his master mason, Henry de Snelleston.[22] It must be noted that this hall range actually consisted of three different structures, the great hall itself at the center, flanked by the chapel on the east and a lesser hall on the west, which were evidently separated from the central structure by timber screens. As can be seen in the accompanying image, this block of buildings is best viewed from above.

Many halls comprised the central chamber in a range of buildings which, unlike that at Conwy Castle, included the lord's solar (the withdrawing chamber) or private apartments on one side and the kitchen and service buildings (the pantry and buttery, or bottlery) on the opposite. The practical arrangement allowed servants to cook, prepare, and serve food while it was still warm and also to pour and carry drink to the hall without taking too much time. Sometimes a screen or cross-wall separated the service rooms from the hall. The passageway between the hall and the service rooms was known as the screens passage. A minstrel's gallery often occupied the upper level of the passage. From the balcony, musicians provided the evening's entertainment. Minstrel's galleries were often very lavishly decorated. Nowadays, only the best preserved halls retain these balconies.

At the far end of the hall, the lord and esteemed guests sat at the high table, which stood on the dais, a raised platform which emphasized the lofty status of the lord and his companions over the rest of the diners, whom they faced. Interestingly, men of lower rank served those of higher status.[23] Behind the dais, a discreetly placed doorway allowed the lord to

Now a mere shell, the enormous great hall at Conwy Castle is best viewed from above, where the relationship between the main chamber and two side chambers is easy to discern. The curious arch is the only one of the eight arches that originally supported a heavy rooftop to survive.

retreat into the solar (the "sun room"), where he (and his wife, if present) could withdraw from the hall, relax or sleep, and continue monitoring discussions and other activities. Some were actually fitted with strategically placed squints or spy holes for just that purpose. Nowadays, most solars look just like any other small room; they are often identified by their position at the upper end of the hall rather than by any distinguishing features.

It is not surprising that the great hall was generally the most ornate chamber in any castle, for not only did the lord use it to impress friends, rivals and important guests with his wealth, cultural sophistication and political stature, he also used it even more frequently to manage his estates and impress (and intimidate) tenants and others who came to the castle to conduct business or obtain or mete out justice. It often served as the lord's personal courthouse. The great hall itself normally occupied the first floor above the basement level of the building, which held the stores. It contained a huge fireplace with fine carvings and at least one set of tall windows, which were adorned with carvings and had seats on either side for guests to enjoy the views or observe the frivolities. Prior to the twelfth century, most halls, particularly those at ground level, were heated with a central hearth, and the ceilings were fitted with louvers which vented the smoke outside. Some had roof ventilators made with pottery, shaped as knights, kings, or priests. Their wide-open eyes and mouths vented the smoke.[24] Late in the twelfth century, wall fireplaces with flues and chimneys began to replace the central hearth.[25]

Of course, not all lords built their halls according to the above plan. Variations could result from a lord's personal whims, his expectations for the hall, or because of space limitations, which were always an issue for castle builders. At Caerphilly Castle, Gilbert de Clare II may have encountered just this problem when he built his great hall block in the inner ward of his concentric castle. The present building, which was refurbished by Hugh le Despenser in the early fourteenth century, contains a range of chambers divided by a crosswall. The larger, western side contained the two-story hall. An ornate chapel and another room, possibly a solar, occupied the upper level on the eastern side; the ground level chamber consisted of the buttery and pantry. The kitchen, however, was located inside a tower positioned on the southern side of hall-block along with an annex and a storehouse. Interestingly, unlike most castles, the raised dais was also located on the eastern side of the hall, and the lord's private apartments were situated beyond the hall's western wall.

An entrance from the inner bailey rather than from the hall gave the lord access to the apartments, now almost completely ruined. At one time, the complex contained several residential chambers, including a large room with a fine tracery window on the side nearest the hall, a round-backed fireplace for heating, and a solar, which once opened to a latrine tower. The lord's personal quarters took up the entire upper level.

Medieval passersby identified the location of a great hall by its grandiose windows, and possibly by the presence of a large chimney. Modern-day visitors can use the same identifiers — conspicuously large fireplaces and lavish windows — to pinpoint the great hall. And, when inside the castle, look for the presence of stone window seats, especially rich ornamentation, and trefoil or quatrefoil designs, all of which typically adorned the great hall. When only a chamber's foundations survive, examining the windows in the curtain wall (or, at least what remains of the windows) that overlooks the spot may help identify what type of building once stood there.

One of the finest examples of a ruined great hall with its associated service buildings can be explored at Kenilworth Castle. During the late fourteenth century, John of Gaunt, Duke of Lancaster and the fourth son of King Edward III, and his master mason, Robert Skyllington,[26] began the castle's transformation into a grand palace by replacing earlier residential buildings with the ornate great hall, the Strong Tower, and the service wing on one side, and the Saintlowe Tower and great chamber on the other. Though now heavily ruined, more than enough remains of this range of buildings to allow modern visitors the pleasure of experiencing something of the castle's medieval grandeur. It is worth noting that, in 1842, a gentleman visiting the site stated, "the Castle looks better as a Ruin."[27]

Now roofless and floorless, the duke's great hall stood two stories high, measured over 90 feet long by 46 feet wide, and was accessed via a particularly lavish main doorway at the first floor level. The basement, also known as an undercroft, was used for storage; it still features a series of decorative red sandstone niches and fragments of columns, which once supported the floor of the hall. Above, the magnificence of the giant six-bay hall (and of John of Gaunt as well) is emphasized by four huge ornate windows with benches for seating, carved tracery, and stone paneling, and an equally impressive fireplace. At one time, the great hall featured a stunning hammerbeam ceiling, comparable to the one still crowning the great hall at Winchester Castle. On the eastern side of the hall at Kenilworth Castle, an unusual polygonal building — the oriel — forms the ideal counterpoint to the lavish doorway mentioned above. With its own fireplace and showy windows, the oriel was a recessed area in the hall reserved for the lord and his guests to enjoy a measure of privacy away from the rest of the visitors but to be able to participate in the activities as they desired.

To complete the block of domestic buildings, the Duke of Lancaster erected the Strong Tower and kitchen on the northern side of the inner bailey, between his great hall and the keep. The three-story tower had a basement for storage; the first floor held the buttery and pantry, which were used to prepare the food and drink for serving in the adjacent hall; and the upper level held living quarters, which were apparently occupied by a member of the household staff, possibly the steward. The tower connected to the kitchen, of which only the foundations of fireplaces and ovens (dating to the fifteenth century) have survived.

Located beyond the oriel, the Saintlowe Tower and a range of buildings, including the great and lesser audience chambers, stood on the opposite side of the great hall from the Strong Tower. Possibly serving as a solar and a private chamber, the two structures were also used for official duties. Nearby, Gaunt's Tower projected outwards towards the ditch. It contained latrines on two levels and residential chambers on the two upper stories. In all, John of Gaunt ensured his grand castle measured up to (and surpassed) the aristocratic standards of the times and contained all the essential structures expected of a man of his stature.

Though greatly ruined, John of Gaunt's ornate great hall still displays the grandeur that made Kenilworth Castle one of the finest palatial fortresses in the realm. A row of decorative niches adorns the walls of the undercroft, above which the great hall itself was lit with fabulous windows and heated with a huge fireplace.

Whenever interior structures are little more than shells, today's visitors can often make reasonable assumptions about how they looked and the activities carried on inside of them by looking for features characteristically associated with certain chambers or areas in the castle. In fact, during the Middle Ages, guests and new residents unfamiliar with the castle's layout were required to assess their surroundings in much the same manner as we can do today, by identifying key architectural elements and placing them in their proper, or at least in a familiar, context. Normally, the great hall was the largest chamber in the castle and contained the most lavish decorations, plastered and painted walls, the tallest and most ornate windows with seats, and an enormous, elaborately carved fireplace. Furnishings were meager at best. Often permanently affixed on the dais, traces of which often survive, the lord's table (also known as the "dormant" table) consisted of a wooden trestle and a long board, which could be removed and pushed out of the way so that other activities could take place in the hall. Alongside the main table, smaller trestle tables, known as "cup boards," supported serving dishes.[28] Candles, oil lamps, and "flambeaux," resin-soaked torches set in wall brackets or sconces, provided light. Some pri-

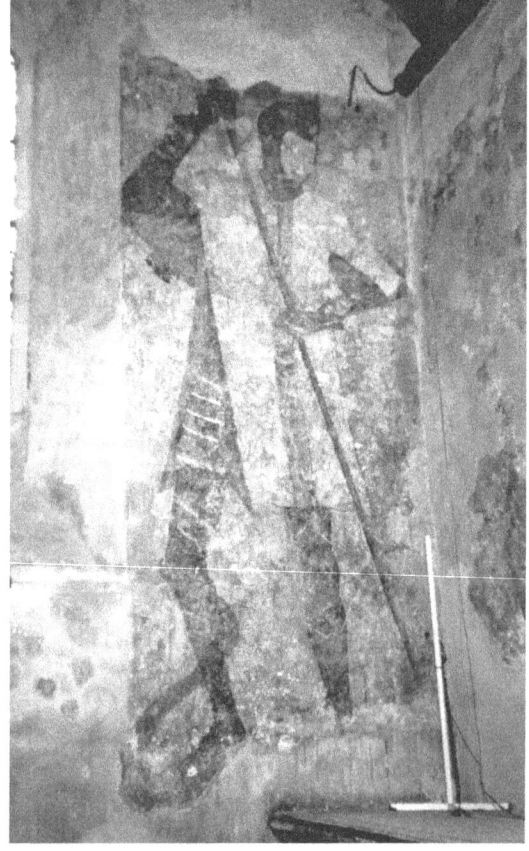

Top: The polygonal oriel on the southern end of Gaunt's great hall was a special chamber inside of which special guests could sit and dine, while still participating in the activity inside the hall. *Left:* Castle chambers were gaily painted with historical and mythological scenes. Remnants often survive. This image of St. George slaying the proverbial dragon decorates the wall of the chapel at Farleigh Hungerford Castle.

vate chambers, including the latrine, had corbels or small platforms for residents to place their candles or small lamps.[29]

Generally speaking, the most elaborately decorated rooms were generally reserved for the lord and his family, and for important guests. Interior walls were whitewashed or coated with plaster, which would hold the mortar in place. Then, they were painted with brightly colored pictures or the occasional mural, or covered with wall hangings (painted cloth) or embroidered tapestries, which not only decorated the room but also insulated it. As with other aspects of a castle, the extent of paintwork depended on the wealth and tastes of the owner. A common design consisted of a series of vertical and horizontal red lines intended to simulate blocks of ashlar and enhance the chamber's image. Examples survive at Hadleigh Castle, where the hall was decorated with red-painted glass, and Marten's Tower at Chepstow Castle.[30] Henry III was known to have adorned many castle walls with green paint and gold stars, and the Rose of Provence, which honored his wife, Eleanor of Provence.[31] Many interior walls were also adorned with wainscoting, a type of wooden paneling that covered only the lower portion of a wall; the panels were often painted white or decorated with colorful designs.

Whereas the solar might merely now look like any other chamber, a castle's service rooms can frequently be identified by the presence of three side-by-side doorways. The central doorway linked to the passage between the buttery and pantry and was used by servants to carry food and drink into the hall and created an air of ceremony and formality that would impress the lord's guests. The outer two doorways opened away from the hall so that servants could make a graceful and relatively unobtrusive exit. This arrangement became the standard by about 1300.[32]

Normally located in the immediate vicinity of the great hall and its service rooms, the kitchen was one of a castle's most important buildings. It is also one of the easiest to identify, even when in ruin. General identifiers include at least one large hearth, the rear of which might contain a bread oven, other ovens, drains, and, rarely, a stone sink. Early castle kitchens often had central hearths, which were later replaced by mural fireplaces. Many castle kitchens were located near the well, as at Old Wardour, and in those cases where only foundations survive, one can make a reasonable assumption that, if the ruins are near the well, they may have once been part of the kitchen, or, perhaps, a residential chamber.

Arguably a castle's most recognizable feature, the well was also its most important. Without a reliable supply of water, life in a castle was impossible. Commonly located close to the keep, the main residential suite or the kitchen block, wells were generally lined with stone and protected by a stone or timber well-house. Today, most wellheads are covered with protective grates which allow visitors to safely peer into the well, some of which still contain water. Sometimes a timber passage linked the well to the kitchen.[33] Some wells were situated inside the keep or in one of the mural towers in order to prevent an enemy from gaining access and poisoning the water supply. At

The most essential feature of any castle was its well. Without a reliable water supply, occupants could not hope to withstand a protracted siege. This well forms the center point of the courtyard at Old Wardour Castle.

Dover, Henry II ensured the integrity of the well by situating the shaft of the well in the thickness of the walls in his mammoth keep. Occupants could only draw water from the well-chamber, which was located on the second story. With the aid of gravity, lead conduits funneled water down to the lower levels which the enemy could not access.[34] An even more creative method was the piping system in the keep at Newcastle-upon-Tyne, where a centrally-positioned pillar fitted with a lead pipe channeled water from the well room in the basement to upper stories.[35]

Diggers often had to bore a hole some dozens of feet deep in order to tap into what would become the castle's main — or only — water source. Wells generally varied from 11 feet to over 200 feet in depth. Among the deepest wells are Beeston, 400 feet; Dover, 350 feet; Windsor, 165 feet; and Bamburgh, 145 feet. Intriguingly, some 172 feet of Dover Castle's well was actually lined with Caen stone, an expensive prospect at best — quarried in France, the yellowish-cream-colored, fine-grained limestone was normally used not for lining wells but rather for building the finest structures, particularly cathedrals and churches, but also some castles. Construction must have involved considerable risk on the part of the miners and masons who worked on the well. It is not surprising that great pains were taken to ensure an ample water supply was accessible prior to settling on a particular building site, and some castles had several wells, including one in the bailey and another in the keep. The well at Caernarfon Castle, among others, was located inside a specially built tower; it channeled water to the adjoining kitchen.

Several castles appear to have been built without wells. In some cases, residents used cisterns to collect rainwater for daily consumption or hauled fresh water into the castle in casks, which they used to store the vital supply. Some cisterns were fed by natural seepage of ground water. Rather than relying upon an interior well, residents at Carreg Cennen Castle instead used two cisterns placed behind the main gatehouse inside the inner bailey to retrieve drinking water. Builders also lined the rock-cut ditch just outside the gatehouse with clay in what archaeologists believe was an attempt to create a cistern-like effect to capture rainwater.[36] This was an unreliable position at best, but it may imply that the occupants felt fairly certain that attackers would never make it through the elongated barbican, over two drawbridges, and through two other gates in order to tamper with the water supply. When visiting a castle, it is always worthwhile to look for streams, creeks, or other fresh water sources that medieval residents may have relied upon for survival. Such water sources are usually easy to spot and sometimes make ideal landmarks to follow when looking for a castle that is off the beaten track.

A late but fascinating example of a kitchen complex can be explored in the outer bailey located immediately behind the great gatehouse at Raglan Castle. Known as the Pitched Stone Court, the bailey itself consists of a rectangular area paved with cobblestones added in the sixteenth century. Around this courtyard, all the domestic activities took place. The hexagonal kitchen tower erected by Earl William Herbert in the fifteenth century stands three stories tall and dominates the northern corner of the bailey. Its dank basement contained the wet larder, which kept fish, meat, cheese, and other items cool until ready for use. The kitchen took up the next level above the wet larder. It still features two huge, double-flued fireplaces fitted with bake ovens and drains, and a servery hatch can be seen alongside the doorway. The tower's upper story has two chambers; the one with an elaborate fireplace and windows with stone seats may have been used to house the clerk of the kitchen.[37]

Just west of the kitchen tower are the scant remains of the pantry and buttery, which

The plain fireplace in the basement of the kitchen range at Old Wardour Castle shows scorching from years of use.

were not added until the mid–1500s. The three-story pantry, now largely identifiable only by its exterior wall, has several windows. The well is located in the courtyard nearby. A passageway once extended past the pantry into the eastern end of the great hall, alongside of which the end wall of the buttery, originally a two-story-high structure with residential chambers on the upper level, still displays the three-door serving arrangement discussed earlier.

One of the more unusual kitchen arrangements survives at "Old" Wardour Castle, built by John, fifth Lord Lovel, in the late fourteenth century. The four-story, hexagonal keep-like structure that forms the core of the site still encloses the central courtyard, from which several doorways led to staircases which in turn led to the upper levels. From one of the doorways, visitors can explore the enormous kitchen block, which filled the ground floor and much of the first story with several huge fireplaces, bread ovens, walk-in cupboards, sinks, and drains that led to storage cisterns in the basement. The pantry and buttery were located between the kitchen and the ornate great hall, which covered the area immediately over the main entrance. The well formed the central feature of the courtyard. In 1643, during the English Civil War, Henry, third Lord Arundell and heir to the property (Sir Thomas Arundell had purchased the site in 1547), besieged the stronghold and brought down the rear walls. Even so, the site remains a fascinating example of a late medieval fortified residence.

During much of the early history of castle building, servants slept on the floors of the chambers where they worked, whether it was in the kitchen or stables. At some castles, the lords slept in the hall with their resident soldiers and servants, who slept on rush-covered floors. It was also common for personal attendants to sleep in the chambers of the lord and lady on a straw pallet or bench. As elsewhere in the castle, bedchambers were sparsely furnished, and visitors frequently had to bring their own bed linens and other items. Lockable wooden chests bound with iron held clothing and other personal items, including valuables. Wooden pegs known as "perches" were used to hang clothes. Sometimes, an antechamber known as the wardrobe was positioned alongside the main bedrooms to store clothes conveniently.[38]

Beds were reserved for the higher status members of the household. They consisted mainly of a wooden frame with leather straps laid crosswise, upon which a feather mattress, pillows, coverlets, linens, and even clothes were laid to create warmth as well as comfort.[39] Linen curtains hung from the ceiling or from railings situated around the bed also helped keep out the chill and give residents a sense of privacy.[40] Chamber pots near the bed allowed occupants to avoid the long, drafty walk to the latrine and its cold stone or wooden seats. Besides the bed, the only other furniture included one or two chairs, a bench, and stools.

During the thirteenth century, privacy became a prized commodity and another symbol of the social distinctions between classes within the castle. As lords began to travel less frequently from estate to estate, castle households began to include the families of servants or higher status residents, each of whom expected to have their own private quarters. As a result, the number of separate residential chambers expanded to accommodate them. They were located in ranges around the inner bailey, in mural towers, and, as mentioned previously, in the keep or gatehouse.

Many castle-builders turned to the quadrangular plan for just this purpose.[41] Not only did the lord and his family occupy their own private apartments, but with the new design, members of the household staff and their families could also reside in individual blocks of chambers, which lined each of the four sides of the inner courtyard created by the four interlocking walls. During the fourteenth and fifteenth centuries, the trend towards comfortable living quarters, equipped with fireplaces and latrines, became entrenched in castle architecture[42]; they were an accepted — and expected — way to visibly demonstrate one's affluence and prominent social status.

Indeed, the form and ornamentation of a castle's windows, fireplaces, and even the walls, symbolically communicated that the owner was a man of cultural sophistication who also had enough financial resources to purchase special stone and to employ specialist craftsmen needed to carve and install the finished products. Generally speaking, the largest and most ornate windows and fireplaces (with the exception of the kitchen) were located on the upper stories of towers and other structures, partly because the primary domestic chambers were on those levels and partly for defensive reasons. Placing smaller windows on the lowest stories lessened the opportunity for an intruder to gain access. So did the iron grilles that covered the exterior of the windows.

Glass was a rare commodity at many castles, not because the windows could not accommodate glass, but because of the sheer expense of manufacturing it. Consequently, those lords who could afford to purchase glass often used it only in the chapel. In fact, it was not until late sixteenth century, when England became a popular market for glass, that many castles (then on their way to becoming grand palaces rather than military structures) acquired huge windows.[43] Before then, it was not unheard of for a lord to remove the glass panes from his windows and take them with him on his journeys around the countryside. In general, only the great halls in the castles of the monarchy and the wealthiest lords contained especially large, glazed windows; they were often decorated with brightly painted floral designs and heraldic emblems and flanked by stone seats. Most castle windows are now open to the elements; even so, some retain fragments of their original carved dressings and painting, so when exploring a castle be sure to look for these features. During the Middle Ages, residents used wooden shutters secured with drawbars, parchment (oiled sheepskin or goatskin[44]), or thin sheets of horn[45] to help keep out the chill, wind, and rain.

In addition to plain slots, the inner end of which splayed to allow more light into rooms on the lower stories, window forms commonly included: the lancet, a narrow frame with a pointed arched head; the trefoil, the top of which was shaped like a three-leaf clover; the quatrefoil, the top of which was shaped like a four-leaf clover or was circular and contained four enclosed foils (lobes); and the oriel, a bay window supported by corbelling, sills, or brackets. Skillfully carved, or dressed, stone, such as Caen limestone imported from France, was used to outline window frames and enhance the decorative effect. Using imported stone greatly increased the expense of completing the windows, but the practice was considered well worth the investment, for it both enhanced the appearance of the castle and, yet again, demonstrated the lord's lofty status. When visiting a ruined castle, particularly one in fragments, notice the design of the windows, for they can provide clues to their function of the chamber they lit and the status of the people who used them.

Likewise, the presence of fireplaces can reveal much about the chamber and the resident's status. In fact, not all chambers were equipped with fireplaces. Consequently, many residents had to make do with finding warmth in the kitchen or great hall or by carrying a portable heater, a brazier, with them to warm the bedroom at night. At times, rooms without fireplaces, such as the guardrooms and servant quarters, could be warmed by heat gener-

Many kitchen fireplaces had tiles or brickwork set in a herringbone pattern which reputedly helped strengthen the back wall and disperse the heat from the fire.

Chimneys were a crucial innovation that resulted in the use of fireplaces instead of central hearths, which vented smoke out an opening in the roof.

ated from the rear of a fireplace in the adjoining room.[46] In the late eleventh century, builders began to shift the hearths from the center of the primary chambers to external walls. To vent the smoke, they constructed simple flues with two loopholes that opened to the outside just a short distance above the hearth itself.[47] Interestingly, the rears of many early fireplaces, such as at Colchester and Canterbury, were laid in a herringbone pattern, which reputedly strengthened the wall and helped prevent cracking from the heat of the fires.[48] Later, tile, brick, or red clay was used to line fireplace backs and hearths; their scorched remains are vivid reminders that real people once used the structures for heat and to cook meals in a world devoid of our modern comforts. In the early twelfth century, castle owners began to upgrade their fireplaces, modifying the jambs into small columns and adorning the lintels with carved chevrons and other symbols,[49] some of which were brightly painted.

During the late thirteenth and early fourteenth centuries, fireplaces acquired projecting hoods and more functional, vertical flues which rose to rooftops where they vented into chimneys.[50] Oftentimes, fireplaces on different levels used the same flue, which was built into the thickness of the walls. During the sixteenth century, castle builders increasingly used chimneys and chimney pots not only to lengthen the flue and improve the removal of smoke[51] but also as decorative devices. Fine examples from this era dot the tower tops and battlements at Framlingham Castle and, later, became a common feature of Elizabethan architecture. Chimneys were embellished with flamboyant designs and unusual cylindrical, polygonal, or square shapes, used brick, terracotta, or metal for the chimney pots, and often arranged them in clusters for heightened dramatic effect. Inside the castle, fireplace hoods colorfully showcased the owner's heraldic pedigree with carved, gilded, and painted artwork and often depicted scenes and figures from classical mythology and the Bible.

Chapels were essential to castle life. Not only did they provide space for daily religious devotion, but they also displayed the owner's piety. Some chapels were erected in special chambers inside towers, and others occupied separate buildings located alongside the castle walls. The chapel at Farleigh Hungerford, shown here, features an underground crypt with lead coffins.

Displays of religious devotion were a critical aspect of castle life, regardless of the strength of that piety. Virtually every castle, at least those built of stone, contained a chapel.[52] Some were located in the keep or in a tower, particularly when space was already limited; others were freestanding or situated in the forebuilding. Many chapels were quite substantial, very ornate, and often featured Caen stone; others were modest chambers. Some chapels stood two stories high, the uppermost level reserved for the lord and his family, who entered from their private chambers, and the lower level for servants. The castles of the greater lords and the monarchy were often fitted with several chapels: Caernarfon had at least four — and possibly as many as seven — private chapels. Even though it was rare for a lord to construct an entire church within the walls of his castle, it did happen. Windsor Castle not only has its share of private chapels, but it also contains arguably England's most impressive freestanding chapel dedicated to St. George, which is akin much more to a cathedral but is characterized as a collegiate church. At Warkworth Castle, the Percys had the option of worshipping in their two-story private chapel inside the great polygonal keep or to attend mass in the now heavily ruined chapel alongside the great gatehouse in the outer bailey. However, it appears that, for Henry, Lord Percy, even two chapels were insufficient to tend to the religious needs of castle residents, and he began construction of a collegiate church about midway between the inner and outer baileys. Unfortunately, only foundations survive of the cruciform building, which was never completed. Still stretching across almost the entire breadth of the bailey, enough masonry survives to reveal the magnitude of the project.

Constructing and furnishing a chapel was an expensive undertaking, so it is not surprising that many lords chose to build their castles close to a parish church or to employ the parish priest to say daily morning mass at the castle. Even today, one of the best ways to find a castle is to locate the parish church, many of which are in much better condition due to their ongoing use over the centuries. For example, Sir Thomas Hungerford built his fourteenth-century fortified residence, Farleigh Hungerford Castle, alongside the parish church of St. Leonard. When his son, Sir Walter Hungerford, expanded the castle, he enclosed the church within its walls and it became the castle chapel. Hungerford then ordered the construction of a new parish church, also dedicated to St. Leonard, about one-half mile to the south. The fascinating chapel features well-preserved wall paintings, several noteworthy tombs, and a basement level crypt containing eight lead coffins dating to the mid-sixteenth century.

Many priests (chaplains) actually lived in a small chamber near a castle's chapel and used an antechamber to change into their vestments. Besides having charge of the chapel, the chaplain (or the chancellor, who had charge of the area containing the altar known as the chancel, in major castles) also performed clerical duties, which included keeping the lord's seal and writing important correspondence. Over time, this position evolved and additional clerical staff was placed under the chaplain's supervision. Some clerks ran errands, assisted with keeping the accounts, or took care of the vessels needed to conduct mass. Almoners dispensed alms and distributed leftover food to the poor.[53]

Nowadays, it is sometimes difficult to distinguish the chapel from other domestic chambers inside a ruined castle; however, a few simple but distinctive features can help visitors identify the important structure. Many chapels had an apse, a D-shaped end that projects outward beyond the curtain wall or the wall of a keep, as at Colchester Castle and inside the White Tower in London, which contains the marvelous Chapel Royal of St. John the Evangelist. Built from Caen stone transported from France, the exquisite two-story chapel was once decorated with paintings, had stained glass windows, and linked to the great chamber and the great hall. It is one of the finest examples of a Norman chapel still in existence in England. When only the foundations of a castle chapel survive, often the survival of the apsidal end can help visitors identify the structure as the chapel, as at Kenilworth, where the remains of the Chapel of St. Mary can be viewed in the outer bailey close to Leicester's stables.

One of the most unusual castle chapels survives in the inner bailey at Ludlow Castle. One of two chapels at the site, the Chapel of St. Mary Magdalene is a single, battlemented cylinder which looks more like a round keep than a chapel. Closer examination reveals a variety of distinctive features. Possibly inspired by the design of the Church of the Holy Sepulchre in Jerusalem, the ornate structure was actually the chapel's nave; the remainder of the chapel was demolished during the late seventeenth century, when Sir Henry Sidney made extensive changes to the castle. Possibly built by Hugh de Lacy or his rival, Sir Joyce de Dinan, in the early twelfth century, the building once also featured a 26-foot-long rectangular chancel, which reached all the way to the curtain wall. Even though Sir Henry made several alterations to the round nave, such as transforming a Norman-era window into a doorway and adding an upper story, much of the original chapel exists, including the Norman archway on the western door with its distinctive chevron pattern and the continuous arcading inside the building.

When considering whether a tower or a chamber in the keep that might have served as the chapel, look for the features that were vital to the performance of morning mass: the piscina (a basin-like depression which held water used to wash the priest's hands or clean the

The charming, freestanding round chapel in the inner ward at Ludlow Castle actually functioned as the nave of a larger structure. Of particular note are the battlements and Norman-era decoration, including zigzag carving on the main doorway.

vessels), a sedile (a stone bench or set of seats reserved for the priest), an aumbry (a wall cupboard used to store the vessels), and the altar (which often survives as a plain slab or a rectangular impression at one end of the chamber). Many times, only one of these items survives, but even on its own, it is a reliable indicator that an otherwise plainly furnished room served as the chapel. For example, the chapel at Carew Castle contains a fine vaulted ceiling, a piscina, and an aumbry in an otherwise plain chamber, which is situated between other plain chambers. The small chamber on the floor above may have been reserved for the lord to hear mass privately.

Latrines were normally incorporated into one or more of a castle's primary buildings or situated inside a separate tower close to the main living chambers. Some were fitted near the wall-walk or along the curtain wall for the convenience of patrolling soldiers. Also known as the garderobe, privy chamber, necessarium, jakes, gong, or draught (draft),[54] the latrine was commonly positioned at the end of a narrow, angled wall passage and frequently accommodated one or more individuals, as at Caerphilly Castle. Latrines are arguably one of a castle's most recognizable features: When exploring the inside of a castle, visitors will often stumble upon the small chambers hidden just off a passageway in the thickness of a wall; and, many are identifiable on the outer walls, as corbelled-out projections overhanging the curtain wall, as at Langley Castle, where the well-preserved garderobe tower still features twelve latrines, four on each floor, or as openings at the base of a tower or close to the base of a tower. Beaumaris Castle had unusual back-to-back latrines with doors and wooden seats, which were

Using the drafty, chilly latrine was one of medieval life's least favorite activities. The lower end of the chute usually opened outside the castle, often dumping the remains into the moat, where the flowing waters would push away the waste. At many castles, such as Conwy, shown here, the chute emptied onto exterior wall foundations or into the dry ditch, which necessitated human intervention to cleanse the spot.

placed periodically along the wall-walk. Interestingly, ventilation shafts rising from the basement level allowed air to circulate through these chambers.

Just like the well, castle latrines bring us into close contact with the real people who lived in a castle. We can readily relate to the discomfort medieval occupants must have felt sitting on a cold slab of slate or wood, the middle of which was nothing more than a gaping hole that opened over a dark, narrow — and quite chilly — shaft. Some latrines were equipped with narrow slots, which allowed daylight into the tiny chambers, but in many cases, users were required to carry their own torches to find their way. So, as mentioned above, during the night residents often preferred to use a chamber pot rather than scrambling to the drafty latrine. The lower end of many chutes dumped its contents into the moat or a stream that ran close to the castle and swept away the waste or into a cesspit at the base of a tower, which was periodically emptied and cleaned by a worker known as the gong farmer (or gang fermor) or a mudator latrinarum. However, it was not uncommon for latrines to empty into the ditch, as can be seen not only at Goodrich, where the huge latrine block in the eastern range still projects outwards on the eastern side of the castle. At sites such as Conwy Castle, the lower, outer ends of the chutes are visible; they dumped their contents onto the masonry walls and bedrock encasing the great fortress.

Iron bars (grilles) were often placed over the opening of the chute in order to prevent unwanted access. The notion of using the filthy shaft for anything other than human waste may seem distasteful, but the chutes were used to store the lord's treasure or as a convenient escape hatch. Indeed, the stone castle at Cilgerran was the scene of just such an event, when it was attacked by Owain ap Cadwgan, Prince of Powys, only a year after its construction in the early twelfth century. Having become enamored with Nest, the wife of owner Gerald de Windsor, who also served as the constable for Pembroke and Carew castles, Owain decided he had to possess the Welsh princess, who was also the daughter of Rhys ap Tewdwr. Before the enemy could gain entry into the castle, however, Gerald escaped down a latrine chute. (His wife awaited a different fate: Nest and her children were abducted by the Welshman, who was actually their kinsman. Owain's followers then plundered the castle, and Nest and her abductor soon embarked on a scandalous affair.)

During the Middle Ages, residents reputedly covered the seat openings with wooden doors to prevent the odor from escaping into neighboring chambers; some were closed with decorative covers, masonry screens, or grotesque masks, and even had wash-basins. The pungent aromas emitting from the latrine chute were said to have deterred moths from invading clothing hung in or close to the latrine; hence its association with the cloakroom or the wardrobe, which derives from the Anglo-Norman word, "garderobe," a word quite familiar to castle visitors. Sometimes, present-day visitors can identify the medieval latrine by the lingering smell.

Castle Ladies, Staff, and Soldiers

Today, ruins are often the only physical evidence we have of the existence of the people who actually lived out their lives in the relatively constricted (and often foul-smelling!) environment offered by castles. However, during the heyday of castle-building, a wide array of people besides the lord lived and/or worked in the buildings that stood in and around the inner bailey. It should be noted as well that, even though movies and books give the impression that castles were fully manned at all times with a permanent garrison, in reality only a skeleton crew of soldiers normally occupied most castles during peacetime. Members of the garrison included knights, squires, the porter or durward (mentioned earlier), guards, watchmen, and men-at-arms. Each soldier had his own role during an attack; for example, as crossbowmen, archers, lancers, or swordsmen.

Known in French as the "chatelaine" (or, the lord's wife), the lady of the castle spent much of her day overseeing the activities of the kitchen staff and keeping an eye on her sizeable group of spinners, weavers, and embroiderers, who not only kept everyone in the castle clothed but also offered companionship to the lady. Her primary companions were ladies-in-waiting, many of whom were noblewomen and wives of prominent lords, and chambermaids, who tended to her personal needs. The lord's wife often had complete charge of the castle when her husband was away on business at another estate or in service to the monarch; at times, she could find herself manning the battlements and leading the garrison against a besieging army.

A chatelaine could quite capably handle the responsibilities left to her while her husband was gallivanting around the countryside and particularly when she had sole ownership, for example during widowhood. Not only did they have the talent and knowledge to plan and carry out the defense of a castle against a siege, these women were also skilled administrators who ensured their workers did their jobs properly, managed the castle's accounts, and carried out other official duties without relying upon their husbands' guidance or permission to make decisions.

Some ladies also made long-lasting decisions about the repairs and construction of new buildings at their castles. For example, in 1327, Alina de Mowbray reacquired Oystermouth Castle after having spent several years in the Tower of London (her husband, John, had participated in a rebellion against King Edward II) and almost immediately began building a grand chapel block alongside the keep. The stunning three-story rectilinear structure still dominates the inner bailey, its square turrets projecting into the inner ward. For a time, the basement served as a kitchen; it contains the remains of a fine fireplace. Though similar to the basement in plan, the first floor chamber held more lavish furnishings, including a large, round-backed fireplace, a garderobe, and several ornate windows, which were once secured with shutters. The chapel itself featured lavish tracery windows rimmed with special stone dressings and carved pieces brought from nearby Neath Abbey. Today, the interior is a shell, but it still features remnants of medieval painting, the remains of an aumbry and piscina, and vaulted recesses in the walls believed to have been used as confessionals.

Depending on the size of the castle and the wealth of the lord, his household staff (those whose primary duties were non-military) would vary in number and composition. The constable's counterpart inside the castle was the steward (from "sty-ward") or seneschal, the most important member of the household who managed the estate, supervised the rest of the staff, and directed events in the great hall. Wielding considerable power of his own, the steward had to know virtually everything that went on at the castle and the surrounding estates, so he also had to be skilled in accounting and legal matters as well as personnel management. In time, the steward's responsibilities became so overwhelming for one man to manage that the position was divided between two men: a steward of the household and a steward of estates.

In addition to the steward, other key members of the household staff included the chamberlain, the chancellor, the chaplain, the keeper of the wardrobe, and the butler (or bottler). Their subordinates were kitcheners, cooks, bakers and baxters, brewers, tapsters, scullions, larderers, poulterers, fruiterers, slaughterers, pantlers, chandlers, washerwomen (laundresses), waterers, cellarers, ewerers, and dispensers. Carders, fullers, dyers, tailors, shearmen, and walkers all worked with cloth and clothing.[55] Perhaps the most distasteful jobs at any castle were those of the gong farmers (or gang fermor), whose main task was to empty and clean the latrine and remove human waste from the castle, and the cup bearers, who had the dubious privilege of tasting drinks for impurities.

Stewards commonly lived in the best servant quarters, sometimes occupying tower chambers. Speculation exists that the square tower in the outer bailey at White Castle may have housed the steward, or perhaps a quartermaster responsible for troops and supplies while they were occupying the outer bailey. The upper floor of the tower, which is part of the outer curtain wall, held a small lodging with a fireplace and private latrine.[56] At Raglan Castle, the steward's quarters were probably located in the so-called Closet Tower, which occupied the southeastern corner of the gatehouse range, near the Pitched Stone Court. The kitchen tower, pantry and buttery, and other servants' quarters were located around this courtyard. From the Closet Tower, the steward had easy access to the structures in the bailey and to the adjoining great hall. Many castle workers, on the other hand, lived in their own houses just outside its walls. At Warwick, for example, both sides of the River Avon on the northeastern side of the castle site are lined with Tudor-era brick and half-timbered houses, many of which were once occupied by the earl of Warwick's servants.

Terminology in This Chapter

Almoner: The clerical worker responsible for charity and ensuring that the poor received alms and leftover food collected from the castle.

Antechamber: A small chamber or vestibule positioned before a larger chamber, such as the lord's audience chambers, in which a person might wait for the lord to receive him or her.

Apron wall: A low-lying wall girding a building, constructed to provide additional defensive protection.

Apartments: The private chambers of the lord, and, at times, of his most important guests.

Apse: (1) The D-shaped or semicircular side of a chamber which projected outwards from the main line of a building; (2) a D-shaped chamber traditionally placed at the eastern end of a church and often projecting outwards from the end of a chapel.

Arrow loops: Another name for arrowslits, generally applied when the base end is rounded. See Chapter 2.

Ashlar: Neatly trimmed, rectangular building stone having a flat cut surface and square edges. Normally applied to outward-facing walls, particularly on the exteriors of keeps and gatehouse towers, they presented a smooth appearance and enhanced the visual appeal of the structure.

Attiliator: The skilled laborer who crafted crossbows.

Audience chambers: Grand chambers specifically designated for the lord or monarch to formally receive guests.

Aumbry: A mural cupboard used for storing valuables, such as sacred vessels and the priest's vestments, typically associated with the castle chapel. When the function of a chamber is difficult to identify from its ruined condition, the presence of an aumbry provides reliable evidence of use as a chapel.

Bailey: The defended courtyard or ward of a castle; open area enclosed by the castle walls. See Chapter 1.

Bakehouse: A purpose-built structure in which the baking of bread and other items occurred. Not every castle had a bakehouse. Most are now little more than ruined foundations.

Baker: An essential member of the kitchen staff who was responsible for baking bread and other items, using ovens in the kitchen or specially constructed bakehouses; also known as a baxter.

Barbican: See Chapter 2.

Barmkin: An area enclosed by a stone wall which provided a moderate degree of defensive support; normally associated with castles and tower houses in Scotland and northern England. Similar to a bailey.

Bastion: An open or solid projecting structure, a turret or tower, placed at a corner or along the wall of a fortification to act as a firing platform from which to defend a castle and also cover dead ground. Normally no higher than the curtain wall, they were often solid rather than filled with chambers.

Battlemented: Fitted with battlements. See Chapter 2.

Baxters: An alternate word for a baker.

Bottlery: See buttery.

Brazier: A portable heater used for warming rooms without fireplaces, in which charcoal or wood was burned to produce heat.

Brewer: The laborer who worked in the brew house, where ale was produced for daily consumption.

Butler: Responsible for the cellar and in charge of large butts and little butts (bottles) of wine and beer. Subordinates might include brewers, tapsters, cellarers, dispensers, cup bearers, and dapifers.

Buttery: The "bottlery"; the storeroom where wine and other drink were dispensed from barrels, usually located between the hall and the kitchen and adjacent to the pantry.

Buttresses, pilaster: A supportive structure which only partially projects outward from a wall; often a decorative feature.

Caen stone: A light-colored, creamy yellow, fine-grained limestone quarried in and transported from Caen, France; favored by William the Conqueror and used by the Normans in Britain and in France as special building material for both castles and churches.

Carboniferous limestone: A common building stone extensively used to construct castles. Formed during the Carboniferous period by the accumulation of shell and coral deposits, the limestone underlies much of England and Wales and parts of Scotland and Europe.

Carder: The worker who brushed cloth to free it of imperfections created during manufacture.

Castellan: See constable.

Cellarer: The servant who tasted the wine for impurities and was responsible to the steward for the activities performed by kitchen staff.

Chamberlain: Responsible for the great chamber, the lord's private chamber (and his confidences), and for overseeing the personal finances of the lord and his castellan; one of the most important members of the lord's staff. Over time, his responsibilities expanded to include collecting revenue in the lord's name. The Lord Chamberlain is still a key officer in the monarch's court.

Chamfer: A beveled face formed by cutting off the corner of a stone or timber structure; the plane formed when the sharp edge or angle of a squared stone block is cut away.

Chancel: The part of church or chapel containing the altar.

Chancellor: The household official or secretary responsible for the chancery and for writing letters and charters on behalf of the king or lord; the role evolved into one of the monarch's most important advisors. In Britain, the Chancellor of the Exchequer now serves as a member of the prime minister's cabinet and is responsible for the nation's finances.

Chancery: The medieval high court which presided over cases of common law and equity; the chancellor's court or office.

Chandler: The person tasked with making candles.

Chantry: A small, private chapel endowed by a patron so that prayers and chants will be said on his behalf.

Chapel: The castle chamber where the lord and his family attended services on a regular basis; smaller, secondary chapels sometimes offered services to the household and other residents. Often identifiable by their fine windows or the presence of a piscina, aumbry, and/or sedile, individual chapel towers graced many castles.

Chaplain: The cleric or priest — a member of the castle staff — who provided spiritual welfare for the lord, his household, laborers, and garrison, and otherwise tended to the chapel. On occasion, he also supervised building operations, functioned as a clerk, and kept castle accounts.

Chevron pattern: The zigzag design typically associated with Norman-era architectural decoration.

Chimney: Hollow aperture that guides the venting of smoke and other fumes from a fireplace to the outside, from the kitchen, great hall or domestic quarters; originally a simple opening in the ceiling which acquired mechanisms, such as flues, and attached them to or embedded them in the walls supporting the fireplace; often elaborately carved chimneys adorned rooftops.

Cistern: Stone-lined containers that collected and stored rainwater, generally located in the inner bailey or within the kitchen block.

Clerestory: The upper level of a Norman church positioned just beneath the roof, containing slender, clear windows; the "clear story."

Clerks: The person who worked with the priest, and, among other tasks, checked material costs and wages and kept accounts.

Cobbler: The laborer who made shoes; also known as a cordwainer.

Constable: The constable or governor of the castle who managed all aspects of castle administration, as well as its contents and facilities in the lord's absence; often occupied the lord's chambers or his own residence over the gate passage.

Cooks: Workers who roasted, broiled, and baked food in the fireplaces and ovens.

Cooper: The worker who made barrels.

Corbel: A projecting stone (or timber) feature on a wall used to support an overhanging parapet, stone platform, turret, or timber beams. At many castles, decorative corbels were positioned on the top of a tower or gatehouse and formed the bases for machicolations.

Courthouse: The purpose-built structure inside of which the lord's court took place.

Cross-wall: A simple but vital structure erected to create a barrier between two chambers or across two areas of the castle.

Crypt: A basement level or underground chamber in a chapel or church used to hold tombs and graves, often of the lords whose castles stood nearby.

Cup bearer: Servant who tasted drinks for impurities prior to being served to the lord and his guests; he also kept drinking cups full during meals. Sometimes performed by a page.

Curtain wall: Arguably the castle's most valuable defenses, erected to enclose a bailey and protect the entire site; the stone wall featured sections of masonry which linked together or hung between two towers (like a curtain), the main gateway, and other structures. Adopted after the Middle Ages, the term refers to the segments of masonry that were built to fill in the spaces between neighboring mural towers. From the French word, "courtine."

Custodian: An alternate word for the constable.

Dapifer: The servant who carried the meat to the dining table.

Dispenser: Also known as a spencer, someone who distributes (dispenses) provisions.

Ditch: The dry moat; see Chapter 2.

Donjon: An alternate word for the great tower or castle keep; the word "dungeon" derives from this French word.

Dovecote: A medieval pigeon house created from bricks or cut stone, the interior of which was lined with pigeon holes used to breed doves and squab (young pigeons prized for the quality of their meat) for the castle food supply.

Draught: An alternate word for the latrine.

Drawbar: A sliding wooden or iron bar, which was moved into place to secure doors in a closed position. The holes into which they were inserted frequently survive in door jambs in the gate passage.

Drawbridge: See Chapter 2.

Durward: The porter or door-ward, responsible for opening and closing the main doors.

Dyer: The servant who dyed cloth in huge heated vats.

Earthworks: Ramparts or fortifications largely made from earth, including mottes and ringworks, enclosure embankments, prehistoric forts, and Anglo–Saxon Era dykes.

Engine-tower: A castle tower purposely built to support a siege engine, as at Criccieth Castle.

Ewerer: The servant who brought and heated water for the lord and his guests.

Fireplace: An enclosed area designed to contain a fire, often built into a wall with a chimneypiece or mantle projecting into the adjoining room. Used to heat a room or for cooking.

Flue: The space or aperture through which smoke and other fumes vented to the outside from the fireplace.

Forebuilding: A key defensive structure which guarded the main entrance to the keep. Projecting outward from the exterior wall, the building screened the entry point and protected the inhabitants from a direct attack.

Fruiterer: The servant responsible for the preparation and care of fruit items.

Fuller: The servant who shrank and thickened cloth fibers by wetting and beating the materials.

Gable: The triangular area formed by a high-pitched or sloping roof.

Gallery: (1) A long chamber or passageway, often positioned along the length of the curtain wall; (2) an elevated room used by the lord and his guests for sitting and socializing, which often offered fine views of the surrounding grounds or the inner bailey.

Garderobe: An alternative term for the latrine chute, privy, or castle toilet, originally a room to store personal items. The term derives from "wardrobe."

Garrison: The military component of a castle. In addition to the constable, a typical peacetime garrison might consist of less than ten men, depending on the size and status of the castle. Larger royal castles and lordship castles could easily function with between 20 and 100 men. Besides knights, men-at-arms, crossbowmen, and archers, support ranks included smiths, porters, and carpenters. In fact, small garrisons were quite capable of thwarting a siege.

Gatehouse: A complex building that protected the main entrance from assault using a variety of defensive mechanisms. See Chapter 2.

Glazier: Workers who cut and shaped glass for windows.

Gong: The latrine.

Gong farmer/gang fermor: The worker responsible for cleaning the latrine chute and removing human waste from the moat, ditch, or other areas of the castle.

Granary: A building used to store grain.

Great hall: The castle's social and administrative center; usually the largest and most lavish room in the castle; hallmarked by carved windows, giant fireplace hoods, and timber-beamed ceilings, heraldic emblems, and a raised dais.

Great tower: An alternate term for the keep.

Grille: An open-work iron grating used to secure a window or doorway.

Guardroom: Chambers specifically used by guards when on duty, commonly located in the gatehouse, often on either side of the gate passage. Some had arrowslits and other defensive devices, but often lacked fireplaces and latrines.

Hall: Often a secondary hall used by the garrison, servants, and residents of lesser status, or by the lord for family occasions when a banquet was not held. See great hall.

Hall-keep: An early version of the rectangular keep, which was shorter than it was wide and dominated by a large hall on the first story. The ground level often contained storage rooms.

Hammerbeam ceiling: The timber equivalent of a stone vaulted ceiling, often seen in great halls or churches, consisting of short horizontal and vertical beams which progressively distribute the weight of a roof across a wide, open area.

Hearth, central: An open fire in the center of a chamber, such as the great hall.

Heraldic emblems: Used to distinguish status, family, or political affiliations, originally sewn onto or otherwise attached to a uniform or armor, the "coat of arms." The emblems often adorn private chambers, fireplaces, or castle gatehouses.

Herringbone masonry: A defining characteristic of Norman-era architecture distinguished by flat stone or brick laid diagonally in mortar rather than horizontally; often arranged in a zigzag pattern resembling the skeleton of a fish.

High-pitched: A roof composed of two steeply sloped sides.

Hooper: An alternate word for a cooper; a barrel maker or maker of wooden tubs, whose main job was to make the hoops that prevented the barrels and tubs from collapsing.

Jakes: An alternate word for the latrine.

Joist holes: Holes cut into walls into which "joists," or horizontal timber beams, which were inserted to support flooring and ceilings; often the only indicators of the exact location of the beams, and, hence, the position of an upper story or ceiling.

Keep: A fortified, self-sufficient tower containing residential chambers. Throughout the medieval period, living in the keep or the dominant mural tower at a castle was a mark of status normally reserved for the lord and his family. From the earliest motte castles, with their timber towers or shell keeps, to the finest stone castles of the Middle Ages, the great keep most visibly distinguished its occupants from other castle dwellers. Also known as the donjon or great tower.

Keep, shell: A stone ring wall encircling the top of a motte which held domestic chambers, the hall, and other facilities, and was used as a residence and an observation post.

Keeper of the wardrobe: One of the lord's closest associates, who tended to his clothing and was in charge of the tailors and laundress.

Kiln: An oven-like structure used to burn lime for use as a component of mortar or to process corn and other grain for brewing.

Kitchen block: Consisting of the main kitchen, buttery and pantry, inside of which all the cooking and food preparation occurred prior to delivery into the great hall, which was usually situated in the adjoining or nearby building. By the late thirteenth century, the three structures were deliberately constructed as a single unit. In many ruins, the arrangement can be identified by the presence of a trio of doorways, a central service door flanked by two others, which led to and from the buttery and pantry. Timber kitchens did exist, but posed a considerable fire risk. Early kitchens had central hearths but, in time, they were replaced by fireplaces, which were built into the curtain wall or into an inner wall. The presence of an oven or large fireplace often pinpoints the location of the castle's kitchen.

Kitchener: A kitchen servant or cook, who also oversaw the serving of food.

Lancet-head: Windows comprised of narrow openings topped with pointed arches, commonly associated with the castle chapel or great hall.

Latrine: Commonly positioned at the end of a narrow, angled mural passage or inside a tower specifically built for that purpose, the latrine consisted of a round hole in the center of a stone seat or wooden, through which human waste dropped. Also known as a garderobe, privy chamber, draught, jakes, necessarium, or gong.

Laundress: The woman in charge of cleaning clothing, linens, and other cloth items.

Louver: An opening in the roof of the hall or a turret which let smoke escape from a central hearth.

Machicolated: Adorned with machicolations.

Machicolations: A series of corbelled openings projecting outwards from the tops of gatehouse or towers, believed to have allowed defenders to safely toss missiles or water down onto enemies or fires below. They also created an ornamental effect, which is commonly associated with castles.

Menagerie: Comparable to a private zoo, where wild and exotic animals were kept by the monarch; often presented as gifts from other monarchs.

Mill, horse: The structure inside of which corn and wheat were ground into flour using the power of horses to move the grinding stones.

Minstrel's gallery: A balcony located at one end of the great hall, inside of which seated musicians entertained the lord and his guests; often situated above the screen and elaborately decorated.

Mint: The structure inside of which coinage was produced.

Motte: See Chapter 1.

Mural chamber: Rooms located within the thickness of a wall, normally situated inside a tower and occasionally within the curtain wall.

Mural tower: Towers positioned along the curtain wall.

Nave: The main or central part of a church or chapel with seating for attendees; normally flanked by aisles.

Necessarium: An alternate word for latrine.

Newel stair: The spiral staircase.

Open-gorged: Towers with open backs or where the upper level was enclosed with timber planks.

Oriel: A large, projecting, curved or polygonal window supported on corbels.

Oubliette: The windowless pit prison, often shaped like a slender cylinder, the only entrance into which was a trapdoor in the ceiling. Prisoners and food were lowered with ropes or baskets into the oubliette from the room above. The name derives from the French word "oublier," meaning "to forget." Also known as a bottle dungeon.

Oven: Usually circular or ovate in design and located in the kitchen or a bakehouse, a feature used for baking bread or heating sand and missiles fired by the siege engines. The presence of an oven at a ruined site is often the only indicator that a kitchen or bakehouse stood on the spot.

Page: The servant who made beds, ran errands, and at times acted as the cup bearer.

Paneling: A decorative wall or door feature comprised of wooden squares, or panels, often with carved designs.

Pantler: The servant who managed the pantry.

Pantry: The service room where bread and other foods were prepared for serving to diners in the hall.

Parliamentarian: Supporters of Parliament and the New Model Army against King Charles I during English Civil War in 1640s. One of the most important was Oliver Cromwell, who became Lord Protector after the final victory of the Parliamentarians over the Royalists.

Piscina: A stone basin with drain holes used by the priest to wash his hands or sacred vessels before or after saying mass. Often set in a niche in the chapel wall. Nowadays, used to identify otherwise ruined chambers as castle chapels.

Plaster: A building material consisting of a mixture of lime and water and other substances such as sand, used to smooth over and seal walls or ceilings in castles and medieval houses; the resulting white color gave some castles their names (for example, the White Tower at the Tower of London, and White Castle in Wales). Oftentimes plastered interior walls were brightly painted with heraldic emblems, human figures, or historical scenes.

Plinth, battered: Projecting stone platforms upon which keeps or wall towers were raised to prevent undermining; the bases sloped inwards and upwards.

Porter: The individual tasked with opening and closing the main doors; also known as the door-ward or durward.

Postern gate: See Chapter 2.

Poulterer: The servant responsible for preparing and tending to the castle's poultry and eggs; a poultry dealer.

Priory: A monastic community administered by a prior.

Prison: Generally associated with the castle dungeon, the prison was a chamber in which hostages were kept until ransom was paid or until other arrangements were completed. Not all prisoners were executed, and many were kept under house arrest. Often located in a chamber in the gate passage, so that the guards could keep a close watch on the prisoners and prevent them from gaining access to the interior of the castle.

Privy chamber: An alternate term for latrine; also used to describe a private chamber or apartment in a royal residence, where the realm's most important advisors met with the monarch.

Quadrangular castle: A late medieval development in castle-building featuring a roughly square plan, towers at the corners, and a main gatehouse.

Quatrefoil: A four-lobed or four-leaved design associated window tops but also as the plan for a few great towers or keeps, such as Clifford's Tower in York.

Ringwork: See Chapter 1.

Roofing: Castle roofs were timber-framed, covered with various materials, including wood, thatch, oak shingles, slates, flagstone, and clay tiles. Because shingles burned easily, many castle builders increasingly chose lead, slate or tiles for roofing. Although expensive, lead was durable and could withstand water and wind. Lead roofs were later stripped away, to be melted for use during battles and for other purposes. Sometimes an undercoating of sand helped dissipate the heat radiating from a lead roof.

Royalists: Supporters of the monarchy.

Sacristy: Normally adjoining the castle chapel, the sacristy was a room used to store sacred vessels and the priest's vestments. The unusual sacristy at Kidwelly Castle is located in a turret attached to the chapel tower.

Sapper: A miner or underminer. See Chapter 2.

Sconce: A wall bracket used to support a burning candle for lighting a passageway or chamber.

Screen: A narrow partition or wall positioned at the lower end of the hall to discreetly obscure the noisy activities occurring in the neighboring pantry and buttery; often situated beneath a minstrels' gallery, erected with stone or timber, and decorated with bright colors.

Screens passage: The passageway between the great hall and the service rooms, which were separated from each other by a screen.

Scullions: Servants responsible for washing and cleaning items in the kitchen.

Sedile: A stone seat or bench designated for use by the priest. Normally positioned on the southern wall of the chapel, it is usually easy to identify if it survives.

Seneschal: The steward.

Servants' quarters: Servants often slept on the floor or on benches in the rooms where they did their daily work. Higher status servants, such as the steward, often had their own living chambers. In time, some castles contained a specific cluster of rooms or a portion of a tower designated for the servants.

Servery hatch: An opening through which food and other items could be placed or removed to be passed between levels in a tower.

Service block: The pantry and buttery, which together normally stood adjacent to the kitchen, so that food and drink could be prepared and quickly delivered to diners in the nearby great hall.

Shearman: Workers who trimmed cloth during its manufacture.

Shutters: Movable wooden devices for sealing crenels, windows, and other wall openings which helped keep out rain and chill and could be slammed shut in case of an attack.

Slaughterer: The servant responsible for slaughtering livestock and preparing meat for storage, salting, or use in meals.

Solar: A chamber normally situated behind the dais-end of the hall, or on the level immediately above, to where the lord and his lady could retreat at the end of a meal or when tired of festivities continuing in the hall but close enough that they could keep aware of the goings-on occurring without them. The room probably acquired its name from its well-lit, traditionally south-facing position. Also known as the withdrawing chamber.

Spinster: A woman who earned her living spinning wool into yarn.

Spiral staircase: Normally positioned in special towers or corners of chambers, the winding staircases linked different stories. Also known as a newel staircase.

Splay: An aperture that widens as it progresses inwards, associated with windows, arrowslits, embrasures, or tower bases.

Springers: The portion of an arch, vault, or set of stones closest to the vertical column to which the arch or vault is attached. Sometimes carved with decorative features.

Squire: A position attained at the age of fourteen while training as a knight. A boy would be assigned to a knight to carry and care for his weapons and horse.

Steward (seneschal): The individual who managed the lord's estate, supervised the castle's household, and directed events in the great hall; arguably the most important person on the castle staff, with the exception perhaps of the constable. The term itself derives from "sty-ward."

Stockhouse: (1) A chamber similar to a prison which held the stocks, devices with boards used to lock prisoners' hands and feet into place, generally for minor crimes; (2) a chamber stocked with dishes, pots, utensils, and food supplies.

Tailor: The individual who cut and crafted clothing.

Timber-framed: A structure built with a basic timber framework, the areas between being filled with various materials, such as wattle and daub, plaster, or brick; at times the timber beams were left exposed to view.

Tower house: Privately fortified residences structurally similar to the rectangular keep, sometimes known as castles of enceinte, most commonly associated with the Scottish border region. See Chapter 2.

Towers: See Chapter 2.

Tracery: Decorative stonework commonly associated with the windows of a great hall or castle chapel.

Treasury: The structure or chamber where the monarch's or lord's most important valuables were stored.

Trefoil: Windows containing three foils, or lobes; three-lobed or three-leaved.

Trestle: A type of dining table with a horizontal beam (the tabletop) and vertical legs forming a framework, which could later be disassembled to provide space in the great hall.

Turret: See Chapter 2.

Twin-towered: Describing a gatehouse with matching drum towers flanking either side of the gate passage

Undercroft: A plain chamber positioned underneath a medieval house or castle, most often barrel-vaulted and used as a storeroom.

Undermine: See Chapter 2.

Unglazed: Windows lacking glass.

Vaulting: An arched ceiling or roof, usually of stone; types of vaulting include barrel vaults, ribbed vaults, and groined vaults.

Vestibule: An antechamber, entrance room, or lobby area positioned before a larger chamber, where arriving guests would wait to be beckoned into the next room, often the great hall or great chamber.

Wainscoting: A type of wooden paneling applied only to the lower portion of a wall, originally used to protect the wall from rising dampness.

Wall-walk: See Chapter 2.

Ward: The bailey or courtyard.

Warden: The individual responsible for the activity in the forest.

Washerwoman: See laundress.

Watergate: See Chapter 2.

Weaver: A worker who cleaned and compacted cloth, and also wove wool into clothing or for other uses.

Well chamber: A small, often round-topped stone shell built to enclose or cover the opening of a well.

Wellhead: The opening of a well, usually in the inner ward, in a well tower, or in the keep.

4

The Manorial Estate

In Chapter 1, we touched on the importance of taking note of a castle's physical location and assessing why builders chose a particular site to erect a castle. In this chapter, the functional relationship between a castle and its surroundings will be examined in greater detail, for every castle was much more than a structure. It was also the administrative center and focal point of an estate, sometimes several estates, which together formed a manor, or a manorial estate. The surrounding lands were farmed and occupied by the peasantry and used as a resource for food and entertainment by the lord and his guests. The land also gave the castle its monetary worth.

Contrary to what we might think today, castles were actually considered to have no value — the surrounding estates gave them monetary worth and gave the lord an income. In 1349, the inquest after the death of Hugh, Lord Despenser, determined that the mammoth castle at Caerphilly had no value "except for reprises and general maintenance costs, though fish from the lakes around it yielded 6s, 7d annually,"[1] and it reverted to the Crown, which continued to use the stronghold well into the fourteenth century. In some ways, the medieval castle was merely the physical manifestation of a much larger enterprise, functioning throughout much of the year, particularly in peacetime, as a great house and administrative center rather than a fortified building built to withstand seizure by covetous enemies. The manorial estate hubbed by a castle teemed with activity, the produce from which could be used to pay rent, to entertain honored guests, or to sell to the highest bidder. Whereas feudalism established lordships and divvied up the landscape in exchange for political and military favors, it was "seignorialism," the separate but intimately associated system better known as manorialism, that enabled a lord (as a tenant-in-chief or landlord) and his tenants to make their living, dominate an area, and establish reputations as men of substance and status.

It is important to realize that references to the "lord" of the manor — or of a castle, for that matter — should be understood to mean the landholder or landlord; the use of the word does not necessarily specify noble or political status of the individual. The majority of these men were petty or lesser lords, including knights and members of the gentry, rather than titled lords (members of the peerage), as we know the term. Their castles or manor houses not only showcased their political clout and social achievement, they were also used in a very direct way to keep these men financially afloat. Even though many manor houses were fortified to some degree and several, such as Bodiam, Kirby Muxloe, and Weobley, are still called castles, most manor houses were never fortified; even fewer rivaled the true castles that are the subject of this book. However, "The vast majority of castles in the English countryside also functioned as manors, representing part of the machinery of rural lordship. Most castles were also the hubs of extensive and often scattered frameworks of estates and centers for the man-

4. The Manorial Estate

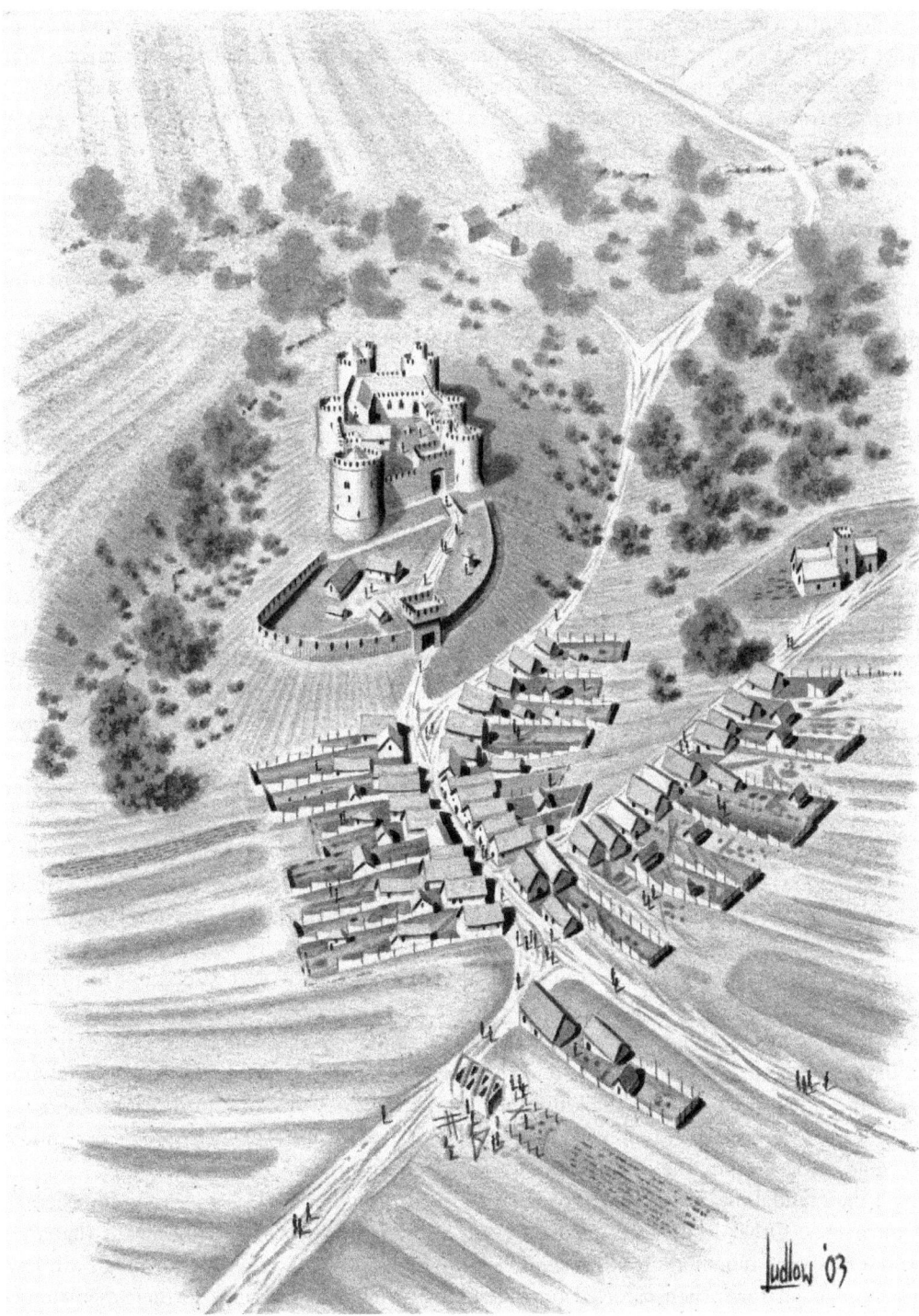

Narberth Castle dominated a steep-sided spur on the southern side of the town, around which a modern road still passes near the ruins and swings uphill past the main entrance. The view of the surrounding countryside was extensive, and visitors arriving at the castle from the south would have identified its gray masonry form from quite some distance away. Town, castle, church, and the landscape were closely associated (courtesy Neil Ludlow).

agement of a wide range of agricultural resources."[2] Even though nowadays we tend to consider castles in isolation from their environment or view them individually as vehicles from which to conduct or thwart a siege, during the Middle Ages they played a vital and ongoing role in the management and maintenance of the local economy, a role that arguably had greater impact on medieval life than the sieges they occasionally encountered.

Landownership and the Feudal Lord

As the Normans gradually took control over the British countryside in the years after the Battle of Hastings, King William I parceled out the land to various owners, including his primary supporters and to his son, during the decades immediately after 1066. William is said to have granted major landholdings, in fact about half of England, to some 200 tenants-in-chief, including most important Norman barons. Another 1,000 men held land worth more than £5, while some 6000 to 7,000 minor landlords held less than a hide of land,[3] an area of about 30 modern acres. Vast conglomerations of land such as the largest lordships, several of which were known as honors, were centered on a castle and its demesne holdings,[4] whereas smaller, more compact lordships, comprised of distinct estates known as fiefs, were largely carved from the existing landscape.

The ease of transferring land ownership from the Saxons to the Normans varied with the political situation, but, in many cases, the conquerors simply took over intact estates previously occupied by Anglo-Saxon leaders and shrewdly carried on the local customs and farming practices, managing the populace much as the English had done prior to the Conquest. They felt little need to create upheaval when the status quo was already working well. However, in some parts of the country, the new overlords chose to re-configure the boundaries, merge estates into huge holdings, and establish new, compact lordships, which they centered around castles in order to bolster their presence in a region or to shore up the defenses of vulnerable areas, such as along the coast, where an attack from Europe was always a possibility, and in parts of the country where native resistance still threatened to erupt, as in Yorkshire, where King William carried out his most devastating campaign against his new subjects, the Harrying of the North, in 1069–1070.[5] Today, Yorkshire is one of England's most heavily castellated regions; it is an ideal destination for exploring a variety of ruined but historically and architecturally significant castles.

In exchange for their fiefs — large or small holdings — and reaping the rewards that came with owning land, Norman lords paid formal homage, swore an oath of fealty, and owed military and other obligations to the king, including knight's service or ministerial service such as serjeanty. For example, rather than providing soldiers for military service, as was required of most castle owners, the de Turbervilles held the lordship of Coity by "serjeanty of hunting"; their feudal obligation was to provide a place for the Lords of Glamorgan and others to hunt game.[6] Other lords were tenants "by free socage," which essentially meant that they paid a rent with money rather than by providing men and equipment for the king's armies.[7] These men, in turn, then parceled out portions of their new holdings to their own subordinates, all of whom were freemen and political peers, through a process known as "subinfeudation," granting men of lesser status rights to hold and use smaller estates. These subordinates became vassals (tenants-in-fee) of the greater lords and owed them service, just as the greater lords were vassals of the monarch. Even though castles were typically erected on the most valuable landed estates,[8] they were also built where and whenever a lesser lord could afford to do so, partly as a way to emphasize his status and partly to meet the defensive needs of the times.

The feudal system just described was a political, military, and social system which bound men together in a relationship of mutual dependence based on personal loyalty that included the promise of faithful service in exchange for the opportunity to own and manage land — and the peasantry bound to it. The arrangement was in fact temporary, for the greater lord or the monarch always had the right to revoke that grant of land and seize the castle. It was only over the course of time that land ownership became hereditary, but even then the monarch could still confiscate it if properly provoked. The histories of individual castles are filled with periods of time when ownership reverted to royal custody, particularly during the minority of the heir but often as the result of a breakdown in the relationship between the king and the castle owner.

The Peasantry in the Manorial System

Whereas the doling out of lands was part and parcel of feudalism, the actual day-to-day work done on the lands, and the interdependent relationships that were forged to reap the benefits from that work, was not strictly feudal. Closely associated with feudalism, manorialism was a system also founded on mutual obligation; however, the key relationship was between a lord or a vassal, who controlled the manorial estates (the landlord) and lived in the castle or manor house, and the peasantry, who lived in traditional houses in neighboring villages and hamlets and worked the lord's lands, in addition to their own. A landlord might be the reigning monarch, an ecclesiastical lord such as a bishop or archbishop, a baron, or other member of the aristocracy.

Manorialism was an economic system whereby the peasants not only worked their own lands — and paid for the privilege of doing so — but they were also required to work the lord's land (the demesne) for a specific period of time each week (week-work) and also during special times of the year, such as the harvest (boon-work). Many peasants were also craftsmen, such as smiths or potters, and made items for sale at the local market. Many were required to labor inside the castle, making repairs to the main structure or the defensive outworks; this type of work would have been familiar to the Anglo-Saxons, who had a similar system in place before the Norman invasion. Some peasants became beekeepers or shepherds.[9] Peasants were required to pay rent in the form of money or payment in kind, which meant giving the lord a portion of their crops or other products. In return, in addition to leasing, or "farming out," their portion of their manorial estate (which could be farm fields or forestry lands) in exchange for a fee, the lord or tenant promised to provide their peasants with a measure of protection. The men who managed the lord's estates — the estate steward, reeve, and bailiff— were generally chosen from the peasantry.

The unofficial moral code of the times regulated the place of the peasant in society: Unlike the landed aristocracy, who were believed to have been born to fight, to keep the peace, and to protect the populace, peasants (the "laboratories"[10]) were born to work for all, to labor for the benefit of everyone else, who had innately superior status. As a result, the peasantry came to be viewed as bound to the land. When a lord or his wife sold an estate or manor, the local peasantry who worked the land was sold as well. Peasants were considered either free or unfree; both categories owed services to the lord, but, whereas freemen were able to sell their lands and move elsewhere, unfree peasants, the serfs, could not. In reality, serfs were bound to the land in an arrangement that passed from generation to generation; they were considered, in essence, a lord's property, but could not be sold separately from the land they tilled.

Serfs could be classified as villeins (villains, or villains), cottars or cottagers (who spent the majority of their time working demesne lands), or bordars (roughly the same as a cottar). However, by about 1180, the distinction between peasant classes became muddy, so those peasants who owed week-work and other service obligations collectively came to be known as villeins. The term derives from the French for "village dweller" and originally connoted free, landholder status. Villeins held their lands in "villeinage" and were categorized as servile in status.[11] According to the *Domesday Book*, compiled during the 1080s, only about 12 percent of the peasantry consisted of freemen or sokemen (who were required to attend the lord's court). Another 40 percent, by far the bulk of the peasantry, were the villeins, who held between 30 and 40 acres of farmland.[12] Over time, serfs were finally able to inherit or purchase the lands they worked. They also gained their freedom through manumission, a formal ceremony during which the lord released them from their bond. Manumission became increasingly common during the twelfth and thirteenth centuries.

Each manor was a self-sufficient unit made up of estates which were farmed or forested or used for breeding animals for food. Land was categorized as arable (for crops, ranging from wheat, barley, rye, oats, and corn to orchards and gardens), meadow (where hay was grown and harvested), parkland and forests, and waste, meaning land not usable for farming. In order to ensure the best and most efficient operation of the manorial estate, not only did each lord appointment officials to represent him and take care of managing his properties and the peasants who worked them, he or his representative also administered the manorial court, which kept the peasants in line and brought him additional income in the form of fines and other taxes.

In order to keep the lands they farmed, the peasantry was constantly subjected to a series of restrictions. If ignored, they might be summoned to the manorial court, which was normally held inside the great hall or in a specially designated chamber, and have fines imposed upon them. Some castles had separate courthouses within the curtain wall; many are now ruined shells, as at Pembroke Castle, their condition making them difficult to distinguish from other structures. At other castles, the court was held at the main gate, where nothing survives to indicate that such activities had occurred. Consequently, it is best to review the castle guidebook or wall plaques to determine if it once had a special structure for managing the manor's governmental affairs.

As mentioned above, the manorial system consisted of mutual relationships whereby the peasantry worked at least part-time for the lord, paying rent in the form of produce or money in exchange for working and living on their own parcels of land. Week-work services depended on the lord's immediate needs and could include making repairs to fences, to the castle itself, or to ancillary structures, such as a barn. Peasants were called upon to plow demesne lands, tend to the gardens, cut and collect corn, scour ditches, trim hedges, gather rushes, feed and care for the lord's livestock,[13] thresh and process grain, milk cows, shear sheep,[14] and do any other work that the lord demanded. These service obligations often interfered with the peasant's own livelihood, particularly during the harvest, when the lord required them for boon-work and took them away from harvesting their own crops to augment the "famuli," peasants regularly assigned to attend to the demesne full time. Angered about having to ignore their own land in favor of the lord's, oftentimes the peasantry would passively resist this obligation, for example, by working as slowly as possible without being obvious or by doing a poor job harvesting crops or making hay.[15] While doing boon-work, however, they were compensated for their labors with hearty meals and drink; for many, this gesture did not make up for the imposition foisted upon them by the lord.

Like other aspects of medieval lordship, the restrictions and obligations placed upon the peasantry were imposed in order to maintain a lord's control of an area and enhance his political clout, while at the same time filling his coffers. The duties were numerous, and often unreasonable, particularly at those times when the lord needed to raise additional funds for projects, such as warfare. For example, besides paying rent and working the demesne lands, peasants were forced to pay a huge fee known as multure to use the lord's mill. In fact, they were prohibited from building their own mills and would even be fined for having hand mills, known as querns, in their homes. Those peasants who took their grain to another lord's mill, where the fees were lower, could find themselves at the manorial court and heavily fined their transgressions.[16] Then, they were required to bake bread for their own consumption in the lord's specially constructed ovens.[17] They were also prohibited from taking fish from the lord's ponds without first paying a fee, from killing the lord's doves, which consumed the grains in their fields, and from hunting game in the lord's forests, which were exclusively reserved for the lord.[18] No matter the purpose, it was common for the lord's representative, normally the bailiff or reeve, to claim a ridiculously high fee for such matters.

By the late twelfth century, the task of ensuring that the peasants were meeting their weekly and seasonal obligations had become quite formidable. To deal with the situation, landlords began to appoint representatives, an estate steward, reeve, or bailiff, to directly manage the demesne estates. With the exception of the steward (or "seneschal"), the officials were usually chosen from among the men living in the local area, who would have had more skill and practical experience working the lands, knew what crops were the best choices given local conditions, weather and soil composition, and was on familiar terms with the other people who lived and worked in the manor. Typically a knight or lesser lord, the estate steward was often a member of the aristocracy who oversaw all of a lord's manors and usually represented the lord at the manorial court.[19] As the lord's primary representative, the estate steward had to know as much as possible about each manor, from its size and capacity to the names of the individuals who managed the estates in his place.

According to a treatise written by Walter of Henley in 1275, the qualities and responsibilities of the office of the steward included:

> (1) knowing the law of the realm, to protect his lord's business and to instruct and give assurance to the bailiffs who are beneath him in their difficulties
>
> (2) making rounds and visiting the manors of his stewardship, and then inquiring about rents, services, and customs ... and about franchises of courts, lands, woods, meadows, pastures, waters, mills, and other things which belong to the manor...
>
> (3) knowing how many acres there are in each field, and thereby to know how much wheat, rye, barley, oats, peas, beans, and dredge on out to sow in each acre....

and much more.[20]

The estate steward or his deputy presided over the manorial court (the "hallmote"), which was held periodically during the year and composed of a dozen local tenants or serfs, who were required to perform this service as part of their manorial obligation. The courts were used to preserve the rights of the lord and to settle disputes between tenants on the manor.

In addition to procedural matters and issues related to tenancy, the court dealt with a broad variety of offenses. At Conisbrough, where one of the realm's finest round keeps still dominates the ruined castle, the infringements ranged from bad plowing on the lord's land to allowing one's cows into the lord's meadow, breaches of the King's peace (for fighting, petty theft, and other public nuisances), eavesdropping, cutting timber without the lord's permission, illegally subdividing one's holdings, and improperly maintaining one's house or fences and walling.[21]

By the end of the thirteenth century, the rents paid by the English peasantry were at their highest point in over a century. Lords increasingly demanded money payments and imposed heavy taxes so that they could maintain their privileged positions within the realm. In all, conditions were becoming unbearable, and, in 1381, the peasantry finally had had enough. Led by Wat Tyler, John Ball, and Jack Straw, they rebelled on a scale never before experienced in England, and even stormed the Tower of London in protest of the taxes levied upon them. The Peasants' Revolt marked the beginning of the end of serfdom in England.

Besides the estate steward, each manor was managed by a full-time bailiff or reeve, who sometimes lived in the manor house or castle during the lord's absence,[22] and their assistant, the hayward, beadle, or messor, who were elected by other manorial tenants to perform these duties. In some ways, the bailiff's job was comparable to that of the steward, just done on a smaller scale. The bailiff generally managed a single manor or two, cautiously walking the estates to ensure the peasants carried out the policy established by the lord and his steward and reap the most profit from demesne lands.[23] In addition to deciding which crops to plant and what animals to breed,[24] the reeve typically supervised the progress of work throughout the day, ensuring the peasants were up early and at work on time, watching over the plowing, planting, harvesting, caring for livestock, and other activities in the fields, and making certain the manor house and its associated farm buildings and implements were in solid repair. He also maintained the demesne accounts, which detailed everything produced on the estates, and reported the results to the bailiff annually.[25] His responsibilities were tremendous, particularly on the largest estates, where demesne lands could cover some 200 to 500 acres of arable, forest, meadow, park, and waste lands, and some reeves took advantage of their position of power over fellow peasants by demanding higher rents and other dues. Visits by the steward or another representative of the lord, including official auditors, attempted to keep this abusive conduct in check.[26]

Exploring the Manorial Landscape

Understanding the manorial system and how castle estates were managed can help modern visitors interpret the landscape surrounding a particular castle and envision how it may have been used when the site was occupied during the Middle Ages. The present-day landscape obviously will not be the same as that farmed and lived upon centuries ago, as towns have expanded into cities and encroached on adjoining open areas, fields have been heavily plowed or built over so that archaeological features no longer survive, and forests have been decimated in the name of progress or necessity. Yet, traces of medieval agricultural lands and remnants of royal forests and parkland still cover the countryside; they frequently retain physical evidence of the medieval practices that produced an income and food for the lord and his household and also kept the peasantry employed. So, when heading to a castle site, be sure to scan nearby undeveloped hillsides and cleared or crop-free land for evidence of medieval farmland.

The sun shines on a field, emphasizing a ridge and furrow system that survives on an open hillside near ancient Grimspound on Dartmoor.

During the Middle Ages, open farmland on a lord's estate was divided into strips which were assigned to and cultivated by different peasant families. Portions of these fields remained the lord's and served as part of his demesne. The rest was allotted to the peasantry in exchange for rent and the other obligations discussed above. In order to ensure a fair distribution of good and poor land, peasants received strips which were scattered across the parcel of land being cultivated. Peasants might farm as many as 30 to 70 individual strips in the different fields. Each strip typically measured eleven yards wide and 220 yards long (a furlong).[27] The plowing process left behind distinctive, elongated, reverse-S-shaped markings, which are known today as ridges and furrows for their distinctive design. They are quite visible in the British landscape, particularly on hillsides or in areas where the sun produces the right type of shadows to emphasize their ongoing existence. The presence of ridge and furrow features frequently indicates a medieval date for a parcel of land. Even though many ridge and furrow strips are not directly associated with castles, when they are present in an area with castle remains, one can reasonably imagine that they were part of the manorial estates governed by that castle. Traces of ridge and furrow cultivation in an area without a castle can point to the site of a deserted medieval village that has yet to be unearthed by archaeologists.

A fascinating survival from the Middle Ages can be found at Laxton, a village in Nottinghamshire with a late-eleventh- or early-twelfth-century motte and bailey castle, which once centered a notable feudal estate. It also served as the administrative center of Sherwood Forest during the twelfth and thirteenth centuries. Besides the castle, medieval relics at Laxton include extensive ridge and furrow features, fishponds, and mill mounds, all of which were commonly associated with medieval manors. Other manorial features known to have existed at Laxton in the seventeenth century include dovecotes, a garden, and orchards. Interestingly, even though modern plowing has leveled the ridges and furrows in certain areas, three open fields are still farmed in strips; efforts are now being made to prevent the destruction of the features in the medieval landscape that are particularly well preserved.[28] Laxton remains one of the finest examples of its kind.

In addition to Laxton, medieval sites associated with ridge and furrow cultivation include both earth and timber and masonry castles, such as Dunstanburgh, Stapleton, Hen Domen, Raby, and Warkworth. At Raby and Warkworth Castles, the ridges and furrows are visible from the sites; at Raby, they actually run right up to the outer curtain wall. These lands were probably abandoned late in the histories of both castles, when they were transformed into palatial complexes.[29]

Arguably, the most important function of the manor was the production of food, which not only fed the lord, his household, and manorial staff, but also sustained the peasant community that was responsible for the cultivation of much of the manorial estate. Foodstuffs also provided the lord with an income from sales at local markets and an income from the rents and fines levied on the peasant population. Lastly, the conditions in which the food stocks were produced, whether by growing crops, milling grain, breeding livestock, doves or fish, or hunting wild game, were crucial to the display of an aristocratic lifestyle, for which castle owners aimed and were expected to emulate.

The presence of dovecotes, rabbit warrens, fishponds, or deer parks, the products from which set a very impressive banqueting table while also providing plenty of food to keep permanent residents fit and full, emphasized a lord's social posture and financial status. Because these structures were expensive to construct and to maintain, only wealthy men could afford them. Just seeing a domed dovecote in the countryside near a castle or manor house reminded medieval passersby that someone of considerable stature lived there. Today, such structures serve as reminders of the past and are reliable indicators that a medieval estate of considerable substance once occupied the site. Some medieval manorial structures, particularly dovecotes, are relatively easy to identify, even when ruined, whereas other buildings are little more than earthen bumps obscured by vegetation or eroded by plowing or wet and windy weather.

During the Middle Ages, four main types of mills were used to grind grain and were powered by a different source: With horses, by hand, with water, or with wind. Particularly difficult to distinguish from other ruins but in their day exceedingly important to the lord and his lordship, mills were a vital source of income for their owners, who, as mentioned above, had the legal right to force their subjects to use the structures or extract a fine from them if they ignored the law. Possession of a mill demonstrated a lord's superior status, just as his castle did. In fact, the two structures were often erected quite close to each other; the proximity bolstered the lord's control over the production, processing, and distribution of the crops that were grown on his demesne and adjoining lands, and was especially valuable in times of surplus.[30] Most mills were granted to millers, local peasants who received wages to operate the mill and collected fees on the landlord's behalf.

Since mills were typically constructed out of timber and thereby prone to rot or fire, today only their stone foundations survive. Generally rectangular in plan, the remains tend to look like any other ruined structure, and it often is only through historical documents and archaeological excavation that the original purpose can be identified. Even so, the existence of a ruined building on the perimeter of the outer bailey, particularly in locations near where land had been cultivated or where other medieval buildings, such as a granary or barn, have been discovered can indicate that it was originally used as a mill. Mills were only rarely erected inside the castle: for example, about midway along the central platform in the outer bailey at Caerphilly Castle, visitors will find an unusual set of steps leading downward into a basement level of the remains of a rectangular structure, which turns out to have been the corn mill. At Middleham Castle, horses were used to mill the grain that was then processed in kilns and transported to the brewhouse to be transformed into ale. As their name suggests, watermills were placed near water sources — including moats — which were used to generate power to turn the massive wheels.[31]

Royal castles regularly operated mills. The mill at Edward I's great concentric castle at Beaumaris was located inside a D-shaped turret strategically positioned immediately alongside the castle dock, which projected into the moat. The moat once connected directly with the Menai Strait, the waters of which still flow onward to the Irish Sea and Atlantic Ocean. A horse-mill stood in the Great Park at Windsor Castle, where four hand-mills (querns) also supported life inside the royal fortress.[32]

Remnants of medieval castle mills can be examined not only at Caerphilly and Beaumaris, but also at Manorbier Castle, where the rectangular foundations of a watermill sit at the base of the castle close to the remains of the medieval fishponds and dovecote. The present structure probably dates to the eighteenth century, but occupies the site of its medieval predecessor. At Hadleigh Castle, visitors can walk to the earthwork remains of a dam, which contained the pond that powered the now buried watermill that once ground wheat into flour in the thirteenth century. A medieval barn stands nearby. At Warwick Castle, the Victorian mill restored in 2002 probably stands on the site of its medieval counterpart. Even though it does not resemble the original mill, it gives visitors an impression of the physical relationship between castle and mill and how they would have worked together.

Mill sites can often be identified by the presence of a small, rounded mound, the center of which might be domed or contain a cruciform-shaped indentation, which once held the tree trunks that supported the mill's revolving central post.[33] Besides grinding grain for the food supply, mills were vital to the medieval iron ore industry, providing the power to flatten the ore for further use, and to the woolen industry, providing the energy for fulling, the process during which wool was cleansed, thickened, and strengthened.[34] Medieval fulling mills were typically powered with water, and, therefore, positioned near a reliable source such as a stream.

In addition to setting aside land for agricultural purposes, lords also divvied up their property in order to breed animals. Not all open grassland as one might assume, medieval deer parks contained substantial pockets of woodland. In addition to the breeding of deer, the land was also used for grazing, timber production, stabling and breeding horses, and keeping other animals. Just as during the Middle Ages, parkland in Britain now often forms the setting for the main approach to a stately residence, such as a castle or lavish home. Many of these vast open areas still function as deer parks (and as status symbols), although nowadays the deer are there primarily for visual enjoyment and to enhance the countryside atmosphere rather than for hunting or the regular provision of venison, which was once reserved for the lord's table.

Increasingly popular throughout the twelfth and thirteenth centuries, medieval deer parks were protected breeding grounds as well as regular venues for the lord's personal entertainment. Serving fresh venison to one's guests was yet another mark of lordly status, and hunting deer was both a favorite pastime and a necessary practice in order to have the valued meat.

Constructing and maintaining a deer park, which averaged about 250 acres, was a costly venture and required constant attention, a huge supply of timber and other materials,[35] and a variety of employees, such as huntsmen and larderers, who butchered and salted the meat.[36] Like crop cultivation, deer farming required skillful management in order to be effective; restrained within the parkland, deer were dependent on the care provided by estate managers for their survival.

In fact, the king was the accepted owner of all of the realm's deer, which included red, roe, and fallow deer (introduced by the Normans), and it was only he who could issue licenses to his vassals to establish their own deer parks.[37] During the decades shortly after the Norman Conquest, the number of deer parks increased from perhaps 20 to 30 to as many as 4,000, not all of which were in use at the same time. Of this total, Wales probably contained about 50 deer parks, while Scotland had another 80. Several castles, such as Barnard Castle, became centers of venison production.[38]

Needless to say, such parkland was highly prized not just by the aristocracy, but also by the peasantry, who trespassed on the lord's land in order to acquire the tasty meat for their own meals and to sell it on the black market.[39] Peasants caught poaching deer were brought before special courts; punishments could be quite severe. Consequently, most parks were enclosed by a pale, an earthen or walled embankment lined with ditches on both sides and topped with a fence or hedge; they were much like the ramparts that originally enclosed the baileys of earth and timber strongholds. Standing some eight to nine feet high,[40] not only did the pale keep out intruders, but it also restricted the movement of deer.[41] Today, it is possible to identify traces of the medieval pale, as at Kenilworth Castle, where several deer parks once occupied the land beyond the great mere west of the majestic red castle and beyond the Brays to the south.[42] In fact, nowadays visitors reputedly can still spot deer wandering in the woodland around the historic site, not too far from the interesting remains of Henry V's pleasance, or banqueting house.

Besides finding traces of the medieval pale, one of the best ways to recognize a medieval park is by the place name. Many castles, such as Fotheringhay, had more than one park, the smallest and closest of which was often known as the "little park" while the largest was called the "great" or "big" park. (It must be noted that this same naming process applies to other features in the manorial landscape, including fishponds: The "servatorium" was the "little pond" and the "vivarium" was the "great pond."[43]) It is likely that the little parks closest to castles were mainly used as venues for non-hunting entertainment, such as the staging of tournaments, or to beautify the grounds immediately outside the castle — at Fotheringhay Castle, the little park (which measured over 27 acres) contained orchards, gardens, and an attractive pond.[44]

Undoubtedly the best known medieval parkland survives at Windsor Castle. Designated as a Site of Special Scientific Interest, Windsor Great Park covers some 5,000 acres of parkland and forest. It still functions as a royal deer park, but at the same time, is a popular tourist destination and offers visitors a variety of recreational activities. Originally it was part of an enormous Norman hunting chase (a private area of forest), but most of the site now dates from the mid-thirteenth century. Other castles with surviving medieval deer parks include Rockingham, where the Big Park dates to 1256. The site was the center of a significant manorial estate, as attested to by the presence of ridge and furrow features, medieval fishponds, rabbit warrens (or pillow mounds), and a hunting lodge.[45] Likewise, Muncaster Castle retains portions of its medieval great park; however, the deer park was redesigned in the eighteenth

Near Bolton Castle, the location of the late-fourteenth-century deer park can be identified by the remains of a hunting tower, which can be found near the present village. Speculation exists that the building functioned as a banqueting tower and also as an observation post to keep track of the deer and other game living in the park.

century. At Manorbier Castle, fragments of the walls that enclosed the medieval deer park survive to the west of the castle site. During the fourteenth century, Restormel Castle was the center of one of the realm's largest deer parks; Edward, the first Duke of Cornwall and better known as the Black Prince, kept some 300 deer here. Sadly, all traces have disappeared. By the mid-fourteenth century, the construction of new deer parks began to go out of fashion, partly due to more pressing matters caused by the devastation of the Black Death, widespread crop failures, and invasions from Scotland. Even so, they continued to be a noticeable feature in the landscape and have persisted in many places to this day.

When the Normans settled Britain, not only did they take over lands occupied by the native population, they also instituted a variety of laws which restricted the use of those lands and imposed considerable fines on those people who flouted them. In fact, William the Conqueror and his successors declared large areas of the new Norman kingdom as "forests," the management and use of which were regulated by what came to be known as "forest law." The process of creating royal forests was known as afforestation. By the time of the *Domesday Book*, the king had created 21 royal forests; during the reign of Henry II, in the mid-twelfth century, one-third of the English landscape was designated as forest, and contained 80 royal forests. Similar to deer parks, but on a much larger scale, medieval forests were a lot more than woodland. In fact, the term itself was a legal term rather than the description of a tree-filled area, as we know the term today. During the Middle Ages, a "forest" was an area of land subject to specific laws where everything in the area, from the trees and natural resources to the wild game and other livestock, was the preserve of the king.

Carved out of land already occupied by the peasantry, the forest not only provided the king with food and a venue for entertaining himself and his guests but the natural resources also gave him (and many local peasants) an income and a source for gift-giving. In addition to expansive stands of trees, forests — including the legendary Sherwood Forest — featured scrubland, heath and moorland, grassland, bogs and marshes, and farmland. Within the forest, wild game, including not just deer but also boar, wolves, and hares, were protected under the law, meaning they could be hunted, but only by the king and those people to whom he granted permission — for a fee. Besides the wildlife and vegetation, the forests also enclosed villages and towns which existed prior to enclosure. Peasant residents had their rights and privileges drastically limited: They could gain access only by paying fees and forest court officials severely punished any infringements. Forest staff included a warden, a forester-in-fee, foresters, agisters, regarders, woodwards, and verderers, who oversaw the different forest activities, ensured no one broke the law (for example, by not "lawing" or removing three claws from the front feet of peasant dogs or gathering dead wood without explicit permission), collected fees and taxes, and attended forest courts.[46] The money raised from collecting fees and fining peasants for breaches of forest law provided the king with a convenient source of extra income.

In addition to enforcing forest law, the king or lord acquired a nice income from using the forest's natural resources. The peasant community who lived in the forest mined coal and iron ore, felled timber for transformation into charcoal, and worked in other forest industries. Many turned to these labor-intensive jobs to supplement the income they gleaned from agricultural work done in their own fields and on the lord's demesne. Forest work could take place during off-season, when crops had been planted but were not yet ready for harvest. Some peasants actually worked as independent contractors in exchange for wages. They worked as charcoal burners, iron or coal miners, smiths, woodcutters, woodworkers (who made items such as bows and arrows, and a variety of tools and vessels), glassmakers, tanners, rope makers (or ropers), and lime burners.

One of the most heavily exploited medieval forests was the Forest of Dean, on the border between England and Wales, where the two main industries were iron and charcoal production. During the thirteenth and early fourteenth centuries, the forest supported scores of royal iron forges and also several smaller, temporary forges, which were not officially recognized by the king.[47] Among his duties, the warden of the Forest of Dean was in charge of a major armaments industry, which involved the mass production of crossbow bolts. He lived at St. Briavel's Castle, situated on the southwestern edge of the forest, where he simultaneously served as the castle's constable. St. Briavel's was a valuable royal arsenal and stored the bolts (also known as quarrels) for distribution when required to support the king's army during a siege.[48] During the thirteenth century, some 500,000 quarrels were reportedly made at the site. The castle also functioned as a manorial court, a prison, and the administrative center for the forest, and it was used by King John and others as a hunting lodge. Other items forged at St. Briavel's included horseshoes, axes, nails, and a variety of tools. Some of the original medieval structure survives in fine condition; nowadays, the site is accessible to the public, but it is used as a youth hostel.

Several castles were deliberately located in or near the edges of medieval forests to perform specific roles tailored to the area and to house members of the forest staff. For example,

Located in the Forest of Dean, where iron mining and forging was a major industry, St. Briavel's Castle was used by the monarchy to store arms and crossbow bolts, scores of which were made at the site.

the Conqueror established Rockingham Forest, which was administered by wardens (or stewards) who lived in Rockingham Castle. They in turn employed landowners of varying status to work as so-called "gentlemen keepers" and "yeoman keepers," who watched over the forest estates, collected fees from the peasantry, and lived in lodges provided by the warden.[49] Peveril Castle, on the edge of the Forest of the Peak, was the administrative center of a thriving lead mining industry as well as a royal castle. Other forest castles, the remains of which still survive, include Marlborough, Pickering, Sauvey, Dunster, and Okehampton.[50]

Besides royal forests, the aristocratic landscape in medieval Britain also contained areas known as chases, smaller versions of the king's forests with varied vegetation, which were granted to high-ranked noblemen, not just secular lords but also ecclesiastical lords, such as bishops. For example, the medieval bishops of Hereford held Colwall Chase, where they bred and hunted deer. The Percys of Northumberland, who owned Alnwick and Warkworth Castles, had the rights to Langstrothdale Chase, where they too hunted game.[51] Place names like these are helpful indicators of how an area was used, especially when the landscape itself has been altered over time.

Deer were not the only wildlife prized by Britain's medieval aristocracy. Manorial lands were also used for breeding and hunting smaller game, such as hares and rabbits, which the Normans reintroduced to Britain in the twelfth century.[52] The animals were considered an excellent source of meat and of fur, which could be used for clothing or sold on the open market. As with deer parks, possession of rabbit warrens emphasized a lord's status among his peers. The term itself derives from the right of free warren, meaning the right to freely hunt small game on one's own estate. Other small game that could be hunted under the right of free warren included foxes, badgers, squirrels, weasels, pheasants, and partridges.[53]

Oftentimes, rabbit warrens were formed out of a larger area of waste, meaning land that was not able to be cultivated. Enclosed by natural and artificial boundaries, including streams, hedges, stone walls, and earthen embankments,[54] they typically covered an area of between nine and 600 hectares.[55] Many warrens were situated within forests and deer parks, where the pale prevented unwanted access and poaching, and also interfered with the animals' diligent efforts to escape. Estate managers known as warreners were responsible for the warrens and lived in special houses, known as warren houses or lodges. Often designed as stone towers, some of these houses functioned as observation posts and even had arrowslits to defend the area from poachers.

Artificial warrens, also known as pillow mounds, rabbit buries, or coney garths (coney is another term for rabbit, particularly an adult rabbit), typically consisted of oblong, flat-topped, earthen mounds. They measured between 45 to 105 feet in length and 15 to 35 feet in width, and stood about two feet high. They could also be square, circular, cigar-shaped, triangular, or, rarely, cruciform in plan. Some were bounded by an outer ditch which helped keep the interior of the mound free from water. Inside the warren, mazes of trenches or tunnels formed the rabbits' home. Sometimes, these were built by human hands and lined with stone slabs for use by the animals; but, just as often, the rabbits took it upon themselves to weave their way underground. Access points were carefully controlled by the warrener so that the animals did not escape.[56] Besides encouraging breeding, the mounds helped protect rabbits from predators, such as foxes.

It has been estimated that between 1,000 and 2,000 warrens existed in the English countryside. Many can still be located, but they are often difficult to distinguish from other landscape features, such as ancient burial sites; many surviving mounds are post-medieval in date. One of the best ways to identify a warren is by a place name or associations with other manorial structures, such as the aforementioned deer parks or with dovecotes and fishponds, which we will discuss shortly. Place names (often names of fields or houses) that suggest links with rabbit warrens include Coney Hill, Coneygarth, Coney Weston, Coneyhurst, Coneysthorpe, and Conegar. In 1597, the name of Toddington Castle was documented as "Toddington Conger Hill," reputedly for its use as a rabbit warren.

Places with "warren" in the name (such as Thetford Warren, where visitors can see an outstanding example of a fortified warren house) clearly suggest use as rabbit breeding grounds. Use of the word "rabbit" with place names is extremely rare; however, sites with names such as Rabbit House indicate use as a warrener's house and give clues to the former presence of a warren at the spot. The mounds survive at several castles, including Rockingham, Penmaen, Neroche, Stapleton, and Laxton. Located in the medieval deer park at Bolton, the Ellerlands contains a well-preserved rabbit warren dotted with pillow mounds.[57] Nearby, the ruined Norton Tower may have been used as an observation tower or as the warrener's house. The remains of several medieval and post-medieval pillow mounds also survive on the Croft Castle estate. Interestingly, during the sixteenth century, the motte at Pleshey Castle was used as a warren.

Another hallmark of medieval aristocratic status was the dovecote, a purpose-built structure designed to house and breed pigeons and their young to supplement the lord's food supply. Alternate words for the dovecote are "doocot" (commonly used in Scotland), "columbarium"

Freestanding dovecotes can be found throughout Britain at castles, monasteries, manor houses, and stately homes. The ruined dovecote at Angle Castle stands in a field north of the tower house; its white exterior and low-lying doorway are quite visible.

(which is Latin, but is sometimes used in conjunction with religious sites such as Ewenny Priory) and "dovecot." Field names such as Dove House Field and Dove's Coat Field, both of which are in Wales, suggest that a dovecote once stood at the site. Like rabbit warrens, dovecotes were said to have been brought to Britain by the Normans. The earliest dovecotes date to the very late eleventh or early twelfth century. Freestanding or embedded into the walls of the castle or an ancillary structure, such as a barn or granary, dovecotes were the legal preserve of the noble class, which included both secular lords and the religious hierarchy in addition to the monarch. As a result, medieval dovecotes are most commonly associated with castles or manor houses, monastic communities, and ecclesiastical structures. However, after the fourteenth century, the laws were relaxed so that landowners of lesser social status also had the right to erect dovecotes, and construction expanded apace. Consequently, many surviving dovecotes date to the post-medieval period. Nevertheless, numerous examples can be found which are directly linked to castles and medieval manorial estates.

Freestanding dovecotes are peculiarly charming structures, which easily attract attention even when surrounded by trees and houses. Many of the earliest examples were constructed in much the same way as stone castles, using rubble filler to create walls which measured between three and five feet in thickness. Arguably the most distinctive dovecotes are squat, whitewashed or plastered, domed cylinders, the insides of which are empty, save for the thick interior walls and row upon row of nesting boxes. Circular dovecote typically measured between 13 and 20 feet across. Other early dovecotes were square in design; their walls averaged between 10 and 30 feet in length.

Reputedly attracted to the white coloration, thousands of pigeons might occupy a single dovecote, which contained on the average between 500 and 1,500 nesting boxes. Some dovecotes held well over 3,000 boxes, but these were quite rare. Each box had to accommodate at least one adult pigeon and two babies, known as squabs, which were considered a real delicacy — just as they are today. The meat of older birds was not as tasty, so they were kept for egg production. In addition to gathering the eggs and squabs for food, workers also collected dove dung, which was used as fertilizer. Their feathers were used for bedding. As time progressed, variations in design and decoration appeared, and many dovecotes featured brickwork patterns and even polygonal plans. Historians estimate that as many as 1,500 dovecotes still survive in England and Wales.

In order to prevent foxes, rats, and other predators (including humans and other birds) from raiding their dovecotes, builders ensured the doorways were as small as possible but still large enough to allow people — who had to carefully crouch to avoid smacking their heads on the masonry — to enter. Normally, the only other opening in the building was at the center of the roof, where a small hole known as an oculus allowed birds to enter and exit as they pleased.[58] Structural features known as string courses, very narrow ledges applied around the circumference of the building, prevented rats from scaling the walls and reaching the boxes. A device known as a potence, which consisted of a wooden pole with arm-like rungs, was placed in the center of the pigeon house. Suspended above the floor, the inventive gadget not only allowed workers to reach the birds and eggs higher up on the walls, it also prevented predators from reaching the boxes.[59]

Dovecotes were often built near agricultural fields, which posed a great problem for the peasants. The birds had a frustrating habit of scouring the fields for grain and seeds and were difficult to keep at bay. Even so, many lords felt that the need to display their social status and to have squab for their tables were greater priorities. Others opted to breed their doves inside the castle walls, which may have lessened the likelihood of crop destruction but was probably more a matter of convenience than of agricultural management. Nowadays, keen-eyed visitors can still identify holes for the pigeon boxes inside keeps, as at Rochester Castle, in towers, as at Bodiam Castle and Ewenny Priory, and on the outer wall of the great hall facing into the inner ward at Manorbier Castle. The lords of Manorbier Castle must have had a particular affinity

The outer wall of the great hall-keep at Manorbier Castle contains a group of pigeonholes, an interior dovecote, which may have housed carrier pigeons.

for dove meat, for in the valley at the base of the castle, where the manorial estates once teemed with crops, orchards, a deer park, woodland, a mill, and fishponds, a second, more classic example of a medieval dovecote still stands tall. Visitors can explore the well-preserved domed, circular structure, which was erected in the thirteenth century.

When exploring the British countryside, you may come across a dovecote that seems to be isolated from other structures. Remember, however, that during the Middle Ages, it would not have been alone, but rather would have been a crucial feature of the larger manorial landscape. For example, a tiny village in West Wales known as Rosemarket features an outstanding example of a dovecote, which is visible from some distance. In fact, in 2006, it was restored to its original pristine condition. Containing some 200 nesting boxes and standing over 17 feet tall, the fine building was apparently constructed, not by the lord of the manor at Rosemarket, but by the Knights of St. John (also known as the Knights Hospitaller), who were based at Slebech, several miles northeast of Rosemarket, where they occupied and ran a religious site known as a commandery (the ruins of which can be visited). After the Dissolution of the Monasteries instigated by Henry VIII in 1537, the commandery was deserted, and the lord of the manor at Rosemarket continued using the dovecote until the manor house too was abandoned.

Of arguably more value to the medieval food supply than doves, fish were not only gathered from the sea and freshwater sources, they were also cultivated on manorial estates. Expensive to construct and costly to maintain, fishponds — also known as fish stews — became increasingly popular from the twelfth century as yet another symbol of aristocratic status and of conspicuous consumption. In fact, place names such as Earl's Pool or Earl's Pond, as at Castle Acre and Clare Castles, reveal medieval usage as fishponds.[60] Fishponds provided both secular and ecclesiastical lords with an ideal substitute for meat on religious holidays and added to the overall aesthetic impression created by one's estate. Available throughout the year, and during winter months in salted or dried forms, fish were also given as gifts or rewards.[61] Maintenance involved routine draining and cleaning of the shallow, artificial ponds and the restocking of fish, such as bream, pike, perch,[62] and carp.[63]

Generally rectangular in shape but also trapezoidal and oblong, both great ponds (vivaria), which were used for intensive breeding programs, and little ponds (servatoria) were constructed on manorial estates[64] and close to castles, such as Kenilworth, where the king maintained a vivarium, and at Windsor, where the Great Park reputedly contained an enormous pond holding some 600 pike, dace, and roach.[65] Normally created by damming a nearby stream or a free-flowing spring and then regulating the flow of the water with sluices, medieval fishponds were lined with clay or timber and enclosed with low-lying embankments no more than three feet high. Many manorial estates contained a series of progressively larger fishponds designed to house fish at different phases of the breeding cycle.[66] As the fish grew, they were transferred to other ponds or harvested as required. Local villagers also prized fish, and were known to have used livestock ponds or mill ponds to breed fish for their own consumption.[67] The residents of Knaresborough Castle also used the mill pond for fish farming.[68]

Some castle owners made shrewd use of their moats as fish stews, as at Leeds, Windsor, Stapleton, and Oakham, where the moat was reshaped into a series of linear fishponds.[69] At York, the River Foss, which flowed close to Clifford's Tower, the impressive motte crowned with a unique five-lobed shell keep, was dammed to create the King's Fishpool, which was recorded as in existence in the *Domesday Book*. The river also fed the mill. Not only did the great pool provide fish for the castle, it also fed residents of the local monastery and the pious,

The expansive grounds located just south of the 78-foot-high great tower erected by William, Lord Hastings, at Ashby de la Zouch Castle contain a series of unusual sunken forms. They are believed to have been ornamental ponds which possibly contained fish.

who abided by the Church's doctrines, which forbade eating meat on holy days. The royal fishponds at Marlborough Castle, now a minor site on a college campus, once provided the fish used to restock other ponds; they were considered among the most important ponds in the realm.[70] Sadly, they no longer survive.

Nevertheless, the remains of fishponds can be seen at many British castles. Often little more than earthwork rectangles enclosing marshy depressions, they sometimes feature stone walls and still contain water. At Manorbier Castle, a major project is now underway to restore the twelfth-century fishponds, which had silted up and become overgrown over the centuries. Located near the ruined corn mill, the elaborate system of fishponds was spring-fed and used sluices to regulate the water level. At Ashby de la Zouch Castle, the fishponds appear as a series of undulating and embanked rectangles positioned near the extensive remains of the late medieval manor house. Beyond the Brays on the southeastern side of the main parking lot at Kenilworth Castle, diligent visitors can spot the remains of several medieval fishponds.

A first glance, each of the above fishponds can be difficult to recognize without taking into consideration their shape and their location relative to the nearby castle. Other castle ponds pose this same problem. For example, the rectangular, undulating, marshy, embanked, deeply enditched structures at Bolingbroke Castle have long been classified as fishponds. However, this characterization has recently been reconsidered. Representatives from Heritage Lincolnshire and English Heritage now believe the large rectangular earthwork in the center of the group may have served as a defensive, earth-built infantry fort during the English Civil War and may have played a role in the siege of the castle by Parliamentary troops in 1643.

Long believed to have been used as fishponds, at least one of the marshy earthworks at Bolingbroke Castle has recently been re-evaluated as a possible Royalist fort erected by the garrison during the English Civil War. In October 1643, the castle was besieged by 6,000 Parliamentarian troops; defenders held out for just over a month before finally surrendering.

However, it is also possible that the structure may have been a pound for keeping stray animals (the grounds are known as the "routyard"), and a line of depressions on the eastern side of the yard may indeed have served as medieval fishponds.[71] So, when wandering Britain's castles, do not despair if you cannot determine with exactness the purpose of the earthworks you encounter. But, with experience, you can make an educated assessment — and, perhaps, modify the opinions of the professionals.[72]

As its name and the above comments suggest, Manorbier Castle once served as the focal point of a substantial but localized lordship. It was the home of the de Barri family, whose most famous son was Gerald, the cleric known as Giraldus Cambrensis, or Gerald of Wales, was born in the castle in the mid-twelfth century. Among his many talents, Gerald was a prolific writer whose works — *The Journey through Wales* and *Description of Wales*— have been republished in recent decades and are widely available. The son of a Norman father, Sir William de Barri, and a Welsh mother, Angharad, the granddaughter of Rhys ap Tewdwr, Prince of Deheubarth, Gerald was proud of his ancestral home, which he described in considerable detail in *The Journey through Wales*. Gerald's writings offer keen insight into how the manorial estates surrounding the castle — and the castle itself— may have appeared and how they were used by his family during the Middle Ages. And they document the existence of the key manorial buildings and agricultural features, the remains of which have been discussed in this chapter:

Only about three miles from Pembroke Castle is the fortified mansion known as Manorbier, that is the house of one Pyrrus (the name, Manorbier, has been variously interpreted as the manor of Pyr; Pyr or Pyrrus probably refers to Abbot Piro of nearby Caldey Island, who lived in the 6th century).... There the house stands, visible from afar because of its turrets and crenellations, on the top of a hill which is quite near the sea and which on the western side reaches as far as the harbour. To the north and north-west, just beneath the walls, there is an excellent fishpond, well constructed and remarkable for its deep waters. On the same side there is a most attractive orchard, shut in between the fishpond and a grove of trees [the lord's chase?], with a great crag of rock and hazel-nut trees which grow to a great height. At the east end of the fortified promontory, between the castle, if I may call it such, and the church, a stream of water which never fails winds its way along a valley, which is strewn with sand by the strong sea-winds. It runs down from a large lake, and there is a water-mill on its bank.... This is a region rich in wheat, with fish from the sea and plenty of wine for sale [manorial estates also had vineyards].[73]

Perhaps best classified as a fortified manor, Gerald's birthplace has long been known as a castle, and indeed possesses all the characteristics of an early stone castle. Erected by the Norman knight, Odo de Barri, in the late eleventh century and expanded throughout the following century by his heirs, the earliest stone structures at Manorbier probably consisted of the impressive hall block, which functioned as a unit unto itself and has been categorized as a hall-keep, and the remnants of the original gateway, now called the Old Tower. In time, the entire site was enclosed with a battlemented curtain wall, a new main gatehouse fronted by a deep rock-cut ditch, and round angle towers.

A trip to Manorbier Castle provides an excellent opportunity to form a visual impression of the physical relationship between a castle or manor house, the manorial estates, and the structures that supported the castle. From the main parking lot at the base of the promontory site, visitors have the option of examining the landscape that once supported the resi-

Acclaimed by Gerald of Wales as "the pleasantest spot in Wales," Manorbier Castle was perched at the edge of a ridge pointing westward towards the sea. The well-preserved site combines all the aesthetic qualities of a fine fortified manor with its original feudal estate, remnants of which survive to the west and north.

dents in the stronghold at the top of the hill, or instead trudging up the steep incline to the castle. No matter which direction one first chooses, before heading that way, take a look at the entire scene and consider the placement of the castle relative to its immediate surroundings: It clearly towers over the area where the peasants would have toiled; and, on the opposite side of the valley in which visitors park, another building, a fine medieval church, dominates the headland, vividly emphasizing the intimate relationship between castle and church during the Middle Ages. Indeed, the Church of St. James the Greater, Apostle and Martyr, played a crucial role in Gerald de Barri's decision to become a priest.

Before heading into the castle, take time to wander the outer bailey, which played a role in the English Civil War, when possession alternated between Royalist supporters of King Charles I and Parliamentarian troops, under the command of Rowland Laugharne, who seized the site in 1645. During this period, the exterior of the castle was strengthened with several fortifications, including the braye, an outer line of defenses built beyond the masonry walls and rock-cut ditch. The center of this structure was revetted with a masonry redan, through which modern-day visitors must pass to access the castle itself. After the Civil War, the site was used as a farm, and the barn in this outer ward may date to that time.[74]

At the base of the rocky headland, the remains of the de Barris' manorial estates spread to the north and west of the main parking lot. Today, much of this land is covered with free-roaming vegetation, but during the Middle Ages, it was used to grow crops and support orchards and vineyards, and probably contained a fine deer park. The real treasures at this location are the structural remains of the corn mill and fishponds, which can be found almost immediately across the narrow lane that passes the parking lot. And, further along the dirt track that leads to these ruins, visitors will find themselves alongside the well-preserved dovecote, the interior of which contains some 250 nesting boxes and can be explored. This building in particular invigorates the site with an awareness of past lives, of the men and women who labored in the fields, or caught fish, gathered pigeon eggs and squab, and of those fortunate enough to have dined on them at the lord's table.

TERMINOLOGY IN THIS CHAPTER

Afforestation: The process of creating royal forests out of lands not originally designed for that purpose; lands and peasant villages within the new forests were then subject to "forest law."

Agisters: During the Middle Ages, the officer of the forest who collected agistment and was subordinate to the verderer.

Agistment: Tax that paid for the right to graze livestock in the forest.

Ale: The main drink of the times, made from grain (barley), malt and yeast, which fermented the mixture. It was better tasting and safer to drink than water.

Bailiff: An official of the lord charged with administering the manor, which was more often the purview of the reeve.

Beadle: A manorial official; one of the reeve's assistants.

Black Death: In 1348, a virulent form of what has long been believed to have been bubonic plague moved from Europe into England and rapidly swept across the British Isles, killing millions of people in its wake. Apparently spread by contact with diseased rats that bore tiny fleas which spread the plague from person to person and also by contact with sick people, the brutalizing disease caused painful lumps in the groin and armpits and then black spots broke out on the body. Most people who contracted the Black Death died within three days. The disease subsided in 1350, but sporadic outbreaks continued into the early fifteenth century. Britain's social, economic, and political systems, and the Church, were severely affected by the devastation of the population.

Bolt: See Chapter Two.

Boon-work: Work done by the peasantry on the lord's demesne lands on special days, such as at harvest time, when the lord's fields were a priority.

Bordar: Comparable to a cottar; a small holder.

Brewer: Brewed ale and cider.

Brewhouse: The building where ale was brewed; often now survives only as foundations and is therefore difficult to distinguish without historical records to reveal that it existed and where it may have been located.

Castellated: (1) An area containing many castles; (2) a style of architecture with castle-like features.

Chases: (1) Stabilizing grooves through which a portcullis was raised and lowered; (2) a groove or shaft in a wall which housed pipes, drains, and chimney flues; (3) the deer park of a medieval lord; (4) the hunting of game.

Columbarium: An alternate word for dovecote, often associated with religious sites such as monasteries.

Commandery: Comparable to a monastic community but operated by the Knights Templar and Knights Hospitaller rather than monks, the hospital of which was used to treat the sick.

Coney garth: An alternate phrase for rabbit warren.

Copyholders: Tenants who possessed a copy of the written entry in the lord's records granting use of a portion of his land, the copyholding. Displaying the copy gave proof of rights to farm the land.

Cottar/cottager: The lowest of the peasant classes, they often worked as swineherds or prison guards, and did odd jobs.

Court house: Structure in which manorial courts or the lord's courts were held.

Deer farming: The deliberate breeding of deer for food and other purposes.

Deer park: Even though the lord and his guests might entertain themselves with a hunt in the castle deer park, the scenic lands, which were enclosed by earthworks and timber or stone walls, primarily functioned as deer farms which provided fresh venison throughout the year. Today, most castle deer parks are little more than forested areas situated just outside the castle walls, but many stately homes still pride themselves on the extent and quality of their deer parks. During the Middle Ages, as now, the presence of a deer park emphasized the status of the property owner, who was required to obtain a royal license to establish the park.

Demesne: The portion of a manorial estate reserved for the lord's personal use, which he farmed as a money-making venture.

Domesday Book: The enormous survey commissioned by William I in 1085 to document and value all the land held by the king and key members of the aristocracy (his tenants-in-chief). Besides learning the exact extent of his possessions within the realm, William intended to use the information to determine what taxes to impose as he funded an army to fight the Danes, who were then threatening to attack Britain. The resulting tome remains one of the medieval world's finest treasures; originally called the Winchester Roll or King's Roll, or sometimes the Book of the Treasury, it became known as the *Domesday Book* in about 1180.

Doocot: See dovecote.

Dovecote: A medieval pigeon house created from bricks or cut stone and often covered with white lime wash or plaster, generally associated with castles, manor houses, and monasteries. Inside, the building was lined with pigeon holes or boxes to encourage nesting and breeding of doves for castle food supply. Young pigeons, known as squabs, were highly prized for the quality of their meat. Owning a dovecote was a badge of success.

Ecclesiastical: Relating to the Church.

Embankments: See Chapter 1.

Famuli: The lord's personal staff; also called the familia.

Feud, in: A parcel land held in exchange for the military service of a single knight.

Feudalism: A political, social, and economic system under which land was granted by a landowner to a subordinate in exchange for military service or other duties (the feudal obligation).

Fief: Land held in feud by a knight or other landowner in feud, in exchange for the military service of a single knight; a fee.

Fish farming: The intentional breeding of different kinds of fish for the lord's food supply.

Fish stew: Alternate term for fishpond.

Fishpond: An artificial pond in which fish of various kinds were bred for the food supply; sometimes the moat was used as a fishpond. A sign of status.

Food: Generally, meals were taken three times a day. A small breakfast of bread and cheese at sunrise was followed between 10 A.M. and noon with the main meal, dinner. Then, towards sunset a lighter supper would be served, consisting of bread, cheese, and perhaps a small dish like a stew. After supper, entertainment might be provided by minstrels, storytellers, acrobats, or contortionists, or games and song enjoyed.

A lord's dinner usually had two to three courses, mainly meats and pastries, bread, wine, or ale (usually the drink of the lowest classes), fruits, cheeses, nuts, and the like. But a feast was something so much more than can be experienced at present-day recreations. Modern banquets fall way short of the mark. Beef, pork, mutton, venison, poultry, fish, eggs, bread, milk, cheeses, vegetables (in lesser quantities, because they were considered "common"), and a profusion of wine, ale, cider, and mead were in ample supply during a feast.

The winter months were a time of scarcity; so, preparations were made during the rest of the year to ensure the availability of meat. Wild animals were always hard to find during the winter, so most of the cattle were eaten. Beef had to be dried, though; otherwise, it would rot if kept for any length of time. Like the meat, fish were salted or smoked for longer preservation.

The lower classes, on the other hand, had a tough time staying alive—and not just in the winter. Their meals mainly consisted of vegetables such as turnips or cabbage, dark breads (deemed not fit for nobler individuals), porridges, an occasional fish, cheese curds, beer, ale, or mead. Indeed, it is a wonder they survived as well as they did, and were able to fend off disease. Ironically, the rich, who should have had better methods of staying healthy, suffered from a variety of ailments, such as scurvy, tooth decay, heart problems, skin eruptions, and infections caused by rotting meat and lack of proper nutrition.

Forests: During the Middle Ages, forests were not the tree-filled areas that we know them as today. Rather, the "forest" was a legal term for an area of land subject to specific laws. Everything in the area, from the trees and natural resources to the wild game and other livestock, was the preserve of the king. Besides trees, forests contained heath, grassland, marshes, and even villages. Parcels of forestland could also be used for cultivation if the land was assarted, or permanently cleared of trees, undergrowth, and other vegetation. Assarting was illegal in royal forests.

Forest law: The use of royal forests was highly regulated, and a set of common rules were implemented to protect the lord's rights within the forest and to protect the venison (the game) and the vert (the vegetation). First imposed by William I, forest law prohibited activities such as hunting game without specific permission, enclosing portions of the forest, and felling and gathering trees for private use. Those peasants who violated forest law found themselves at the forest court, where they could be heavily fined or face physical punishment.

Forest work: In addition to felling trees, most medieval forests supported a number of industries. Besides specialist woodworkers, forests often employed miners, glassmakers, potters, limeburners, charcoal-burners, smiths, tanners, and ropers.

Foresters: Local official responsible for overseeing the enforcement of forest law to ensure that all trees were felled and removed legally. Walking foresters and others who rode on horseback regularly surveyed the portion of the forest for which they were responsible.

Foresters-in-fee: Men granted the hereditary right to hold certain estates in exchange for service in the forests, overseeing the area on behalf of the lord. Equivalent to a warden.

Freeman: The class of peasants who were freely able to earn money, to own and sell the lands they occupied and farmed, and to move away from the manor; despite these freedoms, they also owed rents or other payments to the lord.

Fulling: A phase of the wool-making or cloth-making process, which included cleansing the cloth to remove oils, dirt, or other impurities. The person who performed this task was known as a fuller or walker.

Gardens: Formally laid-out areas which offered the lord and his lady an enjoyable place to spend time and a pleasant venue for entertaining and impressing guests.

Gentry: A class of landholders, generally lower in status than the nobility but often considered part of the aristocracy. The landed gentry became increasingly powerful in the late Middle Ages and in the post-medieval period.

Granary: A building used to store grain.

Harrying the North: In the wake of the Conquest, many Saxons rebelled against Norman rule. Uprisings occurred throughout England, as far north as Durham and Yorkshire. In response, in 1068, William began an extended program of "pacification," which not only included the construction of numerous castles but also the "harrying of the north," during which his soldiers ravaged the countryside, burning crops and destroying Saxon houses in an effort to suppress them for good.

Hayward: Responsible for the "haies" or hedges.

Holding: A parcel of land "held" by a tenant or landlord.

Honor: The great estate of a tenant-in-chief.

Hundred: An administrative or governmental subdivision within a shire or county in England; introduced by the Anglo-Saxons but reorganized by the Normans and maintained in some parts of the country until the nineteenth century. Administered by the shire-reeve (the sheriff) or the steward of the manor to which it was attached, who held hundred courts on a regular basis and collected taxes.

Huntsmen: Men who accompanied the king or a lord on a hunt and were responsible for calling the dogs with a horn, carrying weapons and other implements, and assisting the lord in cornering his prey.

Iron forge: Workshop or forest area where ore was heated and transformed into wrought iron for use in making swords and other items; a smithy, or blacksmith's shop, containing a hearth for heating iron ore and for working molten ore into weapons and utensils.

Knight's service: Part of the feudal obligation: In exchange for the land rewards, noblemen not only swore complete loyalty, they also promised to fight for their ruler upon moment's notice and furnished a number of knights to fortify the standing army. The number of knights owed was often determined by the size and value of the lord's estates.

Laboratories: The peasantry or labor force.

Land: Holding land was a sign of status and vital to the imposition of feudalism in Norman Britain. In fact, land was the realm's — and a lord's — most valuable possession. It provided income as well as power. Manorial lands were considered arable, meaning they could be cultivated for food crops; meadow, for cultivation of hay; parkland and forests, for breeding deer and other game, for harvesting timber, mining, and other industries, and for recreational purposes; and waste, or not usable for farming but useful, for example, as rabbit warrens.

Landlord: The lord of the manor; often a tenant-in-chief who held land from the monarch, which he could then choose to subdivide and bestow upon other men, tenants, who then owed him obligations comparable to the arrangement between the same landlord (a vassal) and the monarch.

Lawing: Declawing; the removal of three claws on the front paws of forest dogs to prevent them from chasing game.

Lord: (1) A person holding land in feud, who owed feudal obligations to a greater lord or the monarch and was also the lord of his own tenants; (2) a feudal landlord; (3) a member of the British peerage.

Lordship: The land under the control of a lord.

Manor: A landed estate (a unit of land) controlled by a lord (landlord), who kept a portion of the land for his own use (the demesne) and farmed out the rest to tenants in exchange for rent, service, or working the lord's land.

Manorial court: Held at the castle or manor house inside the great hall or a chamber specially designated for this purpose and presided over by the steward or another senior representative of the lord; consisted of a group of jurors who made determinations regarding violations of a tenant's manorial obligations, criminal activities, and the imposition of any relevant fines. The "court leet" covered minor infractions of the law, and the "court baron" dealt with more serious crimes related to the management of the manor. Peasants occasionally paid their rent and taxes at manorial courts.

Manorialism: The economic relationship between a lord and his tenants, the peasantry, which involved the exchange of rent, services, and other obligations for the use of a portion of the lord's lands.

Manumission: The official granting of freedom to a peasant; emancipation.

Medieval women: In reality, medieval women had a lot of responsibility and were not at all inferior to men in terms of daily effort. Many peasant women toiled in the fields alongside their families, and some were employed in workshops or as tradeswomen. Women sometimes had the responsibility of running large estates after the death of their husband. They settled local disputes and arranged estate finances, and even took charge of defending castles or manors from attackers. It was also not unknown for medieval women to lead troops into battle.

Unmarried women holding land were powerful and had the same rights as men. However, when a woman married, she forfeited her lands and rights to her husband. Upon his death, she was normally entitled to a third of the lands so that she might support herself. Some unmarried women entered convents or nunneries where they lived a life similar to a monk's. These circumstances afforded them the chance to obtain an education or lead a devout life. Many nuns cared for the sick. Some also became important figures in the community.

Other occupations held by medieval women included shopkeepers, bakers, spinners, alewives (those that brewed the ales), farmers, and silk weavers. There were even some women writers. It was common for a woman to hold more than one job because they were paid much less than men, and in order to make an adequate income they took on extra work. Working as a spinner was the most common occupation. Women spent much of their time spinning wool into coarse thread, and then weaving it into cloth and making garments.

Merchet: A fine or payment owed to the landlord upon the marriage of a peasant man's daughter.

Messor: A reeve's assistant.

Miller: A member of the local peasantry chosen by the lord to operate his mill and charge a fee for its use.

Mills: Powered by water, wind, or horses, mills were primarily built to grind grain into flour for baking and brewing, and were also used in the iron ore and woolen industries. Hand mills, known as querns, were used in homes and kitchens.

Ministerial service: An alternative to knight's service, whereby the tenant provided service other than military duty to fulfill a feudal obligation. See sergeanty.

Motte and bailey castle: See Chapter 1.

Multure: Fee owed to a miller, sometimes in the form of grain, for mill services.

Oculus: The opening at the peak or in the roof of a dovecote through which pigeons could fly into or away from the structure.

Orchard: A field of trees cultivated for their fruit or nuts. During the Middle Ages, people consumed plums, apples, pears, and figs, as well as walnuts, hazelnuts, chestnuts, and almonds.

Pale: A boundary delineating a deer park, composed of an earthen or walled embankment topped with a timber fend or hedge and a ditch on both the outer and inner sides of the bank. Used to keep the animals inside the park and to keep out poachers.

Pannage: The payment of a fee which allowed pigs to roam freely in the lord's parkland or forest for a period of time each year to graze on nuts.

Peasants' Revolt, 1381: The disparate economic, social, and political conditions of the late fourteenth century created a vast gap between the peasantry and their landholding lords. The inequity resulted in one of medieval England's most historic events, the Peasants' Revolt of 1381. Centered on the four counties of Essex, Kent, Suffolk, and Hertfordshire, the uprising involved over 300 villages and hundreds — perhaps thousands — of peasants, the majority of whom were serfs and villeins. Many of the rebels were peasants of considerable status, such as reeves, bailiffs, and others in positions of responsibility; others were members of manorial famuli.[75]

During the centuries since the Norman Conquest, the peasantry became increasingly frustrated with exorbitantly high taxes, ongoing subjugation, high prices, and poor wages. The passage of the Statute of Labourers in 1351, which froze their wage rates and privileges to 1346 levels, added to their burden, already strained by the Black Death two years earlier. Finally, when the government imposed a Poll Tax in 1380 (the third of three such taxes passed within four years), the peasant classes decided they could no longer tolerate the situation. In addition to staging assaults on London and other sites, they displayed their displeasure by stealing their lord's timber, livestock, and hay; by refusing to work demesne lands; by not paying rents or providing other obligatory services; by burning manorial records; and, albeit rarely, by physically assaulting their lords. The rebellion ended with the execution of several leaders, most notably Wat Tyler, and promises by King Richard II to respond to the rebels' grievances and abolish the Poll Tax. The uprising is also known as Wat Tyler's Rebellion.

Pillow mound: An alternate term for a rabbit warren; often the only visible archaeological evidence of the presence of these structures at a medieval or post-medieval site. So named because of their cigar or pillow-like shape.

Pleasance: A pleasure garden. The rectangular remains of the pleasance built by Henry V in 1414 can be explored on the northern side of Kenilworth Castle. At one time, the site, which was enclosed with a series of earthworks and moats, supported the king's timber-framed banqueting hall. To reach the structure, visitors once had to sail in a barge or row a boat across the great mere to a small harbor, which is now completely filled up with grasses. Interestingly, Henry VIII moved the buildings from the pleasance to another site near the main entrance of the castle; the structures no longer survive.

Potence: The central post inside a dovecote from which arm-like appendages projected outwards like steps, which workers climbed to reach the pigeon boxes.

Quern: A hand-mill used to grind grain into flour, normally for personal use.

Rabbit warrens: An artificial or natural structure consisting of a series of tunnels inside of which rabbits lived and bred offspring for the lord's food supply. Also called pillow mounds.

Regarders: Forest officials who made a "regard" every three years to determine what offenses, if any, had been made and if the local officials had concealed the crimes; they then presented the offenses at the forest courts and collected fines for any breaches of forest law.

Reeve: The locally elected official, normally a villager, who was responsible for overseeing work done on the manor.

Ridge and furrow cultivation: During the Middle Ages, open farmland was divided into strips, which the landholder granted to different peasant families to farm in exchange for rents or service. The technology of medieval plowing led to the creation of elongated, reverse-S-shaped strips, which often survive in the British landscape. The presence of these distinctive strips, particularly in the absence of other physical evidence, can be a reliable indicator that the land was once part of a manorial estate.

Right of free warren: The legal right to freely hunt for small game on one's own land.

Secular: Not religious or spiritual; of the State rather than of the Church (ecclesiastical).

Seigneur: The manorial lord.

Seignorialism: An alternate term for manorialism; derived from the French for the lord of the estate, or "seigneur."

Seneschal: An alternate term for the steward.

Serf: The lowest class of the peasantry, the members of which were legally bound to the manorial land they tilled and lived upon in exchange for its use and the protection of the lord. They owed numerous obligations and fees to the lord.

Serjeanty: A feudal obligation whereby the tenant acquired land from the greater lord in exchange for services such as providing lands or gear for hunting, or providing personal or honorary assistance to the lord or monarch, such as carrying the king's banner.

Servatoria: Small fishponds, normally located near the castle, which provided a convenient source of food.

Smallholding: Agricultural property much smaller than the typical farm, normally less than 50 acres in area; often used for grazing or breeding livestock. Peasant smallholders often farmed between 10 and 20 acres of land.

Socage: A fixed payment (usually cash but could also be specific agricultural services) owed to a lord; later replaced knight's service as the preferred means of fulfilling one's feudal obligation. Men who owed socage were often known as socmen or sokemen.

Sokeman: Peasants whose status was almost on a par with freemen, but who were still required to perform certain agricultural services.

Stewards, estate: The responsibilities of the steward expanded tremendously over time, and eventually were divided between two men, one who managed the household and the other — the estate steward — who often managed the manors on the lord's estate. Also known as the seneschal, the estate steward was required to travel from manor to manor to carry out the wide range of duties, including holding the lord's courts and ensuring the reeves were meeting their responsibilities.

String course: A horizontal, projecting molding or band of masonry running along the face of a wall.

Strip farming: See ridge and furrow cultivation.

Subinfeudation: The act of subletting or dividing up a tenancy and granting portions to lesser lords to farm in exchange for military or monetary obligations.

Tanner: A forest-based industry in which the worker, the tanner, used tree bark to "tan" or treat animal hides to make leather; although tanning was illegal in royal forests, the law was often ignored.[76]

Tenant-in-chief: Greater lords who acquired their landholdings directly from the monarch. They then had the right to subdivide their holdings among lesser lords and tenants. The relationships all involved an exchange of services and land for certain feudal or manorial obligations.

Tenants: Individuals who acquired the right to farm and occupy lands from a lord in exchange for service and other obligations.

Venison: Deer meat; was not only part of the castle food supply but also given as gifts.

Verderers: Officials of the royal forests who were responsible for enforcing forest law and for regulating "commoning," the practice of common rights such as grazing ponies and other livestock. Verderers are still appointed to supervise activities in the New Forest, the Forest of Dean, and Epping Forest.

Vert: Vegetation in the royal forest.

Villein: Feudal tenants who are members of the peasantry; serfs.

Vineyards: Fields used to cultivate grapes for making into wine.

Vivaria: The large fish ponds, which were used for large breeding programs.

Walker: See fulling.

Warden: The individual appointed to manage the entire forest on behalf of the monarch.

Warren: (1) An area of waste land set aside to breed rabbits for consumption; (2) a term used for an earthen mound (artificial or natural) containing tunnels, in which rabbits lived.

Warrener: Estate manager responsible for maintaining the lord's rabbit warrens, who often lived in a special lodge which acted both as a residence and as an observation post to keep poachers at bay.

Week-work: Regular work performed on the lord's demesne lands in addition to that on the peasant's own parcel of land.

Woodward: A manorial official who supervised work in the forest and was responsible for the trees and the vert.

5

The Castle Experience

Throughout this book, various ways to approach and explore castle ruins have been suggested to the reader: taking in the entirety of its surroundings; considering the role of the castle within the region, as indicated by its physical position and associated natural features; imagining how it would have functioned not only as a military base and as a residence but also as an administrative center and a manor house; and identifying landscape features, the relics from the past, and structural elements scattered around a site which might have been associated with a castle or the peasantry who supported it. It is also worthwhile to consider how various architectural features and the layout of the property displayed the owner's social, financial, and political positions vis-à-vis his neighbors, his peers, his monarch, and his rivals, and to also envision their roles in ceremonial and leisure time activities.

Stepping towards Discovery

One of the best ways to experience castles is to begin by exploring the greatest and best preserved, such as the Tower of London, Windsor Castle, or Dover Castle. Each of these sites contains a vast repository of British history; their physical makeup actually traces the development of the monarchy from the defeat of the Anglo-Saxons by the Normans through to modern times. Despite their current roles as heavily visited tourist attractions, each of these massive castles offers visitors access to the past through their structural remains, which preserve the wide array of features that were integral to every castle in the realm. For example, each of these royal fortresses features a central keep and adjoining baileys, lengthy curtain walls, complex gateways, and powerful settings that display the supremacy of the monarch. The powerful rectangular keeps at Dover and the Tower of London are, arguably, the most impressive and best surviving examples of their type, and Windsor's round keep still crowns a substantial motte at the core of the site. Both the Tower of London and Dover Castle developed from relatively simple Norman-era strongholds into concentric fortresses; both carried out military roles well into the twentieth century. Of particular note, the Windsor estate retains extensive physical evidence of its role as an enormous manor as well as a key royal residence.

However, even though the great fortresses contain the keys to castle exploration, visitors can find themselves somewhat overwhelmed by the enormity of the sites — and by the sometimes chaotic presence of so many other visitors. Even though these castles should be on everyone's list of "must sees," they can seem strangely stark, alienated from their medieval past, and almost lifeless. For this author, the ideal setting for exploring a castle is quiet solitude, when the throngs have departed or where the site is off the beaten track. In many cases, this approach to exploring castles means deliberately avoiding the more popular tourist destinations in favor of the lesser known — but historically and archaeologically valuable — sites. This suggestion is not to say, however, that Britain's most famous castles should not be explored, but rather that the most intimate, revealing experiences one can have at a castle occur when one's senses and imagination are not blocked by the presence of a lot of other people. Then, one's curiosity can be released, and the overall experience of the place and one's awareness of its past will be heightened.

Exploring a castle at one's own pace encourages each individual to get the most from each site. It can be quite exciting to discover hidden treasures, such as medieval graffiti, mason's marks, carved masonry faces, traces of wall paintings, latrine chutes, roosting holes, and charred fireplaces, or larger manmade structures, such as Civil War earthworks, fishponds, gardens, or town walls. Always take in the entire scene, from the distant approach to the castle to nearby natural features, such as streams, which may have provided the castle's water supply or ran the lord's corn mill. Making educated conclusions about the relationship between the castle and the uses of these features will greatly enrich your experience.

Besides carrying a camera and a pair of waterproof shoes or boots with good tread to safely wander the sites, take a detailed map in order to locate the castles you hope to visit. Of invaluable benefit for anyone exploring Britain are the series of maps known as Ordnance Survey (OS) maps, particularly the older green Pathfinder and Landranger series (in fact, the older, the better, as newer maps now leave off many out-of-the-way sites). Originating in 1791 as part of a defense project to survey the English countryside, these meticulously measured, diligently drawn maps detail virtually every inch of land within Great Britain. They identify public footpaths, trails, and access points across public and private lands. Using what are known as grid references, these wonderful maps pinpoint the exact locations of castles, earthworks, and many other relevant features, including standing buildings, post offices, inns, public houses, private houses, streams, and even place names, which will dramatically aid your search. They are available on the Internet and from local shops, bookstores, and Tourist Information Centres in Britain.

An enjoyable way to explore castles is to base oneself in a particular locality where a number of castles exist in a variety of conditions. For example, Pembrokeshire has at least two occupied medieval castles (one of which offers overnight stays), several restored stone castles, one heavily ruined stone castle, a bishop's castle, a tower house, and numerous earth and timber fortifications, the finest of which is at Wiston. All of these sites are within easy driving distance of each other. Several can be seen from far away, which allows visitors to gain an understanding of the strategic value of the structure's position relative both to the defensive nature of the site and to the prestige of the owner.

After reaching the property, pause before heading into the castle itself. Try to identify traces of an outer bailey or an enclosing ditch at a motte or ringwork site now isolated in a farmer's field. Try to identify the location of these features at castles where later construction may have covered them. Then, when examining the ruins, imagine how the masonry pieces may have appeared when the castle was originally occupied. Also consider how the castle was used, who may have lived inside, and how well the structure would have performed during a siege. Look closely for evidence of medieval life, such as remnants of scorched stone or bake ovens, plasterwork and paint, corbelled platforms where candles once dripped wax, and elements of religious worship (soldiers often carved tiny crosses in prison walls) or self-aggrandizement, such as sculpted images of the lords or their heraldic emblems. Be aware of any odoriferous reminders of sanitation limitations (some latrine chutes do actually retain an aroma of the past) and imagine using the slate or wood-covered facilities on a rainy winter's evening.

Heraldic emblems can be found on many castle ruins. Owners took pride in their heritage and ensured visitors were well aware of their place within the medieval social order. These emblems adorn the main gateway at Bodiam Castle.

Do not expect to immediately recognize all the features of a castle. It is only over a period of time and visiting a variety of castles that one can begin to make educated assessments about the parts that lay strewn around a site. In fact, some castle ruins still stump the experts, most of whom have explored dozens of sites and studied their details extensively. This author's best suggestion is for beginning castle explorers to simply explore each site, absorbing the ambience while looking closely at its architectural features. I originally began exploring castles simply because they were historic, medieval structures and exuded tremendous aesthetic appeal. For me, at that time, the histories were of secondary importance to the remains. Even though my interest has expanded over time to include the histories behind the sites, I firmly believe that exploring the ruins is essential to truly understanding the castle's role in the Middle Ages. Perhaps even more important is recognizing that these structures, crumbling and barren though they may now be, were actually occupied by real people. This awareness enlivens the sites and invigorates my experience of castles.

In order to gain the most from my visits, I always purchase the castle's guidebook, if available, prior to entering the site and open it to the plan of the castle. As I roam the ruins, I repeatedly refer to the booklet, not just to verify my own assessment of what I am seeing but also to discover if I have missed a notable feature. These books are invaluable aids for exploring a castle. Later, when there is time to read the text more carefully, be sure to fit together any missing or confusing pieces. Some guidebooks contain artist's renditions of how the castle would have looked during different phases of its existence, which can trigger one's imagination and expand one's appreciation of the place.

Considering the Context — Churches and Towns

Recently, castle researchers have begun focusing on the context of the castle within its setting and have come to recognize that the landscape close to the castle was often manipu-

Artists' renditions of ruined castles give us immediate access to the past and are of particular benefit when actually examining the ruins. Neil Ludlow's interpretation of Narberth Castle shows the castle as it would have looked in the sixteenth century (courtesy Neil Ludlow).

lated for ceremonial purposes as well as for farming and other activities. As much as possible when visiting a castle site, be sure to take in the entirety of its surroundings, the lay of the land, unusual mounds or dips, and also pre- and post-medieval structures. They can fill in gaps in one's understanding of the history of the site and open one's mind to a broader range of possible activities that occurred there. Consideration of the relationship between a castle and other structures in the vicinity, such as medieval or post-medieval houses or churches, will enhance one's experience of the castle site and increase one's awareness of the inter-connectivity between the castle and its surroundings. Many castle towns, such as Warwick and Pembroke, still have the medieval houses of household staff and other castle workers. Those at Warwick line both sides of the River Avon just outside the castle property; many are occupied and survive in fine condition, their exteriors quite visible from the battlements and also approachable (but do not trespass!).

And, as mentioned earlier, castles and churches often still stand in close proximity to each other. In locations where the castles are difficult to find or are said to have vanished, just head towards the parish church, the tower of which generally can be seen above other buildings and keep on the lookout for the castle. While there, seize the chance to expand the castle experience by taking in the church as well. If open, head inside and look for effigies, wall paintings, and tombs associated with the former owners of the castle. Many are adorned with lifelike portraits of the dead and symbols that reveal personal achievements or participation in historic events such as the Crusades. Also stroll through the adjoining graveyard and look for aging tombs that have associations to the lords of the castle.

Always place a castle in the context of its surrounding landscape, where you can often identify related structures. Beyond the walls at Warwick Castle, for example, homes once occupied by castle servants and other supporters still line local streets.

In addition to the construction of churches, new towns also developed in response to the presence of a new castle, which not only served as the power base for the region's overlord but also provided an excellent place for the exchange of goods and labor services. Not surprisingly, market towns such as Haverfordwest and Pickering often grew up in a castle's shadow. Besides protecting the town's residents and controlling access, the main gate through the walls served as a stopping point where tolls were collected before merchants or peasants could proceed into the town to sell their goods.[1] The construction (and repair) of a town's walls was largely funded by a special tax known as murage.

Medieval churches often contain the remains of the lords of the castle and their families and descendants. Inside the chapel at Farleigh Hungerford Castle, visitors will discover well-preserved paintings on the walls and on the tombs of the Hungerford family, which are also decorated with life-like effigies.

Other towns, however, appeared in order to populate the spot with supporters of the lord or monarch and became centers of colonization, known as planted or plantation towns. Edward I was particularly adept at establishing planted towns, which he used to keep the Welsh at bay late in the thirteenth century. In fact, when he decided to build his mammoth concentric castle at Beaumaris, Edward ordered the relocation of the native population to another place on the Isle of Anglesey. That town became known as Newborough.

At Beaumaris and other Edwardian castles, the adjoining towns were not only dominated by the king's new fortresses, but they were also enclosed by a circuit of towered stone walls. Inside, Edward established each town according to a symmetrical grid plan. Intended to keep the colonists safe from rebelling invaders and also to provide an additional line of defense for the castles themselves, these town walls were at least six feet thick, rose twenty feet high, and featured numerous mural towers, many of which were open-gorged. In addition to fulfilling a defensive function, they also visibly reminded the native Welsh of their defeat at the hands of the English army.

Many castles are located in, adjacent to, or near a set of medieval town walls. Some formed a circuit which ended at the castle or enclosed the castle. The walls in castle towns, as at Denbigh, Conwy, Caernarfon, York, Tenby, Chester, and Newcastle-upon-Tyne, remain in such good condition that visitors can walk along extensive portions and explore tower interiors. Town walls often had a variety of defensive features, just like the stone castles nearby.

The lengthy towered walls at Conwy extend from the castle itself to the opposite side of the town, where they peak, and then continue around the rest of the town and back to the castle. Almost completely intact, the walls featured open-gorged towers, which resembled the mighty fortress.

For example, the impressive walls at Conwy, which still extend for three-fourths of a mile, features three twin-towered gateways, twenty-one round towers placed at fifty-yard intervals, and a continuous wall-walk. The inner side of the open-gorged towers had timber bridges, which could be removed during an attack to effectively isolate that portion of the wall and its flanking towers.

The immense wall enclosing Newcastle-upon-Tyne and its castle was erected during the thirteenth and fourteenth centuries, partly to keep Scottish invaders at bay. Funded by town residents, the town defenses stretched over two miles and featured seventeen towers with 10-foot-thick walls standing some 25 feet high, six main gates, and several smaller towers and postern gateways. The ditch around the exterior measured 36 feet wide and was over 14.5 feet deep. Portions of the castle and wall, most notably the great rectangular keep and the Black Gate, a barbican erected by Henry III in front of the town's north gate, survive in excellent condition.

Tenby's medieval walls are, undeniably, the town's finest feature, unlike the castle, which pales in comparison. Much of the walling was saved from ruin in 1873 when a local man named Dr. Charter obtained an injunction to prevent the town corporation from pulling them down. Dating to the late thirteenth century but altered several times, the stone wall completely ringed the town, except for the expanse along the southern waterfront, which had its own natural defenses and was reinforced with masonry at several points. Archaeological evidence indicates that a bank and ditch probably fronted the original, weakly constructed town walls, which were replaced after the Welsh devastated Tenby in 1260.

Of Tenby's four original gateways and numerous rounded towers, only one gate and seven towers survive along the western side of the town. The most elaborate and largest of these massive towers, known locally as the Five Arches or St. George's Gate, was actually a D-shaped barbican defended with arrowslits. It led visitors toward a simple inner gateway, known as the South or West Gate (due its position midway along the western length of walling). A set of steps leading from the adjacent wall-walk allowed access to the portcullis mechanism situated above the gateway. To the south, three smaller towers still project from the wall; two are round and the third, located between them, is rectangular (it may be a later addition).

The medieval town walls at Pembroke, only a few miles east of Tenby, also once enclosed the entire town; extensive sections are still quite visible. The stone walls attached directly to the western and eastern sides of the castle, such that town and castle formed a single unit. The complete circuit had six round towers (four of which remain) and three gateways, one of which was twin-towered (no longer survives). Near the castle's Westgate Tower, fragments of the medieval gate can be identified, including a portion of the southern side and springers. On the southeastern side of Pembroke, a round tower known as Goose's Lane Tower (now only a fragment), the Gazebo Tower (the upper half of which was replaced with a modern structure), and the Gun Tower defended the town. At the northeastern end, Round Turret and Barnard's Tower dominated the walls. Barnard's Tower still stands three stories, retains its battlements, although they are in poor condition, and is accessible from the town wall. On the first floor level, visitors will find a garderobe, arrowslits, and a portcullis groove. The second story features a round-backed fireplace, a window, and additional arrowslits. A fine section of town wall then runs southeast from Barnard's Tower.

Whenever visiting a castle site, in addition to exploring any town walls, be sure to notice the layout of the town, for the design of a medieval town often points to the position of its

Tenby's Five Arches Gate functioned as a barbican and defended one of several entrances through the medieval town walls. The arches were later additions to the original structure, which is crowned with battlements and arrowslits.

castle. The grid plans of medieval towns make a great finding aid for people looking for the castle. The main street (sometimes called High Street), which normally bisected the grid, ran directly from the castle through the center of the town, where burgage plots, residences, and shops lining both sides of the road. At Longtown (also known as Ewyas Lacy), in Herefordshire, the motte and bailey castle dominates the head of the elongated village that gave it its name. The main road actually passes through the castle site, which is particularly notable for the impressive round keep that crowns the substantial motte and its well-preserved earthwork enclosure.

Appreciating the Ruins

The most invasive and long-lasting problem found at many castle sites is caused by a disrespectful attitude, which takes form of tossing trash or other waste into wells, towers, or moats or onto the ground, or vandalizing the remains with graffiti and paint or by removing, chipping, or carving the stonework. Even though medieval graffiti and trash can reveal much to archaeologists about life and conditions during past times, when present-day visitors carelessly or selfishly chose to leave something of themselves behind at a castle, they show a callous disregard not only for the past, which survives and imbues each site, but also for the present and the future, when other castle enthusiasts, visitors from home and abroad, students, castellologists, and other researchers will explore the castle. Sadly, some local authori-

Pembroke is an excellent example of a medieval walled town. The towered walls extended around the town from two sides of the great castle, enclosing residences, burgage plots, and other structures, some of which are still in use. This artist's rendition displays the castle as it would have appeared in about 1500. Note the towered castle walls, the outer and inner baileys, William Marshal's round keep, and the position of the barbican, in front of the main gatehouse (courtesy Neil Ludlow).

ties have had to restrict public access to their castles due to vandalism and other types of unsavory behavior.

In fact, the condition of every ancient or historic monument directly depends on the attitude of the public to it. Always treat the remains — no matter whether they are part of the castle, town walls, or associated structures — with utmost care. It would be a tragic mistake to alter the historical integrity of the place just because of a misstep, careless disregard for the fragility of the site, or because the site is already ruined and one mistakenly thinks it would make little difference if what does survive is damaged further.

Earth and timber castles in particular are extremely vulnerable to erosion, which results not just from rain, wind, and gravity, but also from humans and livestock clambering along the fragile embankments, loosening the soil, and causing slippage. At masonry castles, the footsteps and itchy fingers of visitors can cause damage to stonework that has been poorly consolidated or has been weakened by vegetation growing into cracks, porous rock, or mortar. Even at restored castles that are maintained on a regular basis, the public's frequent use of the spiral staircases causes unintentional wear to the stone steps (the newels). Visitor traffic can also result in problems such as the dislodging of stones from the mortar and makes the already sizeable expense of maintaining a castle site even higher. One key reason why so many castles were in ruin by the sixteenth century was the prohibitively high cost of their repair and upkeep. Many owners neglected their castles and eventually chose to abandon them altogether rather than bankrupt themselves trying to make repairs.

However, there is much more to the conservation of castle sites than just the expense of returning them to their medieval state, something much less concrete but equally — if not more — important. Clearly, the state of preservation of Britain's castles varies dramatically from one site to the next. One might wonder why some of the great castles, such as Caerphilly or Kenilworth, are ruins, whereas others, such as Caernarfon or Leeds, seem in almost perfect condition. Others may find it equally perplexing that many of Britain's most historically important castles, such as Fotheringhay and Pontefract, which were once substantial stone structures, now contain almost no masonry. The fact is that even the greatest of Britain's surviving medieval castles, except for those that have been occupied more or less continuously, lingered as ruins well into modern times.

For example, it is now almost impossible to imagine that the royal fortresses at Caernarfon, Conwy, Harlech, and Beaumaris, along with the town walls that enclosed them, were ruins overgrown with vegetation and crowded with structures that had no place in a castle. Photographs taken in the nineteenth century show that the castles were empty, overgrown shells; fortunately, a substantial amount of medieval masonry also survived and provided a solid foundation upon which to base repair work. Nevertheless, ruins they were, their walls crumbling and rooftops decaying, just like the majority of castles in the realm, many of which are in dire need of attention before they disappear altogether.

Logically, one can understand how the expense of reconstructing such sites would prohibit everyone but the wealthiest individuals and public agencies from funding a return to their original condition. In the above cases, each castle's overall condition and historical relevance must have justified extensive conservation, the funding of which came from a variety of sources, including the local government or wealthy owners. Rather than merely viewing castle ruins as piles of junk and convenient quarries for building materials, many people believed they were valuable enough to warrant large expenditures of money, time, and labor to preserve — and to preserve them as ruins rather than to rebuild them.

The primary theme of this book is that, regardless of their size and the extent to which they survive, ruined castles are exciting, vital places worthy of exploration and admiration. They should be evaluated, envisioned, and enjoyed in their own right for their aesthetic qualities, as well as their histories and architectural achievements. This is not a new notion. During the seventeenth, eighteenth, and nineteenth centuries, artists such as Samuel and Nathaniel Buck, Edward Webb, Henry Gastineau, and J. M. W. Turner, antiquarians such as J. R. Cobb and Sir Ivor Philipps, and Victorian citizens were attracted by ruins and their romantic settings and memorialized them in paintings, engravings, novels — and as ruins. Ruins even became the focal point for Sunday outings, when members of the social elite donned their finest garb and strolled through the sites. Amateur archaeologists and military and architectural historians also devoted themselves to the pursuit of the past as attested to by ancient and medieval ruins, and in that way encouraged their preservation.

Some early preservation advocates argued that the best approach was the full-scale restoration of individual sites, returning a castle, for example, to the period of time considered to have the greatest historical value. However, during the nineteenth century, men such as John Ruskin and William Morris denounced this practice, which was in vogue at the time, railing against the "Victorian passion for wholesale remodeling of ecclesiastical buildings and other large-scale restoration projects on castles such as Caernarfon."[2] Their passion for retaining (preserving) the historical integrity of monuments such as castles and churches led to the formation of the so-called Anti-Scrape Movement to oppose practices such as scraping away historical plasterwork, painting, and surface masonry, which revealed deeper levels but destroyed more recent work.

John Ruskin, writer, poet, artist, lecturer, and controversial social critic, was an early advocate for preserving ruins as ruins and leaving them as the authentic historic relics that they are. Ruskin vigorously supported a policy of preserving ruins with as little intervention as possible, an approach to preservation which he laid out in his book *The Seven Lamps of Architecture*, published in 1849. Any other attitude, he believed, was a grave mistake, for it resulted in a structure that had never existed. To restore it would not only be a disservice to the original builders, whose thoughts and workmanship we can never know, but also would be based purely on conjecture.[3]

For Ruskin, the value of a historic monument, even in ruin, was its age, and the fact of its continued existence:

> The greatest glory of a building is not in its stones, nor in its gold. Its glory is in its Age, and in that deep sense of voicefulness, of stern watching, of mysterious sympathy, nay, even of approval or condemnation, which we feel in the walls that have long been washed by the passing wavers of humanity. It is in their lasting witness against men, in their quiet contrast with the transitional character of all things, in the strength which, through the lapse of seasons and times, and the decline and birth of dynasties, and the changing face of the earth, and of the limits of the sea, maintains its sculptured shapeliness for a time insuperable, connects foreign and forgotten ages with each other, and half constitutes the identity, as it concentrates the sympathy, of nations ... it is not until a building has assumed this character, till it has been encrusted with the fame, and hallowed by the deeds of men, till its walls have been witnesses of suffering, and its pillars rise out of the shadows of death, that its existence, more lasting as it is than that of natural objects of the world around it, can be gifted with even so much as these possess, of language and life.[4]

To press his point further, Ruskin emphasized, "We have no right whatever to touch them. They are not ours."

Ruskin's reverence for the past, especially as embodied in its aging buildings, sparked the Anti-Scrape Movement. He was instrumental in shaping the thinking of William Morris, poet, artist, writer, and socialist who, among his other achievements, was prominent in the Arts and Crafts Movement. In 1877, Ruskin, Morris, and architect Philip Webb founded the Society for the Protection of Ancient Buildings, or SPAB, the manifestation of the Anti-Scrape attitude.

In writing the SPAB manifesto, Morris proclaimed that, during the previous fifty years, the increasing interest in ancient monuments had "done more for their destruction than all the foregoing centuries of revolution, violence and contempt." The manifesto, which is the basis of the society's philosophy even today, bemoaned the "strange idea of the Restoration of ancient buildings ... [as] a most fatal idea, which by its very name implies that it is possible to strip from a building this, that, and the other part of its history — of its life that is — and then to stay the hand at some arbitrary point, and leave it still historical, living, and even as it once was." The practice, in Morris's view, resulted in "a feeble and lifeless forgery."[5]

The SPAB's founders supported a minimalist approach to ruins, preserving as much as possible of the site but with as little intrusion as possible, rather than transforming it into something that never actually existed or tearing away pieces of its history in order to measure up to some arbitrary ideal of what was valuable about the site. They recognized that conserving the entire site as found rather than saving portions from only one era would limit the likelihood of making errors that would be too costly to fix or would permanently distort or destroy what remained of the original structure. Out of this realization, the Society decided to identify and list all as of yet unrestored ancient buildings in an effort to prevent any insensitive, and therefore inaccurate, changes.[6] Some 150 years later, SPAB still advocates the same principles: to "repair not restore" historic structures, to "use responsible methods" when working on a site, to "complement not parody" when adding new work to an aging site, to perform "regular maintenance" but only "essential work," to use compatible materials, to distinguish new work from the old, and to respect the age of the structural features, because "age can confer a beauty of its own."[7] They also publish a list of properties that need repair, renovation, or conversion, which is available to members, whom they believe would make "sympathetic and principled owners."

What was it about ruins that appealed to the romanticists, antiquarians, historians, writers, artists, tourists, and, indeed, the everyday citizen, up to the present day? The Anti-Scrapists emphasized the beauty of aging ruins, and even Ruskin recognized that ruins, which he considered historic entities, stirred one's emotions. In 1903, Alois Riegl, an Austrian art historian, professor, and founder of the Vienna School of Art History, attempted to clarify what made the preservation of structures he characterized as "unintentional" monuments (including ruins) so vitally important. In his thought-provoking essay "The Modern Cult of Monuments: Its Character and Its Origin," Riegl distinguished between intentional monuments, those features deliberately erected to commemorate an event or a person, and unintentional monuments, including ruins, which were created for some other purpose but in the end became valued for their actual relationship to the past, as we perceive it today.

As unintentional monuments, ruins have both "age-value" and "historical-value," qualities which, while valid, created contradictory approaches to restoration of monuments. For Riegl, "ruins appear more picturesque the more advanced their state of decay…. Age-value manifests itself immediately through visual perception and appeals directly to our emotions."[8] Not only was a ruin valuable for its actual age but also for its increasing beauty as it decayed. When a site has age-value, all building phases should be preserved but with minimal intervention. This concept is consistent with the philosophies touted by Ruskin and the Anti-Scrape Movement. On the other hand, having historical value results in the restoration of a monument to a specific point in its history but, at the same time, to the unavoidable destruction of newer building phases in order to "faithfully" reach the site's original state, its most important historical period.[9]

Riegl also discussed the concepts of "use-value" and "art-value," what he considered as "present-day values." In order for a monument to have use-value, it must serve some productive purpose. However, redeveloping decaying historic sites into something new and economically useful, perhaps a business building or a restaurant, is inconsistent with its age-value, its historical-value, and its authentic aesthetic appeal. The result would be nothing less than the destruction of the site itself.

Even today, the perception of what makes an aged site valuable is fairly subjective and professionals in the heritage sector still debate the issue. As more and more nations involve themselves in the preservation of their heritage, the debate widens. In 2003, the International Council on Monuments and Sites (ICOMOS) held their fourteenth General Assembly and Scientific Symposium. Their theme? "Place, memory, meaning: preserving intangible values in monuments and sites." These values include the site's aura, its spiritual message, and the feeling value.

In April 2008, English Heritage, the public body charged with advising the government on England's ancient and historic monuments, published "Conservation Principles: Policies and Guidance for the Sustainable Management of the Historic Environment,"[10] official policy based on the results of a consultation that involved members of the heritage sector and also the public. Similar in many respects to what Riegl identified and the Anti-Scrapists realized over a century ago, English Heritage concludes that each site has to be assessed relative to the different heritage values it possesses. With the relevant values in mind, decisions can be made about site management and conservation, the role the place should take within the local and broader communities in which it exists, and how it will be presented to the public.[11] There are four primary heritage values which give meaning to a place: (1) evidential value: "the potential of a place to yield primary evidence about past human activity"; (2) historical value: "the ways in which the present can be connected through a place to past people, events and aspects of life"; (3) aesthetic value: "the ways in which people derive sensory and intellectual stimulation from a place"; and (4) communal value, which "relates to the meanings of a place for the people who relate to it, and whose collective experience or memory it holds." Within each category are subcategories, such as the spiritual value of the place, "which is generally dependent on the perceived survival of the authentic fabric or character of the place from the past."[12]

When we look at ancient monuments such as Caernarfon, Harlech, and Conwy, we can easily see that their empty, albeit heavily restored, shells were once impressive medieval castles, Harlech perhaps more aesthetically pleasing than the two other castles. We are aware of their histories, including their associations with Edward I and the struggle for Welsh independence. We recognize their special significance and are not surprised that they draw scores of visitors each year. We may even thank the governmental bodies for restoring the sites as comprehensively as they did, even if they remain largely ruined. Even major ruins such as Kenilworth and Raglan, where conservationists more closely followed a "conserve as found" policy, are clearly castles; these aging structures have notable histories as well as visual appeal. However, when it comes to other, more ruinous sites, such as Caergwrle, Farleigh Hungerford, or even Corfe, some visitors doubt that they are truly castles, even though the sites have their own, significant histories, contain physical evidence of past lives, and can extract an emotional response from us. Why? Sadly, nowadays many people have been charmed into believing that, even today, centuries after their construction and later abandonment, medieval castles should look like those they see in the movies or like those that still house the royal family or like one of the flamboyant castellated mansions that appeared around Britain during the eighteenth and nineteenth centuries.

It is important to understand that, for several reasons, the majority of castles in Britain had already fallen into ruin, at least to some degree, by the sixteenth century, as John Leland documented on his rounds throughout the countryside on behalf of Henry VIII. As stated earlier, many times, owners could not afford the castle's upkeep. Consequently, they chose either to move to other residences that fit with the architectural styles of the times, to sell off the contents and the castle, to farm them out to tenants, or to abandon them and allow them to continue to decay. Not surprisingly, ruins increasingly became an integral part of the landscape as castles became obsolete or were abandoned. Nevertheless, many were repaired and served during the English Civil Wars of the 1640s. Afterwards, Parliamentarian troops pulled down or blew up the walls or battlements of many castles in order to prevent them from returning to action against the new government. In fact, relatively few castles have persevered as livable homes. And, those that are still occupied regularly require an enormous financial outlay to maintain. Nowadays, castle owners often lease out parts for weddings, as film venues, or to renters, put on special events or living history re-enactments, or open some wings to paying tourists to help fund necessary repairs and ongoing structural maintenance.

Prior to the twentieth century, relatively few castles received financial and restorative attention from the Crown. The first preservation project paid for by the government took place in 1845 at Newark Castle, which was then held by the monarchy. The consolidation work cost £650.[13] At Caernarfon Castle, the constable, Sir Llewelyn Turner, carried out extensive (but somewhat defective) restoration work between 1870 and 1900 on behalf of the government.[14] But it was not until 1882, five years after the founding of SPAB, that the Ancient Monuments Protection Act, Britain's first piece of legislation aimed at protecting historic and prehistoric sites, was signed into law. Then, it took until 1913 and the passage of the Ancient Monuments Consolidation and Amendment Act for the government (initially as the Office of Works and later the Ministry of the Environment) to finally acquire the legal right to take monuments into care and to ensure the sites received what they deemed to be proper restoration and management. Even so, most early restoration efforts were privately funded projects

Built on the site of a Roman station and possibly an earlier Iron Age hillfort, Caergwrle Castle is an interesting mix of Welsh and English design features. Today little remains of Dafydd ap Gruffydd's castle, most of the structure being rebuilt by Edward I in about 1283. The Anti-Scrape Movement would have vigorously supported the preservation of this historical site as the ruin we see today.

The first royal castle to be restored in the modern era, mighty Newark Castle lines the River Trent. The scene is deceiving, for the opposite side, which faces into the town, is heavily ruined. In recent years, archaeological excavations and conservation work have occurred at the castle.

on privately owned property.[15] Consequently, several of Britain's most impressive castles are the legacies of rich and influential individuals, such as the earls of Powis, Lord Curzon, and the marquesses of Bute, who had the ambition, foresight, and finances to tackle the monumental challenge of restoring the castles in their possession.

In 1776, the marquesses of Bute acquired the hulking concentric ruin at Caerphilly along with other castle sites in and around Cardiff, Wales. Finally, in 1871, the third marquess of Bute, John Patrick Crichton-Stewart, initiated the first reconstruction work at Caerphilly. Then, in 1890, he commissioned architect William Frame to draw up a series images of the castle in order to begin a full-scale restoration of the site. However, it took his son, the fourth marquess, John Crichton-Stewart, to transform the ruins into the site we see today — the third marquess had turned his attention to the restoration of nearby Cardiff Castle and the complete reconstruction of Castell Coch, the fairy-tale "Red Castle" just north of Cardiff.

Caerphilly Castle is in many ways the classic concentric fortress. Erected by Gilbert de Clare II in the 1260s, the castle was inspired by Kenilworth Castle and featured a complex series of water and stone defenses designed to thwart the most formidable of enemies, and undoubtedly to proclaim the preeminence of its lord, one of the most influential noblemen in Edward I's court. De Clare, Earl of Gloucester and Lord of Glamorgan, was also Edward's rival and building such a monumental stronghold would have declared to his king that he considered himself at least equal in stature. Caerphilly Castle had a relatively short lifespan. By 1539, it had begun to decay and even became a quarry for building materials. After participating in the English Civil Wars a century later, the castle's defenses were destroyed, the great lake-like moats drained, and the site abandoned to the ravages of time, weather, and uncontrolled undergrowth. The task of restoring the extensive ruins proved quite daunting.

Investing some £125,000 (roughly the equivalent of £22 million in modern currency), the fourth marquess of Bute carried out what has been characterized as "the most comprehensive and carefully researched restoration work ever undertaken in Britain."[16] From 1928 to 1930, Crichton-Stuart not only cleared the site of ivy and vegetation which was destroying the stability of the stonework, he embarked on a large-scale, meticulously conducted rebuilding program which, in essence, produced the castle that visitors can explore today. Ironically, had Lord Bute not undertaken this project, the castle would probably have remained a complete ruin, the masonry cleared and consolidated and the site made safe for public exploration, but not rebuilt.[17] However, thanks to the work done by the fourth marquess and his huge retinue of employees, the State was in a position in 1950, when it acquired the site, to complete Bute's project and reflood the lakes. Even though a ruin, the great restored castle, with its mighty stone and water defenses, honors the ingenuity of its builders and the men who restored it.

The restoration of other castles fell to avid antiquarians who had the knowledge, resources, and determination to tackle the extensive, labor-intensive projects. Barrister and antiquarian, J. R. Cobb, for example, played a major role in the consolidation of Pembroke, Manorbier, and Caldicot Castles. Cobb purchased Caldicot Castle in 1885 with the intention of restoring the structure to use as a residence. About five years earlier, he had leased Manorbier Castle, built a private house inside the medieval barn, and did extensive restoration work at that site. His stated approach to restoration work reflected the attitude of the times: "One, never to remove an ancient stone except to put a similar sound one in its place or to bring to light one more ancient. Two, never to add anything without evidence that it had existed before."[18] Even though Cobb did take creative license when restoring some elements of the castles under his care, his restoration of the main gatehouse at Caldicot Castle remains one of its finest features; it was here that Cobb lived for a time. Today, conservation work at the castle is ongoing. The present emphasis is on preserving the buildings using medieval techniques rather than on reconstruction work such as done by Cobb.[19]

The issue of whether to "conserve as found" or to "restore" ruins has long plagued the British government. Even though the Office of Works had "gradually adopted a policy against the wholesale restoration and rebuilding of ancient monuments,"[20] before 1913 they had no legal authority to block projects such as those undertaken by the Butes and J. R. Cobb. In fact, the State actually tried to halt the restoration work at Caerphilly Castle, which Lord Bute had begun without their knowledge or consent (which was not required until 1913) and went against their "conserve as found" policy, but the project continued after some conciliatory efforts were made on both sides and Bute agreed to fully survey and record the work for the State. Indeed, the restoration of Caerphilly Castle was the very type of situation that SPAB and other Anti-Scrape preservationists had wanted to prevent: In the end, some castles were heavily restored; many are now the focus not only of the tourist trade but also of a huge investment in time and money. Other castles were consolidated, the ruins neatly shored up to allow safe public access. Still others, certainly the lesser known and smallest sites, have been left in their "natural" state, vegetation overgrowing and penetrating the unstable masonry, earthworks eroding, stonework crumbling due to a lack of intervention in the destructive process of aging. The Anti-Scrapists might have welcomed this last approach (even though it ultimately leads to the complete loss of many sites), but would have reacted with despair and disdain at the large-scale restoration projects carried out not only by the likes of Bute and Cobb, but by the State as well.

Despite the best of intentions, it has been virtually impossible for the Office of Works and its successor agencies to adhere to the "conserve as found" philosophy. Each project must be evaluated according to its particular situation, the condition of the masonry and other features, and what seems to be the most pressing concern. Over time, different inspectors have made their own determinations about which parts of a particular monument are significant and which are unimportant, extraneous, or even confusing[21] and removed or replaced them as they saw fit. It is undeniable that many of the efforts undertaken by the British government, both in England and Wales, have produced remarkable monuments, but, in doing so, they stripped away an unknown number of features from other periods (both pre- and post-medieval) which would now be considered integral pieces of their historical makeup. For example, during the 1950s at Framlingham Castle, the Ministry pulled out the first floor of the eighteenth-century poorhouse that occupied the site of the medieval great hall, only one wall of which had survived.[22] The most notable

Antiquarians and amateur historians were responsible for the restoration of several of Britain's finest castles. J. R. Cobb was an avid castle enthusiast, who financed and spearheaded the restoration of Pembroke, Manorbier, and Caldicot Castle, shown here.

structure still standing in the inner bailey in the mid-twentieth century, the poorhouse was an otherwise intact building which played a key role in the later history of the castle. Ruskin, et al., would have railed against this destruction, claiming the converted building was "a lie from beginning to end."[23]

Caernarfon Castle, Edward I's headquarters in North Wales, is one of the world's best known and most visible medieval castles. Not only did the imposing fortress receive considerable international attention when it served as the venue for the investiture of Charles as the Prince of Wales in 1969, but in 1988 it was chosen by UNESCO for inclusion on its list of designated World Heritage Sites, along with the castles at Conwy, Harlech, and Beaumaris and their associated town walls. Having walls that mirror those constructed by the Holy Roman Emperor, Constantine, to enclose his capitol city at Constantinople (now known as Istanbul), Caernarfon Castle's outstanding condition and unique design directly contributed to its placement among the world's greatest medieval structures. Yet, many people would be shocked to know that, in 1815, a report written by Robert Jones, a local surveyor and architect, stated that the castle was "in a most ruinous state" and that the entire structure was greatly dilapidated.[24] Nevertheless, the castle was still in use: Two areas stored blasting powder, another two areas stored ammunition, one area served as a guardroom for the local militia, and a sixth area was used by the harbormaster. In addition, tenants occupied the Eagle Tower, Edward I's private residence, and also a part of the ditch. Jones advised the Commissioners of Woods, Forests and Land Revenues, to whom he reported, to offer the castle for sale at a price of £500; however, they chose not to follow his recommendation and the castle continued to decay.

In 1845, a concerted effort was finally made to rectify the situation at Caernarfon and Commissioners hired famed architect, Anthony Salvin, to oversee repairs and consolidation work at the castle. Even though he would probably have tackled the complete restoration of the ruinous castle, Salvin "concentrated on urgent repair, leaving restoration to his successors."[25] Consequently, it was another fifty years before Sir Llewelyn Turner, deputy constable, financed and commanded a major restoration project, intending not only to make essential repairs, but to take the building work several steps farther to return the castle "to its pristine state ... [so that] this and future generations [would gain] an infinitely better idea of the life of our early kings and rulers than can be guessed from inspecting a ruin, of which there are plenty so badly decayed that they hardly admit of reparation." This attitude persists in some corners of the heritage sector as well as in the minds of some visitors.

For the next three decades, Sir Llewelyn applied his own policy towards the consolidation and conservation of the castle, one that clearly digressed from the "conserve as found" policy reputedly supported by the government. Turner had insisted on being in total control of the project from the start and the government essentially gave him all the room he wanted to do as he wished to the castle. This action ultimately led to the irretrievable loss of structures and features Turner decided had little value but which may in fact have revealed much more about the history and development of the site had they been left standing. For example, he removed a mound of earth and vegetation situated in the upper bailey, which, interestingly enough, was found to contain a limekiln and stone vaults. Researchers theorize that this mound may actually have been the original motte castle.

With Turner's death in 1903 came the end of the major restoration project he had spearheaded for three decades. A new survey of the castle was undertaken. It was determined not only that much of the structure remained in extremely poor condition despite Turner's efforts and that the castle needed consolidation rather than more restoration, but also that many of the "improvements" made by Turner were defective or already in need of repair. After they officially took over the castle in 1908, the newly renamed Office of Works removed much of Turner's work and applied their policy of conserving as found. Today, Caernarfon Castle is only partly restored, the ruins largely consolidated and made safe for public access.[26] As at many castle sites around England and Wales, however, consolidation work and other modifications, such as better access for the disabled, are virtually continuous.

Throughout the twentieth century, and now into the twenty-first, additional legislation has been enacted to protect historic sites and ruined castles. Arguably the most important, the Ancient Monuments and Archaeological Areas Act, was passed in 1979. The Act set the guidelines for categorizing and protecting the nation's vast array of heritage sites as "scheduled ancient monuments" or "listed" structures. It primarily emphasized identifying and classifying particular sites so that they would have continuous protection against the devastating impact of development. Ironically, at the time of writing this book, the government was again

Virtually derelict in 1815, Edward I's spectacular headquarters at Caernarfon Castle was consolidated and partially restored to its medieval grandeur, with building programs guided by architect Anthony Salvin, amateur historian (and deputy constable) Sir Llewelyn Turner, and, finally, by the efforts of the Ministry of Works.

revising its conservation policies and guidance, ostensibly to stay on track with changing social norms, political correctness, and technological advances of the times. One of the changes under consideration was the elimination of the designation/listing system now in place.

Besides defining what factors give a site value, discussed above, English Heritage's "Conservation Principles: Policies and Guidance for the Sustainable Management of the Historic Environment" now lays out priorities for the repair, restoration, or conservation of ancient and historic monuments. Even though they continue to support the "conserve as found" philosophy, in practice it is impossible to achieve, as individual sites differ significantly. In reality, it is an ideal towards which the professionals strive.[27] In their consultation report, English Heritage identifies several ways to treat sites they label as "significant places," which are decaying or need professional attention to keep from crumbling.[28] Beyond "routine management and maintenance," options include: (1) "periodic renewal," such as re-covering roofs, which involves more than limited intervention; (2) "repair" and "adaptation," which includes "the use of materials or techniques with proven longevity, and which are close matches for those being repaired or replaced" and, therefore, are less likely to cause future harm to the site, this option allows for the use of modern rather than traditional materials under certain circumstances, such as when traditional materials are particularly vulnerable to corrosion or weathering; (3) "intervention to increase knowledge of the past"—in essence the archaeological excavation option—which is only acceptable when the gains in knowledge outweigh the irreversible (but minimal) destruction caused by the effort; (4) "restoration" of the site, if the project meets five specific criteria, such as that "there would be no obvious incongruity through creating something that has never previously existed as an entity"; and (5) "new work and alteration."

Interestingly, the document specifically addresses the remains of castles which were deliberately slighted after the English Civil War, a "historically-significant event," emphasizing that such sites should NOT be restored:

> Attempts to restore those exceptional places that have survived as ruins would deny their strong visual and emotional evidence of important historic events. Ruins — real or contrived — can also play a major role in designed landscapes, define the character of places, or be celebrated in art. Even so, their restoration or adaptive re-use may be justified if the alternative is loss.... Retaining gutted shells as monuments is not likely, in most cases, to be an effective means of conserving surviving fabric, especially internal fabric never intended to withstand weathering nor is this approach likely to be economically sustainable. In such cases, it is appropriate to restore to the extent that the evidence allows, and thereafter to apply the policy for new work.[29]

Like the Anti-Scrapists and the countless others who sought to preserve Britain's historic ruins, the writers of this report continue to advocate that, as much as possible, any work done to a historic monument minimize the destruction of the surviving historical/authentic fabric, which is always part of both archaeological and restoration work.

Historic monuments, particularly those that have yet to be excavated or studied in depth, are potential repositories of great knowledge and physical evidence of the past. When excavated and consolidated, all efforts should be made to retain as much as possible of all phases of a site's existence, not just the era someone subjectively deems to have special value. Yet, in recent decades, approaches to this task have differed greatly, not only from site to site but also between England and Wales. It seems to this author that the reasons for these inconsistencies are myriad, but partly based on the notion that many aging, lesser known sites will provide little economic return for the substantial amount of money that would have to be invested in order to conserve them. Projected visitor numbers at smaller sites, which are often freely accessible, must pale in comparison to sites such as Dover, Bodiam, or Harlech, which draw scores of paying guests each year. Furthermore, some sites, including Cardigan Castle, have been hastily assessed as having had an inconsequential impact on regional or national history. What's more, reports of problems, such as the progressive destruction of the motte at Castell Caereinion by the intrusion of graves, have been dismissed because the governing body relies upon community representatives to provide reliable information about their condition rather than visiting the site for themselves, even though they are tasked to review them periodically.

Although many castles are in the care of national or local governing bodies, who have taken over the management and maintenance of the sites from private owners, scores of others remain in private hands, not just the descendants of the lords who once dominated the kingdom but also the average farmer or landowner upon whose lands the castles happen to be located. In many cases, the care and maintenance of the historic site is limited at best or ignored completely, not necessarily because of the owner's attitude but often due to the legal restrictions placed on them by the governmental agencies that regulate such things. It is frustrating to come upon a castle site where the farmer who owns the property wants to consolidate the remains, to clear them of trash and vegetation, and to stabilize them, but where the heritage agency responsible for the site prevents this from occurring. Fortunately, in recent years, at least in Wales, a scheme known as Tir Gofal has been established to encourage farm-

Scores of motte and ringwork castles dot the British landscape. Many have been neglected, and others, such as at Castell Caereinion, have been intruded upon, by quarrying, building works, and grave digging.

ers to get involved with the conservation of historic and archaeological features on their land through training, funding, and professional support.

It is equally frustrating to come upon a castle site where the owners refuse to allow intervention from heritage representatives so that the structure may be made safe for public access. Besides the expense of conserving ruins, they would also rather not have the public crawling around their property, possibly injuring themselves or harming their possessions, than consolidate and preserve the ruined site. Curiously, in at least one case, visitors are allowed to follow a public footpath across private property that is overlooked by castle ruins but are prevented from an up-close examination of the historic site itself. The Ancient Monuments and Archaeological Areas Act of 1979 does allow for the State to compulsorily take a site into their care, but normally the governmental bodies prefer the softer, more tactful approach of encouraging owners to focus their financial resources on the most urgent problems, often with the aid of a grant-package coordinated with the local authority. Owners of sites which are particularly dangerous to the public have the option of giving them to the national heritage body or to place it in guardianship while retaining the freehold, or lifetime control, of the property.[30]

At times, public sympathy can sway the plight of a ruin, as with the case of Cardigan Castle, which was in private hands until just recently. Without the unceasing efforts of the *Tivy-Side* newspaper, town councilor Glen Johnson, who also happened to be the castle's historian, and local citizens, the decrepit structure might no longer be standing. For decades,

The most recent Welsh stone castle to be fully excavated by archaeologists and then consolidated to allow visitors, Dolforwyn Castle was erected by Llywelyn ap Gruffydd in the 1270s, but English troops under Edward I's command virtually leveled the castle some four years later.

the site had lain undisturbed. Its owner refused to sell or give up the historic castle and allowed it fall into abject ruin. In 2001, Cadw declined to take the castle into guardianship and the Ceredigion County Council, cautious about investing an enormous amount of money in salvaging the site, also attempted to back away. However, the Castle in Crisis Campaign pushed ahead, garnering as much attention as possible about the issue. Early in 2002, the castle was finally offered for sale, for the incredible price of £1.5 million. This time, the county council took positive steps responding to a 4,000-signature-strong petition to acquire the castle and decided to impose a compulsory purchase order on the site after negotiations with the sellers failed. However, the order was unnecessary, and the sale finally went through once the council paid £500,000. Clearance, consolidation, and archaeological excavation have been carried out, enough to allow the Friends of Cardigan Castle to open the site to visitors for some days each summer.

Many castle sites have either never been excavated or only partially excavated by archaeologists; so, much remains hidden underneath decades of accumulated vegetation, soil, and waste. In some cases, the lack of excavation relates to the status of the site — for example, whether or not it has been placed in State guardianship — at other times, the expense involved in a full-scale excavation prohibits archaeological work and consolidation of the site for posterity and public enjoyment. Nowadays, developers call in archaeologists to construction projects, such as when fragments of an old structure or even skeletons are uncovered by backhoes or to conduct what are known as "watching briefs," during which they stand by, ready to excavate limited areas of the site in the event that archaeological remains are found.

During the 1970s and 1980s, though, archaeologists began what in many cases was years and years of excavation work at castles and other heritage sites. In Wales, for example, several stone castles under the care of Cadw, including Llanblethian (St. Quentin's), Dryslwyn, Dinefwr, Montgomery, Laugharne, and Dolforwyn, have been rigorously excavated and conserved. Dolforwyn Castle, which Cadw and its predecessor, the Office of Works, have owned since 1967,[31] was the last independent native Welsh castle to be completely excavated. It was only in 1980 that a decision was made to fully excavate the site. Not only was the castle so heavily degraded that it cried out for clearance and conservation, the re-emergence of the Welsh independence movement and the striving for a national consciousness and individual identity separate from England also supported the decision to excavate.[32] From 1981 to 2000, archaeologists and volunteers cleared collapsed rubble and the overgrowth of vegetation, documented their finds, and revealed the full extent of the surviving monument, which was built by Llywelyn ap Gruffydd, the last native Prince of Wales, in the 1270s. Cadw carried out consolidation work at the same time as the archaeological excavations were underway, and Dolforwyn Castle was opened to the public in 2000. Even though none of the surviving structures stand to their full extent, the basic layout of the castle, and its interior buildings, can be explored.

Local authorities and special trusts are also undertaking conservation work at castles in their care. At the time of writing, Llantrisant Castle, another ruinous castle built and used by the de Clares and now managed by the Rhondda Cynon Taf County Borough Council, was being prepared for possible restoration work. Even though the masonry remains have long been heavily overgrown and are confined to a relatively small portion of the property, work is being done to remove the intrusive vegetation and then conserve the masonry ruins and walls of the ringwork castle, which has never been archaeologically excavated. Likewise, plans are underway to restore Hopton Castle, now that the Hopton Castle Preservation Trust has received a grant to the tune of £880,000 from the Heritage Lottery Fund. And, as mentioned above, the Ceredigion County Council only recently purchased Cardigan Castle, with the intention of consolidating the site, preserving the scanty remains, and using the site for some as of yet undecided purpose.

In 1995, Wigmore Castle, the last substantial stone castle in England yet to be fully

During the thirteenth century, when round towers became fashionable, Richard de Clare strengthened Llantrisant Castle with a stone keep, which may have replaced an earlier timber tower. Christened as the "Raven Tower" and also known as "Giguran" ("gigfran" means "raven" in Welsh), the keep probably once stood about 46 feet high and had walls over 10 feet thick. Restoration work is presently underway to return the castle to something of its original glory.

Wigmore Castle was the site of considerable drama during its history, primarily because of the controversial roles of its owners, the Mortimers, in the courts of their monarchs. The castle is still comprised of tiers, levels of masonry and earthen embankments that rose successively to the highest point, which the ruined shell keep crowns. The last great English stone castle to be consolidated, the site was deliberately kept in its "natural" state.

excavated and consolidated, was transferred to the care of the State. Unlike in Wales, where both archaeological excavation and site consolidation were deemed appropriate for several noteworthy stone castles, the English government chose to go experimental at Wigmore, despite its direct associations with the monarchy and the notorious Mortimer family, and a history dating to 1069. At Wigmore, English Heritage applied its "conserve as found" policy with zeal. Something of a test case for England, the site was neither excavated nor restored, and instead only essential repairs were made to stabilize the fragile masonry. The bulk of the castle was left as it was found, archaeological deposits minimally disturbed and vegetation still running wild, so that visitors can explore a ruin in its natural, unaltered state.[33] As a result, much of the historic fabric remains buried "to maintain the very special atmosphere of the site."[34] When visiting Wigmore Castle, one can easily see that it was once an enormous structure and encompassed much more than the central part of the site, where the masonry is so brittle. Even though English Heritage claims that the work done (or not done!) at Wigmore is intended "to set the standard for the conservation of manor ruins into the early twenty-first century," one can only hope that, in time, more of the site, which disappoints rather than informs, will be consolidated and shared with both the interested public and professional researchers.

Emphasis at many castle sites is now on restoring non-masonry features, such as timber hoarding, in order to display how they looked or functioned over time. Some of these modifications help visitors gain a fuller appreciation for the history or function of a site. Unfortunately, some efforts create a circus-like, inauthentic atmosphere filled with phony cannons puffing nauseating smoke, as at majestic Dover Castle, which is such an imposing,

5. The Castle Experience

Seen just prior to recent excavation and consolidation work, Narberth Castle now barely resembles the artist's rendition of the site on page 171 above. Even so, it is well worth exploring and should be honored not only for its scenic views of the Welsh countryside but even more for its historical and aesthetic value and for having steadfastly endured the ravages of time and neglect.

complex site that it does not need the artificial props and noisy exhibitions to crowd the great keep and interfere with one's appreciation of the authentic structure. Ruskin and Morris would have vehemently condemned this kind of presentation. They also would have protested against the modern trend towards "dumbing down" the educational experience at castle sites, which seems to be increasingly pervasive, as if visitors today cannot use their own imagination — perhaps with the aid of a guidebook, audio-tour, or unobtrusively placed plaques — to appreciate the value of the ruins. Castles and other monuments in Britain are now being presented as little more than backdrops against which artificial light-and-sound displays and re-enactments titillate visitors. This kind of show may entertain and lure paying guests but it does little to increase their appreciation of the historic site, especially when the displays block views of the actual structure. After all, the real drama is still contained in the stones, earthworks, timber, and carved remains of the actual castle; a reconstruction can never match the original, even if the original is a mass of ruins.

Whether you begin as an armchair explorer or see your first castle in person, each visit can be an enchanting and educational experience. Unlike viewing castles on television and in the movies, which are often portrayed fancifully or used as sets for the action at hand, one can only gain a real, sensory understanding of their histories, physical makeup, and intrinsic value by wandering through the baileys, scrambling up the spiral staircases into darkened towers and narrow passages, and examining the battlements and residential chambers. Every castle is unique. Some are in better condition than others. Some are still occupied by Britain's nobility, but many more are not. Yet, each remains a testament to the people who designed them, who lived and worked in and around them, and who fought for freedom from the lords who owned them. We pay tribute to them and acknowledge our ties with them each time we pause to contemplate the ruins they left behind. Unlike their human occupants, the crumbling walls and aging earthworks have survived the passage of time, sometimes with grace and beauty, sometimes with decay and collapse, but always having the ability to merge space and time, present and past, into a cohesive whole.

Terminology in This Chapter

Burgage: A narrow plot of land in a medieval town owned by the king or a greater lord containing a house and facing the main street, which a person could rent by paying money to the lord or, less commonly, performing services.

Effigies: Carved figures adorning tombs or the walls of a church, intended to resemble the dead person they are honoring.

Grid plans: A common medieval town plan consisting of at least two or three main roads bisected at approximately right angles by two or three other roads to form a grid pattern.

Local authorities: The local, town, county, or regional governmental bodies responsible for, among other tasks, managing the ancient and historic monuments under their control.

Murage: A toll or tax paid to build or repair the walls of a fortified town.

National heritage bodies: The main governmental organizations responsible for managing the care and maintenance of Britain's castles: English Heritage, for England, and Cadw, for Wales. The National Trust is a charity and independent of the government; it is responsible for some castles, including those at Bodiam and Corfe.

Planted towns: Colonizing a town with one's supporters, an effort normally resulting in the forced removal of the native population.

Scheduled ancient monuments: Legally protected archaeological sites or historic buildings of national importance. The governments of England and Wales (and Scotland) are required to compile and maintain a "schedule" or list of ancient monuments of national importance. Monuments included in the schedule have statutory protection. The intent is to protect the site for the future. In order to modify the site, owners must obtain legal permission and follow a specific set of guidelines.

Town walls: A circuit of stone or earthen walls with towers and gateways enclosing a medieval town, which provided defense, a means of controlling access, and at times reiterated the authority of the lord or king who built them along with a castle. Their defensive features were generally the same as and complemented those of the associated castle.

Appendix: Castles Mentioned

England

Alnwick Castle, Northumberland— motte castle originally built by Yves de Vescy in 1096, transformed into a stone castle in the twelfth century, the second largest inhabited castle in England, now the residence of the dukes of Northumberland, located on the outskirts of Alnwick.

Arundel Castle, West Sussex— motte castle originally built by Roger de Montgomery shortly after the Conquest, acquired stone defenses in the mid-twelfth century, now the residence of the dukes of Norfolk, located near the Arundel town center.

Ashby de la Zouch Castle, Leicestershire— fortified manor erected in the twelfth century, converted into a castle by William, Lord Hastings, in the fifteenth century, managed by English Heritage, located in the Ashby de la Zouch town center.

Bamburgh Castle, Northumberland— the seat of the kings of Bernicia in the sixth century AD, Robert de Mowbray, Earl of Northumberland, possibly erected an earth and timber castle on the site as early as 1095, after which it was besieged and seized by William II; stone enclosure castle dominated by the four-story great keep erected by Henry II in about 1160, privately owned, located on the eastern side of the town of the same name.

Barnard Castle, County Durham— late eleventh-century ringwork erected by Bernard de Balliol, later transformed into a substantial stone castle with a three-story-high round keep, managed by English Heritage, located in the town of the same name.

Beeston Castle, Cheshire— built in 1220 by Ranulf de Blundeville, managed by English Heritage, located on a steep-sided hilltop northwest of the village of the same name.

Berkeley Castle, Gloucestershire— motte castle erected by William FitzOsbern shortly after the Conquest, transformed into a stone castle by Robert FitzHardinge in the twelfth century, site of Edward II's imprisonment and murder in 1327, lived in by the same family for over 900 years, located near the Berkeley town center.

Berkhamsted Castle, Hertfordshire— motte castle built shortly after the Conquest by Robert de Mortain, William I's half-brother, located just off the town center, next to the railway station.

Bishop's Castle, Shropshire— motte castle erected in about 1100, shell keep added in the late twelfth century, located on private property in the village of the same name.

Bishopton Castle, County Durham— motte castle erected by Roger de Conyers in about 1143, never converted to stone, located at Bishopton, a few miles northeast of Darlington.

Bodiam Castle, East Sussex— quadrangular castle constructed by Sir Edward Dalyngrygge in 1385, many castellologists currently believe this was a fortified manor house rather than a castle, managed by the National Trust, located near the village of the same name.

Bolingbroke Castle, Lincolnshire— stone enclosure castle constructed by Ranulf de Blundeville in the 1220s, located near the Bolingbroke village center.

Bolsover Castle, Derbyshire— eleventh-century motte castle with great tower erected in 1173, rebuilt in the seventeenth century by Sir Charles Cavendish as a grand residence, with remains of wall paintings, a conduit house, pleasure gardens and the indoor riding school erected in the mid-seventeenth century by Sir William Cavendish, Duke of Newcastle, managed by English Heritage, located in Bolsover.

Bolton Castle, North Yorkshire— quadrangular castle begun by Richard, Lord Scrope, in 1379, partly refurnished, privately managed, in the village of the same name.

Bramber Castle, West Sussex— motte castle

erected in about 1070 by William de Braose, converted into a stone castle in the twelfth century, managed by English Heritage, located in the village of the same name.

Cambridge Castle, Cambridgeshire—motte built by William the Conqueror in about 1068 on the remains of a Saxon settlement, converted into a stone enclosure castle by Edward I, robbed of most of its masonry in the fourteenth century, managed by the local authority, on Castle Hill in Cambridge.

Canterbury Castle, Kent—two castles stand near each other in this cathedral city: (1) Dane John, said to be the original motte castle erected possibly by William the Conqueror immediately after the Battle of Hastings, (2) stone enclosure castle dominated by great rectangular keep built in the early twelfth century, managed by local authority, located in the city center.

Castle Acre, Norfolk—motte castle erected by William de Warenne in 1080 as a country house, converted into a stone enclosure castle in the twelfth century, managed by English Heritage, located in the village of the same name.

Castle Neroche, Somerset—motte castle probably erected by Robert de Mortain in the late eleventh century on the site of an earlier Iron Age hillfort and Saxon settlement, also known as Castle Rache, on private property with a walking trail near the hamlet of Curland.

Castle Rising, Norfolk—enormous ringwork castle erected in 1138 by William d'Albini, contains one of the finest Norman-era keeps in England, managed by English Heritage, located just southwest of the town center.

Chester Castle, Cheshire—motte castle erected in about 1069 by Hugh d'Avranches on behalf of William the Conqueror, acquired stone defenses in the twelfth century, associated with circuit of towered walls that enclose the entire town, managed by English Heritage and local authority, located in the city center.

Clare Castle, Suffolk—motte castle built by Richard FitzGilbert, ancestor of the de Clare family, in about 1070, shell keep added in twelfth century, managed by local authority, located within Clare Castle Country Park.

Clavering Castle, Essex—possible ringwork castle identified as Richard's Castle in the *Anglo-Saxon Chronicle*, erected in about 1052 possibly by Richard FitzWimarc, located in the village of the same name.

Clifford Castle, Herefordshire—motte castle erected in 1069 by William FitzOsbern, converted to stone in the thirteenth century, managed by local authority, located on western side of village of the same name.

Clifford's Tower, North Yorkshire—one of two motte castles in York, Clifford's Tower is by far the finest with its unique quatrefoil, or four-lobed, shell keep, erected in 1069 by William the Conqueror and originally topped with a wooden tower, managed by English Heritage, located in the city center near the medieval walls. Look for second motte (Baile Hill), which stands nearby.

Clun Castle, Shropshire—motte castle built in about 1099 by Robert de Say, stone defenses added in 1140, managed by English Heritage, located near the town center.

Colchester Castle, Essex—stone castle with impressive great keep constructed in 1075 by William the Conqueror, managed by local authority, located in the town center.

Conisbrough Castle, South Yorkshire—motte castle erected by William de Warenne in about 1070, transformed by Hamelin Plantagenet, Henry II's illegitimate half-brother, into monumental stone castle with unique round keep in the twelfth century, managed by English Heritage, located in the town center.

Corfe Castle, Dorset—earth and timber castle erected by William I in about 1080, transformed into substantial royal stone enclosure castle in twelfth century, managed by the National Trust, located in the village center.

Cowdray Castle, West Sussex—sixteenth-century castellated residence begun by Sir William FitzWilliam to replace an earlier manor house on the site, better known as Cowdray House, managed by private trust, located on the grounds of Cowdray Park, Midhurst.

Croft Castle, Herefordshire—quadrangular castle begun in the late fourteenth century by Richard Croft, rebuilt in the late fifteenth and sixteenth centuries and transformed into the present castellated manor house, further alterations in the eighteenth century, managed by the National Trust, located near the village of Yarpole, five miles northwest of Leominster.

Dover Castle, Kent—one of Britain's greatest stone enclosure castles, with extensive, well-preserved remains spanning the entire history of castle building from the Norman Conquest to modern times when it was used during the Cold War, concentric design with towered walls enclosing Henry II's enormous great keep, also features the remains of a Roman pharos, an Anglo-Saxon church, and underground tunnels, managed by English Heritage, located in the Dover town center.

Dunstanburgh Castle, Northumberland—stone enclosure castle erected by Thomas, Earl of Lancaster, in 1313, owned by the National Trust and managed by English Heritage, located near the village of Craster, about seven miles northeast of Alnwick.

Dunster Castle, Somerset— motte castle built by William de Mohun shortly after the Conquest, transformed into a stone enclosure castle in the thirteenth century, then into a castellated country house in the seventeenth century, and finally rebuilt in the late nineteenth century, managed by the National Trust, located in the village of the same name.

Ewyas Harold Castle, Herefordshire— one of England's earliest motte castles, probably erected prior to the Conquest in about 1050 by Osbern Pentecost, also known as Pentecost's Castle, refortified by William FitzOsbern in about 1067, shell keep added in twelfth century, on private property, public access allowed, located in the village of the same name.

Exeter Castle, Devon— one of Britain's earliest ringwork castles, erected by William I in about 1086, also known as Rougemont Castle for its red stone, acquired stone defenses in the twelfth century, managed by local authority, located in the city center.

Farleigh Hungerford Castle, Somerset— stone enclosure castle begun in about 1370 by Sir Thomas Hungerford, impressive family chapel, managed by English Heritage, located in the village of the same name.

Farnham Castle, Surrey— substantial motte castle erected in 1144 by Henry de Blois, Bishop of Winchester, destroyed by Henry II in 1155 and rebuilt with an impressive shell keep and other structures in the triangular inner bailey, official residence of the bishops of Winchester for 900 years, bishop's palace has been leased by the Overseas Service College since 1962, great keep managed by English Heritage, located just north of town center.

Fotheringhay Castle, Northamptonshire— motte castle erected by Simon de Senlis in about 1100, birthplace of King Richard III, execution site of Mary, Queen of Scots, managed by the local authority, located in the village of the same name, about 12 miles south of Stamford.

Framlingham Castle, Suffolk— stone enclosure castle erected by Roger Bigod in 1189, managed by English Heritage, located in the town center.

Gloucester Castle, Gloucestershire— motte castle erected by William the Conqueror shortly after the Conquest, masonry added in the twelfth century, eventually used as the local prison but was demolished when the jail was expanded in the eighteenth century, no above-ground remains survive.

Goltho Castle, Lincolnshire— motte castle erected in about 1080 on the site of an Anglo-Saxon defended enclosure probably built two centuries earlier, altered again in the twelfth century, located in Goltho village, approximately ten miles northeast of Lincoln and two miles southwest of Wragby.

Goodrich Castle, Herefordshire— earth and timber castle begun by Godric Mappestone in about 1101, great rectangular keep added by Henry II in the late twelfth century, by the late thirteenth century it had become a substantial stone enclosure castle, managed by English Heritage, located just northeast of the village of the same name.

Hadleigh Castle, Essex— stone enclosure castle erected in 1230 by Hubert de Burgh, expanded in the fourteenth century, managed by local authority, located in Hadleigh Castle Country Park in Hadleigh.

Hastings Castle, East Sussex— motte castle built in 1066 by William the Conqueror, acquired stone defenses in the twelfth and thirteenth centuries, managed by the local authority, located in the town center.

Hedingham Castle, Essex— originally a ringwork castle, transformed by Aubrey de Vere III in about 1140 into a stone enclosure castle with one of England's finest rectangular keeps, privately owned, located just northeast of the village of Castle Hedingham.

Hereford Castle, Herefordshire— motte castle erected in about 1052 by Ralph, Earl of Hereford, restored by William FitzOsbern in 1067, fortified with stone in the twelfth century, largely destroyed in the 1650s, managed by the local authority, located near Hereford Cathedral.

Hopton Castle, Shropshire— motte castle erected in twelfth century by the de Hopton family, square stone keep added to low-lying motte in the fourteenth century, besieged by Parliamentarians in 1644 and much of the Royalist garrison massacred, on private property, managed by Hopton Castle Preservation Trust.

Huntingdon Castle, Cambridgeshire— motte castle and several baileys built by William the Conqueror in 1068 on Saxon fortifications, passed to King David I of Scotland, destroyed by Henry I in 1170s, remains located on Castle Hill, in town center.

Kenilworth Castle, Warwickshire— probably begun as a motte castle by Geoffrey de Clinton in the early twelfth century, acquired stone defenses and a strong rectangular keep by mid-century, broad water defenses known as the great mere constructed by the mid-thirteenth century when the castle became one of the most formidable fortresses in Britain, in 1266 Henry III's forces successfully staged a major siege against supporters of Simon de Montfort and the barons' rebellion, visited by Queen Elizabeth I in the seventeenth century, managed by English Heritage, located on the western side of town of the same name.

Kirby Muxloe Castle, Leicestershire— quadrangular castle/fortified manor house begun in the 1480s by William, Lord Hastings, but never completed due to his untimely execution, interesting brickwork and moat system, managed by English Heritage, located in the village of the same name.

Knaresborough Castle, North Yorkshire— earth and timber stronghold erected in the late eleventh century by Serlo de Burg, acquired stone defenses and a rectangular keep in the twelfth century, managed by local authority, located just west of the town of the same name.

Langley Castle, Northumberland— H-plan, four-story tower house erected by Thomas de Lucy in the mid-fourteenth century, damaged by Henry IV in 1404, passed to the Earls of Derwentwater, James and Charles, Viscounts Langley, in the seventeenth century, the men were executed on Tower Hill for their roles in the failed Jacobite Risings, purchased in 1882 by Cadwallader Bates, who restored the castle, now a luxury hotel, located near Haydon Bridge.

Laxton Castle, Nottinghamshire— motte castle probably erected by Robert de Caux in the late eleventh or early twelfth century, managed as part of the Crown Estate, located just north of the village of the same name.

Leeds Castle, Kent— attractive stone enclosure castle begun by Robert de Crevecoeur in the early twelfth century on the site of an Anglo-Saxon manor, most of present site dates to the time of Edward I, castle was popular with Henry VIII and Queen Anne Boleyn, extensively restored in the twentieth century by Lady Baillie, managed by private foundation, located six miles southeast of Maidstone, east of the village of Leeds.

Lewes Castle, East Sussex— one of Britain's rare castles with two mottes, built in 1068 by William de Warenne, larger motte features a fine shell keep, second motte known as Brack Mount, impressive fourteenth-century barbican stands close to main gateway, managed by Sussex Past, the Sussex Archaeological Society, located in the Lewes town center.

Lincoln Castle, Lincolnshire— the second of two English castles having two mottes (see Lewes Castle), the original motte was begun in 1068 by William the Conqueror, acquired stone defenses in 1115 and a shell keep, managed by local authority, located in the city center near Lincoln Cathedral.

Lodsbridge Castle, West Sussex— motte castle also known as Lodsworth Castle, erected in the thirteenth century, possibly reused as a windmill mound in about 1700, private property, located two miles east of Midhurst.

Longtown Castle, Herefordshire— motte castle built in early twelfth century probably by Hugh de Lacy, also known as Ewyas Lacy Castle, round shell keep added in twelfth century, medieval borough and grid plan survive, managed by English Heritage, located in the village of the same name.

Ludlow Castle, Shropshire— stone enclosure castle begun in the late eleventh century by Roger and Hugh de Lacy, passed to the Mortimers and then the Plantagenets, notable for unusual round chapel and four-story gate-keep, owned by the Earls of Powis, located in the Ludlow town center.

Marlborough Castle, Wiltshire— motte castle erected by Roger, Bishop of Salisbury, on behalf of William the Conqueror in about 1067, acquired stone defenses and shell keep during the twelfth century, also known as the Mount, privately owned, on the grounds of Marlborough College.

Middleham Castle, North Yorkshire— ringwork castle erected in about 1086 by Alan "the Red," extended by Robert FitzRandolph, who built the great keep in 1170, later owned by the Nevilles, this was Richard III's favorite castle, managed by English Heritage, located in the town center.

Muncaster Castle, Cumbria— early fourteenth-century pele tower erected by the Penningtons whose ancestor, Alan de Penitone, first acquired the land in 1208, the tower was incorporated into the nineteenth-century castellated residence now dominating the site, privately owned, located just east of the village of the same name.

Newark Castle, Nottinghamshire— stone enclosure castle built by Alexander, Bishop of Lincoln, in about 1130, King John died here in 1216, managed by private trust, located in the town center.

Newcastle-upon-Tyne Castle, Northumberland— motte castle built by Robert Curthose, the eldest son of William the Conqueror, in about 1080, transformed in the twelfth century into a stone enclosure castle with a huge rectangular keep, owned by the local authority but managed by the Society of Antiquaries of Newcastle-upon-Tyne, located in the city center.

Norwich Castle, Norfolk— imposing motte castle begun in 1067 by William FitzOsbern, stone defenses and great keep added in the early twelfth century, managed by local authority, located in the city center.

Nottingham Castle, Nottinghamshire—motte castle built by William the Conqueror in 1068, masonry defenses and a rectangular keep added in the late twelfth century, the duke of Newcastle replaced the remains of the medieval site with a private residence in the seventeenth century, managed by local authority, located in the city center.

Oakham Castle, Leicestershire—motte castle featuring one of the finest surviving examples of a medieval great hall in Britain, erected in the late twelfth century by Walkelin de Ferrers, managed by local authority, located in the town center.

Okehampton Castle, Devon—motte castle built in 1070 by Baldwin de Brionne, masonry defenses added in the twelfth century, castle rebuilt in 1297 by Hugh Courtenay, managed by English Heritage, located just southwest of the town center.

Orford Castle, Suffolk—stone enclosure castle with well-preserved, unique great tower erected by Henry II in 1165, managed by English Heritage, located just southwest of the town center.

Oxford Castle, Oxfordshire—earthen enclosure to which motte was added by Robert d'Oilly in about 1071, acquired stone defenses in twelfth century, used as county prison until 1996, privately owned, now part of a hotel, located in the city center.

Pevensey Castle, East Sussex—William the Conqueror's first English castle, a partial ringwork erected in 1066 inside remains of Roman fort, masonry defenses added by Robert de Mortain in about 1100, managed by English Heritage, located just southwest of the town center.

Peveril Castle, Derbyshire—stone enclosure castle begun in 1080 by William de Peverel, great keep added by Henry II in 1176, also known as the Castle of the Peak, managed by English Heritage, located just south of Castleton village.

Pickering Castle, North Yorkshire—motte castle erected by William I shortly after the Conquest, masonry defenses added in the twelfth century and later, managed by English Heritage, located in the town center.

Pleshey Castle, Essex—motte castle probably built by Geoffrey de Mandeville in the twelfth century, stone keep and defenses added later, managed by local authority, located in the village of the same name.

Pontefract Castle, South Yorkshire—motte castle begun in the late eleventh century by Ilbert de Lasci (Lacy), acquired substantial masonry defenses including towered walls during twelfth century, prison for James I of Scotland, Charles, the Duke of Orleans, and Richard II (who died there), managed by local authority on behalf of the monarchy, located in the town center.

Raby Castle, County Durham—quadrangular castle begun by Ralph, Lord Neville, in 1378, now a castellated stately home incorporating the medieval remains, owned by Henry, Lord Barnard, located about one mile east of Staindrop village, eight miles northeast of the town of Barnard Castle.

Restormel Castle, Cornwall—ringwork castle erected in the twelfth century by Baldwin FitzTurstin, crowned with thirteenth-century shell keep, managed by English Heritage, located in the village of the same name.

Richard's Castle, Herefordshire—motte castle possibly built in 1052 by Richard le Scrop, acquired polygonal stone keep in the twelfth century, on private property, located in the village of the same name about five miles southwest of Ludlow.

Richmond Castle, North Yorkshire—stone enclosure castle begun in 1071 by Alan "the Red," rectangular keep added a century later, managed by English Heritage, located on a hilltop overlooking the village center.

The Rings, Dorset—well-preserved siege castle built by King Stephen's troops preparing to attack nearby Corfe Castle in 1139 and reused during the English Civil War, constructed as a ringwork castle, on private property, located about 300 yards southwest of the castle in the village of Corfe Castle.

Rochester Castle, Kent—motte castle erected shortly after the Conquest at the site of a Roman town, owned by the bishops of Rochester, enclosure wall with towers was added in 1088, the four-story great tower—the tallest Norman keep in England—was begun in 1127, King John successfully besieged the castle in 1215 during the Magna Carta wars, managed by English Heritage, located alongside the River Medway and Rochester Cathedral.

Rockingham Castle, Northamptonshire—motte castle built by William the Conqueror shortly after the Conquest, masonry defenses added in the twelfth and thirteenth centuries, privately owned, located one mile north of the borough of Corby.

St. Briavel's Castle, Gloucestershire—ringwork castle erected in the twelfth century by Miles FitzWalter, seized by Henry II in 1160, substantial masonry defenses added by Edward I in the late thirteenth century, now used as a youth hostel, located in the village of the same name.

Sauvey Castle, Leicestershire—twelfth-century ringwork castle, masonry defenses probably erected by King John in the thirteenth century, used as a forest castle/hunting lodge, on private property, located near Withcote, about six miles southwest of Oakham.

Scarborough Castle, North Yorkshire—enclosure castle erected in 1130 by William le Gros, rectangular keep erected by Henry II, managed by English Heritage, located on the northeastern side of the town center.

Shrewsbury Castle, Shropshire—motte castle built in 1067 by William the Conqueror, acquired stone defenses including a shell keep in the twelfth century, managed by local authority, located in the town center.

South Mimms Castle, Hertfordshire—motte castle erected by Geoffrey de Mandeville in about 1140, also known as South Mymms, on private property, located west of Potters Bar, just off M25, northeast of the tiny village of the same name.

Stafford Castle, Staffordshire—motte castle begun in 1070 by William the Conqueror, stone defenses rebuilt by Ralph de Stafford in 1348, also known as Burton Castle, managed by local authority, located on the western side of town.

Stapleton Castle, Herefordshire—motte castle probably erected by Hugh FitzOsbern or his son in the mid-twelfth century, property of the Say family in the thirteenth century, remains of seventeenth-century manor house survive, near village of same name, about one mile southeast of Presteigne.

Toddington Castle, Bedfordshire—motte castle also known as Conger Hill possibly built by the Tracy family, on private property, located near the church on the north side of town.

Tonbridge Castle, Kent—motte with three moats, erected by Richard FitzGilbert in the late eleventh century, impressive oval shell keep, five-story great gatehouse added by Richard de Clare in the early thirteenth century, possibly inspired the design of the inner gatehouse at Caerphilly Castle, built by Richard's son, Gilbert de Clare II, used in World War II, managed by local authority, located in Tonbridge town center.

Tower of London, London—motte castle built by William the Conqueror in 1067, the great rectangular keep—the White Tower—constructed in 1077 dominates the site, repeatedly added to over the centuries until the stone enclosure castle acquired a concentric design, towered walls enclose palatial and medieval buildings, a complete church, and a military depot, used as a residence, a prison, a treasury, a mint and armory, now a World Heritage Site, managed by Historic Royal Palaces on behalf of the monarchy, located in the city center.

Wardour (Old) Castle, Wiltshire—stone enclosure castle built by John, Lord Lovel, in 1393, dominated by unusual hexagonal tower, managed by English Heritage, located about five miles northeast of Shaftesbury.

Warkworth Castle, Northumberland—motte castle possibly erected in the late eleventh century by Robert de Mowbray or, more likely, by Henry, Earl of Northumberland, who held the site in about 1140, converted into a stone enclosure castle later in the same century, remodeled by Henry, Lord Percy, and his son, Henry "Hotspur," in the late fourteenth century, features a unique polygonal great keep, managed by English Heritage, located on the southern side of the town of the same name.

Warwick Castle, Warwickshire—motte castle erected by William the Conqueror in about 1068, masonry defenses added in the twelfth century and later, now one of England's best preserved castles, owned and operated by The Tussaud's Group who purchased the castle from the Earl of Warwick in 1978, located in the town center.

Wigmore Castle, Herefordshire—motte castle probably built by Ralph de Mortimer shortly after the Conquest, stone defenses extended in the twelfth century to include a polygonal shell keep, managed by English Heritage, located in the village of the same name.

Winchester Castle, Hampshire—motte castle built by William the Conqueror in 1067, acquired stone defenses in the twelfth century, with the exception of the magnificent great hall built by Henry III (the finest of its type surviving in England), only fragments of stonework remain because the Law Courts built in 1974 covered most of the medieval site, managed by local authority, located in the city center.

Windsor Castle, Windsor—motte castle begun in 1067 by William the Conqueror, continuously expanded with new structures to become the largest occupied castle in the world, the official royal residence features a shell keep, towered walls, gateways, state and private apartments, and St. George's Chapel, owned and managed by the Crown, located in the town center.

Worcester Castle, Worcestershire—motte castle erected in 1069 by William de Mowbray, converted to stone by King John in 1204, used as a prison and, in the nineteenth century, as a quarry for building stone which destroyed the castle, originally located on the site of the present College Green.

York Castle—see Clifford's Tower.

WALES

Aberystwyth Castle, Ceredigion— diamond-shaped castle erected by Edward I after his first campaign against the Welsh in 1277, managed by local authority, located on waterfront just off the town center.

Angle Castle, Pembrokeshire— the only surviving Welsh tower house, erected in the late fourteenth century by the Shirburns, located just north of the village road. Also look for the dovecote, a ruined two-story hall-house, and the medieval parish church.

Beaumaris Castle, Anglesey— the last of Edward I's great fortresses in North Wales begun in 1294/5, considered the perfect example of a concentric plan, never completed, managed by Cadw, now a World Heritage Site, located in the town center.

Builth Castle, Powys— motte and bailey castle erected by Philip de Braose in about 1100, attacked by the Welsh on several occasions, finally seized by Edward I in 1277, and completely rebuilt and transformed into a stone castle with a stone keep and curtain wall with towers, largely destroyed after a fire in the seventeenth century, only the extensive earthworks now survive, owned by local authority, located in town center.

Caerau Castle, Glamorgan— ringwork castle possibly erected by the bishops of Llandaff, located inside a large hillfort on the southern side of the village, near Cardiff, freely accessible with permission.

Caergwrle Castle, Flintshire— the last of the native Welsh castles, small stone enclosure castle with several towers built by Dafydd ap Gruffydd in 1277 on a site occupied by the Romans and other groups, destroyed by Edward I in 1282, located in the town center.

Caernarfon Castle, Gwynedd— intended as Edward I's headquarters in North Wales, the figure-eight design begun in 1283 features polygonal towers and masonry resembling the walls of Constantinople, managed by Cadw, now a World Heritage Site, located in the town center.

Caerphilly Castle— Gilbert de Clare II's great concentric fortress highlighted by extensive water defenses, begun in the late 1260s, managed by Cadw, located in the town center.

Caldicot Castle, Monmouthshire— motte castle built by William FitzOsbern in about 1067, expanded into a stone enclosure castle, restored by antiquarian J.R. Cobb in the nineteenth century, managed by local authority, located in the town of the same name.

Cardiff Castle, Glamorgan— William the Conqueror's first motte castle in Wales, built in 1081 on the remains of several Roman forts, fine shell keep, site extended in modern times, managed by local authority, located in the city center.

Cardigan Castle, Ceredigion— stone enclosure castle originally erected as a timber castle by Gilbert FitzRichard de Clare in 1110, seized by the Welsh under the leadership of Rhys ap Gruffydd, the Lord Rhys, in 1165, who rebuilt it in stone, site of the first national eisteddfod held to celebrate the completion of the castle in 1176, owned and managed by local authority, located on the southern side of town overlooking the river.

Carew Castle, Pembrokeshire— stone enclosure castle with four huge corner towers, begun in the twelfth century by Gerald de Windsor and extensively modified over time, managed by Pembrokeshire Coast National Park Authority, located in the village of the same name.

Carreg Cennen Castle, Carmarthenshire— originated in the twelfth century as a Welsh-built stone enclosure castle, major alterations done after Edward I seized the castle in 1277, managed by Cadw, located off the beaten track about four miles southwest of Llandeilo.

Castell Caereinion, Powys— small motte castle located in church graveyard in the village of the same name.

Castell Coch, Glamorgan— originated as an earth and timber castle, now a stone enclosure castle rebuilt by the third marquess of Bute in the late nineteenth century on the remains of a medieval castle built by Gilbert de Clare II in the late thirteenth century, managed by Cadw, located at Tongwynglais.

Castell Talyfan, Glamorgan— overgrown ringwork castle with stone remains, erected in the twelfth century, on private property three miles west of Cowbridge.

Castell-y-Bere, Gwynedd— native Welsh stone enclosure castle erected in about 1221 by Llywelyn ab Iorwerth, managed by Cadw, located off the beaten path near Abergynolwyn.

Castlemartin Castle, Pembrokeshire— ringwork castle, on private property but visible from road, located at eastern end of the village of the same name.

Chepstow Castle, Monmouthshire— stone enclosure castle (hall-keep) begun in about 1070 possibly by William FitzOsbern, several building phases expanded the structure, managed by Cadw, located in the town center.

Cilgerran Castle, Pembrokeshire— stone enclosure castle built by William Marshall II in 1223 to replace the timber castle erected by Gerald de Windsor in 1108, managed by Cadw, located in the village of the same name.

Coity Castle, Glamorgan— ringwork castle

with substantial earthworks and stone remains, begun in the twelfth century by Payn de Turberville, managed by Cadw, located near the parish church in the village of the same name.

Conwy Castle, Conwy — impressive figure-eight-shaped stone enclosure castle begun in 1283 by Edward I, associated with extensive circuit of medieval town walls, managed by Cadw, now a World Heritage Site, located in the town center.

Criccieth Castle, Gwynedd — triangular-shaped stone enclosure castle erected by Llywelyn ab Iorwerth in the early thirteenth century, seized by Edward I in 1283 and altered, managed by Cadw, located in the town center.

Crickhowell Castle, Powys — motte castle built by the Turberville family in the early thirteenth century, stone improvements, including a shell keep, added by Sir Gimbald Pauncefoot in about 1300, ruins of gateway and two large towers survive next to the motte, managed by local authority, located on south side of town center.

Denbigh Castle, Denbighshire — stone enclosure castle with polygonal towers erected in 1282 by Henry de Lacy, managed by Cadw, located on a hilltop overlooking the town center. Also look for the medieval town walls.

Dinefwr Castle, Carmarthenshire — main seat of the native Princes of Deheubarth, held by the Lord Rhys in 1163, pentagonal courtyard castle with an impressive round keep, managed by the National Trust, located in Dinefwr Park, near Llandeilo.

Dolforwyn Castle, Powys — rectilinear stone enclosure castle built by Llywelyn ap Gruffydd in 1273, seized by Edward I in 1282, managed by Cadw, located off the beaten track near Abermule, about four and a half miles southwest of Montgomery.

Dolwyddelan Castle, Gwynedd — stone enclosure castle dominated by restored rectangular keep, probably erected by Llywelyn ap Gruffydd, his birthplace — a motte — can be seen to the south, managed by Cadw, located on private property but accessible to the public.

Dryslwyn Castle, Carmarthenshire — stone enclosure castle erected in the thirteenth century by Maredudd ap Rhys, captured by Edward I in 1287, managed by Cadw, located off the beaten track about two and a half miles west of Llandeilo.

Ewenny Priory, Glamorgan — extensive remains of fortified priory begun in twelfth century by William de Londres, includes thirteenth-century curtain wall, towers and gatehouse, and priory church, medieval remains managed by Cadw, located on private property in the village of the same name.

Ewloe Castle, Flintshire — Welsh-built castle begun in 1150 by Owain Gwynedd, converted to stone by Llywelyn ab Iorwerth in the early thirteenth century, notable D-shaped tower, managed by Cadw, located in Wepre Park but freely accessible from lay-by on B5125, about six miles northeast of Mold.

Flint Castle, Flintshire — the first of Edward's great stone enclosure castles in Wales, erected in 1277 after his initial campaign against the Welsh, dominated by the round donjon, managed by Cadw, located just off the town center.

Harlech Castle, Gwynedd — one of Edward I's great stone enclosure castles, concentric design dominated by great gatehouse, begun in 1283 just after the king's second campaign against the Welsh, seized by Owain Glyndwr in the early fifteenth century, managed by Cadw, now a World Heritage Site, located in the village of the same name.

Haverfordwest Castle, Pembrokeshire — stone enclosure castle originally built by Tancred the Fleming in about 1110, managed by local authority, located in the town center.

Hen Domen, Powys — sometimes known as Old Montgomery, substantial motte and bailey castle erected in 1070s by Robert de Montgomery, archaeological excavations uncovered several building phases, on private property alongside a minor road just over a mile north of Montgomery.

Henry's Moat, Pembrokeshire — motte castle damaged by quarrying, also known as Castell Hendre, located adjacent to the village church.

Kidwelly Castle, Carmarthenshire — originating in the twelfth century as a substantial D-shaped ringwork, converted by Roger de Caen into an impressive stone enclosure castle in the late thirteenth century, managed by Cadw, located in the village of the same name.

Laugharne Castle, Carmarthenshire — recently restored stone enclosure castle begun as a ringwork in 1115 by Robert Courtmain, stone defenses added by Guy de Brian IV in the mid-fourteenth century, managed by Cadw, located in the village of the same name.

Llanblethian Castle, Glamorgan — ringwork modified by the de Quentin family into a stone enclosure castle with a twin-towered gatehouse and keep, also known as St. Quentin's and St. Quintin's Castle, managed by the local authority, located in the village of the same name.

Llandovery Castle, Carmarthenshire — motte castle erected by Richard FitzPons in the early twelfth century, seized by the Welsh but regained by the Normans and refortified in stone in the mid-twelfth century, D-shaped tower, managed by the local authority, located in the village center.

Llantrisant Castle, Glamorgan — ringwork castle fortified in stone by Richard de Clare in 1246, attacked by the Welsh several times, served as a prison for Edward II, fragments of great tower and other structures survive, local authority recently began a consolidation project at the site, located on a hill in the town center.

Manorbier Castle, Pembrokeshire— originally an earth and timber castle erected by Odo de Barri in about 1093, converted into a stone enclosure castle dominated by a hall-keep in the twelfth and thirteenth centuries, fine example of a manorial center, privately owned, located in the village of the same name. Dovecote, fishponds, and mill foundations visible at base of castle.

Monmouth Castle, Monmouthshire— stone enclosure castle begun in about 1071 by William FitzOsbern, birthplace of the future King Henry V, managed by Cadw, located in the town center.

Montgomery Castle, Powys— stone enclosure castle built by Henry III in 1223 to replace Hen Domen, managed by Cadw, overlooks the town center, freely accessible via public footpath.

Narberth Castle, Pembrokeshire— enclosure castle erected in the mid-thirteenth century by Andrew Perrot, had a great tower and five corner towers, recently excavated and consolidated, owned by local authority, located on eastern side of town center.

Nevern Castle, Pembrokeshire— also known as Castell Nanhyfer, probably begun in the twelfth century by Robert FitzMartin, changed hands frequently between Welsh and Normans, notable for having two mottes, managed by Cadw, on hilltop overlooking St. Brynach's Church in the village of the same name.

New Moat, Pembrokeshire— motte castle surrounded by a wet ditch, on private property, freely accessible via public footpath.

Newcastle Bridgend Castle, Bridgend— ringwork castle begun by Robert FitzHamon in early twelfth century, polygonal curtain wall added by William, Earl of Gloucester, later in the century, managed by local authority, located on a hilltop overlooking the center of Bridgend next to St. Leonard's Church.

Ogmore Castle, Gower— ringwork castle with extensive stone remains, begun in about 1106 by William de Londres, masonry keep added by Maurice de Londres in the 1120s, managed by local authority, located off the beaten track in the village of the same name, about four miles southwest of Bridgend.

Oystermouth Castle, Gower— ringwork castle begun in 1099 by William de Londres, converted to stone enclosure castle in the early twelfth century, managed by local authority, located in the town center.

Pembroke Castle, Pembrokeshire— the seat of the earls of Pembroke, begun by Arnulf de Montgomery as a motte and bailey castle in about 1092, refortified in stone by William Marshal and his heirs from the late twelfth to mid-thirteenth century and then by William de Valence late in the thirteenth century, notable for Marshal's powerful round keep and the de Valence gatehouse and towered walls, managed by private trust, located in town center. Also look for medieval town walls and ruins of neighboring Monkton Priory with dovecote.

Penrice Castle, Gower— stone enclosure castle erected by Robert de Penres II in about 1237 to replace ringwork castle located about one-half mile away, the largest stone castle on the Gower Peninsula, on private property alongside a public footpath, located near hamlet of same name.

Powis Castle, Powys— original motte and bailey castle either survives as Domen Castell, some 300 meters to the west, or was covered over during the construction of the later castle, the present red sandstone castle-cum-stately home incorporates the medieval stone castle, also known as the Red Castle, privately owned, located just south of Welshpool.

Raglan Castle, Monmouthshire— impressive late medieval stone enclosure castle begun by Sir William ap Thomas in about 1430, possibly built on the site of an earlier motte and bailey, notable for the Yellow Tower of Gwent (the great polygonal keep), the great twin-towered gatehouse, and elaborate carvings, managed by Cadw, located just north of the village of the same name, about seven miles southwest of Monmouth.

Rhuddlan Castle, Denbighshire— diamond-shaped, concentric castle with two twin-towered gatehouses, erected by Edward I in 1277 just after he defeated the Welsh, replaced motte castle (Twthill) which survives to the south, managed by Cadw, located just west of the village of the same name.

Skenfrith Castle, Monmouthshire— originally a motte castle possibly erected by William FitzOsbern late in the eleventh century, converted into a stone enclosure castle by Hubert de Burgh in the early thirteenth century, three-story round keep is the most notable feature, located off the beaten track in the village of the same name, managed by Cadw, about seven miles northwest of Monmouth.

Sycharth Castle, Denbighshire— late-eleventh- or early-twelfth-century motte and bailey castle with partially wet ditch, best known for its associations with Owain Glyndwr in the late fourteenth and early fifteenth centuries, fragments of stone structures have been uncovered, on private property, freely accessible via public footpath.

Tenby Castle, Pembrokeshire— fragments of

twelfth-century stone enclosure castle, probably originated as an earth and timber stronghold, owned by local authority, located on promontory overlooking harbor. Also explore the town walls and Five Arches barbican.

Tretower Castle, Powys— motte and bailey castle begun in 1100 by the Picard family, first stone shell keep built in about 1160, towered curtain wall and second cylindrical tower erected inside shell keep in about 1220, managed by Cadw, located just off the A40 in the village of the same name midway between Abergavenny and Brecon, adjacent to Tretower Court.

Walwyn's Castle, Pembrokeshire— ringwork castle of which little history is known, by the thirteenth century it was part of the estate of the de Brian family, located next to the church.

Weobley Castle, Gower— fortified manor house built in the thirteenth century by David de la Bere, managed by Cadw, located on private property just west of Llanrhidian but fully accessible to the public.

White Castle, Monmouthshire— originated as an earth and timber castle, possibly built by William FitzOsbern in the late eleventh century, converted into a stone enclosure castle in the late twelfth century when it acquired a small rectangular keep and the curtain wall, Prince Edward, the future Edward I, extensively remodeled the castle during the mid-thirteenth century, managed by Cadw, located off the beaten track about eight miles west of Abergavenny.

Wiston Castle, Pembrokeshire— the county's finest motte and bailey castle erected by Wizo the Fleming in the early twelfth century, remains of a polygonal shell keep, extensive earthworks, managed by Cadw, located off the beaten track about seven miles northeast of Haverfordwest, in the village of the same name.

SCOTLAND

Caerlaverock Castle, Dumfries and Galloway— unusual triangular castle begun in 1280 by the Maxwells to replace the earlier earth and timber castle which survives nearby, water-filled moat, round corner towers, twin-towered gatehouse, and lavishly decorated interior walls, managed by Historic Scotland, located off the beaten track about seven miles south of Dumfries.

Crathes Castle, Aberdeenshire— classic L-plan tower house begun in 1533 by the Burnetts of Ley, who served as royal foresters, managed by Historic Scotland, located about fifteen miles west of Aberdeen.

Hermitage Castle, Border— impressive enclosure castle with powerful corner towers, similar to an H-shaped tower house, originally built by Nicholas, Lord de Soulis, in the 1240s, but rebuilt in the 1360s by Sir Hugh de Dacre and then completely revamped by William, first Earl of Douglas, into the present stronghold, it passed to the Earls of Bothwell in about 1400, and has important associations with Mary, Queen of Scots, and James Hepburn, fourth Earl of Bothwell, managed by Historic Scotland, located off the beaten track near Hawick.

Inveraray Castle, Argyllshire— grand stately castellated home designed in the Scottish baronial style and begun in 1720 for the Campbell Dukes of Argyll, who still own the property, located near village of same name.

Threave Castle, Dumfries and Galloway— classic five-story, rectangular tower house built in 1370 by Archibald, "the Grim," third Earl of Black Douglas, on an island in the River Dee accessible only by boat, managed by Historic Scotland, located about a mile west of the village of Castle Douglas.

REPUBLIC OF IRELAND

Blarney Castle, County Cork— well-preserved tower house begun in 1446 by Dermot McCarthy, King of Munster, eventually sold to Sir James St. John Jefferyes, Governor of Cork, in 1688, well known for its kissing stone, said to "give people the gift of gab," located in the village of Blarney near the River Martin, about five miles northwest of Cork, privately owned.

Bunratty Castle, County Clare— Built on the site of a Viking settlement, the first castle at the site — earth and timber — was built by the Normans in 1250, Thomas de Clare erected the first stone castle in the late thirteenth century, the castle was repeatedly assaulted, destroyed and restored by the Irish and the English until 1475, when it was owned by the O'Briens, who became Earls of Thomond during the reign of Henry VIII, modern restoration work began in the 1940s, managed by Shannon Heritage on behalf of the Irish government, located about eight miles west of Limerick, specializes in medieval banquets.

ISLE OF GUERNSEY (CROWN POSSESSION)

Chateau des Marais, Guernsey— ringwork established in 1244 in the English Channel, also known as Ivy Castle, managed by the States of Guernsey, located on the northeastern side of the island.

Chapter Notes

Chapter 1

1. In the Harry Potter book series, Dumbledore is part of a wizarding organization called the Wisengamot. It is very similar to the witenagemot but turns into a very bad entity in the last few books, as it was exploited to bring evil into the wizarding world.
2. Mark Gardiner, "Shipping and Trade between England and the Continent during the Eleventh Century," in *Anglo-Norman Studies XXII Proceedings of the Battle Conference*, ed. Christopher Harper-Bill (Woodbridge: Boydell & Brewer, 1999), pp. 78–79. See also David Howarth's account of the invasion in *1066: The Year of the Conquest* (New York: Viking Press, 1977).
3. John R. Kenyon, e-mail message to author, April 9, 2007.
4. John R. Kenyon, *Medieval Fortifications* (Leicester: Leicester University Press, 1990), 7.
5. Ibid., 24.
6. David Martin, et al., *A Re-interpretation of Hastings Castle, Hastings, East Sussex* (Commissioned by Hastings Borough Council, 1999), 19, 22.
7. Robert Higham and Philip Barker, *Timber Castles* (London: B.T. Batsford, Ltd., 1992), 14.
8. N. J. G. Pounds, *The Medieval Castle in England and Wales* (Cambridge: Cambridge University Press, 1994), 57.
9. Ibid., 35.
10. Helen Clarke, *The Archaeology of Medieval England* (Oxford: Basil Blackwell, Ltd., 1986), 110.
11. Marc Morris, *Castle* (London: Pan Books, 2004), 29.
12. Kenyon, *Fortifications*, 7.
13. Derek Renn, *Norman Castles in Britain* (London: John Baker Publishers Ltd., 1973), 314.
14. Pounds, 13; Clarke, 124–126; Kenyon, *Fortifications*, 22.
15. Kenyon, *Fortifications*, 35.
16. Ibid., 27, 35.
17. Ibid., 98.
18. Ibid., 35.
19. Ibid., 127.
20. Ibid., 128.
21. Richard Eales, "Royal Power and Castles in Norman England," in *Anglo-Norman Castles*, edited by Robert Liddiard (Woodbridge, Suffolk: The Boydell Press, 2003), 50.
22. See Robert Higham's "Timber Castles — A Reassessment," in *Anglo-Norman Castles*, edited by Robert Liddiard (Woodbridge, Suffolk: The Boydell Press, 2003), 105–118, for a fuller discussion.
23. Stephen Friar, *The Sutton Companion to Castles* (Stroud: Sutton Publishing, 2003), 53–54.
24. R. Allen Brown, "Royal Castle-Building in England 1154–1216," in *Anglo-Norman Castles*, edited by Robert Liddiard (Woodbridge, Suffolk: The Boydell Press, 2003), 147.
25. Frank Bottomley, *The Castle Explorer's Guide* (New York: Avenal Books, 1983), 188.
26. Brown, "Royal Castle-Building," 151.
27. David Macaulay, *Castle* (Boston: Houghton Mifflin, Company, 1977), 18.
28. Bottomley, *Castle Explorer's Guide*, 40.
29. Brown, "Royal Castle-Building," 135.
30. Tom McNeill, *Castles* (London: B. T. Batsford, Ltd./English Heritage, 2006), 37.
31. Bottomley, *Castle Explorer's Guide*, 22.
32. Ibid., 189–190.

Chapter 2

1. O. H. Creighton, *Castles and Landscapes: Power, Community and Fortification in Medieval England* (London: Equinox, 2002), 35.
2. Oliver Creighton and Robert Higham, *Medieval Castles* (Princes Risborough: Shire Archaeology, 2003), 14.
3. Tom McNeill, *Castles* (London: B. T. Batsford, Ltd./English Heritage, 2006), 27.
4. Creighton, *Castles and Landscapes*, 42.
5. Ibid., 43.
6. A. J. Taylor, Dr., *The King's Works in Wales 1277–1330* (London: HMSO, 1974), 319.
7. John R. Kenyon, *Medieval Fortifications* (Leicester: Leicester University Press, 1990), 83.
8. Colin Platt, *Dover Castle* (London: English Heritage, 1988), 15.
9. Kenyon, *Medieval Fortifications*, 73.
10. D. J. Cathcart King, *The Castle in England and Wales: An Interpretative History* (Beckenham, Kent: Croom Helm, Ltd., 1988), 121.
11. Paul Barker, *Warwick Castle* (Warwick: Warwick Castle, Ltd., 1990), 29–30.
12. Ron Shoesmith, *Castles & Moated Sites of Herefordshire* (Almeley: Logaston Press, 1996), 114.
13. Joseph Gies and Frances Gies. *Life in a Medieval Castle* (New York: Harper & Row, 1974), 27–28.
14. Margaret Wade Labarge, *A Baronial Household of the Thirteenth Century* (London: Eyre & Spottiswoode, 1965), 69.
15. Robin Mackworth-Young, *The History & Treasures of Windsor Castle* (London: Pitkin-Britannia, 1982), 2.
16. John Martin Robinson, *Arundel Castle* (Arundel: Arundel Castle Trustees Ltd., n.d.), 2.
17. Robert Liddiard, *Castles in Context: Power, Symbolism and Landscape, 1066 to 1500* (Macclesfield: Windgather Press, 2005), 39, 41, 78.

18. Christopher Gravett and David Nicolle, *The Normans Warrior Knights and their Castles* (Oxford: Osprey Publishing, 2006), 201.
19. Richard Eales, "Royal Power and Castles in Norman England," in *Anglo-Norman Castles*, edited by Robert Liddiard (Woodbridge, Suffolk: The Boydell Press, 2003), 61.
20. Ibid.
21. King, *The Castle*, 21.
22. Charles Coulson, "The Castles of the Anarchy," in *Anglo-Norman Castles*, edited by Robert Liddiard (Woodbridge, Suffolk: The Boydell Press, 2003), 180.
23. Marc Morris, *Castle* (London: Pan Books, 2004), 58.
24. Eales, "Royal Power and Castles," 64.
25. Richard Eales, "Castles and Politics in England 1215–1224," in *Anglo-Norman Castles*, edited by Robert Liddiard (Woodbridge, Suffolk: The Boydell Press, 2003), 384.
26. Ibid., 386.
27. Anne Savage's translation of the *Anglo-Saxon Chronicle* (London: Guild Publishing, 1988) is just one of several versions readers will find of use when researching this particular era of British history.
28. Liddiard, *Anglo-Norman Castles*, 36.
29. Creighton, *Castles and Landscapes*, 126.
30. Christopher Dyer, *Making a Living in the Middle Ages: The People of Britain, 850–1520* (New Haven and London: Yale University Press, 2002), 81.
31. Ibid., 80.
32. Liddiard, *Anglo-Norman Castles*, 148.
33. Christopher Dyer, e-mail message to author, January 22, 2008.
34. The Friends of Sconce and Devon Park discuss the history of the fortifications in some detail on their website: *http://www.sconceanddevonpark.org*.
35. An interesting discussion of the siegeworks at Colchester can be found on the website of the Colchester Archaeological Trust, *http://www.catuk.org/index.html*.

Chapter 3

1. Frank Bottomley, *The Castle Explorer's Guide* (New York: Avenal Books, 1983), 152.
2. John R. Kenyon, *Medieval Fortifications* (Leicester: Leicester University Press, 1990), 104.
3. Bottomley, *Castle Explorer's Guide*, 190.
4. A. J. Taylor, *Conwy Castle and Town Walls* (Cardiff: Cadw, 1998), 43.
5. Neil Guy, "Pevensey Castle," *The Castle Studies Group Journal* 19 (2005–6): 53; email message to author, July 1, 2007.
6. David Thackray, *Bodiam Castle East Sussex* (London: The National Trust, 1995), 11.
7. Lindsay Clarke, "Tower Menagerie Home to Barbary Lions — Official." *Londonist. http://londonist.com/2008/03/scientists_at_t.php*.
8. James Owen, "Medieval Lion Skulls Reveal Secrets of Tower of London Zoo," *National Geographic News. http://news.nationalgeographic.com/news/2005/11/1103_05110 3_tower_lions.html*.
9. BBC News. "Big cats prowled London's tower." *http://news.bbc.co.uk/1/hi/sci/tech/4371908.stm*.
10. Robert Liddiard, *Castles in Context: Power, Symbolism and Landscape, 1066 to 1500* (Macclesfield: Windgather Press, 2005), 46.
11. Most modern castellologists, including McNeill, Gravett, and Marshall, agree with this view of castles. The conflict arises when it comes to the military role that castles played during the Middle Ages and beyond. Recently, there has been a significant push towards viewing castles less as military structures and more as purely residential buildings designed in an aristocratic style that emphasized castellation. See Chapter 5 for more.
12. Christopher Gravett and David Nicolle, *The Normans: Warrior Knights and their Castles* (Oxford: Osprey Publishing, 2006), 146.
13. Liddiard, *Castles in Context*, 47.
14. Ibid., 53.
15. Philip Dixon and Pamela Marshall, "The Great Tower at Hedingham Castle: a Reassessment," *Anglo-Norman Castles*, edited by Robert Liddiard (Woodbridge, Suffolk: The Boydell Press, 2003), 298.
16. Liddiard, *Castles in Context*, 53; Dixon & Marshall, 306.
17. Dixon & Marshall, "Hedingham Castle," 306.
18. Berie Morley, *Peveril Castle* (London: English Heritage, 1990), 19.
19. Ibid., 19; The Official Site of the British Monarchy, "History of the Monarchy: Malcolm IV." *http://www.qm memorial.gov.uk/output/Page110.asp*.
20. John R. Kenyon, e-mail message to author, February 5, 2008; Oliver H. Creighton, e-mail message to author, July 10, 2007.
21. Stell, Geoffrey, *Exploring Scotland's Heritage Dumfries and Galloway* (Edinburgh: HMSO, 1986), 91.
22. Taylor, *Conwy*, 23.
23. Tom McNeill, *Castles* (London: B. T. Batsford, Ltd./English Heritage, 2006), 71.
24. Joseph Gies and Frances Gies, *Life in a Medieval Castle* (New York: Harper & Row, 1974), 64.
25. N. J. G. Pounds, *The Medieval Castle in England and Wales* (Cambridge: Cambridge University Press, 1994), 189.
26. Adrian Pettifer, *English Castles: a guide by counties* (Woodbridge, Suffolk: The Boydell Press, 1995), 258.
27. Derek Renn, *Kenilworth Castle* (London: English Heritage, 1999), 18.
28. John Gibson, *Anatomy of the Castle* (Saraband, Scotland: MetroBooks, 2001), 164.
29. Bottomley, *Castle Explorer's Guide*, 103.
30. Kenyon, *Medieval Fortifications*, 116, 124.
31. Margaret Wade Labarge, *A Baronial Household of the Thirteenth Century* (London: Eyre & Spottiswoode, 1965), 33.
32. McNeill, *Castles*, 75.
33. Bottomley, *Castle Explorer's Guide*, 194.
34. Gravett and Nicolle, *The Normans*, 159.
35. The Castle Keep, Newcastle Upon Tyne, "Guide Ground Floor." *http://museums.ncl.ac.uk/keep/keepguide/keep_guide_groundfloor.htm*.
36. Kenyon, *Medieval Fortifications*, 157–158.
37. John R. Kenyon, *Raglan Castle* (Cardiff: Cadw, 2003), 34.
38. Gies and Gies, *Life in a Medieval Castle*, 69.
39. Labarge, *Baronial Household*, 34–35.
40. Gibson, *Anatomy of the Castle*, 166.
41. Liddiard, *Castles in Context*, 61.
42. Ibid., 64.
43. Marc Morris, *Castle* (London: Pan Books, 2004), 229.
44. Bottomley, *Castle Explorer's Guide*, 196.
45. Gravett and Nicolle, *The Normans*, 148.
46. Gies and Gies, *Life in a Medieval Castle*, 62.
47. Sidney Toy, *Castles: Their Construction and History* (New York: Dover Publications, Inc., 1984), 114.
48. Toy, *Castles*, 114; Bottomley, *Castle Explorer's Guide*, 63.

49. Toy, *Castles*, 114.
50. Bottomley, *Castle Explorer's Guide*, 63.
51. National Monuments Record. "NMR Components Thesaurus." http://thesaurus.english-heritage.org.uk/thesaurus.asp?thes_no=546.
52. Pounds, *The Medieval Castle*, 224.
53. Gies and Gies, *Life in a Medieval Castle*, 105–106.
54. Bottomley, *Castle Explorer's Guide*, 145.
55. Philip Warner, *The Medieval Castle: Life in a Fortress in Peace and War* (New York: Barnes and Noble Books, 1993), 195.
56. Jeremy Knight, *The Three Castles* (Cardiff: Cadw, 2000), 41.

Chapter 4

1. The Royal Commission on Ancient and Historical Monuments in Wales, *The Early Castles from the Norman Conquest to 1217*, edited by C. J. Spurgeon (London: HMSO, 1991), 71.
2. O. H. Creighton, *Castles and Landscapes: Power, Community and Fortification in Medieval England* (London: Equinox, 2002), 177.
3. Christopher Dyer, *Making a Living in the Middle Ages: The People of Britain, 850–1520* (New Haven and London: Yale University Press, 2002), 85.
4. Ibid., 106.
5. Judith A. Green, *The Aristocracy of Norman England* (Cambridge: Cambridge University Press, 2002), 48, 50.
6. Lise Hull, *Castles of Glamorgan* (Almeley: Logaston Press, 2007), 77.
7. Green, *Aristocracy*, 160.
8. Ibid., 180.
9. Richard Muir, *The English Village* (New York: Thames and Hudson, 1980), 69.
10. Judith M. Bennett, *A Medieval Life: Cecilia Penifader of Brigstock, c. 1295–1344* (Boston: McGraw-Hill College, 1999), 3.
11. Dyer, *Making a Living*, 140.
12. The National Archives, "World of Domesday, the social order." www.nationalarchives.gov.uk/domesday/world-of-domesday/order.htm.
13. H.S. Bennett, Life on the English Manor: A Study of Peasant Conditions 1150–1400 (London: Cambridge University Press, 1971), 108.
14. Dyer, *Making a Living*, 122.
15. Bennett, *A Medieval Life*, 110.
16. Dyer, *Making a Living*, 132.
17. Bennett, *A Medieval Life*, 130.
18. Ibid., 137.
19. Joseph Gies and Frances Gies, *Life in a Medieval Castle* (New York: Harper & Row, 1974), 50.
20. Internet Medieval Sourcebook, "Medieval Sourcebook: Manorial Management & Organization, c. 1275." http://www.fordham.edu/halsall/source/1275manors1.html.
21. Conisbrough Court Rolls, "The Manor Court." http://www.hrionline.ac.uk/conisbrough/find/manor_court.html.
22. Bennett, *A Medieval Life*, 162.
23. Leon Carroll Marshall, *Readings in Industrial Society—Study in the Structure and Functioning of Modern Economic Organization* (Chicago: University of Chicago Press, 1929), 63–64.
24. Dyer, *Making a Living*, 126.
25. Gies and Gies, *Life in a Medieval Castle*, 53; Bennett, *A Medieval Life*, 167.
26. Dyer, *Making a Living*, 122.
27. David Hall, "Medieval fields in their many forms," *British Archaeology* 33 (April 1998). http://www.britarch.ac.uk/BA/ba33/ba33feat.html.
28. Trent and Peak Archaeological Trust, "The Laxton Village Survey." http://mahan.wonkwang.ac.kr/link/med/economy/agricul/laxsurv.html.
29. Matthew Johnson, *Behind the Castle Gate: From Medieval to Renaissance* (London: Routledge, 2002), 45.
30. Creighton, *Castles and Landscapes*, 182.
31. Ibid., 183.
32. N. J. G. Pounds, *The Medieval Castle in England and Wales* (Cambridge: Cambridge University Press, 1994), 193.
33. Richard Muir, *The NEW Reading the Landscape: Fieldwork in Landscape History* (Exeter: University of Exeter Press, 2000), 64.
34. Muir, *English Village*, 91.
35. Jean Birrell, "Deer and Deer Farming in Medieval England," *The Agricultural History Review* 40 (1992): 119.
36. Ibid., 122.
37. Muir, *New Reading*, 126.
38. Robert Liddiard, *Castles in Context: Power, Symbolism and Landscape, 1066 to 1500* (Macclesfield: Windgather Press, 2005), 103.
39. Birrell, "Deer and Deer Farming," 114.
40. Ibid., 119.
41. Liddiard, *Castles in Context*, 102.
42. Johnson, *Behind the Castle Gate*, 137, 144.
43. Liddiard, *Castles in Context*, 102–103.
44. Creighton, *Castles and Landscapes*, 190.
45. English Heritage, "Parks and Gardens." http://www.eng-h.gov.uk/ArchRev/rev94_5/parks.htm.
46. Buckinghamshire County Council, "Bernwood Forest: Royal Forests & Forest Law." http://www.buckscc.gov.uk/medieval_life/bernwood/history2.htm.
47. Jean Birrell, "Peasant Craftsmen in the Medieval Forest," *The Agricultural History Review* 17 (1992): 91–92, 97–98.
48. Creighton, *Castles and Landscapes*, 187.
49. Cottinghamhhistory.co.uk. "Rockingham Forest." http://www.cottinghamhistory.co.uk/Rockinghamforest.htm.
50. Creighton, *Castles and Landscapes*, 186–187.
51. Yorkshire Dales National Park Authority, "Out of Oblivion: A Landscape Through Time." http://www.outofoblivion.org.uk/hunting.asp.
52. Muir, *New Reading*, 128.
53. Historic Herefordshire Online, "The Medieval Countryside of Herefordshire." http://www.smr.herefordshire.gov.uk/education/Medieval_Countryside.htm.
54. Legendary Dartmoor, "The Dartmoor Rabbit." http://www.legendarydartmoor.co.uk/rabb_its.htm.
55. English Heritage, "Monuments Protection Programme Monument Class Description Warrens September 1998." http://www.eng-h.gov.uk/mpp/mcd/wrn.htm.
56. Ibid.
57. Yorkshire Dales National Park Authority. http://www.outofoblivion.org.uk/record.asp?id=478.
58. English Heritage, "Monuments Protection Programme Monument Class Description Dovecotes December 1989." http://www.eng-h.gov.uk/mpp/mcd/sub/dove.htm.
59. Klara Spandl, "Exploring the Round Houses of Doves," *British Archaeology* 35 (June 1998). http://www.britarch.ac.uk/ba/ba35/ba35feat.html.
60. Liddiard, *Castles in Context*, 107.
61. Ibid., 184.
62. Historic Herefordshire Online. "The Agricultural Landscape: Fishponds." http://www.smr.herefordshire.gov.uk/education/Fishponds.htm.
63. Muir, *New Reading*, 132.
64. Liddiard, *Castles in Context*, 103.

65. Pounds, *The Medieval Castle*, 199.
66. Muir, *New Reading*, 196.
67. Historic Herefordshire Online, "The Agricultural Landscape: Fishponds." *http://www.smr.herefordshire.gov.uk/education/Fishponds.htm*.
68. Pounds, *The Medieval Castle*, 199.
69. Creighton, *Castles and Landscapes*, 184–185.
70. Ibid., 185.
71. Penny Ward, e-mail message to author, April 2, 2008.
72. Howard Giles, e-mail message to author, May 25, 2007. Giles's research and extensive understanding of the site, Civil War fortifications, and the history of Bolingbroke Castle led those responsible for managing the site (English Heritage and the Heritage Trust of Lincolnshire) to reconsider their own opinions on the subject and, ultimately, to — at least tentatively — agree with Giles.
73. Lewis Thorpe, *Gerald of Wales: The Journey through Wales and The Description of Wales* (London: Penguin Books, 1978), 150.
74. Lise Hull, *Castles and Bishops Palaces of Pembrokeshire* (Almeley: Logaston Press, 2005), 139.
75. Christopher Dyer, *Everyday Life in Medieval England* (London and New York: Hambledon and London, 2000), 192–219.
76. Birrell, "Deer and Deer Farming," 103–104.

Chapter 5

1. C. J. Bond, "Anglo-Saxon and Medieval Defences," *Urban Archaeology in Britain, CBA Research Report* 61 (1987). *http://ads.ahds.ac.uk/catalogue/adsdata/cbaresrep/pdf/061/06107003.pdf*.
2. Peter Humphries, e-mail message to author, November 21, 2007.
3. A. G. Krishna Menon, "Conservation in India: a search for direction." *http://www.architexturez.net/+/subject-listing/000233.shtml*.
4. Scott Demel, "Architectural Additions." *http://www.demel.net/th-ch1.html*.
5. William Morris, "Manifesto of the Society for the Protection of Ancient Buildings (SPAB)." *http://www.marxists.org/archive/morris/works/1877/spabman.htm*.
6. Pamela Todd, *William Morris and the Arts and Crafts Home* (San Francisco: Chronicle Books, 2005), 33.
7. The Society for the Protection of Ancient Buildings, "SPAB's purpose." *http://www.spab.org.uk/html/what-is-spab/spabs-purpose*.
8. Demel, "Architectural Additions."
9. Thordis Arrhenius, "The Fragile Monument: On Riegl's Modern Cult of Monuments," *http://www.cadw.wales.gov.uk/upload/resourcepool/masonry%20notes%20english7511.pdf*.
10. English Heritage, "Conservation Principles: Policies and Guidance for the Sustainable Management of the Historic Environment." *http://www.english-heritage.org.uk/upload/pdf/ Conservation_Principles_Policies_and_Guidance_April08_Web.pdf*.
11. Ibid., 37.
12. Ibid., 27–32.
13. Pamela Marshall and John Samuels, *Guardian of the Trent: The Story of Newark Castle* (Newark: Newark Castle Trust, 1997), 40.
14. Humphries, November 21, 2007.
15. Ibid.
16. Ibid.
17. Ibid.
18. Andrew Helme and Annie Rainsbury. *Caldicot Castle, Great Fortress of the Gwent Levels* (Caldicot: Caldicot Castle & Country Park, Monmouthshire, 2005).
19. Anita Badhan, e-mail message to author, November 13, 2007.
20. Humphries, November 21, 2007.
21. Jeremy Ashbee, e-mail message to author, January 29, 2008.
22. Ibid.
23. Menon, "Conservation in India."
24. Richard Avent, "The Conservation and Restoration of Caernarfon Castle, 1845–1912," *The Modern Traveller to Our Past: Festschrift in Honour of Anne Hamlin*, edited by Marion Meek (Belfast: DPK Publishing, 2006), 344.
25. Ibid., 347.
26. Ibid., 344–351.
27. Richard Turner, e-mail message to author, March 7, 2008.
28. English Heritage, "Conservation Principles," 51–59.
29. Ibid., 56–57.
30. Richard Avent, "Cadw and Castle Conservation," Castle Studies Group newsletter, 1999–2000. *http://www.castlewales.com/cadw_rsk.html*.
31. Lawrence Butler, "Dolforwyn Castle: Prospect and Retrospect," *The Medieval Castle in Ireland and Wales*, edited by John R. Kenyon and Kieran O'Conor (Dublin: Four Courts Press, 2003), 150.
32. Ibid.; John R. Kenyon, e-mail message to author, March 4, 2008.
33. English Heritage, "Historic Properties: Midlands." *http://www.eng-h.gov.uk/ArchRev/rev95_6/hp_mids.htm*.
34. English Heritage, "Wigmore Castle, Hereford," *Archaeology Review* 4:19 (1996–97). *http://www.eng-h.gov.uk/archrev/rev97_8/cas4.htm*.

Bibliography

Arrhenius, Thordis. "The Fragile Monument: On Riegl's Modern Cult of Monuments." http://www.cadw.wales.gov.uk/upload/resourcepool/masonry%20notes%20english7 511.pdf.

Ashbee, Jeremy. E-mail message to author (November 21, 2007).

Avent, Richard. "Cadw and Castle Conservation." Castle Studies Group newsletter, 1999–2000. http://www.castlewales.com/cadw_rsk.html.

_____. "The Conservation and Restoration of Caernarfon Castle, 1845–1912," The Modern Traveller to our Past: Festschrift in Honour of Anne Hamlin, edited by Marion Meek. Belfast: DPK Publishing, 2006.

_____. Laugharne Castle. Cardiff: Cadw, 1995.

_____. "William Marshal's building works at Chepstow Castle, Monmouthshire, 1189–1219," The Medieval Castle in Ireland and Wales, edited by John R. Kenyon and Kieran O'Conor. Dublin: Four Courts Press, 2003.

Badhan, Anita. E-mail messages to author (November 13, 2007; March 4–6, 2008).

Barker, Paul. Warwick Castle. Warwick: Warwick Castle, Ltd., 1990.

Barthel, Diane L. Historic Preservation: Collective Memory and Historical Identity. Piscataway, NJ: Rutgers University Press, 1996.

BBC News. "Big cats prowled London's tower." http://news.bbc.co.uk/1/hi/sci/tech/4371908.stm.

Bennett, H. S. Life on the English Manor: A Study of Peasant Conditions 1150–1400. London: Cambridge University Press, 1971.

Bennett, Judith M. A Medieval Life: Cecilia Penifader of Brigstock, c. 1295–1344. Boston: McGraw-Hill College, 1999.

Birrell, Jean. "Deer and Deer Farming in Medieval England," The Agricultural History Review 40 (1992): 112–12, http://www.bahs.org.uk/40n2a2.pdf.

_____. "Peasant Craftsmen in the Medieval Forest," The Agricultural History Review 17 (1969): 91–107. http://www.bahs.org.uk/17n2a2.pdf.

Bond, C. J. "Anglo-Saxon and medieval defenses," Urban Archaeology in Britain, CBA Research Report 61 (1987). http://ads.ahds.ac.uk/catalogue/adsdata/cbaresrep/pdf/061/06107003.pdf.

Bottomley, Frank. The Castle Explorer's Guide. New York: Avenal Books, 1983.

Bradbury, Jim. The Medieval Siege. Woodbridge, Suffolk: The Boydell Press, 1992.

Brown, R. Allen. "Royal castle-building in England 1154–1216," Anglo-Norman Castles, edited by Robert Liddiard. Woodbridge, Suffolk: The Boydell Press, 2003.

Buckinghamshire County Council. "Bernwood Forest: Royal Forests & Forest Law." http://www.buckscc.gov.uk/medieval_life/bernwood/history2.htm.

Butler, L. A. S. Denbigh Castle and Town Walls. Cardiff: Cadw, 1990.

_____. Denbigh Castle, Town Walls and Friary. London: HMSO, 1976.

Butler, Lawrence. "Dolforwyn Castle: prospect and retrospect," The Medieval Castle in Ireland and Wales, edited by John R. Kenyon and Kieran O'Conor. Dublin: Four Courts Press, 2003.

Cambria Archaeology. www.cambria.org.uk/news.htm, 2007.

Challis, Keith. "Settlement Morphology and Medieval Village Planning: A Case Study at Laxton, Nottinghamshire." Tran Thoroton Soc Nottm (106) 2002.

Clarke, Helen. The Archaeology of Medieval England. Oxford: Basil Blackwell, Ltd., 1986.

Clarke, Lindsay. "Tower Menagerie Home to Barbary Lions — Official," Londonist. http://londonist.com/2008/03/scientists_at_t.php.

Columbia Encyclopedia, Sixth Edition, 2001–2007. "Manorial System." http://www.bartleby.com/65/ma/manorial.html.

Conisbrough Court Rolls. "The Manor Court." http://www.hrionline.ac.uk/conisbrough/find/manor_court.html.

Coulson, Charles. "The Castles of the Anarchy," Anglo-Norman Castles, edited by Robert Liddiard. Woodbridge, Suffolk: The Boydell Press, 2003.

Creighton, O. H. Castles and Landscapes: Power, Community and Fortification in Medieval England. London: Equinox, 2002.

_____. E-mail messages to author (June 5, 2007; July 10, 2007; December 21, 2007).

Creighton, Oliver, and Robert Higham. Medieval Castles. Princes Risborough: Shire Archaeology, 2003.

Demel, Scott. "Architectural Additions." http://www.demel.net/th-ch1.html.

_____. "Architectural Additions." http://www.demel.net/th-ch2.html.

Department for Culture, Media and Sport. "Draft Heritage Protection Bill, April 2008." http://www.culture.gov.uk/Reference_library/Publications/archive_2008/pub_drafthpb.htm.

Dixon, Philip, and Pamela Marshall. "The Great Tower at Hedingham Castle: A Reassessment," Anglo-Norman Castles, edited by Robert Liddiard. Woodbridge, Suffolk: The Boydell Press, 2003.

Drage, C. "Urban castles," Urban Archaeology in Britain, CBA Research Report (61) 1987. http://ads.ahds.ac.uk/catalogue/adsdata/cbaresrep/pdf/061/06108001.pdf.

Dyer, Christopher. Everyday Life in Medieval England. London and New York: Hambledon and London, 2000.

_____. *Making a Living in the Middle Ages: The People of Britain, 850–1520*. New Haven and London: Yale University Press, 2002.

_____. E-mail messages to author (May 28, 2007; January 22, 2008).

Eales, Richard. "Castles and Politics in England 1215–1224," *Anglo-Norman Castles*, edited by Robert Liddiard. Woodbridge, Suffolk: The Boydell Press, 2003.

_____. "Royal Power and Castles in Norman England," *Anglo-Norman Castles*, edited by Robert Liddiard. Woodbridge, Suffolk: The Boydell Press, 2003.

English Heritage. "Conservation Principles: Policies and Guidance for the Sustainable Management of the Historic Environment." http://www.english-heritage.org.uk/upload/pdf/Conservation_Principles_Policies_and_Guidance_April08_Web.pdf.

_____. "Historic Properties: Midlands." http://www.eng-h.gov.uk/ArchRev/rev95_6/hp_mids.htm.

_____. "Monuments Protection Programme Monument Class Description Dovecotes, December 1989." http://www.eng-h.gov.uk/mpp/mcd/sub/dove.htm.

_____. "Monuments Protection Programme Monument Class Description Warrens September 1998." http://www.eng-h.gov.uk/mpp/mcd/wrn.htm.

_____. "Parks and Gardens." http://www.eng-h.gov.uk/ArchRev/rev94_5/parks.htm.

_____. "Wigmore Castle, Hereford," *Archaeology Review* 4:19 (1996–1997). http://www.eng-h.gov.uk/archrev/rev97_8/cas4.htm.

Friar, Stephen. *The Sutton Companion to Castles*. Stroud: Sutton Publishing, 2003.

Fryde, E. B. *Peasants and Landlords in Later Medieval England*. Stroud: Sutton Publishing, 1996.

Fujita, Haruhiko. "William Morris and the 'Anti-Scrape,'" *The Japanese Society for Aesthetics* (46:4,) abstract. http://ci.nii.ac.jp/naid/110003714187/en.

Gardiner, Mark. "Shipping and Trade between England and the Continent during the Eleventh Century," *Anglo-Norman Studies XXII Proceedings of the Battle Conference*, edited by Christopher Harper-Bill. Woodbridge, Suffolk: Boydell & Brewer, 1999.

Gibson, John. *Anatomy of the Castle*. Saraband, Scotland: MetroBooks, 2001.

Gies, Joseph, and Frances Gies. *Life in a Medieval Castle*. New York: Harper & Row, 1974.

Giles, Howard. Email message to author (May 25, 2007).

Gravett, Christopher, and David Nicolle. *The Normans Warrior Knights and their Castles*. Oxford: Osprey Publishing, 2006.

Green, Judith A. *The Aristocracy of Norman England*. Cambridge: Cambridge University Press, 2002.

"Guide Ground Floor," The Castle Keep, Newcastle upon Tyne. http://museums.ncl.ac.uk/keep/keepguide/keep_guide_groundfloor.htm.

Guy, Neil. "Pevensey Castle," *The Castle Studies Group Journal* 19 (2005–6): 49–55.

_____. E-mail message to author (July 1, 2007).

Hall, David. "Medieval fields in their many forms," *British Archaeology* 33 (April 1998). http://www.britarch.ac.uk/BA/ba33/ba33feat.html.

Hammond, Peter. *Her Majesty's Royal Palace and Fortress of the Tower of London*. London: Historic Royal Palaces, 1993.

Helme, Andrew, and Annie Rainsbury. *Caldicot Castle, Great Fortress of the Gwent Levels*. Caldicot: Caldicot Castle & Country Park, Monmouthshire, 2005.

Higham, Robert. "Timber Castles—A Reassessment," *Anglo-Norman Castles*, edited by Robert Liddiard. Woodbridge, Suffolk: The Boydell Press, 2003.

Higham, Robert, and Philip Barker. *Timber Castles*. London: B. T. Batsford, Ltd., 1992.

Historic Herefordshire Online. "The Medieval Countryside of Herefordshire." http://www.smr.herefordshire.gov.uk/education/Medieval_Countryside.htm.

_____. "The Agricultural Landscape: Fishponds." http://www.smr.herefordshire.gov.uk/education/Fishponds.htm.

"History of the Monarchy: Malcolm IV." The Official Site of the British Monarchy. http://www.qmmemorial.gov.uk/output/Page110.asp.

Hull, Lise. *Castles and Bishops Palaces of Pembrokeshire*. Almeley: Logaston Press, 2005.

_____. *Castles of Glamorgan*. Almeley: Logaston Press, 2007.

Humphries, Peter. E-mail messages to author (November 7, 2007; November 9, 2007; November 21, 2007; December 27, 2007).

_____. "Prospect of Caernarfon (English abridged)." Exhibition write-up, n.d.

_____. "Rebuilding a Castle: The Restoration of Caerphilly." Exhibition write-up, 2007.

ICOMOS. "Principles of Preservation." http://www.icomos.de/einfuehrung.php.

Internet Medieval Sourcebook. "Medieval Sourcebook: A Manorial Court: 1246–1249." http://www.fordham.edu/halsall/source/manor-pleas.html.

_____. "Medieval Sourcebook: Manorial Management & Organization, c. 1275." http://www.fordham.edu/halsall/source/1275manors1.html.

Johnson, G. K. *Castles in Crisis*. Cardigan: Tivy-Side Advertiser, 2002.

Johnson, Matthew. *Behind the Castle Gate: From Medieval to Renaissance*. London: Routledge, 2002.

Keay, Anna. "The Presentation of Guardianship Sites," *Transactions of the Ancient Monuments Society* 48 (2004): 7–20.

Kenyon, John R. "Kidwelly Castle, Carmarthenshire: The Reinterpretation of a Monument," *The Medieval Castle in Ireland and Wales*, edited by John R. Kenyon and Kieran O'Conor. Dublin: Four Courts Press, 2003.

_____. *Medieval Fortifications*. Leicester: Leicester University Press, 1990.

_____. E-mail messages to author (April 9–10, 2007; June 1, 2007; June 15, 2007; July 9, 2007; August 9, 2007; September 2, 2007; November 6–8, 2007; January 30, 2008; February 5–6, 2008; March 4, 2008).

_____. *Raglan Castle*. Cardiff: Cadw, 2003.

King, D. J. Cathcart. *The Castle in England and Wales: An Interpretative History*. Beckenham, Kent: Croom Helm, Ltd., 1988.

Knight, Jeremy. *The Three Castles*. Cardiff: Cadw, 2000.

Kreis, Steven. "Lecture 21: Feudalism and the Feudal Relationship," *The History Guide*. http://www.historyguide.org/ancient/lecture21b.html.

Labarge, Margaret Wade. *A Baronial Household of the Thirteenth Century*. London: Eyre & Spottiswoode, 1965.

Legendary Dartmoor. "The Dartmoor Rabbit." http://www.legendarydartmoor.co.uk/rabb_its.htm.

Liddiard, Robert. *Castles in Context: Power, Symbolism and Landscape, 1066 to 1500*. Macclesfield: Windgather Press, 2005.

Macaulay, David. *Castle*. Boston: Houghton Mifflin Company, 1977.

Mackworth-Young, Robin. *The History & Treasures of Windsor Castle*. London: Pitkin-Britannia, 1982.

Manco, Jean. "Researching the History of Dovecotes." *Researching Historic Buildings in the British Isles*. http://www.buildinghistory.org/Buildings/Dovecotes.htm.

Manorbier Medieval Fishponds Restoration Group. http://www.manorbier-fishponds.org.uk/pageone.html.

Marshall, Leon Carroll. *Readings in Industrial Society—Study in the Structure and Functioning of Modern Economic Organization*. Chicago: University of Chicago Press, 1929.

Marshall, Pamela, and John Samuels. *Guardian of the Trent: The Story of Newark Castle*. Newark: Newark Castle Trust, 1997.

Martin, David, Barbara Martin and Christopher Whittock. *A Re-interpretation of Hastings Castle, Hastings, East Sussex*. Commissioned by Hastings Borough Council, 1999.

McNeill, Tom. *Castles*. London: B. T. Batsford, Ltd./ English Heritage, 2006.

Menon, A. G. Krishna. "Conservation in India: A Search for Direction." http://www.architexturez.net/+/subject-listing/000233.shtml.

Morley, Berie. *Peveril Castle*. London: English Heritage, 1990.

Morris, Marc. *Castle*. London: Pan Books, 2004.

Morris, William. "Manifesto of the Society for the Protection of Ancient Buildings (SPAB)." http://www.marxists.org/archive/morris/works/1877/spabman.htm.

Muir, Richard. *The English Village*. New York: Thames and Hudson, 1980.

_____. *The NEW Reading the Landscape: Fieldwork in Landscape History*. Exeter: University of Exeter Press, 2000.

National Archives. "World of Domesday, the Social Order." http://www.nationalarchives.gov.uk/domesday/world-of-domesday/order.htm.

National Monuments Record. "NMR Components Thesaurus." http://thesaurus.english-heritage.org.uk/thesaurus.asp?thes_no=546.

National Trust. *Corfe Castle Dorset*. London: The National Trust, 2000.

Oldham, Tony. "The Mines of the Forest of Dean." http://www.mike.munro.cwc.net/mining/tony_o/fod_01.htm.

Owen, James. "Medieval Lion Skulls Reveal Secrets of Tower of London Zoo," *National Geographic News*. http://news.nationalgeographic.com/news/2005/11/1103_051103_tower_lions.html.

Petzet, Michael. "Place, Memory, Meaning: Preserving Intangible Values in Monuments and Sites." Introductory lecture, ICOMOS 14th General Assembly and Scientific Symposium. http://www.international.icomos.org/victoriafalls2003/papers/4%20-%20Allocution%20Petzet.pdf.

Pettifer, Adrian. *English Castles: A Guide by Counties*. Woodbridge, Suffolk: The Boydell Press, 1995.

Platt, Colin. *Dover Castle*. London: English Heritage, 1988.

Pounds, N. J. G. *The Medieval Castle in England and Wales*. Cambridge: Cambridge University Press, 1994.

Prestwich, Michael. *Armies and Warfare in the Middle Ages: The English Experience*. New Haven and London: Yale University Press, 2003.

Raby, F. J. E. *Framlingham Castle*. London: HMSO, 1984.

Renn, Derek. *Caerphilly Castle*. Cardiff: Cadw, 1997.

_____. *Goodrich Castle*. London: English Heritage, 1998.

_____. *Kenilworth Castle*. London: English Heritage, 1999.

_____. *Norman Castles in Britain*. London: John Baker Publishers Ltd., 1973.

Robinson, David M., ed. *Tretower Court and Castle*. Cardiff: Cadw, 1990.

Robinson, John Martin. *Arundel Castle*. Arundel: Arundel Castle Trustees Ltd., n.d.

"Rockingham Forest." http://www.cottinghamhistory.co.uk/Rockinghamforest.htm.

Royal Commission on Ancient and Historical Monuments in Wales, The. *The Early Castles from the Norman Conquest to 1217*. Edited by C.J. Spurgeon. London: HMSO, 1991.

Royal Forest Society, The. "The Hunting Forests and Chases." http://www.rfs.org.uk/thirdlevel.asp?ThirdLevel=4&SecondLevel=1.

Savage, Anne. *The Anglo-Saxon Chronicles*. London: Guild Publishing, 1988.

Shoesmith, Ron. *Castles & Moated Sites of Herefordshire*. Almeley: Logaston Press, 1996.

Society for the Protection of Ancient Buildings, The. "SPAB's purpose." http://www.spab.org.uk/html/what-is-spab/spabs-purpose.

Spandl, Klara. "Exploring the Round Houses of Doves," *British Archaeology* 35 (June 1998). http://www.britarch.ac.uk/ba/ba35/ba35feat.html.

Stell, Geoffrey. *Exploring Scotland's Heritage Dumfries and Galloway*. Edinburgh: HMSO, 1986.

Taylor, A. J. *Conwy Castle and Town Walls*. Cardiff: Cadw, 1998.

_____. *The King's Works in Wales, 1277–1330*. London: HMSO, 1974.

Thackray, David. *Bodiam Castle East Sussex*. London: The National Trust, 1995.

Thorpe, Lewis. *Gerald of Wales: The Journey through Wales and The Description of Wales*. London: Penguin Books, 1978.

Todd, Pamela. *William Morris and the Arts and Crafts Home*. San Francisco: Chronicle Books, 2005.

Toy, Sidney. *Castles: Their Construction and History*. New York: Dover Publications, Inc., 1984.

Trent and Peak Archaeological Trust. "The Laxton Village Survey." http://mahan.wonkwang.ac.kr/link/med/economy/agricul/laxsurv.html.

Turner, Richard. E-mail message to author (March 7, 2008).

Ward, Penny. E-mail messages to author (January 25, 2008; February 19, 2008; April 2, 2008).

Warner, Philip. *The Medieval Castle: Life in a Fortress in Peace and War*. New York: Barnes and Noble Books, 1993.

_____. *Sieges of the Middle Ages*. London: Penguin Books, 2000.

Warwick Castle. "Discover Our History." http://www.warwick-castle.co.uk/plan_your_day/history.asp.

Welsh Assembly Government. "Heritage Protection for the 21st Century." http://www.cadw.wales.gov.uk/upload/resourcepool/Heritage%20Protection%20White%20Paper1669.pdf.

_____. "The Repair and Preservation of Masonry: Technical Conservation Note 1." http://www.cadw.wales.gov.uk/upload/resourcepool/masonry%20notes%20englih7511.pdf.

Wickham Parish Council. "Discover the Forest of Bere." http://wickham.parish.hants.gov.uk/new_page_51.htm.

Yorkshire Dales National Park Authority. "Out of Oblivion: A Landscape through Time." http://www.outofoblivion.org.uk/hunting.asp.

_____. http://www.outofoblivion.org.uk/record.asp?id=478.

Index

Abbey Cwmhir 3
Abbey of Fecamp 14
Aberystwyth (castle) 79, 82, 201
ab Iorwerth, Llywelyn 79, 202
Accommodation *see* Living quarters
Administrative center 140, 153; *see also* Purpose
Adulterine castles 74, 79
Aethelred 11
Afforestation 161
Agisters 152, 161
Agistment 161
Alan "the Red" 198, 199
Ale 161
Alexander, Bishop of Lincoln 198
Almoner 133
Alnwick (castle) 58, 82, 107, 155, 195
Altar 129
The Anarchy 20, 22, 36, 73, 74, 76, 79, 80; *see also* Empress Matilda; King Stephen
Ancient Monuments and Archaeological Areas Act 186, 189
Ancient Monuments Consolidation and Protection Act 182
Ancient Monuments Protection Act 182
Ancillary structures 64
Angharad 159
Angle (castle) 112, 155, 201
Anglo-Saxon army 15
Anglo-Saxon Chronicle 16, 36, 76
Antechamber 115, 124, 133
Antiquarians 178, 184
Anti-Scrape Movement 179, 181, 182, 184, 188
Apartments *see* Living quarters
ap Cadwgan, Owain 131
ap Gruffydd, Dafydd 182, 201
ap Gruffydd, Llywelyn 3, 79, 190, 191, 201, 202
ap Gruffydd, Rhys (the Lord Rhys) 202
ap Rhys, Maredudd 202
Apron wall 133
Apse 133
Apsidal 80, 82, 95, 128
ap Tewdwr, Rhys 131, 159
ap Thomas, William 58, 107, 110, 203

Aquitaine, Eleanor of 108
Arable 144
Arbalest 82; *see also* Crossbow
Archaeological excavations 190–192, 193
Archibald "the Grim" 204
Aristocratic landscape 153
Arms 80
Arrow 80
Arrowloops 133
Arrowslits 52, 53, 68, 71, 80, 82, 84, 133
Arsenal 152
Artist's renditions 141, 170, 171
Arts and Crafts Movement 179
Arundel (castle) 28, 31, 32, 35, 37, 64, 67, 68, 81, 195
Arundell, Sir Thomas 123
Ashby de la Zouch (castle) 158, 195
Ashlar *see* Stone, building
Attiliator 133
Aubrey, John 3
Audience chambers 133
Aumbry 129, 132

Baggage train *see* Siege train
Baile Hill (castle) *see* Clifford's Tower
Bailey 37, 87, 133; inner 3, 80, 88–89, 95, 96, 113–114, 122; outer 63–64, 66, 67, 68, 80, 88, 132
Bailiff 77, 143, 145, 146, 161
Baillie, Lady 197
Bakehouse 115, 133, 137
Baker 133
Balcony 116; *see also* Minstrel's gallery
Ball, John 146
Ballista 81, 86; *see also* Siege, engines
Bamburgh (castle) 122, 195
Barbican 36, 37, 60, 62, 71, 81, 85, 104, 204
Barker, Philip 27
Barley 161
Barmkin 111, 133
Barnard (castle) 150, 195
Baronial style 204
Barons' rebellion 74, 102, 197
Barrels 134

Bastions 83, 94, 95, 133
Bates, Cadwallader 198
Battering ram 81; *see also* Siege, engines
Battle Abbey 15
Battlements 51, 58, 59, 81, 82; stepped 112; *see also* Crenellations
Baxter 133
Bayeux (castle) 25
Bayeux Tapestry 13, 16, 23, 25, 27, 39
Beadle 146, 161
Beauchamp, Thomas 56
Beaumaris (castle) 32, 46, 62, 78, 81, 129, 149, 173, 178, 185, 201
Bedchambers 90, 123, 124, 125
Beds 124
Beeston (castle) 55, 122, 195
Belfry 81; *see also* Siege, engines
Berkeley (castle) 24, 27, 195
Berkhamsted (castle) 18, 28, 195
Big pond 150
Bigod, Hugh 73
Bigod, Roger 36, 93, 113, 197
Birds 156
Bishop's (castle) 24, 195
Bishops of Llandaff 201
Bishops of Winchester 195
Bishop's palace 195
Bishopton (castle) 39, 195
Black Death 161, 165
The Black Prince 116, 151
Blarney (castle) 112, 204
Blockade 81; *see also* Siege
Bloet, Elizabeth 107, 110
Bodiam (castle) 10, 31, 45, 88, 89, 114, 115, 140, 156, 170, 188, 195
Boley Hill (castle) 101; *see also* Rochester Castle
Boleyn, Anne 198
Bolingbroke (castle) 158–159, 195
Bolingbroke, Henry 55
Bolsover (castle) 108, 195
Bolton (castle) 114, 151, 154, 195
Boon-work 77, 81, 143, 145, 162
Bordar 144, 162
Bore 81; *see also* Ram; Siege engines
Bottle dungeon 137; *see also* Oubliette
Bottlery *see* Buttery

Brack Mount (castle) *see* Lewes Castle
Bramber (castle) 43, 195–196
The braye 161
The Brays 69, 150, 158
Brazier 133
Bretons 15
Brewer 133, 162
Brown, Lancelot "Capability" 3
Buck, Nathaniel 178
Buck, Samuel 178
Building a stone castle 32–36
Builth (castle) 6, 82, 201
Bunratty (castle) 112, 204
Burgage 194
Burhs 17, 23, 37; *see also* Saxon settlements
Burnetts of Ley 204
Burton (castle) *see* Stafford
Butler 133
Buttery and pantry 99, 116, 119, 121, 122, 123, 133, 137; *see also* Kitchen
Buttresses: pilaster 133; pyramidal 48
Buttressing 102

Cadw 190, 191, 194
Caen stone *see* Stone, building
Caerau (castle) 200
Caergwrle (castle) 181, 182, 201
Caerlaverock (castle) 50, 203–204
Caernarfon (castle) 55, 56, 66, 67, 78, 82, 95, 96, 122, 127, 173, 178, 179, 181, 182–183, 185–186, 187, 201
Caerphilly (castle) 6, 30, 32, 35, 236, 40, 63, 74, 81, 82, 95, 997, 104, 105, 128, 132, 140, 149, 178, 183, 201
Caldicot (castle) 184, 185, 201
Cambridge (castle) 24, 196
Campaign castle 37
Campbell dukes of Argyll 204
Canterbury (castle) 18, 99, 100, 101, 103, 196
Carboniferous limestone *see* Stone, building
Carder 133
Cardiff (castle) 201
Cardigan (castle) 188, 189–190, 191, 201
Carew (castle) 83, 129, 131, 201
Carpentarius 37, 81
Carreg Cennen (castle) 62, 78, 122, 201
Carter 37, 81
Carvings 116
Castell Caereinion (castle) 24, 201
Castell Coch (castle) 183, 201
Castell Hendre (castle) *see* Henry's Moat
Castell Nanhyfer (castle) *see* Nevern Castle
Castell Talyfan (castle) 30, 201
Castell-y-Bere (castle) 7, 201
Castellan 38, 64

Castille, Eleanor of 110
Castle Acre (castle) 196
Castle definition 37
Castle of the Peak (castle) *see* Peveril
Castle Rache (castle) *see* Neroche
Castle Rising (castle) 19, 104, 105, 196
Castle studies: revisionists 9, 10, 102, 104; traditionalists 9
Castlemartin (castle) 29, 201
Castles *see* individual castle names
Cat 81, 85; *see also* Siege, engines
Catapult 81; *see also* Siege, engines
Cavaliers 38, 83
Cavendish, Sir Charles 195
Cellarer 134
Cementarius 37
Centre Guillaume le Conquer'ant 13
Ceredigion County Council 190, 191
Cesspit 130
Chamberlain 134
Chamfer 134
Chancel 134
Chancery 134
Chandler 134
Chantry 134
Chapel of St. Mary 128
Chapel of St. Mary Magdalene 128, 129
Chapel Royal of St. John the Evangelist 128
Chapels 127–129, 132, 134, 137, 138
Chaplains, 134; *see also* Priests
Charcoal 152
Charcoal burners 152
Charlemagne 23
Charles, Duke of Orleans 199
Charles I 38, 74, 83, 102, 137
Chase, hunting 150, 153, 162
Chateau des Morais (castle) 21, 204
Chatelaine 131
Chepstow (castle) 24, 36, 60, 67, 80, 82, 98, 113, 121, 201
Chester (castle) 24, 173, 196
Chevron pattern 134; *see also* Norman style; Stone, building
Chimney 126, 134
Church 128, 161
Churches 172
Cider 162
Cilgerran (castle) 47, 49, 50, 78, 131, 201
Cistern 28, 37, 66, 122, 134
Clare (castle) 196
Clavering (castle) 16, 18, 196
Clerestory 134
Clerks 134
Clifford (castle) 24, 196
Clifford's Tower (castle) 24, 31, 157, 196
Cloth-making 163
Clun (castle) 27, 196
Coal 152
Coat of arms 80
Cobb, J. R. 71, 178, 184, 185, 201
Cobbler 134

Coity (castle) 201–202; lordship of 142
Colchester (castle) 15, 83, 128, 196
Collegiate church 127
Columbarium 154; *see also* Dovecote
Colwell Chase 153
Commandery 162
Commissioners of Woods, Forests and Land Revenues 186
Communing 167
Conan the Little 99
Concentric 32, 37, 81, 200, 201
Coney garths 154, 162; *see also* Rabbit warrens
Conger Hill 200
Conisbrough (castle) 93, 196
Conservation 178, 180, 181, 184, 186, 187, 188, 193
"Conserve as found" 181, 184–185, 186, 187
Constable 38, 64, 81, 134
Constantine, Holy Roman Emperor 56, 185
Constantinople 56, 185, 201
Consuetudines et Iiusticie 73
Context 170
Conwy (castle) 35, 56, 62, 67, 78, 82, 88, 90, 93, 95, 115, 116, 117, 130, 173, 174, 178, 181, 185, 201
Conwy town walls 174–175
Cooks 134
Cooper 134
Copyholder 162
Corbels 91, 92, 94, 116, 134
Cordwainer 134
Corfe (castle) 21, 22, 35, 67, 68, 69, 83, 95, 196
Costs 32, 33, 34
Cottar/cottager 144, 162
Counterweight 81, 86; *see also* Siege, engines; Trebuchet
Court baron 164
Court house 116, 117, 134, 144, 162
Court leet 164
Court, manorial 77, 144, 145, 146, 152, 164
Courtenay, Hugh 199
Courtine 134
Courtmain, Robert 202
Courtyard castle, pentagonal 202 *see also* Stone castles
Cowdray (castle) 196
Cowper, John 45
Craftsmen 64, 143
Crathes (castle) 112, 204
Crenel 81, 82, 85
Crenellations 58, 59, 81, 82
Criccieth (castle) 78, 79, 135, 201
Crichton-Stewart, John 183, 184
Crichton-Stewart, John Patrick 183
Crickhowell (castle) 6, 154, 201
Croft, Richard 196
Cromwell, Oliver 55, 74–75, 86
Cross-loops 80
Cross-oillets 52, 82
Cross-wall 116, 134

Crossbow 82
Crossbow bolts 152; *see also* Quarrels
Crow's nest 86
Crypt 127, 128, 134
Cup bearer 134
Curtain wall 134; *see also* Walls
Curthose, Robert 198
Curzon, Lord 183

D-shaped 202; *see also* Apsidal
Dais 116; *see also* Great hall
d'Albini, William 19, 102, 105, 196
Dalyngrygge, Sir Edward 88, 195
Dane John (castle) 100, 101; *see also* Canterbury Castle
Dapifer 135
David I, King of Scotland 195
d'Avranches, Hugh 24, 66, 196
de Balliol, Bernard 195
de Barri, Odo 160, 203
de Barri, William 99, 159
de Blois, Henry 195
de Blois, William 73
de Blundeville, Ranulf 195
de Braose, Philip 201
de Braose, William 43, 195
de Brian, Guy, IV 202
de Brian family 203
de Brionne, Baldwin 199
de Burg, Serlo 198
de Burgh, Hubert 53, 74, 197, 203
de Caen, Roger 202
de Cardiff family 22, 202
de Caux, Robert 198
de Clare, Gilbert FitzRichard 201
de Clare, Gilbert, II 49, 73, 74, 118, 183, 196, 200, 201
de Clare, Richard 191, 196, 200, 202
de Clare, Thomas 204
de Clinton, Geoffrey 102, 197
de Conyers, Roger 195
de Corbeil, William, Archbishop of Canterbury 102
de Crevecouer, Robert 198
de Dinan, Sir Joyce 128
Deer parks 148, 149, 150, 151, 153, 154, 161, 162
Defenders, stone 82
Defenses, water 37, 47
de Ferrers, Walkelin 199
de la Bere, David 203
de Lacy, Henry 55, 114, 201
de Lacy, Hugh 128, 198
de Lacy, Roger 99, 198
de Lasci, Ilbert 199
de Londres, Maurice 203
de Londres, William 203
de Louvain, Adeliza 19, 105
de Lucy, Thomas 198
de Mandeville, Geoffrey 25, 200
Demesne 82, 140, 144, 152, 162, 164, 167; *see also* Manorial estates
de Mohun, William 196
de Montfort, Simon 74, 110, 198
de Montgomery, Arnulf 66, 203

de Montgomery, Roger 24, 27, 195, 202
de Mortain, Robert 14, 20, 195, 196, 199
de Mortimer, Ralph 200
de Mowbray, Alina 132
de Mowbray, John 132
de Mowbray, Robert 195, 200
de Mowbray, William 200
Denbigh (castle) 56, 62, 85, 114, 116, 173, 201
de Penitone, Adam 198
de Penres, Robert II 203
de Peverel, William 108, 199
de Say, Robert 196
de Senlis, Simon 197
de Snelleston, Henry 116
de Soulis, Lord 204
de Stafford, Ralph 200
de Turberville, Payn 202
de Turbervilles 142, 202
de Valence, William 54, 55, 62, 65, 71, 203
de Vere, Aubrey III 104, 105, 197
de Vescy, Yves 195
de Warenne, William 55, 195, 196, 198
de Windsor, Gerald 131, 201, 202
Dinan (castle) 25
Dinefwr (castle) 191, 202
Dispenser 135
Dissolution of the Monasteries 157
Ditch 44, 46, 47, 38, 62, 67, 69, 82, 85, 130, 135; *see also* Moat
Ditcher 38, 82, 84
d'Oilly, Robert 199
Dol (castle) 25
Dolforwyn (castle) 78, 190, 191, 201–202
Dolwyddelan (castle) 78, 202
Domen Castell (castle) *see* Powis Castle
Domesday Book 38, 144, 151, 157, 162
Dominarium 97
Donjon 82, 97, 135; *see also* Keeps
Doocot *see* Dovecote
Doors 51, 68, 69, 71, 82, 84
Dovecot *see* Dovecote
Dovecote 22, 38, 113, 135, 148, 154, 155–157, 162, 165, 166, 203
Dover (castle) 10, 32, 24, 53, 55, 74, 81, 99, 103–104, 105, 110, 128, 132, 168, 188, 192, 196
Draughts *see* Latrine
Drawbar 82
Drawbar holes 71, 82
Drawbridge 49–51, 62, 82
Dryslwyn (castle) 191, 202
Dudley, Robert 49, 103
Dungeon 54, 82, 85, 135
Dunstanburgh (castle) 148, 196–197
Dunster (castle) 153, 196
Durward 135
Dux Anglorum 12
Dyer 135
Dykes 38

Earl's Pond 157
Earl's Pool 157
Earls of Bothwell 204
Earls of Derwentwater 198
Earls of Douglas 204
Earls of Powis 183
Earth and timber 38, 177
Earthen enclosure castle 19, 38; *see also* Ringworks
Earthworks 38, 135
Edgar, the Aetheling 12
Edith, daughter of Godwin 11
Edmund Ironside 11, 12
Edward I 38, 39, 43, 45, 47, 55, 56, 69, 73, 78, 79, 81, 82, 86, 88, 95, 97, 173, 181, 182, 183, 185, 186, 187, 190, 196, 198, 199, 200, 201, 202, 203, 204
Edward II 36, 91, 195, 203
Edward of Woodstock *see* The Black Prince
Edward the Confessor 11, 12, 16, 39
Effigies 194
Eisteddfod 201
Elizabeth I 49, 95, 198
Embrasures 82, 83, 85
Enclosure castle 32
Engineer 83, 84
English Civil Wars 38, 55, 68, 69, 74, 83, 102, 107, 123, 137, 158, 159, 161, 181, 183, 188, 199; fortifications 83, 158–159
English Heritage 181, 187, 192, 194, 195, 197, 198, 200
Epping Forest 167
Equipment 34
Escalade 83, 86; *see also* Siege
Ethelfleda's Mound (castle) 65, 95, 96; *see also* Warwick Castle
Eustace, Count, of Bologne 15, 16
Ewenny Priory (castle) 156, 202
Ewerer 135
Ewloe (castle) 78, 79 202
Ewyas Harold (castle) 16, 18, 196–197
Ewyas Lacy (castle) *see* Longtown Castle
Exeter (castle) 18, 37, 81, 197
Exploring castles *see* Visiting castles

Famuli 144, 162
Farleigh Hungerford (castle) 120, 127, 128, 173, 181, 197
Farming *see* Ridge and furrow system
Farming, deer 150, 162; *see also* Deer parks; Food production
Farming, fish 162; *see also* Fishponds; Food production
Farming out 143
Farnham (castle) 27, 197
Fealty 38
Feast 163
Fees 165
Fergant, Count Alan 15
Feudal obligation 142, 164, 166
Feudal summons 83

Feudalism 23, 77, 83, 140, 142–143, 152
Feuds 23, 39, 162
Fiefs 23, 38, 142, 162
Fighting platform 38, 59, 60, 84; *see also* Hoarding
Fines 145; *see also* Fees
Fireplaces 84, 90, 115, 117, 118, 122, 125, 126, 135; *see also* Central hearth; Chimney, Hearth
First sight 5
Fish stews 157; *see also* Fishponds
Fish 157–158
Fishponds 22, 148, 157–160, 162, 166, 167, 202
FitzAlan, Richard 67
FitzGilbert, Richard 196, 200
FitzHamon, Robert 22, 203
FitzHardinge, Richard 195
FitzMartin, Robert 203
FitzOsbern, Hugh 200
FitzOsbern, William 24, 36, 195, 196, 197, 198, 201, 202, 203
FitzPons, Richard 202
FitzRandolph, Robert 198
FitzTurstin, Baldwin 199
FitzWalter, Miles 199
FitzWimarc, Richard 196
Flemings 78
Fletchlings 80; *see also* Arrow
Flint (castle) 45, 82, 97, 202
Floors 90, 91
Flue 135; *see also* Chimney; Fireplaces
Food 163; production 148, 149–160, 162, 163, 165
Foraging 84
Forebuilding 135
Forest of Dean 152, 167
Forest of the Peak 153
Forest work 163
Foresters-in-fee 163
Forests 144, 151–153, 163; jobs 152, 153, 163, 204; law 151–152, 161, 163
Fortitudinem 73
Fossatore 38, 44, 82, 84
Fosse 73
Fotheringhay (castle) 5, 71, 150, 197
Foundations 38
Framlingham (castle) 93, 126, 185, 197
Freemason 38
Freemen 144, 163; *see also* Peasantry
Fruiterer 135
Fuller 135
Fulling 163; mills 149
Furnishings 119, 120, 121, 124

Gabion 39, 84
Gable 135
Gallery 135
Game 152, 153, 154, 162; *see also* Deer parks; Rabbit warrens
Gardens 163, 195
Garderobe 84, 131, 135; *see also* Latrine

Garrison 131, 135
Gastineau, Henry 178
Gate passage 51, 71, 84, 91
Gate towers 36
Gatehouse 51, 53, 55, 60, 65, 67, 68, 69, 84, 113, 114, 135, 202
Gateway 51, 53, 63, 66, 84, 85, 87, 104, 160, 175
Gaunt, John of 103, 118, 119
Gaveston, Piers 110
Gentlemen keepers 153
Gentry 163
Geoffrey, Fifth Count of Anjou 36, 80
Gerald of Wales (Giraldus Cambrensis) 159–160
Glamorgan, Vale of 21
Glass 121, 124, 128
Glassmakers 152
Gloriette 69
Gloucester (castle) 24, 197
Glyndwr, Owain 78, 202, 203
Godwin, Earl of Wessex 12
Goltho (castle) 93, 197
Gong 135; *see also* Latrine
Gong farmer (gang fermor) 130, 135
Goodrich (castle) 30, 37, 46, 48, 49, 62, 81, 130, 197
Gower Peninsula 21
Granary 28, 39, 135, 163
Grand Tour 2
Great hall 99, 105, 115, 116, 117, 118, 119, 135, 198
Great mere 150, 165
Great park 149, 150, 157
Grid plan 173, 175, 194, 198
Grilles 130, 135
Grimspound, Dartmoor 147
Grooves 51, 85
Guardroom 39, 68, 84, 135
Guernsey, Isle of 21
Gundulf, Bishop 101
Gunloops 53, 80, 84
Gutters 93
Gwynedd, Owain 202
Gynour 84

Hadleigh (castle) 121, 149, 197
Hall 39, 99, 116, 135; *see also* Great hall
Hall-keep 39, 98, 99, 135, 160, 201, 203
Hallmote *see* Manorial court
Hammerbeam ceiling 118, 135
Harald Hardrada, king of Norway 12, 13, 39, 41
Hares and rabbits 153
Harlech (castle) 46, 47, 55, 78, 79, 82, 178, 181, 185, 188, 202
Harold II (Godwinson) 11, 12, 13, 15, 16, 17, 23, 24, 39, 77
Harry Potter 1
Harrying of the North 142, 163–164
Harthaknut 12
Hastings 12, 13, 14
Hastings (castle) 23, 25, 197

Hastings, William, Lord 10
Haverfordwest (castle) 72, 78, 172, 202
Hawkesworth, Colonel 102
Hayward 146, 164
Hearth 121; central 117, 126, 135
Hedingham (castle) 104–105, 197
Hen Domen (castle) 27–28, 31, 50, 148, 202
Henry I 30, 36, 69, 78, 80, 99, 102, 195
Henry II 34, 53, 73, 74, 100, 103, 104, 108, 109, 110, 122, 196, 197, 199
Henry III 74, 97, 99, 102, 109, 121, 197, 200, 203
Henry IV *see* Bolingbroke, Henry
Henry of Monmouth (Henry V) 79, 150, 165, 203
Henry VII 95
Henry VIII 157, 165, 181, 199, 204
Henry, Earl of Northumberland 200
Henry "Hotspur" 200
Henry, Lord Barnard 199
Henry, Lord Percy *see* Percy, Henry, fifth Lord
Henry, Third Lord Arundell 122
Henry's Moat (castle) 29, 45, 202
Hepburn, James, Earl of Bothwell 204
Heraldic emblems 58, 80, 95, 125, 126, 135, 170
Herbert, William 58, 122
Hereford (castle) 16, 18, 197
Heritage Lottery Fund 192
Hermitage (castle) 111, 204
Herringbone masonry 35, 39, 109, 124, 126, 135; *see also* Stone, building
Hewer 39
High-pitched 135
Higham, Robert 27
Hillfort 39, 201
Historic monuments 188
Historic Scotland 204
Hoarding 38, 39, 59, 60, 68, 84
Hodman 39
Holding 164
Homage 39, 142
Honor 142, 164
Hooper 135
Hopton Castle Preservation Trust 192
Hornwork 83, 84
Houses 172; staff 64, 132
Hugh, Lord Despenser 140
Hungerford, Sir Thomas 128, 197
Hungerford, Sir Walter 128
Hunting 162; lodge 200
Huntingdon (castle) 24, 197
Huntsmen 150, 164

Ingeniator 39, 84
International Council of Monuments and Sites (ICOMOS) 180
Interpretation 5, 6, 7, 24, 31, 72, 76, 89, 90, 91, 107, 111, 113, 115,

116, 118, 119, 121, 123, 125, 128, 130
Inveraray (castle) 112, 204
Ireland 112
Iron age forts 18, 196; see also Hillforts
Iron forges 164
Iron ore industry 149, 152
Isabella, Queen 36, 91

Jakes see Latrine
James I 199
James of St. Georges, Master 82
John, Fifth Lord Lovel 122
John, King 69, 74, 81, 84, 97, 100, 104, 152, 198, 199, 200
Johnson, Glen 189
Joist holes 91, 93, 116, 135; see also Hammerbeam ceiling, Timber-framed
Jones, Robert 185
The Journey Through Wales 159, 160
Jousting 84
Justiciar 84

Keep 19, 30, 36, 39, 53, 55, 58, 67, 69, 76, 84, 90, 94, 97–111, 114, 122, 135, 156, 168, 176, 177, 185, 191, 195, 196, 197, 198, 199, 200, 201, 202, 203, 204; see also Tower, great
Keeper of the wardrobe 135
Kenilworth (castle) 37, 49, 69, 84, 102, 103, 104, 118–120, 128, 150, 157, 158, 175, 178, 181, 183, 197–198
Kidwelly (castle) 138, 202
Kiln 39, 135
Kirby Muxloe (castle) 10, 45, 197
Kitchen 99, 115, 116, 118, 121, 122, 123, 135, 137; see also Buttery and pantry
Kitchener 135
Knaresborough (castle) 157, 197
Knight 84
Knights Hospitaller 157, 162
Knights of St. John see Knights Hospitaller
Knight's service 164; see also Feudalism
Knights Templar 162
Knut 11, 12, 14

L-plan 112, 204; see also Tower houses
Laboratories 143, 164
Lady 131–132
Lancet-headed 135; see also Windows
Land 144, 164; ownership 142–143, 163; see also Demesne; Manorial estates
Landlord 84, 140, 143, 164; see also Lord
Landscape, manorial 157
Langley (castle) 129, 198
Langley, Charles (viscount) 198

Langley, James (viscount) 198
Langstrothdale Chase 153
Larderer 150
Latrine 48, 59, 84, 97, 102, 109, 115, 123, 129–131, 136
Laugharne (castle) 113, 191, 202
Laugharne, Rowland 161
Laundress 136
Lawing 152, 164
Laxton (castle) 147, 154, 198
Laxton village 147–148
Layout 67, 88, 97, 102
Lead mining 153
le Despenser, Hugh 36, 91, 118
Leeds (castle) 157, 178, 198
Legislation 182, 186, 188
le Gros, William 200
Leland, John
le Scrop, Richard 199
Lewes (castle) 26, 27, 55, 198
License to crenellate 31, 39
Lime production 152
Lincoln (castle) 24, 27, 198
Lions 97
Listed structures 186
Lists 84, 86
Little park 150
Little pond 150
Living quarters 28, 64, 113, 119, 124, 133
Llanblethian (castle) 99, 191, 202
Llandovery (castle) 6, 202
Llantrisant (castle) 191, 202–203
Llantrithyd (castle) 21, 22, 28, 202
Llantrithyd Place 22
Local authorities 194
Location see Setting
Lodsbridge (castle) 24, 198
Longtown (castle) 176, 198
Lord 84, 140, 164; lordship 142, 164; see also Landlord
Lord Curzon 183
The Lord of the Rings 1
The Lord Rhys 202
Louis, the French Dauphin 100
Louver 136
Ludlow (castle) 99, 128, 129, 198
Ludlow, Neil 141, 171, 177

Machicolations 59, 60, 68, 84, 94, 113, 136
Madame Tussaud's 200
Magna Carta 74, 84, 199
Mangonel 81, 85; see also Onager, Siege engines
Manor 144, 164
Manor houses 22, 140; fortified 10, 38
Manorbier (castle) 83, 99, 149, 156, 159–161, 184, 185, 202
Manorial estates 76, 82, 140–160
Manorial obligations 145; see also Manorialism; Payments; Rent
Manorialism 140, 143, 164
Manumission 144, 164
Mappestone, Godric 197

Maps, Ordnance Survey (OS) 29, 169
Markets 172
Marlborough (castle) 153, 158, 198
Marquesses of Bute 183
Marshal, William 36, 55, 64, 66, 74, 105, 177, 203
Marshal, William II 201
Mary, Queen of Scots 5, 197, 204
Mary Tudor 100
Mason 37, 40; see also Master mason
Mason's marks 75, 85
Master craftsman 40
Master mason 40; see also Master James of St. Georges
Matilda, Empress 20, 36, 73, 80, 104
Maurice the Engineer 103
Maxwells 204
McCarthy, Dermot 204
Meadow 144
Medieval town walls 173–176, 194, 201, 203
Menagerie 85, 97
Merchet 165
Merlon 81, 82, 83, 85
Messor 146, 165
Meurtrières 52, 62, 84, 85
Middleham (castle) 149, 198
Mill 145, 148, 149, 165; corn 160, 161; fulling 149; horse 136; water 149
Miller 165
Miner 38, 85, 138; see also Fossatore; Sapper
Ministerial service 165; see also Serjeanty
Minstrel's gallery 116, 136
Mint 97, 137
Missiles 85; see also Siege, engines
Moat 44, 45, 47, 69, 82, 85, 157; see also Ditch
Moated site 40
Molding 40
Monkton Priory 203
Monmouth (castle) 24, 202
Montgomery (castle) 27, 191, 202
Moral code 143
Morris, William 178, 179, 193
Mortar 40
Mortimers 192, 198
Mottes 18, 21, 23–31, 32, 36, 40, 65, 68, 85, 95, 99, 106, 176, 196, 197, 198, 199, 201, 202, 203
Movies 1, 4
Multure 145, 165
Muncaster (castle) 150, 198
Murage 172, 194
Mural chamber 137
Mural passage 85
Murder holes 52, 62, 84, 85

Names, field 155
Names, tower 95
Narberth (castle) 141, 171, 193, 202
National heritage bodies 194; see

also Cadw; English Heritage; Historic Scotland
National Trust 194
Natural resources 152
Nave 137
Neath Abbey 132
Necessarium 37; *see also* Latrine
Neroche (castle) 154, 196
Nest 131
Nevern (castle) 202
New Forest 167
New Moat (castle) 29, 202
New Model Army 137; *see also* English Civil Wars
Newark-on-Trent (castle) 83, 182, 183, 198
Newborough 173
Newcastle Bridgend (castle) 51, 202
Newcastle-upon-Tyne (castle) 34, 74, 83, 122, 173, 198
Newcastle-upon-Tyne town walls 175
Newel stair 137; *see also* Stairways
Norman Conquest 11, 12–15, 16–17, 24, 36, 39, 76–79, 142, 137, 163, 195
Norman style 92
Normandy 73
Norton Tower 154
Norwegians 12, 13, 14
Norwich (castle) 24, 25, 27, 198–199
Nottingham (castle) 24, 34, 198

Oakham (castle) 157, 198
O'Briens, Earls of Thomond 204
Occupations 165
Oculus 165
Odo, bishop of Bayeux 13, 15, 16, 20, 101, 102
Office of Works 182, 184
Ogmore (castle) 45, 202–203
Okehampton (castle) 153, 198–199
Old Wardour (castle) 3, 121, 123, 200
Onager 85; *see also* Mangonel, Siege engines
Open-gorged 93, 137, 173, 174, 175; *see also* Towers
Orchards 160, 161, 165
Ordericus Vitalis 76
Orford (castle) 73, 199
Oriel 118, 119, 120, 125, 137
Oubliette 85, 137
Outwork 85; *see also* Barbican
Oven 121, 137
Oxford (castle) 24, 34, 199
Oystermouth (castle) 203

Pacification *see* Harrying the North
Page 137
Painting 40, 90, 114, 120, 121, 124, 126, 132, 195
Pale 150, 165
Pannage 165
Pantler 137
Parapet 85

Parkland 144, 149
Parliamentarians 38, 83, 86, 102, 137, 181
Pauncefoot, Sir Gimbald 202
Payments 143, 145, 152
Peasantry 44, 76–79, 81, 85, 140, 143–146, 152, 162, 166
Peasant's Revolt (1381) 146, 165
Pembroke (castle) 17, 46, 54, 60, 61, 62, 64, 65, 66, 69–71, 72, 95, 104, 105, 111, 113, 115, 116, 131, 144, 160, 172, 184, 185, 203
Pembroke town walls 175, 177
Pembrokeshire 169
Penrice (castle) 3, 4, 203
Penningtons 198
Pentecost, Osbern 196
Pentecost's (castle) *see* Ewyas Harold
Penthouse 85
Percy, Henry, fifth Lord 58, 106, 127, 200
Percys of Northumberland 153
Perrot, Andrew 203
Pevensey (castle) 13, 14, 20, 93, 94, 199
Peveril (castle) 36, 74, 107–110, 153, 199
Pharos 196
Philipps, Sir Ivor 178
Picard family 110, 203
Pickering (castle) 28, 153, 172, 199
Pigeons 156; boxes 156; *see also* Dovecote
Pillow mounds 154, 165; *see also* Rabbit warrens
Pipe Rolls 34, 40
Piscina 128, 132, 137
Pit prison 85, 87; *see also* Oubliette
Place names 24, 29, 150, 153, 154, 157
Plan *see* Layout
Plantagenet, Hamelin 93, 196
Plaster 40, 90, 137
Pleasance 150, 165
Pleshey (castle) 154, 199
Plinth, battered 103
Poaching 150
Poll Tax of 1380 165
Pontefract (castle) 71, 75, 199
Pope Innocent III 84
Portcullis 51, 52, 62, 68, 71, 84, 85
Porter 135, 137
Portico 40
Post holes 40
Postern 69, 85
Potence 156, 165
Powis (castle) 78, 203
Preservation 178, 179, 182, 184, 188
Priests 128
Princes of Deheubarth 202
Priory 137; fortified 137, 201; *see also* Ewenny Priory
Prison 137; *see also* Bottle Dungeon; Dungeon; Oubliette; Pit prison
Privy chamber 137; *see also* Latrine

Purpose 6, 9, 10, 11, 37, 69, 71, 113, 117, 140, 153
Putlog holes 40, 113

Quadrangular castles 40, 114, 124, 137
Quareator 40
Quarrel 85
Quern 166

Rabbit warrens 148, 153, 154, 162, 166
Raby (castle) 148, 199
Raglan (castle) 36, 58, 59, 83, 94, 106, 107, 115, 122, 132, 181, 203
Ralph, Earl of Hereford 197
Ralph, Lord Neville 199
Ram 81, 85; *see also* Battering ram; Bore; Siege engines
Ramparts 40; *see also* Embankments; Palisades
Ravelin 83
Reconstruction 178
Redan 83
Redoubt 83
Reeve 77, 85, 143, 145, 146, 166
Regarders 152
Religion 127
Rendability 74, 85
Rennes (castle) 25
Rent 143, 146
Restoration 180, 184, 185, 188, 191
Restormel (castle) 151, 199
Restrictions 144, 145
Revetment 25, 85
Rhondda Cynon Taf County Borough Council 191
Rhuddlan (castle) 34, 36, 43, 45, 82, 203
Richard I 93
Richard II 75, 165, 199
Richard III 5, 95, 197, 198
Richard, Lord Scrope 195
Richard's (castle) 16, 18, 199
Richmond (castle) 35, 99, 100, 199
Ridge and furrow system 147, 148, 166
Riegl, Alois 180, 191
Right of free warren 154, 166
The Rings (castle) 20, 21, 22, 83, 199
Ringworks 18–23, 24, 38, 40, 47, 65, 105, 195, 196, 200, 201, 202, 203
River Foss, York 157
Robert, Count of Eu 23
Robert of Normandy 73
Robin Hood 1
Rochester (castle) 74, 101–102, 103, 104, 113, 156, 199
Rockingham (castle) 150, 153, 154, 199
Rockingham Forest 153
Roger, Bishop of Salisbury 198
Roman sites 14, 18, 19, 27, 95, 101, 196, 199, 201
Romance of ruins 178, 179

Romanesque style 92
Roofs 92, 93, 97, 115, 137
Ropemakers 152
Rosemarket 157
Rougement (castle) *see* Exeter
Roundheads 38, 83
Royalists 38, 83, 137
Ruins 1–4, 8, 11, 71, 76, 79, 109, 111, 114, 118, 128, 131, 148, 161, 168–169, 171, 176, 177, 178–180, 181, 182, 183, 186, 188
Ruskin, John 178, 179, 185, 193

Sacristy 138
St. Briavel's (castle) 152, 153, 199
St. George's Chapel 67, 200
St. Georges d'Esperanche (castle) 39
St. John Jeffryes, Sir James 204
St. Quentin's (castle) *see* Llanblethian
St. Quintin's (castle) *see* Llanblethian
Sally port 85
Salvin, Anthony 186, 187
Sapper 85, 102, 138
Sauvey (castle) 153, 199–200
Saxon settlements/cemeteries 15, 18, 19, 24, 37, 76, 95, 196
Say family 200
Scaffolding 41
Scaling ladder 86
Scarborough (castle) 74, 199
Scheduled ancient monuments 186, 194
Sconces 83, 138
Scotland 111–112
Screen 116, 138
Screens passage 138
Scullions 138
Scutage 86
Secular 166
Sedile 129, 138
Seigneur 166
Seignorialism 140, 166
Seneschal 132, 166; *see also* Steward
Serfs 23, 143–144, 166
Serjeanty of hunting 142, 166
Servant quarters 132, 138
Servatorium 150, 166
Servery hatch 138
Service block 138; *see also* Buttery and pantry; Kitchen
Setting 21, 34, 42–44, 107
The Seven Lamps of Architecture (1849) 179
Shams 3, 4, 59
Shearman 138
Sheriff 164
Sherwood Forest 147, 151
Shirburns 200
Shire-reeve *see* Sheriff
Shrewsbury (castle) 24, 199
Sidney, Sir Henry 128
Siege 63, 81, 83, 84, 85, 86, 100, 102, 137; castle 14, 41, 199; engines 41, 81, 84, 85, 86, 102; tower 81, 86 (*see also* Belfry); train 86
Siegeworks 83, 86
Skenfrith (castle) 46, 203
Skyllington, Robert 118
Slater 41
Slaughterer 138
Slebech 157
Sleeping chambers *see* Bedchambers
Slighting 75, 83, 86, 182
Sluice gates 45, 86
Smallholding 166
Smith 152
Socage 142, 166
Society for the Preservation of Ancient Monuments (SPAB) 179–180, 182, 184
Sokeman 166
Solar 97, 99, 116, 117, 138
Somerset, Dukes of 58
South Mimms (castle) 25, 199–200
Spinster 138
Spiral staircase 138; *see also* Newel Stair; Stairways
Splay 86
Springald 86
Springers 92, 113, 138
Spur 86
Squabs 167
Squire 138
Stables 86
Stafford (castle) 24, 200
Stairways 59, 69, 71, 90, 91, 115, 138
Stamford Bridge 39, 77
Stapleton (castle) 148, 154, 157, 200
Status and symbolism 7, 14, 18, 24, 69, 72, 73, 79, 97, 98, 104–110, 113, 116, 117, 120, 124, 135, 140, 148, 149, 153, 154, 162, 164, 170
Statute of Labourers 165
Stephen, King 20, 22, 25, 36, 62, 73, 79, 80, 199
Steward 13, 138, 143; estate 145, 146, 166
Stigand, Archbishop of Canterbury 20
Stockhouse 138
Stone, building 32–33, 34, 35, 36, 37, 38, 39, 40, 91, 115, 122, 125, 127, 133
Stone enclosure castles 31–41
Storm poles 83
Straw, jack 146
String courses 156, 166
Strip farming 147, 148, 166
Strongholses 112
Structures, standard in castles 114
Stukeley, William 3
Subinfeudation 23, 41, 142, 166
Sycharth (castle) 79, 203

Tailor 138
Talbot, Thomas Mansel 4
Tancred the Fleming 202
Tanner 152, 166
Tenant 166
Tenant-in-chief 142, 166
Tenby (castle) 173, 203–204
Tenby town walls 175, 176
Thatcher 41
Thetford Warren 154
Thomas, Earl of Lancaster 196
Threave (castle) 111, 204
Tiltyard 84, 86; *see also* Lists
Timber-framed 64, 92, 138
Tir Gofal 188
Timber structures 28, 30
Tivy-Side newspaper 189
Toddington (castle) 154, 200
Tombs 172, 173, 194
Tonbridge (castle) 199, 200
Tools 33
Tostig (Godwinson) 12, 13, 41
Tower houses 41, 111–113, 138, 201, 204
Tower of London (castle) 10, 15, 20, 32, 35, 36, 40, 62, 74, 81, 82, 95, 97, 104, 105, 128, 132, 137, 146, 168, 200–201
Towers 53, 54, 55, 56, 58, 66, 71, 80, 86, 90–97, 105, 118, 132, 173, 186; great 97–108, 135; *see also* Keep
Towns: medieval 172 (*see also* Medieval town walls); planted 173, 194; walled 69, 70, 93; *see also* Medieval town walls
Tracery 41, 138; *see also* Stone, building
Tracy family 179
Treasury 139
Trebuchet 81, 86; *see also* Siege, engines
Trefoil 139; *see also* Windows
Trestle 139
Tretower (castle) 46, 107, 110–111, 203
Truce 86
Turner, J.M.W. 178
Turner, Sir Llewelyn 182, 186, 187
Turret 86
Turris magnus 97; *see also* Keep; Tower, great
Twin-towered 51, 53, 55, 62, 67, 69, 86, 95, 104, 135, 175, 203
Twthill 203; *see also* Rhuddlan Castle
Tyler, Wat 146, 165

Undercroft 91, 118, 142, 139
Undermining 53, 85, 87, 102, 107
UNESCO 185
Unglazed 139
Unlicensed 87; *see also* Adulterine castles

Value of ruins 179, 180–181
Vassal 23, 41, 142
Vaughan, Roger 110
Vaughan, Thomas 110
Vaulting 91, 92, 129, 138, 139
Venison 166, 167; *see also* Deer parks; Farming, deer

Verderers 152, 161, 167
Vert 167
Vestibule 139; *see also* Antechamber
Viking settlement, construction on 204
Village dwellers 144
Villein 144, 167
Vineyards 160, 161, 167
Visiting castles 29, 31, 63, 160–161, 164–170, 172, 176–181, 192–193
Visual effect 72–73, 76–78, 88, 106, 118
Vivarium 150, 167

Wainscoting 121, 139
Wales 78–79, 112, 113
Walker 167
Wall-walk 59, 81, 85, 87
Walls 53, 62, 67, 82, 102, 103, 116
Walter of Henley 145
Walwyn's (castle) 29, 203
Ward 86, 139; *see also* Bailey
Warden 139, 152, 153, 167
Wardour (Old) (castle) *see* Old Wardour
Warkworth (castle) 95, 106, 127, 148, 153, 200
Warren 167; *see also* Rabbit warrens
Warrener 167
Wars of the Roses 55, 87, 107
Warwick (castle) 24, 28, 31, 32, 37, 56, 57, 58 62, 65, 81, 95, 96, 132, 149, 172, 200

Washerwoman 139
Water sources 122
Watergate 87, 96
Weapons 80
Weaver 139
Webb, Edward 178
Webb, Philip 179
Week-work 77, 86, 143, 144, 167
Well chamber 139
Wellhead 139
Wellington, Duke of 97
Wells 67, 121, 122, 123, 139
Welsh Marches 24
Weobley (castle) 10, 140, 203
White (castle) 35, 37, 40, 45, 69, 84, 98, 113, 132, 137, 203
White Tower (castle) *see* Tower of London
Whitewash 35, 120
Wicket 87
Wigmore (castle) 24, 191–192, 200
William I (the Conqueror, Duke of Normandy) 11, 12, 13, 14, 15, 16, 17, 18, 20, 23, 24, 25, 30, 38 41, 65, 73, 99, 101, 107, 142, 163, 195, 196, 197, 198, 199, 200, 201
William II (Rufus) 73, 101–102
William, Earl of Gloucester 203
William, Lord Hastings 158, 195, 198
Winchester (castle) 18, 34, 116, 118, 200

Windelsora 24
Windlass 51, 71, 85, 87
Window seats 118
Windows 86, 97, 115, 118, 124–125; *see also* Oriel
Windsor (castle) 24, 27, 28, 31, 32, 34, 67, 72, 122, 127, 149, 150, 157, 168, 200
Wiston (castle) 28, 29, 30, 78, 169, 203
Witan/witenagemot 11
Wizo the Fleming 30, 204
Wogan 46
Women 164; *see also* Chatelaine; Lady
Wood-making 163
Woodcutters 152
Woodward 152, 167
Woodworks 152
Worcester (castle) 24, 200
World Heritage Sites 185, 200, 201, 202

Yellow Tower of Gwent 58, 107, 203; *see also* Raglan Castle
Yeomen keepers 153
York (castle) 173; *see also* Clifford's Tower

Z-plan 112; *see also* Tower houses
Zoo *see* Menagerie